C000178330

CADE'S LOCOMOTIVE GUIDE

Written by
Dennis Lovett and Leslie Wood

Edited by
Reg Cade and Barry Gallafent

Published by
Marwain Publishing Limited,
Marwain House,
Clarke Road,
Mount Farm, Milton Keynes,
MK1 1LG.

Printed by
Star Standard Industries
Jurong Town
Singapore

Distributed by
Marwain Publishing Limited, Milton Keynes, England
Telephone: 01908 643022
www.cadeslocomotiveguide.co.uk

ISBN 1 - 905963 - 03 - 3

Cover Photograph
LMS Princess Coronation Class 'Duchess of Hamilton' *courtesy of Milepost 92½*

Introduction

It came as a bit of a shock to us, the authors, to realize that it is almost 30 years since Reg Cade of Marwain approached us as officers of his local model railway club, to respond to his suggestion of producing a book about locomotives for modellers. Reg's idea was simple, it gave historical background to the models that were available to purchase in model shops. We both thought it a good idea and offered to assist in creating a draft on the Britannia Class locomotives, so that the outcome could be discussed with manufacturers, retailers and potential customers. Little did we realize, that a few weeks later the go ahead would be given and we were to be the joint authors! Two more volumes appeared in successive years, and in 1988 a new combined volume hit the shelves. Despite the passage of time, Marwain are still asked for copies and to reconsider a reprint. So here we are again!

In the intervening years there have been many changes both in the full size railway industry and also in the world of model manufacturing. Todays mass produced models surpass everything that went before both in looks, accuracy and performance. Some manufacturers have long gone, but many of their former products can still be obtained secondhand from specialist toy fairs, model railway exhibitions and internet auction sites such as e-bay. Only the Hornby and Graham Farish brands have survived since the first book appeared, and in the case of Farish, it is due to the company changing hands and passing to Bachmann in 2000.

Both of us have spent most of our working lives in the railway industry, which since the last book appeared has undergone considerable change. British Rail has been replaced by a large number of private sector companies, and in many cases these too have passed into railway history to be replaced by others due to mergers, takeovers and franchise changes.

Todays railway modellers have far more ready to run locomotives to choose from than our readers did back in 1979. The contribution by companies such as Bachmann, Dapol, Farish, Heljan, Hornby and Vi-trains has given us more choice to a standard that was only obtained back then by a handful of leading modellers.

The models we purchase and run on our layouts are only as good as the subjects they portray. We now have a great choice of steam locomotive models, thanks to the heritage railway movement for restoring large numbers of them. We also have a national railway network far more colourful than even the Pre-Grouping companies that existed prior to 1923, and one where constant changes throw down endless challenges to us all.

The number of classes that are described in this book show just how far our railway and model railway industries have progressed since this title first emerged.

Dennis Lovett and Les Wood
September 2007

Index

Drummond, D	Caledonian Railway	1882-1890
	London & South Western Railway	1895-1912
Fowler, Sir Henry	London, Midland & Scottish Railway	1925-1931
Gresley, Sir Nigel	Great Northern Railway	1911-1922
	London & North Eastern Railway	1923-1941
Hawksworth, F.W.	Great Western Railway	1941-1947
Holden, S.D.	Great Eastern Railway	1908-1912
Hughes, G	Lancashire & Yorkshire Railway	1904-1922
	London & North Western Railway	
	London, Midland & Scottish Railway	1923-1925
Ivatt, H.G.	London, Midland & Scottish Railway	1945-1947
Peppercorn, A.H.	London & North Eastern Railway	1941-1946
Riddles, R.A. CBE	British Railways	1948-1953
Stanier, Sir William	London, Midland & Scottish Railway	1932-1944
Stirling, J.	South Eastern Railway	1878-1898
Thompson, E.	London & North Eastern Railway	1941-1946
Urie, R.W.	London & South Western Railway	1912-1922
Wainwright, H.S.	South Eastern & Chatham Railway	1899-1913
Worsdell, W	North Eastern Railway	1090-1910

101 Class 0-4-0 T
Great Western Railway

Introduced:	1902
Allocation:	Great Western Railway
Locomotive Nos:	101
Last of Class Withdrawn:	1911
Number Built:	1
Preserved Examples:	None
Duties:	Works Shunter, Swindon
Technical Data:	**Tractive Effort:** (85%) - 11,492 lb **Loco Weight:** 28 tons 13 cwt **Loco Driving Wheels:** 3' 8" dia **Cylinders:** (2) - 13" x 22" **Valve Gear:** Joys Outside

The 0-4-0 tank locomotive No.101 was an experimental locomotive built in 1902. It was an oil burner and adopted a system devised by Holden. In 1903 a Lentz boiler replaced the original boiler. Despite these modifications, No.101 was not a success and a period of out of use followed.

In 1905 the locomotive was converted from oil burning to coal burning, and a bunker was added to carry coal. The small oil tanks were replaced with larger pannier tanks to carry water, thus greatly altering the appearance of the locomotive.

Although originally intended for use elsewhere, No.101 spent its entire working life within the confines of Swindon Works as a works shunter, surviving in its rebuilt form until 1911 when it was withdrawn.

The locomotive carried standard G.W.R. green livery throughout its life.

Hornby Class 101

Hornby produced a ready to run OO gauge model in 1978 portraying the locomotive in its post 1905 coal burning condition. It has also appeared in a number of fictitious industrial liveries over the years. This model is currently available.

14xx Class 0-4-2 T
Great Western Railway

Introduced:	1932
Designed By:	C B Collett
Allocation:	Great Western Railway, later British Railways Western Region.
Locomotive Nos:	4800 - 4829, built in Swindon 1932/1933. 5800 - 5819, built in Swindon 1932/1933. (See Text) 4830 - 4859, built in Swindon 1934/1935. 4860 - 4874, built in Swindon 1936. 4800-4874 were renumbered 1400-1474 in 1946.
Last of Class Withdrawn:	1964
Number Built:	75 (14xx) 20 (58xx)
Preserved Examples:	1420 1450 1442 1466
Duties:	Light branch line duties.
Technical Data:	**Tractive Effort:** (85%) - 13,900 lb **Loco Weight:** 41 tons 6 cwt **Loco Driving Wheels:** 5' 2" dia **Cylinders:** (2 inside) - 16" x 24" **Valve Gear:** Stephenson with slide valves.

The 14xx Class (classified 48xx until 1946), was built at Swindon as replacements for the ageing fleet of 517 Class 0-4-2 Tanks which had been built during the 1870's for branch line duties.

They were of similar design to their predecessors, although various modifications were made from earlier designs, larger cabs were provided with better shelter for the footplate staff.

Under Churchward, many of the 517 Class had been fitted for auto train working. These push/pull trains worked on a similar principle to todays multiple units in that they allowed the train to be driven from both ends. The auto coaches had a cab at one end, which when coupled to the locomotive the other end, allowed the unit to be driven from the cab or locomotive depending on the direction of travel. When the unit was being driven from the coach, the fireman remained on the locomotive to attend to his duties. This system avoided running round at terminal stations. On the better patronised services, the locomotive was 'sandwiched' between two or more auto coaches. All of the seventy five 14xx Class were fitted for push/pull working.

At first the Class were designated 48xx Class, but in 1946 they were reclassified 14xx Class, and re-numbered accordingly. This allowed the previous numbers to be re-allocated to 28xx Class 2-8-0 locomotives.

A further 20 locomotives were constructed and classified 58xx Class, these were not initially fitted for push/pull working and had to run round their trains on reaching their destination in the normal way. Ten of these locomotives however, were converted to push/pull working between 1936 and 1938.

GWR Class 14xx *Photograph courtesy of Colour Rail*

The 14xx Class found their way to most of the Great Western Railways branch lines. They were taken into British Railways stock on Nationalisation in 1948, and survived well into the 1960's when the publication of Dr. Beeching's plans for the reshaping of British Railways had a profound effect on them. Many branch lines were subsequently closed, or worked by diesel multiple units, and thus the Class became redundant.

In G.W.R. days, standard green livery was applied; after Nationalisation B.R. black livery was carried, and later lined green livery became standard. Both B.R. crests were carried according to the period.

Hornby Class 14xx

Airfix produced a OO guage ready to run model in 1978. Follwoing the collapse of the Airfix company, the tools pased to Mainline in 1981and dapol in 1985. They were sold to Hornby and the model improved and re-introduced in to the Hornby range in 1997 and is currently available.

N guage, Dapol introduced a ready to run model in 2004.

2721 Class 0-6-0 PT
Great Western Railway

Introduced:	1897
Designed By:	W Dean
Allocation:	Great Western Railway, later British Railways Western Region.
Locomotive Nos:	2721 - 2800 (No.2800 was re-numbered 2700 in 1912)
Last of Class Withdrawn:	1950
Number Built:	80
Preserved Examples:	None
Duties:	Shunting
Technical Data:	**Tractive Effort:** (85%) - 15,935 lb (a); 20,260 lb (b) **Loco Weight:** 47 tons **Loco Driving Wheels:** 4' 7½" dia **Cylinders:** (2 inside) - 17½" x 24" (a); 17" x 24" (b) later locos **Valve Gear:** Stephenson

The 2721 Class were the final version of the 1854 Class Saddle Tank, from which they were derived. Construction was of three different styles, Nos. 2721-2778 were fitted with flush top boilers; Nos. 2779-2795 were fitted with extended smokeboxes and tanks; whilst Nos. 2796-2800 were fitted with Belpaire boilers and piston valves.

Experiments were made by converting No.2796 from a saddle tank to a panier tank in 1904. Eventually all locomotives were converted into pannier tanks. 31 of the Class were fitted with enclosed cabs, and the vast majority of locomotives had their bunkers increased to 3¼ tons capacity.

Whilst the cylinder diameter was reduced to 17", the boiler pressure on some locomotives was raised from the original 150 lb psi to 180 lb psi, which resulted in the higher tractive effort quoted.

Hornby Class 2721

The locomotives were used extensively in South Wales, although they were allocated in small numbers to other divisions. They were used as shunting locomotives, and were withdrawn from service between 1945 and 1950. Four of the Class served as works shunters during their latter days. The Rhondda & Swansea Bay Railway acquired No.2756 for a short period during 1921/1922 and it was temporarily re-numbered to No.33 in its stock.

On Nationalisation in 1948, 44 of the Class entered B.R. stock. As the locomotives were soon withdrawn, they did not receive a repaint, nor were they fitted with smokebox numberplates. G.W.R. standard green livery was carried throughout their working lives.

Hornby introduced a OO gauge ready to run model in 1980. The model is currently available.

2301 Class (Dean Goods) 0-6-0
Great Western Railway

Introduced:	1883
Designed By:	W Dean
Allocation:	Great Western Railway, later British Railways Western Region. Others loaned to other companies for short periods saw service overseas during two World Wars.
Locomotive Nos:	2301 - 2360 2381 - 2399 All built Wolverhampton 2400 - 2499 2500 - 2580
Last of Class Withdrawn:	1957
Number Built:	260
Preserved Example:	2516
Duties:	Initially used on Goods trains, later used on Mixed Traffic duties mainly in Wales.
Technical Data:	**Tractive Effort:** (85%) - 17,120 lb (a); 18,140 lb (b) **Loco Weight:** 36 tons 16 cwt **Loco Driving Wheels:** 5' 2" dia **Cylinders:** (2 inside) - 17" x 24" (a); 17½" x 24" (b) later locos **Valve Gear:** Stephenson with slide valves

The Dean Goods 0-6-0 locomotives (Class 2301) first appeared in 1883, and for 75 years served not only the Great Western Railway, but other railways at home and overseas.

Designed primarily as a goods locomotive, they were also used on passenger trains from time to time, notably in Wales. Being of lightweight construction, they were permitted to run without restriction on all lines on the system. They were not subjected to the G.W.R. route colouring classification, thus the Class was particularly versatile. As a result, almost every G.W.R. shed received an allocation, although from 1920 they were rarely found in Devon and Cornwall.

Not all of the Class were identical, and as with most large Classes, variations crept in.

Acknowledgements

Marwain Publishing Limited would like to express their grateful thanks to the following organisations for their assistance in compiling this publication:-

Hornby Plc., Westwood, Margate, Kent.   www.hornby.com

Bachmann Europe Plc., Barwell, Leicestershire.   www.bachmann.co.uk

Union Mills Models, Braddan, Isle of Man.

Hattons of Liverpool.   www.hattons.co.uk

Milepost 92½, Newton Harcourt, Leicestershire.   www.milepost92-half.co.uk

Colour Rail, Chesham, Buckinghamshire.

Chief Mechanical Engineers

The appointment of a Chief Mechanical Engineer was always an important one. The position was responsible for the locomotive and rolling stock development, as well as looking after existing equipment.

The rise to this position was a slow one. It is sometimes difficult to imagine that these men started as ordinary apprentices in a railway workshop. Later they worked through various departments and many acted as assistants to the then C.M.E.. Often C.M.E.'s were appointed from other companies, having held the number two position with a rival railway for some years.

A list of C.M.E.'s responsible for the design of steam locomotives described in this book is given below. With the advent of Nationalisation, standardisation and dieselisation, the appointment of Chief Mechanical Engineer is no longer the prominent post it was in previous eras.

Adams, W.	London & South Western Railway	1878-1895
Billington, L.B.	London, Brighton & South Coast Railway	1911-1912
Bullied, O.V.	Southern Railway	1937-1947
Churchward, G.J.	Great Western Railway	1902-1921
Collett, C.B.	Great Western Railway	1922-1941
Cudworth, J	South Eastern Railway	1845-1876
Dean, W	Great Western Railway	1877-1902

GWR Class 2301 Dean Goods *Photograph courtesy of Colour Rail*

When other railways suffered a shortage of motive power, the G.W.R. came to the assistance of other companies and loaned out several members of the Class. Amongst those to benefit in this way was the London & North Western Railway.

Around 1907 the G.W.R. was suffering from a glut of 0-6-0 goods locomotives, and a shortage of 2-6-2 tanks. Having no capacity to build new locomotives, 20 Dean Goods locomotives (Nos. 2491-2510) were withdrawn and rebuilt as 39xx 2-6-2 tanks (Nos. 3901-3920).

The Railway Operating Division (R.O.D.) acquired 62 of the Class for service in France in 1917. Most of these later returned to Britain, but two locomotives were sold off to a foreign operator in 1919. At the outbreak of the Second World War in 1939, the War Department acquired 108 of the class for service overseas. Most went to France and passed into enemy hands following the retreat to Dunkirk in 1940. Many were subsequently recovered as the allies advanced in the latter stages of the war. Others saw service in China, Tunisia and Italy. Amongst those called up for War Department service were several locomotives which the G.W.R. had recently withdrawn. They were immediately reinstated at the outbreak of war.

When hostilities ceased in 1945, withdrawal of the Class was stepped up. By Nationalisation, only 54 locomotives remained in service, most of which survived until the introduction of British Railways Standard Class 2 2-6-0's in the early 1950's.

By 1955 the Class had been reduced to two, and one of these (No.2516) was selected for preservation.

Hornby Class 2721

In G.W.R. days the locomotives carried standard green livery, and on Nationalisation carried unlined black.

Originally tooled by Airfix, this OO gauge ready to run model was not released by them but appeared in the Mainline range in 1983. The tooling was sold to Dapol and reappeared in 1986 before being sold to Hornby. It was upgraded and reintroduced by Hornby in 1998. Although it is not in the current catalogue, it is available.

2251 Class 0-6-0
Great Western Railway

Introduced:	1930
Designed By:	C B Collett
Allocation:	Great Western Railway, later British Railways Western Region.
Locomotive Nos:	2200 - 2299 3200 - 3219
Last of Class Withdrawn:	1965
Number Built:	120
Preserved Example:	3205
Duties:	Mixed traffic on both main and branch lines.
Technical Data:	**Tractive Effort:** (85%) - 20,155 lb **Loco Weight:** 43 tons 8 cwt **Loco Driving Wheels:** 5' 2" dia **Cylinders**: (2 inside) - 17½" x 24" **Valve Gear**: Stephenson with slide valves.

GWR Class 2251 *Photograph courtesy of Colour Rail*

With the grouping of 1923, the Great Western Railway took over control of several lines, mostly in Central Wales, which were of very light construction. They were therefore unable to cope with anything but the lightest of locomotives.

Under Churchward's reign as Chief Mechanical Engineer at Swindon, no 0-6-0 tender locomotives had been built. Emphasis had been placed on building large powerful locomotives for freight and passenger work, and the motive power departments had to rely on ageing Dean Goods 0-6-0's to undertake pick-up duties.

Construction of the Dean Goods locomotives first commenced in 1883, and in the late 1920's they were still found on main line pick-up freight trains. Their replacement, or re-employment, on less arduous tasks was becoming a matter of some importance. Collett decided to design a new Class of 0-6-0 tender locomotive (the 2251's) which would allow the Dean Goods locomotives to be transferred to the lightly constructed lines.

Construction of the new class took place at Swindon and commenced in 1930. In all, eight batches were built and the Class eventually totalled 120 units. The last two members of the Class (Nos. 3218 & 3219) were not completed until after Nationalisation in 1948.

The Class were fitted with the standard No.10 taper boiler and were the first locomotives of the 0-6-0 arrangement to be designed around this boiler. Other 0-6-0's had in fact been fitted with the No.10 taper boilers during overhauls. The 2251 Class were also fitted with generously proportioned cabs, with side windows and plenty of protection from the elements. These were great improvements when compared with the small cabs fitted to the Dean Goods locomotives, and proved popular with the train crews. Those locomotives built during the Second World War (Nos. 2211-2240) were not fitted with cab windows due to the blackout regulations then in force, but these were soon fitted when hostilities ceased.

In G.W.R. days most main line depots had an allocation for working mostly pick-up goods trains along main lines. In B.R. days they were often noted on cross country and branch line trains. In addition to working freight trains, they were also employed on passenger trains, and were officially classified as mixed traffic locomotives.

Livery in G.W.R. ownership was unlined green. B.R. at first painted them in unlined black, although many of the Class were later turned out in black or green livery with full lining.

Bachmann GWR Class 2251

Mainline produced a OO gauge ready to run model in 1979. A few were made for Replica in 1989 just before Kader established Bachmann in the UK in the same year. It was given a major upgrade before being re-introduced by Bachmann in 1998. It remains available.

Peco introduced a ready to run N gauge model in 2007.

38xx County Class 4-4-0
Great Western Railway

Introduced:	1904
Designed By:	G J Churchward
Allocation:	Great Western Railway.
Locomotive Nos:	3473 (later No.3800)* 3474 - 3482 (later Nos. 3831 - 3839)* 3801 - 3830 All built in Swindon from 1904 to 1912. * Re-numbered from 1912.
Last of Class Withdrawn:	1933
Number Built:	40
Preserved Examples:	None
Duties:	Express Passenger
Technical Data:	**Tractive Effort:** (85%) - 20,530 lb **Loco Weight:** 58 tons 16 cwt **Loco Driving Wheels:** 6' 8½" dia **Cylinders:** (2) - 18" x 30" **Valve Gear:** Stephenson with slide valves.

Why the G.W.R. 38xx County Class 4-4-0's were built remains one of the unanswered mysteries of locomotive history. They were constructed for express passenger working over the Bristol and South Wales lines, but were quickly replaced by Star Class 4-6-0's. They eventually moved from depot to depot as newer and more powerful locomotives made them redundant.

The first locomotive No.3474 was built at Swindon in 1904. Further batches followed in 1906 and 1911/12. Locomotives not numbered in the 38xx series were re-numbered accordingly (see numbering details above). The later batch included several minor modifications. They were built with superheaters whereas the earlier locomotives had these fitted from 1909. One or two locomotives were reboilered, and one locomotive ran with a Bulldog type boiler for a short time.

Hornby Class 38xx

Once replaced from main line work between London (Paddington) and Bristol/South Wales, the Counties found work between Birmingham and Bristol, where civil engineering structures restricted use of larger locomotives. A similar restriction applied between Shrewsbury and Hereford. Weight restrictions between Birmingham and Bristol were lifted in 1927. The Counties were also allocated to secondary mainline depots, such as Didcot and Taunton, for mainline pilot duties and intermediate passenger services. All of the class were scrapped between 1930 and 1933. At the time of withdrawal most of the class were allocated to Oxford.

The 38xx Class carried G.W.R. standard lined green livery throughout their service lives.

Hornby produced a OO gauge ready to run model in 1981. It was last produced in 1995.

45xx Class 2-6-2 T
Great Western Railway

Introduced:	1906
Designed By:	G J Churchward
Allocation:	Great Western Railway, later British Railways Western Region.
Locomotive Nos:	4500 - 4554, built 1906-1915. 4555 - 4599, built 1924-1929. 5500 - 5574, built 1924-1929.
Last of Class Withdrawn:	1964
Number Built:	175

Preserved Examples:

4555	5526	5542
4561	5532	5552
4566	5538	5553
4588	5539	5572
5521	5541	

Technical Data:
Tractive Effort: (85%) - 21,250 lb
Loco Weight: 57 tons. Locos 4575 onward, 61 tons
Loco Driving Wheels: 4' 7½" dia
Cylinders: (2) - 17" x 24"
Valve Gear: Stephenson with slide valves.

The 45xx Class were a development of Churchward's earlier 44xx Class 2-6-2 tanks, which in turn had been developed from Churchward's original 2-6-2 T No.99 (later re-numbered 3100).

The 45xx's were almost identical to the earlier 44xx Class. The major difference was the fitting of larger diameter driving wheels (4' 7½") compared to the 4' 1½" diameter wheels fitted to the 44xx's.

The first locomotives (Nos. 2161-2180) were built at Stafford Road Works in Wolverhampton between 1906 and 1908, and were the last locomotives to be built there. The second batch (Nos. 2181-2190) were built at Swindon from 1909. In 1912 re-numbering took place and the locomotives were re-numbered 4500-4529. Seven further batches were built and construction ceased in 1929.

GWR Class 45xx *Photograph courtesy of Milepost 92½*

The first locomotives (Nos. 4500-4574) were fitted with flat tank tops. When construction recommenced with No.4575 in 1927, tank capacity was increased by some 300 gallons. Plus, to give additional capacity for coal, locomotives constructed from 1924 (Nos. 4555 onwards) were fitted with larger coal bunkers.

The 45xx Class were used essentially for branch line duties on both passenger and freight trains. They were allocated mainly to depots in Cornwall, Devon, Somerset, South Wales and Worcestershire, and to depots for work on the former Cambrian Railways lines in Central Wales.

The London area saw very little of the Class. Two locomotives were allocated to Southall Depot in London for a brief period in the mid 1920's, for working the Brentford branch freight trains.

Bachmann Class 45xx

Bachmann Class 4575

For working branch line trains in the Cardiff area, 15 of the Class were fitted for push/pull working in 1953. Engines allocated to Taunton were fitted with automatic staff changing apparatus, for working single track lines in that area.

The first locomotive was withdrawn in 1950. As branch lines closed, or diesel multiple units took over, large scale withdrawals took place.

In G.W.R. days the livery was unlined green. From 1948 onwards the Class were painted British Railways unlined black. Later, several of the Class received standard B.R. lining. At the end of the 1950's some of the Class were repainted in green livery with full lining, both B.R. crests being carried according to the period.

Lima introduced a ready to run OO gauge model in 1978. This was not available after 1993 and following the demise of Lima the tools were taken over by Hornby. It has not been re-introduced.

Bachmann introduced a model in 2003 and the 4575 version in 2004.

57xx Class 0-6-0 PT
Great Western Railway

Introduced:	1929
Designed By:	C B Collett
Allocation:	Great Western Railway, later British Railways Western, London Midland and Southern Regions. Also London Transport.

Locomotive Nos:

Group a:

3600 - 3799	7700 - 7799
4600 - 4699	8700 - 8799
5700 - 5799	9600 - 9682
6700 - 6749	9711 - 9799

Group b:
6750 - 6779
Introduced in 1948 with steam brakes and increased weight.

Last of Class Withdrawn:	1966 (BR); 1971 (London Transport)
Number Built:	852

Preserved Examples:

3650	7752
3738	7754
4612	7760
5764	9600
5775	9629
5786	9649
7714	9681
7715	9682

Duties: Mixed (as described in text).

Technical Data: **Tractive Effort:** (85%) - 22,515 lb
Loco Weight: 47 tons 10 cwt (a); 49 tons (b)
Loco Driving Wheels: 4' 7½" dia
Cylinders: (2 inside) - 17½" x 24"
Valve Gear: Stephenson with slide valves.

GWR Class 57xx *Photograph courtesy of Milepost 92½*

The first of the 57xx 0-6-0 pannier tanks was introduced in 1929. The Class, which eventually totalled 852, was built between 1929 and 1950. They were similar in appearance to the rebuilt 27xx Class, which in turn had been developed from the earlier 1813 Class. Construction took place at Swindon, and in the works of outside contractors, to provide work during the depression years.

The 57xx Class were versatile locomotives, found on all parts of the Great Western Railway system (later British Railways Western Region), performing a multitude of tasks. These ranged from branch line freight and passenger trains, to empty stock working between Paddington and Old Oak Common.

Not all the locomotives had the same type of cab. The later units were fitted with larger cabs which gave additional protection for the crew. The locomotives numbered in the 67xx series were not permitted to be used on passenger trains as they were not fitted with vacuum brakes nor the Great Western ATC apparatus.

Spark arresting chimneys were fitted to No.7713 during 1937, and No.5757 was fitted in 1938. During World War II, Nos. 3709, 3721, 4601, 5710, 5744, 5752, 7709, 8738, 8757 and 9722 were similarly converted. These were allocated to Didcot for working in the Milton Trading Estate, and also on the adjacent Ordnance Depot near Stevenson.

During 1958, Nos. 4634, 4672, 4686, 4692, 4698 and 9770 were allocated to the Southern Region at Nine Elms (South London) for working empty stock into and out of Waterloo. ATC shoes were removed, and two additional lamp brackets were fitted to suit the S.R. Disc Route Headcodes. Nos. 4610, 4616, 4626, 4630 and 4631 were shedded at Dover (sub shedded to Folkestone) to power the boat trains up the steeply graded Harbour Branch, which had severe weight restrictions, and no larger locos were permitted.

Other locomotives working off the original Western Region were allocated to Bath and Templecombe (ex Somerset & Dorset), as well as Yeovil (Pen Mill) and Wrexham.

The first withdrawals took place in 1956, and the last of the Class was withdrawn from B.R. service in 1966. 57xx's however, remained in revenue service with London Transport, to whom B.R. had sold them after withdrawal until June 1971. These were numbered L89 - L99 and finished in the distinctive London Transport lined red livery. These were used on engineers trains and rubbish trains to Watford tip. The Class were all allocated to Neasden Depot. Other locomotives were sold to the National Coal Board for work at N.C.B. colleries. Many of the preserved locos listed above, are those originally sold to London Transport.

In Great Western days, the locomotives were finished in unlined G.W.R. green livery. In B.R. days they were painted black, and at least one was known to be lined out. Both B.R. crests were carried according to the period.

Bachmann Class 57xx

Bachmann Class 8750

Gaiety were the first to introduce a ready to run OO model in 1951. It utilised both the Tri-ang 2 rail and Hornby Dublo 3 rail chassis depending on the owners preference.

In 1971, Tri-ang Hornby introduced their OO version before it passed to Hornby. In 1987 the tooling was modified to become 'Duck' in the Thomas the tank engine series and is still available in this form.

Mainline introduced their version in 1981 using tooling produced by Kader. It was made for Replica in 1986 but after Kader commenced its Bachmann operation in the UK in 1989 production ceased. Reintroduced in 1998, an upgraded version was introduced as part of the Bachmann range in 1999. A new version using new tooling was introduced in 2005. It remains available.

Bachmann also produce the 8750 version which it introduced in 1999. It is still available.

Graham Farish introduced a N gauge ready to run model in 1994. After Bachmann took over the company in 2000, the model was upgraded and reintroduced in 2002. It is still available.

94xx Class 0-6-0 PT
Great Western Railway

Introduced:	1947
Designed By:	F W Hawksworth
Allocation:	Great Western Railway, later British Railways London Midland and Western Regions. Remainder of Class delivered after Nationalisation.
Locomotive Nos:	9400 - 9499 8400 - 8499 3400 - 3409

Last of Class Withdrawn:	1965

Number Built: 210

Preserved Examples: 9400
9466

Duties: Passenger & Freight Trains. Also Shunting, Banking and Empty Stock workings.

Technical Data: **Tractive Effort:** (85%) - 22,515 lb
Loco Weight: 55 tons 7 cwt
Loco Driving Wheels: 4' 7½" dia
Cylinders: (2 inside) - 17½" x 24"
Valve Gear: Stephenson with slide valves.

GWR Class 94xx *Photograph courtesy of Colour Rail*

The 94xx's were developed from the 57xx 0-6-0 pannier tanks, and were designed at Swindon by F. W. Hawksworth, the last in a long line of G.W.R. Chief Mechanical Engineers. The 94xx's had the largest panniers of all the G.W.R. 0-6-0 tank locomotives with a water carrying capacity of 1300 gallons.

The first locomotive emerged from Swindon in early 1947, and by Nationalisation (1st January 1948) ten locomotives were in service, all had superheated boilers.

The Class was built in eight batches, and all bar the initial batch (Nos. 9400-9409), were built by sub-contractors without superheated boilers. These were the work of Robert Stephenson & Hawthorns Ltd., Bagnalls and the Yorkshire Engine Company (working as sub-contractors themselves for the Hunslet Engine Company). The last ten locomotives (Nos. 3400-3409), were constructed during 1955 and 1956.

The 94xx's were originally intended as replacements for the ageing 0-6-2 tanks, which had been absorbed by the G.W.R. at the 1923 grouping from companies in South Wales. Others of the Class were used on short distance passenger and freight workings. Early members of the Class were fitted with vacuum brakes for passenger duties, but later examples were not so fitted, and therefore were restricted to freight duties. The 94xx's were used for shunting in yards whilst in the London area, examples worked empty stock trains in and out of Paddington. Seven locomotives (Nos. 8400-8406) were transferred to the London Midland Region in 1957, and then allocated to Bromsgrove for banking trains up the Lickey incline on the Bristol to Birmingham line.

Due to the dieselisation programme, the working life of these extremely powerful locomotives was cut short.

The first ten locomotives (Nos. 9400-9409) were the only members of the Class to carry G.W.R. green livery, the rest were painted B.R. unlined black livery throughout their working lives.

Lima Class 94xx

Graham Farish introduced a ready to run OO gauge model in 1961. This model continued in production until 1979.

Not surprisingly Graham Farish chose to replicate its OO model as one of its two initial N gauge locomotives in 1971. After Bachmann acquired the company in 2000, the model was upgraded and reintroduced in 2003. It is still available.

Lima introduced a ready to run OO gauge model in 1978. It was last available in 1994. The tools passed to Hornby in 2005 when it acquired Lima, but the model has not been re-introduced.

Saint Class 4-6-0
Great Western Railway

Introduced: 1902

Designed By: G J Churchward

Allocation: Great Western Railway, later British Railways Western Region.

Locomotive Nos: 100, Re-numbered 2900, Built 1902.
                         98, Re-numbered 2998, Built 1903.
                         171, Re-numbered 2971, Built 1903.
                         172 & 179 - 190, Re-numbered 2972 & 2979 - 2990, Built 1905.
                         173 - 178, Re-numbered 1973 - 1978, Built 1905.
                         2901 - 2910, Built 1906.
                         2911 - 2930, Built 1907.
                         2931 - 2955, Built from 1911-1913.
                         All built in Swindon.

Last of Class Withdrawn:	1953

Number Built: 77

Preserved Example: One replica is being constructed from a Hall Class locomotive (see text).

Duties: Express Passenger.

Technical Data:

Tractive Effort:	(85%) - 20,530 lb Nos.100 & 98;	
	23,090 lb Nos.171 & 173-178;	
	23,382 lb Nos.2902-2910; 21,457 lb No.2901;	
	24,395 lb Nos.2941-2955	
Loco Weight:	67 tons 16 cwt No.100;	
	68 tons 6 cwt No.98;	
	70 tons 4 cwt No.171;	
	71 tons 14 cwt Nos.173-178;	
	72 tons Nos.2902-2910 & 2901;	
	74 tons Nos.2941-2955.	
Driving Wheels:	6' 8½" dia	
Cylinders:	(2) - 18" x 30" Nos.100, 98, 171 & 173-178;	
	18 1/8th" x 30" Nos.2902-2910;	
	18 3/8th" x 30" No.2901;	
	18½" x 30" Nos.2941-2955.	
Valve Gear:	Stephenson with piston valves (No.2935 was rebuilt with Poppett Valve Gear in 1931).	

GWR Saint Class *Photograph courtesy of Colour Rail*

The departure from Swindon Works of No.100 in 1902, caused a great deal of axcitement. This locomotive was to become the prototype on which all future large Great Western motive power would be based.

No.100 (later No.2900), being a prototype loco, had different cylinders, valve gears and frames from the remainder of the Class. It was originally built with a parallel boiler with Belpaire casing. It was reboilered in 1903 with the standard No.1 boiler, in 1910 with a superheated boiler, and again in

1912 when it received a long cone boiler. It was initially named Dean, being renamed William Dean a few months later. At first nameplates were fitted to the splashers (above the front driving wheels), but later, to comply with standard G.W.R. practise, they were relocated above the centre drivers.

A second prototype, No.98 (later No.2998), emerged from Swindon in 1903. It had a short cone boiler incorporating a tapered firebox, which was similar to the standard No.1 boiler in dimension etc.. Alterations were made to the cylinders and valve gear, the latter having ten inch piston valves.

At the end of 1903 a third loco, No.171 Albion (later No.2971), was built on almost identical lines to No.98. Boiler pressure was increased to 225 lbs p.s.i., which in turn increased the tractive effort. It ran for three years (from 1904 to 1907) as a 4-4-2 to allow it to be tested alongside the De Glehn Atlantics.

Thirteen 4-4-2's followed in 1905, Nos. 172 and 179-190, along with six 4-6-0's, Nos. 173-178. The 4-4-2's were known as the Scott Class until being rebuilt in 1912/13 as conventional Saints (4-6-0's).

The next batch, Nos. 2901-2910, left Swindon in 1906. Although they were regarded as the first true production run of the Class, they had variations in types of boiler fitted, some having short cone and others the long cone boiler. No.2901 had a short cone boiler with Schmidt superheaters, another variation from the previous batch was the different cylinder size (18 1/8" dia.), which increased tractive effort to 23,382 lb. No.2901 was again non standard, having 18 3/8" dia. cylinders and 200 lbs p.s.i. working pressure, reducing the tractive effort considerably to 21,457 lb. Reboilering of many of the batch took place between 1907 and 1912. All of these locomotives were named after 'Ladies'.

The Saints proper were all built at Swindon during 1907. Slight alterations were made to the frames, whilst the boilers were of the long cone type. The only other difference from the previous locos, was the fitting of screw reversing, as opposed to the hand levers previously used.

The final batch (Nos. 2931-2955) were named after 'Courts', and were all built at Swindon between 1911 and 1913. They were two tons heavier than earlier locos. The cylinder diameter on No.2941 was increased to 18½" dia., and this later became the standard which all locos subsequently received, except No.2900.

In 1924 No.2925 St Martin, was rebuilt to become the prototype Hall Class locomotive, being re-numbered No.4900.

Initially the locomotives were used on principal expresses between London Paddington and the West Country. As numbers increased they spread to other routes, and were used on Wolverhampton, South Wales and Cheltenham trains. As more powerful locomotives were introduced, they were allocated to less arduous duties (circa 1920). The first withdrawals took place in 1931, and by the Second World War only 48 remained in service. The need for wartime motive power reprieved those remaining, and they found themselves back in the top links, often working heavy passenger and troop trains.

On Nationalisation in 1948, 47 locos remained in service. The withdrawal of these was fairly rapid with the last loco, No.2933 'Bibury Court', being withdrawn in January 1953.

Hornby Saint Class

At first G.W.R. lined green livery was carried, although during the First World War lining was not replaced if repainting took place. Lining was replaced later. After Nationalisation, several locos received B.R. lined black livery.

The Great Western Society at Didcot are currently converting a Hall Class back into a Saint Class 4-6-0. Completion of No.2999 'Lady of Legend' is anticipated in 2010/2011. The chassis is currently at Ian Riley's Bury workshop awaiting the boiler (not yet complete) before delivery to Didcot.

> Hornby introduced a ready to run OO model in 1986. It was last produced in 1998.

43xx Class 2-6-0
Great Western Railway

Introduced:	1911 93xx Class (shown*) introduced 1932
Designed By:	G J Churchward. 93xx* C B Colett
Allocation:	Great Western Railway, later British Railways Western Region.
Locomotive Nos:	4300 - 4399 5300 - 5399 6300 - 6399 7300 - 7321 7322 - 7341 (originally Nos. 9300-9319) see text
Last of Class Withdrawn:	1964
Number Built:	175
Preserved Examples:	5322 7325
Duties:	Mixed Traffic.

Technical Data:

Tractive Effort:	(85%) - 25,670 lb
Loco Weight:	62 tons as built; 64 tons 5300 Series (65 locos); 65 tons 6 cwt 7300/9300 Series with side window cab
Driving Wheels:	5' 8" dia
Cylinders:	(2) - 18½" x 30"
Valve Gear:	Stephenson with piston valves.

In 1909 a member of Churchward's staff visited Canada, and he observed Canadian mixed traffic 2-6-0's in service. On his return he reported his findings to Churchward, and as a result the G.W.R. contemplated construction of a similar locomotive for its own use.

The 43xx series were all constructed between 1911 and 1916. No.4300 was constructed in 1916, and Nos. 5300-5399 were built between 1916 and 1920. Modifications were made to this series from 1927, following flange wear problems on the front driving wheels. The buffer beam was moved forward by some twelve inches, extending the frames; more weight was added (2 tons); and the pony truck relocated to give more side play. 65 locomotives were treated in this way, and they were

GWR Class 43xx *Photograph courtesy of Colour Rail*

Nos. 5300-5302, 5304, 5305, 5307-5309, 5313-5315, 5318, 5320, 5322, 5325-5329, 5331-5335, 5337, 5338, 5340-5344, 5351-5354, 5357-5366, 5368, 5369, 5372-5374, 5376, 5378, 5379, 5381-5384, 5386-5391 and 5393. These received their corresponding numbers in the 83xx series (i.e. No.5300 became 8300). Those still remaining in service were converted back to their original condition from 1944, when withdrawal of 4-4-0 types created a vacuum in the locomotive fleet. 53 locomotives were rebuilt to 53xx Class specification, they were Nos. 5300, 5302, 5305, 5307, 5309, 5313-5315, 5318, 5320, 5322, 5325-5328, 5331-5335, 5337, 5338, 5340, 5341, 5343, 5344, 5350, 5351, 5353, 5357-5362, 5364, 5365, 5368, 5369, 5372-5374, 5376, 5377, 5378, 5381, 5382, 5384, 5386, 5388, 5390, 5391 and 5393.

The 63xx batch were built at Swindon between 1920 and 1925, continuing with the 73xx series, with No.7319 being completed in 1922. Nos. 7320-7321 were constructed at Swindon in 1925.

The last batch, Nos. 9300-9319, were built in 1932, and were fitted with improved cabs which included side windows. These were re-numbered into the 73xx series, becoming Nos. 7322-7341, between 1956 and 1959. They were built originally as the 83xx conversions, with longer extended frames and increased weight at the front end. When this modification was no longer required, they were converted to the 73xx type and re-numbered accordingly. They retained their improved cab features.

The Class were true mixed traffic types, appearing in a wide spectrum of duties on all parts of the Great Western system. In B.R. days they worked regularly over the Southern Region, West of England, mainline between Plymouth (Friary) and Exeter Central. During the First World War, Nos. 5319-5326 and 5328-5330 were in service with the Railway Operating Division (R.O.D.) in France between 1917 and 1919.

The first withdrawals took place in 1936, and the last in 1964. At Nationalisation in 1948, 241 locomotives remained in service. As far as can be ascertained, only one locomotive was converted to oil burning (No.6320).

It was originally intended to withdraw all of the 2-6-0's and replace them with Grange and Manor Class 4-6-0's, utilising various parts from the 2-6-0's. 100 locomotives (replaced by 80 Granges and 20 Manors) were so affected, before the outbreak of the Second World War revised this modernisation programme.

In G.W.R. days the Class were painted in unlined green livery. B.R. originally painted them in unlined black livery, but No.7313 received standard lined, mixed traffic, black livery. Later examples were painted in lined green, whilst others appeared in unlined green. British Railways in full or either crest was carried according to the period.

Bachmann Class 43xx

Mainline introduced a OO gauge ready to run model in 1981 using Kader owned tooling. After Kader set up Bachmann in the UK in 1989 the model was upgraded and added to the catalogue in 2000. It is still available.

56xx Class 0-6-2 T
Great Western Railway

Introduced:	1924
Designed By:	C B Collett
Allocation:	Great Western Railway, later British Railways Western Region.
Locomotive Nos:	5600 - 5699 6600 - 6699 Built at Swindon from 1924 to 1928.
Last of Class Withdrawn:	1966
Number Built:	200
Preserved Examples:	5619 6634 5637 6686 5643 6695 5668 6697 6619
Duties:	Mixed Traffic.
Technical Data:	**Tractive Effort:** (85%) - 25,800 lb **Loco Weight:** 68 tons 12 cwt; 66xx Class weighed 15 cwts more **Loco Driving Wheels:** 4' 7½" dia **Cylinders:** (2 inside) - 18" x 26" **Valve Gear:** Stephenson with piston valves.

With the grouping of the Railways in 1923, the Great Western Railway absorbed most of the railway companies operating in South Wales. This area included many coal mines and steelworks which

GWR Class 56xx *Photograph courtesy of Colour Rail*

required much heavy freight movement. To cope with this work, the pre-grouping companies had each developed their own form of freight locomotives, the most popular of which being the 0-6-2 Tank.

The G.W.R. was not keen to continue this practice at first, but eventually did carry on the tradition in 1924 with the building of No.5600 at Swindon.

Eventually 200 of the Class were built with the last locomotive emerging from Swindon in 1928. The vast majority were sent to work in South Wales, others were allocated to the Bristol, Worcester, Wolverhampton and London areas.

Duties consisted mainly of freight work, although the Class were often found on passenger trains, notably in the Welsh Valleys, where they worked alongside the later B.R. standard Class 3 2-6-2 tanks and on cross country routes.

The G.W.R. painted the class in standard unlined green livery. This was replaced after Nationalisation by B.R. unlined black. Some locomotives later appeared in lined passenger green, with further examples appearing in lined black livery.

Bachmann Class 56xx

Trix Twin produced the first ready to run model in 1959. Although it was for use on OO gauge railways it was produced in 3.8mm to the foot rather than 4mm. It was not produced after 1964.

At the time that the Trix Twin model was being developed, Hornby Dublo were planning their own OO model. They dropped it but all the drawings had been completed. Michael Foster produced a model from these drawings for Hornby Dublo enthusiasts in 2001. It is no longer available.

Mainline introduced a further OO version in 1984 using new tooling produced by Kader. When Kader opened the Bachmann operation in the UK in 1989 it was retooled to Blue Riband standards before being introduced in 2003.

Hall Class 4-6-0
Great Western Railway

Introduced:	Prototype 1924. Production Locos 1928. Hawksworth modification to Collett design 1944.
Designed By:	C B Collett from a design by Churchward. Modified Halls designed by F W Hawksworth (shown by *).
Allocation:	Great Western Railway, later British Railways Western Region.
Locomotive Nos:	4900 - 4999 5900 - 5999 6900 - 6958 6959 - 6999* 7900 - 7929* * Modified Halls
Last of Class Withdrawn:	1965
Number Built:	259

Preserved Examples:

4920 Dumbleton Hall	6960* Raveningham Hall
4930 Hagley Hall	6984* Owsden Hall
4936 Kinlet Hall	6989* Wightwick Hall
4953 Pitchford Hall	6990* Witherslack Hall
4965 Rood Ashton Hall	6998* Burton Agnes Hall
4979 Wootton Hall	7903* Foremarke Hall
5900 Hinderton Hall	7927* Willington Hall
5952 Cogan Hall	* Modified Halls.
5972 Olton Hall	

Duties:	Mixed Traffic.
Technical Data:	**Tractive Effort:** (85%) - 27,275 lb **Loco Weight:** 75 tons **Loco Driving Wheels:** 6' 0" dia **Cylinders:** (2) - 18½" x 30" **Valve Gear:** Stephenson with slide valves.

In 1924 Collet modified No.2925 St. Martin, one of Churchward's Saint Class 4-6-0's. Collett fitted 6' 0" driving wheels, altered the cylinders in relation to the driving axle, and fitted a Castle Class cab.

GWR Hall Class *Photograph courtesy of Milepost 92½*

Before the go-ahead for construction of a new class was given, further modifications were made to the pitch of the boiler and the fitting of outside steam pipes. No.2925 became No.4900, but still retained the name St. Martin.

During 1928, 80 locomotives entered service, with a further 178 on order.

F.W.Hawksworth, then Chief Mechanical Engineer, modified the design for a further batch of 70 locomotives, construction of which commenced in 1944. Included in the alterations was the fitting of a larger superheater, and the use of one-piece plate frames. The standard No.1 boiler was fitted and alterations were made to the cylinder/smokebox saddle arrangements. Minor modifications were also made to the front end. This batch were known as Modified Halls.

The locomotives were used throughout the Great Western system, later British Railways Western Region, for mixed traffic duties. They were often found on express passenger trains, deputising for larger locomotives, and proved to be sprightly performers when given the chance.

All, apart from one locomotive, entered B.R. service on Nationalisation in 1948. The absentee was No.4911, which was scrapped in 1941 after receiving a direct hit from a bomb.

Bachmann Hall Class

A variety of different tenders were paired with the Halls during their working lives. The first locomotives to be delivered were paired with 3500 gallon tenders of the Churchward type. The 4000 gallon tenders, as fitted to the Castle Class, were paired with the majority of locomotives. The Modified Halls were paired with the flat sided 4000 gallon tenders of Hawksworths design. In around 1946, 11 locomotives were converted to oil burning, but had been re-equipped for coal burning by 1950.

No.6990 was involved in the 1948 interchange trials, working between Manchester and Marylebone (London) on the ex Great Central Railway main line. In later years, these locomotives worked regularly along this line, on inter-regional workings, via the Banbury to Woodford Halse link line.

In G.W.R. days the Class were finished in lined green livery. B.R. painted them in unlined black, but some later appeared in lined black or lined green. British Railways in full or either crest was carried according to the period.

Tri-ang Hornby produced the first OO gauge ready to run model in 1966. It became part of the Hornby range but has not been available since 1983. Bachmann introduced their model of the Modified Hall in 1997. This was originally tooled by Kader for Mainline but was not released by them. Some were manufactured for Replica before Kader established its own company Bachmann in the UK in 1989. The model of the original series appeared in 2005.

In N gauge, Graham Farish introduced their model in 1973. It was upgraded after Bachmann acquired the company in 2000 and re-released in 2003.

61xx Class 2-6-2 T
Great Western Railway

Introduced:	1931, developed from earlier designs
Designed By:	C B Collett
Allocation:	London area. Great Western Railway, later British Railways Western Region.
Locomotive Nos:	6100 - 6169
Last of Class Withdrawn:	1966
Number Built:	70
Preserved Example:	6106
Duties:	Suburban duties from London (Paddington).
Technical Data:	**Tractive Effort:** (85%) - 27,340 lb **Loco Weight:** 78 tons 9 cwt **Loco Driving Wheels:** 5' 8" dia **Cylinders**: (2) - 18" x 30" **Valve Gear**: Stephenson with piston valves.

The 61xx Class locomotives were, like many others, developed from earlier designs. Collett's 61xx Class owes its beginnings to No.99, which was designed by Churchward in 1903. This locomotive was re-numbered 3100 in 1912, and became the first of the 31xx Class. In all, 40 locomotives were constructed, and following re-numbering in 1929, became the 51xx Class. Further batches were

GWR Class 61xx *Photograph courtesy of Colour Rail*

added and these locomotives were numbered 5100-5199 and 4100-4179, totalling 180 locomotives. The last batch were constructed at Swindon, under Collett, between 1939 and 1949.

The 61xx Class were almost identical to the earlier 51xx and later 81xx Classes (Nos. 8100-8109). They did however, have an increased boiler pressure (225 lbs p.s.i.) which resulted in a greater tractive effort.

The 61xx's spent their working lives on the Paddington suburban services. They were required to haul heavy trains at quite fast speeds, and due to the increased boiler pressure, were able to cope well with traffic demands.

When the diesel multiple units began to infiltrate onto the Paddington suburban lines, the 61xx's were relegated to parcels and empty stock workings, some moving to other parts of the region (e.g. Neyland, Gloucester, Tyseley, Severn Tunnel Junction).

A later development of the 61xx Class came with the building of ten locomotives of the 81xx Class (Nos. 8100-8109). The only difference between these and the 61xx Class was the fitting of 5' 6" diameter driving wheels, as opposed to the 5' 8" wheels fitted to the 61xx's. These locomotives worked suburban services around Bristol and Birmingham.

In G.W.R. days, standard unlined green livery was carried. B.R. applied both lined black and lined green liveries to the Class. British Railways in full or either crest was carried according to the period.

Hornby Class 61xx

Graham Farish were the first to introduce a ready to run OO model in 1951. It has not been available since 1971.

Ten years later in 1961, Tri-ang introduced a TT version for its short lived range. This has not been available since the mid 1960s.

The 61xx Class was chosen by Airfix when it entered the ready to run market in 1977. These tools passed to Mainline, Dapol and in 1998 to Hornby. Hornby reintroduced it in 1999 after upgrading it.

Not surprisingly Graham Farish chose to replicate its OO model in N gauge in 1977. After Bachmann acquired the company in 2000, the model was upgraded and reintroduced in 2003. It is still available.

Manor Class 4-6-0
Great Western Railway

Introduced:	1938
Designed By:	C B Collett
Allocation:	Great Western Railway, later British Railways Western Region.
Locomotive Nos:	7800 - 7829
Last of Class Withdrawn:	1966
Number Built:	30

Preserved Examples:

7808 Cookham Manor	7821 Ditcheat Manor
7802 Bradley Manor	7822 Foxcote Manor
7812 Eriestoke Manor	7827 Lyndham Manor
7819 Hinton Manor	7828 Odney Manor
7820 Dinmere Manor	

Technical Data:

Tractive Effort: (85%) - 27,340 lb
Loco Weight: 68 tons 18 cwt
Loco Driving Wheels: 5' 8" dia
Cylinders: (2) - 18" x 30"
Valve Gear: Stephenson with piston valves.

The first of the Manor Class 4-6-0's entered service after leaving Swindon works in 1938. They were smaller versions of the Grange Class which had been introduced in 1936, and utilised parts from withdrawn 43xx Class 2-6-0's.

The Manors were built with smaller boilers, and had lighter axle loadings for working mixed traffic duties over cross country and branch lines of light construction.

They were, at first, very poor steamers and were not up to the standard for which Swindon had become renowned. Two further batches, each comprising of ten locomotives, were built surprisingly to the original design without modification. By 1951 it had become clear that something had to be done to remedy the situation, and No.7818 was sent to Swindon for tests. Following alterations to the draughting system, No.7818 emerged, at long last, as a free steaming locomotive, and was therefore

GWR Manor Class *Photograph courtesy of Milepost 92½*

capable of undertaking duties more efficiently. The rest of the class were treated accordingly, and their popularity increased dramatically with the footplate staff.

Whilst the Class was allocated to depots mostly in South West and Central Wales, it was on the former Cambrian Railways (Shrewsbury to Aberystwyth/Pwllheli route) that they achieved their fame. The Cambrian Coast Express was revitalised in 1954 and conveyed through coaches from Paddington to Aberystwyth, and also to Barmouth and Pwllheli. The Paddington to Shrewsbury section of the journey was usually King or Castle hauled, and at Shrewsbury a Manor took charge for the remainder of the journey, complete with headboard. Manors performed this duty until early 1966 when the locomotives were withdrawn, and standard Class 4-6-0's were drafted to the line. Eventually, the Paddington-Shrewsbury-Birkenhead services were transferred to London Midland Regions Euston-Wolverhampton-Shrewsbury route, and the Cambrian Coast Express faded into oblivion, only to be reintroduced for steam specials on the line in 1987.

In G.W.R. days the locomotives were finished in unlined green livery. They subsequently appeared in B.R. black, and later lined green. British Railways in full or either crest was carried according to the period.

Bachmann Manor Class

Mainline introduced a ready to run OO model in 1981 using tools owned by Kader. When Kader formed Bachmann in the UK in 1989, the Manor Class locomotive was introduced into the range the following year. It is currently available.

Grange Class 4-6-0
Great Western Railway

Introduced:	1936
Designed By:	C B Collett
Allocation:	Great Western Railway, later British Railways Western Region.
Locomotive Nos:	6800 - 6879. Built in Swindon from 1936 to 1939.
Last of Class Withdrawn:	1965
Number Built:	80
Preserved Examples:	None
Duties:	Mixed Traffic.
Technical Data:	**Tractive Effort:** (85%) - 28,875 lb **Loco Weight:** 74 tons **Loco Driving Wheels:** 5' 8" dia **Cylinders:** (2) - 18½" x 30" **Valve Gear:** Stephenson with piston valves.

The first of the 80 Grange Class 4-6-0's appeared in 1936, utilising wheels and motion from an identical number of withdrawn 43xx Class 2-6-0's. It was intended to replace all the 43xx's with either Grange or Manor Class locomotives, but with the outbreak of the Second World War, this plan was put to one side and never resumed. The last Grange was built in the summer of 1939, it was No.6879 Overton Grange.

GWR Grange Class *Photograph courtesy of Colour Rail*

The Granges were reduced versions of the Hall Class 4-6-0's, but with smaller driving wheels and raised footplate above the cylinders. The original 43xx Class cylinders were not retained, and slightly larger cylinders were fitted. Both 3500 and 4000 gallon tenders were used with this class.

Duties were almost identical to those performed by the larger Hall Class. Both types were given the Great Western Railway red route restriction, due to heavy axle loadings. The Class were allocated to principal depots on the West of England mainline, between London-Birmingham-Birkenhead and in South Wales. After Nationalisation they ventured onto the former Great Central mainline, working to Leicester Central via the Banbury-Woodford Halse link line. The Class were seen on a wide variety of duties, ranging from express passenger to freight workings. They were also used on banking duties, particularly over the South Devon banks on the West of England mainline. The last locomotives survived until late 1965 when steam on the Western Region ended. Both Oxford and Banbury held allocations at the end, when Nos. 6815, 6819, 6829, 6838, 6847-6849, 6856, 6859, 6872 and 6876 were scrapped.

The Grange Class were first turned out in unlined green livery. After Nationalisation they carried B.R. mixed traffic lined black livery, later appearing in lined green. British Railways in full or either crest was carried according to the period.

Hornby Grange Class

> Both Bachmann and Hornby announced a new Grange Class locomotive in 2004 after years of modellers requesting a ready to run model. To avoid duplication the Hornby model was introduced in 2005 and Bachmann opted for the Hall Class in original condition.

Castle Class 4-6-0
Great Western Railway

Introduced:	1923
Designed By:	C B Collett
Allocation:	Great Western Railway, later British Railways Western and London Midland Regions.
Locomotive Nos:	4073 - 4099 5000 - 5099 7000 - 7037
Last of Class Withdrawn:	1965
Number Built:	171

Preserved Examples:

4073 Caerphilly Castle	5051 Drysllwyn Castle
4079 Pendennis Castle	5080 Defiant
5029 Nunney Castle	7027 Thornbury Castle
5043 Earl of Mount Edgcumbe	7029 Clun Castle

Duties: Express Passenger

Technical Data:
Tractive Effort: (85%) - 31,625 lb
Loco Weight: 79 tons 17 cwt
Loco Driving Wheels: 6' 8½" dia
Cylinders: (4) - 16" x 26"
Valve Gear: Inside Walschaerts with rocking shafts (piston valves).

The ancestry of the Great Western Railway Castle Class 4-6-0, can be traced back to Churchward's Star Class 4-6-0 of 1906. The Castles were larger versions with detail alterations which included longer frames, larger fireboxes, and an increase in the cylinder size. A new cab was designed to greatly increase the comfort of the footplate staff. The Star cabs were primitive and draughty, and did not give staff adequate protection from the elements. Another identification feature was the double bend steam pipes from the outside cylinders, and a new design of boiler was fitted.

GWR Castle Class *Photograph courtesy of Milepost 92½*

The first of the class was released from Swindon in August 1923. In all, 171 Castles were to be built from 1923 to 1953 in twelve different batches. Sixteen of the locomotives were conversions from the Star Class, and one of the rebuilds included the Great Western's only Pacific locomotive, 'The Great Bear'. Various modifications were made over the years to locomotives in the class. 66 of the class were fitted with double chimneys during rebuilding. 5 were converted to oil firing in 1946, but only lasted for some two years in that condition. No.5005 was streamlined, in similar vein to the King Class No.6014, but this did not last long either. Between 1946 and 1947, several locomotives were fitted with three or four row superheaters and double chimneys as appropriate.

The Castles were soon appearing in front of the public; No.4037 Caerphilly Castle appeared at the 1924 Wembley Exhibition alongside the L.N.E.R. No.4472 Flying Scotsman. This in turn led to the

1925 Interchange Trials between the two companies. No.5000 Launceston Castle was later sent on loan to the L.M.S. to work between Euston (London) and Carlisle. No.4082 Windsor Castle took part in the centenary celebrations of the Stockton & Darlington Railway in 1925. No.4082 later became the 'Royal' engine following a visit to Swindon by King George V, who was allowed to open the regulator and drive the locomotive.

All the class were originally named after famous castles. During the late 1930's and early 1940's, several locomotives were renamed after Warplanes and Earls. When these names were carried, a small plate, 'Castle Class', was affixed to the nameplates under the main name. The last of the class to be built, No.7037, was named 'Swindon' by the then Princess Elizabeth, during a visit to Swindon in November 1950.

The Castles were found on express passenger duties on all Great Western (later British Railways Western Region) main lines, from their introduction until the first withdrawals took place at the end of 1958. By 1964 only 14 locomotives remained in service, and these then became part of the London Midland Regions allocation following alterations to the regional boundaries north of Oxford.

These remaining Castles did not last long, and Paddington lost its last Castle hauled trains in 1965. Fortunately, eight of the Class survive in private ownership. No.4079 Pendennis Castle was exported to Australia in 1977, and repatriated in July 2000.

The Class, in G.W.R. days, carried lined green livery. After Nationalisation, B.R. lined green livery was applied. British Railways in full or either crest was carried according to the period.

Hornby Castle Class

Hornby Dublo introduced the first OO gauge model in 1957. After the company closed in 1964, the tooling passed to G & R Wrenn and sold initially under the Tri-ang Wrenn label. When Wrenn closed in 1992 the tooling passed to Dapol and subsequently to the new Wrenn company. It has not been reintroduced.

Also in 1957, Tri-ang introduced a TT ready to run model but this has not been available since the mid-1960s.

Airfix introduced a new OO ready to run model in 1980 which then passed to Mainline, Dapol and Hornby in 1998. It was upgraded before reintroduction and is currently available from Hornby.

In N gauge, Graham Farish introduced a ready to run model in 1982. After the company was acquired by Bachmann the model was upgraded before being reintroduced in 2003. It is still available in the Graham Farish range.

10xx County Class 4-6-0
Great Western Railway

Introduced:	1945
Designed By:	F W Hawksworth
Allocation:	Great Western Railway, later British Railways Western Region.
Locomotive Nos:	1000 - 1029. Built at Swindon from 1945 to 1947.
Last of Class Withdrawn:	1964
Number Built:	30
Preserved Examples:	None
Duties:	Mixed Traffic.
Technical Data:	**Tractive Effort:** (85%) - 32,580 lb **Loco Weight:** 76 tons 17cwt **Loco Driving Wheels:** 6' 3" dia **Cylinders:** (2) - 18½" x 30" **Valve Gear:** Stephenson link with piston valves.

The Hawksworth designed County Class was the final development of the Great Western Railway two cylinder 4-6-0's, which had commenced with Churchward's Saint Class in 1902.

GWR County Class *Photograph courtesy of Colour Rail*

During the Second World War, Swindon Works had undertaken construction of Stanier's LMS Class 8F locomotives for the War Department and Ministry of Supply. When this work was nearing completion, the G.W.R. decided to build a further batch of 4-6-0's as an interim period before commencing work on a Pacific (4-6-2). It was originally intended to use a Castle Class boiler, strengthened as required to accept a higher steam pressure of 280 psi. Following completion of the Class 8Fs, the G.W.R. had several castings left over and decided to utilise these. A boiler, very similar to the LMS Stanier Class 8F, was designed and fitted to the first of the Class (No.1000).

The Counties differed from G.W.R. tradition in several ways. They were fitted with a continuous splasher over the driving wheels, which caused problems regarding the fitting of nameplates to the Class. A new design of tender (4000 gallons) with flat sides was used.

The County Class was designed for mixed traffic work. After some good work initially, the Class soon developed a reputation for bad steaming. In the mid 1950's, No.1009 was recalled to Swindon to undergo draughting tests, and as a result a new style of double chimney was fitted. Most of the Class later received these also. It is worth noting that No.1000 was built with a double chimney, but the rest of the Class reverted to a single chimney during construction. Following these modifications, the Counties, like the Manors, emerged completely transformed and put up some good performances from then on.

The Class were allocated between main depots including Old Oak Common (London), Bristol (Bath Road), Newton Abbot, Truro, Laira (Plymouth), Penzance, Wolverhampton (Stafford Road) and Neyland in West Wales.

The Counties were delivered in full G.W.R. lined green with copper embellishments. Appearing as they did at the end of the Second World War, when most locomotives were running in black, the re-appearance of pre-war G.W.R. livery caused a great deal of excitement. In B.R. days, mixed traffic lined black was first applied, although all later carried B.R. brunswick green livery. 'British Railways' in full, or either crest, would have been carried according to the period.

Hornby County Class

Dapol produced a OO gauge ready to run model in 1985. This passed to Hornby in 1998 and is still currently available.

28xx Class 2-8-0
Great Western Railway

Introduced:	1903
Designed By:	G J Churchward. Nos. 2884-3866 built to Collett's modified design from 1938.
Allocation:	Great Western Railway, later British Railways Western Region.

Locomotive Nos:	2800 - 2899
	3800 - 3866
	All built at Swindon.
Last of Class Withdrawn:	1965
Number Built:	165

Preserved Examples:

2807	2873	3814
2818	2874	3822
2857	2885	3845
2859	3802	3850
2861	3803	3862

Duties: Heavy Freight.

Technical Data: **Tractive Effort:** (85%) - 35,380 lb
Loco Weight: 75 tons 10 cwt (a); 76 tons 5 cwt (b) Collett locos
Loco Driving Wheels: 4' 7½" dia
Cylinders: (2) - 18½" x 30"
Valve Gear: Stephenson with piston valves.

The 165 examples of this Class were built in three distinct batches. The first batch (Nos. 2800-2830) were constructed between 1903 and 1907, the second batch (Nos. 2831-2883) were constructed between 1911 and 1919, and the third batch (Nos. 2884-3866) were constructed between 1938 and 1942, long after Churchward had been succeeded by Collett.

GWR Class 28xx *Photograph courtesy of Colour Rail*

The first locomotive left Swindon as No.97 in 1903, and it retained its number until around 1912 when it became No.2800.

The prototype locomotive was followed by a production run in 1905, taking the opportunity to make minor modifications before commencing construction. When construction re-commenced in 1911, the cylinder size was increased, and earlier locomotives were later altered as they passed through works. Further locomotives were constructed in 1938 when Collett made several minor improvements, the most important feature being the fitting of side windows to the cabs which gave train crews more protection from the elements. The locomotives completed after the outbreak of the Second World War had blackout panels instead of windows, but when hostilities ceased these were replaced by windows.

When the last batch was nearing completion, the War Department considered constructing a further 60 units for service overseas. However, this did not come to anything, and eventually the LMS Class

8F 2-8-0 became their choice. The 8F's were constructed at various works, and Swindon built some 80 of them.

The class were found on most parts of the former G.W.R. system, usually working heavy coal trains. For this purpose, many were allocated to depots in South Wales for working trains to London and the Midlands. When the British Rail Standard Class 9Fs began to infiltrate onto the Western Region in the 1950's, many were relegated to ordinary freight and pick-up goods trains. They were often used on parcel trains and occasionally on passenger trains, notably for special occasions when the Traffic Department was hard pressed to find alternative motive power.

20 locomotives were converted to oil burning between 1945 and 1947. These were re-numbered in the 48xx series. All had been converted back to coal firing by early 1950, and returned to the former numbering.

When delivered, No.97 (later No.2800) carried lined black livery. The production locomotives carried unlined green, until British Railways days when they carried unlined black. British Railways in full or either crest was carried according to the period.

Hornby Class 28xx

Hornby produced a OO ready to run model in 1993. It is currently available.

King Class 4-6-0
Great Western Railway

Introduced:	1927
Designed By:	C B Collett
Allocation:	Great Western Railway, later British Railways Western Region. Restricted to certain routes (please see text).
Locomotive Nos:	6000 - 6029
Last of Class Withdrawn:	1962
Number Built:	30
Preserved Examples:	6000 King George V 6023 King Edward II 6024 King Edward I
Duties:	Express Passenger.

Technical Data: **Tractive Effort:** (85%) - 40,300 lb
                                     Loco Weight: 89 tons
                                     Loco Driving Wheels: 6' 6" dia
                                     Cylinders: (4) - 16¼" x 28"
                                     Valve Gear: Inside Walschaerts with rocking shafts.

The Great Western Railway was a very publicity conscious organisation, taking great delight in proclaiming its Castle Class as the most powerful locomotives in the British Isles. All was well until the Southern Railway constructed its Lord Nelson Class 4-6-0's in 1926. These had a tractive effort of 33,500 lb, compared with the 31,625 lb of the G.W.R.'s Castle Class. Waterloo, as can be imagined, took great delight in claiming the title from G.W.R.. The powers at Paddington were not amused, so C.B.Collett, the Chief Mechanical Engineer, commenced the design work on what was to become the King Class.

GWR King Class *Photograph courtesy of Milepost 92½*

The main problem confronting Collett was the 20 ton axle loading. He asked for this to be increased so that he could build a bigger locomotive. He was eventually given a limit of 22½ tons within which to work, whilst the Civil Engineer undertook the necessary job of strengthening bridges along the West of England line as far as Plymouth.

The first of the Kings emerged from Swindon Works in June 1927, with the tractive effort of 40,300 lb. The publicity team once again proclaimed that the G.W.R. had the most powerful locomotives. The first of the Class, No.6000 King George V, was sent on a tour of important stations along the West of England line. It was then shipped to the USA to take part in the centenary celebrations of the Baltimore & Ohio Railroad, and during the celebrations the locomotive acquired its famous inscribed bell and cabside medallions.

The 30 members of the Class were initially restricted to just three routes; Paddington to Plymouth, Paddington to Bristol and Paddington to Birmingham/Wolverhampton. Some additional routes were added in British Railways days. The Kings were always found at the head of the most prestigious express passenger trains, and continued on these duties until withdrawal commenced in the early 1960's.

In the B.R. Interchange Trials of 1948, No.6013 King Henry VI was set to work on the Kings Cross route. It did not greatly impress and was soon returned to the Western Region.

As years passed, the Kings were modified and improved. In 1935 No.6014 King Henry VII was streamlined, but this did not enhance its looks or running a great deal, and most of the fittings were soon removed. The streamlined cab was, however, retained until withdrawal. In early B.R. days (1948) they were fitted with four row superheaters, mechanical lubricators for cylinders and piston valves. In 1955 the final development took place, No.6015 was fitted with double blastpipe and double chimney, and over the following three years the rest of the Class were so treated.

The arrival of the Western Class 52 diesels in 1962 ousted them from their final duties on the Paddington to Birmingham/Wolverhampton line, and the class were all withdrawn by the end of 1962. All except three of the class have been cut up.

In G.W.R. days lined green livery was carried. B.R. first turned them out in an ultramarine B.R. blue, before returning them to their more acustomed brunswick green. British Railways in full or either crest was carried according to the period.

Hornby King Class

Graham Farish introduced a OO gauge ready to run model in 1951. It was produced until 1953.

It was another 26 years before Lima introduced their model in 1977. This model has not been available since 1993 and is unlikely to be reintroduced despite the tooling passing to Hornby in 2005. Hornby have their own version which they introduced in 1978 and upgraded in 2003.

Graham Farish introduced a N gauge ready to run model in 2000 just before the company was taken over by Bachmann. It was upgraded by Bachmann and reintroduced in 2003.

SR Rebuilt West Country *Photograph courtesy of Milepost 92½*

A1 & A1X Class 'Terrier' 0-6-0 T
London, Brighton & South Coast Railway

Introduced:	1872
Designed By:	W Stroudley
Allocation:	London, Brighton & South Coast Railway, later Southern Railway, later British Railways Southern and Western Regions. Others saw service with the South Eastern & Chatham Railway, Newhaven Harbour Company, Isle of Wight Central Railway, Shropshire & Montgomery Railway, Edge Hill Light Railway, Freshwater Yarmouth & Newport Railway, The Kent & East Sussex Railway, The Weston Clevedon & Portishead Railway, London & South Western Railway and the Great Western Railway etc.. In Australia, eight locomotives were constructed to the same design for use on the New South Wales Government Railway.
Locomotive Nos:	70 - 75, built 1872. 64 - 69, built 1874. 53 - 63, built 1875. 47 - 52, built 1876. 41 - 46 and 76, built 1877. 35 - 40, built 1878. 77 - 84, built 1880. All built at Brighton. L.B. & S.C.R. later prefixed numbers by 6xx. S.R. prefixed numbers again by 2xxx. B.R. prefixed numbers again by 3xxxx.
Last of Class Withdrawn:	1963
Number Built:	50
Preserved Examples:	72 Fenchurch 55 Stepney W11 Newport 32662 Martello W8 Freshwater 32670 Poplar 50 Sutton 78 Knowle 54 Waddon 82 Boxhill
Duties:	Suburban, Branch Passenger and Shunting.
Technical Data:	**Tractive Effort:** (85%) - 7,650 lb (A1); 10,695 lb (A1X) **Loco Weight:** 27 tons 10 cwt (A1); 28 tons 5 cwt (A1X) **Loco Driving Wheels:** 4' 0"dia **Cylinders:** (2 inside) - 12" x 20" (A1); 14 3/16ths" x 20" (A1X) **Valve Gear:** Stephenson with slide valves.

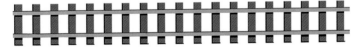

LB & SCR Class A1X *Photograph courtesy of Colour Rail*

The London, Brighton & South Coast Railway required a fleet of new locomotives for working its London suburban area trains. Stroudley commenced work in 1870, and three types of locos were designed before the final design was accepted. Construction commenced in 1872 and had not gone very far before Stroudley changed boiler details. Originally it was intended to use a domeless boiler, but this was altered to a larger boiler with a dome.

Problems were experienced with the first six locomotives' cylinders. These were modified after all other locos had been fitted with a new type of cylinder from new. These locos were designated Class A, later becoming Class A1. They were nicknamed 'Terriers'. Nearly all were sent new to London for suburban work, which they were well suited for with their close coupled wheels. Several were used on the East London line, and were named after localities served by that line.

Modifications were carried out over the years, as was the fitting of experimental equipment. Following an accident in 1901, the Board of Trade Inspector recommended that improvements be made to the feed pumps.

Newhaven Harbour (Sussex) was owned by an independent company who worked closely with the L.B. & S.C.R.. Following an accident involving their own two locos, they borrowed two Terriers. They purchased No.72 'Fenchurch' in 1898, and in subsequent years leased Terriers from the L.B. & S.C.R. as required.

In the late 1890's, locomotives were still in use on the Wimbledon, Bognor Regis, Hayling Island and East Southsea branches. They had been relegated from most of the rapidly expanding London suburban services, due to lack of power. In 1899, The Locomotive Committee recommended the withdrawal of all but 15 locos over a four year period.

The Isle of Wight Central Railway acquired No.75 'Blackwall' in 1899. They subsequently purchased No.40 'Brighton', No.69 'Peckham' and No.84 'Crowborough'. Realising the apparent 'boom' in the second-hand Terrier market, surplus engines were advertised for sale. The engineering firm of

Pauling & Co. was engaged in building the Great Western/Great Central joint line via High Wycombe, and they purchased five locos for use on construction trains, they were No.36 Bramley, No.39 Denmark, No.49 Bishopgate, No.52 Surrey and No.57 Thames. Three were scrapped after completion of this work in 1902, and the other two were re-sold for use possibly in South America. The Kent & East Sussex Railway purchased No.70 Poplar and No.71 Wapping. The London & South Western Railway purchased No.46 Newington and No.68 Clapham, initially for service of the Axminster to Lyme Regis branch. The South Eastern & Chatham Railway acquired No.54 Waddon, initially for use on the Isle of Sheppey. Eight of the Class were sold after the First World War, Nos. 637 and 638 went to the Admiralty for use in Scotland, No.667 to a firm who later re-sold it to a Derbyshire colliery, Nos. 673 and 674 to The Edge Hill Light Railway, and Nos. 679, 681 and 683 to the Admiralty. Three of the Admiralty locos, Nos. 638, 681 and 683, were re-sold to The Shropshire & Montgomery Railway. The London & South Western Railway re-sold its No.734 (L.B. & S.C.R. No.646) to the Freshwater Yarmouth & Newport Railway on the Isle of Wight. No.643 was sold to the Weston Clevedon & Portishead Railway in 1925. This company purchased a second Terrier, No.2653, in 1937. When this line went into liquidation in 1940, the Great Western Railway was principal creditor, and acquired the assets of the line, including its two Terriers. The G.W.R., after working on them at Swindon, put them into service in the Bristol Docks. The better of the two locos (ex L.B. & S.C.R. No.643), was put into service at Taunton and Bridgwater, finishing at Newton Abbot in 1950 (G.W.R. No.5 Portishead).

Changes to the numbering system took place from 1900, the original two digit numbers being prefixed by 6xx. Another major change was the fitting of new boilers and larger cylinders, designed by Marsh, from 1911 to Nos. 644, 647, 653, 655, 661-663, 673, 677-679 and 680. These locomotives were reclassified A1X. New boilers were also provided for three locos, previously sold out of service Nos. 40 and 84 of the I.O.W.C.R., and the Newhaven Harbour loco (ex L.B. & S.C.R. No.72). These were altered between 1913 and 1918. From 1919, four L.B. & S.C.R. A1 locos were similarly treated, Nos. 635, 643, 650 and 659.

At the Grouping in 1923, the L.B. & S.C.R. had fourteen A1X's and two A1's in service. The Southern Railway, however, took over the four I.O.W.C.R. Terriers, plus one from the Freshwater Newport & Yarmouth Railway. In 1927, after the acquisition of The Newhaven Harbour Company, a further example was taken into stock.

The Isle of Wight locomotives were numbered with a 'W' prefix, and from the later 1920's all received names. They were running at this time as follows: No.W2 Freshwater, No.W3 Carisbrooke, No.W4 Bembridge, No.W9 Fishbourne, No.W10 Cowes, No.W11 Newport and No.W12 Ventnor. Nos. W2, W4, W9 and W10 were returned to the mainland in the mid 1930's, the nameplates being acquired by the 02 Class 0-4-4 T's on their departure. Of those remaining, some numbers were altered, and the four remaining locos ran as No.W8 Freshwater, No.W11 Newport, No.W13 Carisbrooke and No.W14 Bembridge. No.W14 left for the mainland around 1936. The three remaining Terriers survived until 1949. Under the 1931 S.R. re-numbering scheme, all three digit numbers were prefixed by 2xxx.

On the mainland, Terriers saw service on shunting, shed pilot or branch line duties. Fratton Shed (Portsmouth) had a large allocation for working the Hayling Island branch from Havant. Others were in service stock, principally as works shunters at Brighton and Lancing.

At Nationalisation in 1948, one A1 and thirteen A1X locomotives were passed onto the new owners by the Southern Railway. The Great Western Railway added one of the former W.C. & P.R. locos, and the previously independent Kent & East Sussex Railway provided another example. All S.R. numbers were prefixed by 3xxxx.

The ex G.W.R. locomotive (No.5 Portishead) was used as shed pilot at Newton Abbot until 1950 when it was returned to the stock shed at Swindon. Here it remained for some years before withdrawal. Brighton works closed in 1959 and the Terrier, previously in departmental stock, was returned to service stock, albeit briefly. From 1963, the Terriers were also removed from Lancing Works, when USA 0-6-0 T's were transferred there. Newhaven lost its Terrier workings also in 1963, as did the Hayling Island branch which was closed to passenger services at the end of 1963. Following the closure of Fratton Shed, the Hayling branch locomotives had been allocated to Eastleigh.

No.32646 spent many years on static display outside a Hayling Island public house, before being donated to the Isle of Wight Steam Centre at Haven Street.

On delivery, the locomotives carried Stroudley's yellow livery with green lining. From 1905 they carried umber with black/gold lining. After grouping, some appeared in Southern green, whilst some service locos appeared in black. Unlined green was applied to one locomotive before the remainder of the Class were painted unlined black. B.R. painted the unlined black, but all later received lined black. British Railways in full or either crest was carried according to the period. Those in service with other companies carried the liveries of the company concerned.

Hornby LB & SCR Class A1X

Dapol introduced a OO gauge ready to run in 1989. Following the sale of the tools to Hornby in 1996, the model was upgraded and reintroduced in 1998. It remains available.

Class R1 0-6-0 T
South Eastern & Chatham Railway

Introduced:	1910
Designed By:	Wainwright. Rebuild of Stirling R Class
Allocation:	South Eastern & Chatham Railway, later Southern Railway, later British Railways Southern Region.
Locomotive Nos:	10, 47, 69, 107, 127, 147, 154, 174, 335, 337 and 340.
	Numbering was not consecutive and tended to be allocated in the

order of locos entering service, and not in batches as on other railways.

Prefixed letter A in Southern Railways list. Later prefixed 10xx for two digit numbers, and 1xxx for three digit numbers.

B.R. added 3xxxx from 1948.

Last of Class Withdrawn: 1960

Number Built: 13

Preserved Examples: None

Duties: Shunting and Pilot work.

Technical Data:
Tractive Effort: (85%) - 18,480 lb; 18,780 lb Whitstable Line loco
Loco Weight: 46 tons 15 cwt; Whitstable line loco 46 tons 8 cwt
Loco Driving Wheels: 5' 2" dia; Whitstable Line loco 5' 1" dia
Cylinders: (2 inside) - 18" x 26"
Valve Gear: Stephenson.

SE & CR Class R1 *Photograph courtesy of Colour Rail*

By the mid 1880's, the South Eastern Railway was desperately short of shunting locomotives, possessing only a handful of ageing Cudworth designed tanks. Therefore, any loco available on shed would be press-ganged into service to shunt the yards.

In 1887, Stirling was asked to design eight six-coupled tank locomotives, which were constructed at the company's Ashford Works. The first of the new locos, designated Class R, entered service in the summer of 1888. These locos had open sided cabs to allow maximum look out facilities, but in return offered little comfort to the train crews during inclement weather. Seventeen more locos were constructed between 1890 and 1898, this time offering better protection due to the fitting of the Stirling cabs, which were of rounded design. Four locos, Nos. 10, 77, 124 and 147, had smaller Urie pattern chimneys fitted to allow them to be used on the Canterbury to Whitstable line, which had a restricted loading gauge.

Following the amalgamation of the South Eastern and London, Chatham & Dover Railways in January 1899, they entered S.E. & C.R. stock. Initially, the R Class were fitted with domeless boilers, but from 1910 Wainwright fitted 13 of the Class with his H Type domed boiler. These locos were reclassified Class R1. Wainwright designed new cabs, and these were fitted to all but Nos. 10 and 147, which were used on the Canterbury to Whitstable line.

In 1923, the Southern Railway took over and all 13 locomotives entered Southern stock. To meet tight clearances on the Canterbury to Whitstable line, No.1010 was fitted with a stovepipe chimney and Ross pop safety valves. Nos. 1147, 1339 and 1069 were treated likewise, although in the case of Nos. 1339 and 1069, it was necessary to remove the Wainwright cabs and revert back to the Stirling rounded cabs, removed from the redundant R Class locos. Other boiler mountings were cut down to improve clearances at the same time. This line closed in 1952 and, despite a brief reprieve due to floods in 1953, was lifted in 1954.

In addition to the Canterbury to Whitstable duties, the R1's were allocated to other depots for shunting duties, including Ashford, St. Leonards, Bricklayers Arms and Folkestone Junction. At Folkestone, the R1's became the mainstay of the steeply graded harbour branch. In addition to shunting work they were used as pilots on the heavy boat trains, and it was not uncommon for two locos to head the train with a third banking from the rear. They continued on these duties until 1959 when ex G.W.R. pannier tanks were drafted onto the line. This was the end for the R1's, and once the pannier tanks had become established, the last locos were withdrawn from service in 1960.

At Nationalisation in 1948, all 13 locomotives survived to enter the British Railways service, although No.1127 did not survive for long, being withdrawn in early 1949.

Various liveries were carried over the years. All entered service in S.E.R. black, which after 1900 was changed to S.E. & C.R. brunswick green. During the First World War, locos were painted in S.E. & C.R. austerity grey. In Southern ownership, goods black livery was applied and continued under B.R.. British Railways in full or either crest was carried according to the period.

Wrenn SE & CR Class R1

Hornby Dublo introduced a ready to run OO gauge model in 1959 and it was only available as a 2 rail locomotive and was the first from the company to have a plastic body. After the closure of the Meccano operation in 1964, the tools passed to Tri-ang and it was re-released under the Tri-ang Wrenn label in 1968. After the collapse of the Tri-ang empire in 1971, Wrenn then became independent again in 1972 and continued to produce the model until retirement resulted in the sale of the company to Dapol in 1993. The model did not reappear under Dapol ownership and despite the sale of the Wrenn tooling to G & R Wrenn (Mordvale) in 2001, it has not reappeared.

Class L1 4-4-0
Southern Railway

Introduced:	1926
Designed By:	R L Maunsell
Allocation:	Southern Railway, later British Railways Southern Region.
Locomotive Nos:	A753 - A759, after 1931 became 1753 - 1759. A782 - A789, after 1931 became 1782 - 1789. All built by North British Locomotive Co. in 1926. BR added 3xxxx to the 1931 numbers.
Last of Class Withdrawn:	1962
Number Built:	15
Preserved Examples:	None
Duties:	Express Passenger, later less arduous services although often used by double heading on heavy boat trains.
Technical Data:	**Tractive Effort:** (85%) - 18,910 lb **Loco Weight:** 57 tons 16 cwt **Loco Driving Wheels:** 6' 8" dia **Cylinders:** (2 inside) - 19½" x 26" **Valve Gear:** Stephenson.

SR Class L1 *Photograph courtesy of Colour Rail*

The L1 Class, built in Southern Railway days, follow a fairly long line of development from the Wainwright ex Class D 4-4-0s which were introduced in 1902, many of which being rebuilt with Belpaire fireboxes between 1931 and 1937. Wainwright then developed the Class E, already fitted with Belpaire fireboxes, between 1905 and 1909, several being rebuilt by Maunsell from 1919 as Class E1. During 1914, by which time Maunsell had taken over from Wainwright, the Class L was introduced, designed by Wainwright, which were the final locos built for the SE&CR.

By 1923, the London to Folkestone boat trains were too heavy for a Class L to handle, whilst the Civil Engineer had eased weight restrictions on the SE&CR main line, and thus Maunsell produced the Class L1 4-4-0, which was based on the rebuilt Class E1s which had larger diameter driving wheels (instead of 6' 6" dia), larger diameter cylinders (increased by ½") which raised the tractive effort from 18,410 lb to 18,910 lb. Unlike the previous Classes D, D1, E, E1 and L, which had a SE&CR flare sided tender with coal plate, a slab sided 3,500 gallon tender was paired with these locos.

Whilst Maunsell introduced the King Arthur 4-6-0s in 1924 and the Lord Nelson 4-6-0s in 1926, the L1s still performed their intended duties on the Eastern Section boat trains, being shedded at Bricklayers Arms or Dover. With the introduction of the Merchant Navy and Battle of Britain/West Country Pacifics, the L1s were reduced to less arduous work on the Charing Cross to Hastings route, although they were often used to pilot the Pacifics on the heavy 'Night Ferry', working consisting of the British gauge 'Wagon-Lits' sleeping cars.

When introduced, and again after the 1939-1948 war, the locos appeared in Malachite green until about 1953. During the war black was applied, whilst in BR days lined black livery was applied and they carried either crest according to the period.

Tri-ang Hornby SR Class L1

Tri-ang introduced a OO Gauge ready to run model in 1960. The tooling passed to the new Tri-ang Hornby company in 1965 after the take over of the Meccano empire, and then to the new Hornby company in 1972. The model has not been produced since 1972.

M7 Class 0-4-4 T
London & South Western Railway

Introduced:	1897
Designed By:	Dugald Drummond
Allocation:	London & South Western Railway, later Southern Railway, later British Railways Southern Region.

Locomotive Nos:	21 - 60, 104 - 112, 123 - 125, 126*, 127 - 133, 241 - 256, 318 - 324, 328, 356, 357, 374 - 379, 479 - 481 and 667 - 676.

All built at Nine Elms & Eastleigh 1897-1911.

* No.126 was rebuilt in 1921 (see text).

The following locomotives were fitted with steam reversing gear, and had an extended front end:
21, 27-29, 45-60, 104-111, 125, 128, 129, 131, 328, 379, 480 and 481.

B.R. added 30xxx to these numbers.

Last of Class Withdrawn:	1964
Number Built:	105
Preserved Examples:	30053 245
Duties:	Suburban or Branch Passenger and empty Stock Working.
Technical Data:	**Tractive Effort:** (85%) - 19,755 lb **Loco Weight:** 60 tons 1 cwt; Extended/Modified locos 62 tons **Loco Driving Wheels:** 5' 7" dia **Cylinders:** (2 inside) - 18½" x 26" **Valve Gear:** Stephenson with slide valves.

L & SWR Class M7 *Photograph courtesy of Colour Rail*

The Class M7 tanks were designed primarily for suburban work out of London (Waterloo). Construction of the class commenced in 1897 at the company's Nine Elms Works in London, where a total of 95 locomotives were built prior to closure of the works. The remaining 10 engines were built at Eastleigh after the workshops were moved there. As in most classes, there were minor variations between locos. The major modification was that some locos were increased in overall length by some 15 inches (see Data Tables).

On entering service, the Class M7's proved extremely powerful for tank locomotives of this type, and had a fair turn of speed. This led to them being tried on semi-fast trains from Waterloo to Portsmouth and Bournemouth. This train working continued until a derailment brought a hasty curtailment to these activities. For branch line work, many were later fitted with push/pull apparatus. Others members of the class were used for empty stock workings and station pilot duties, particularly at Waterloo. Urie, when Chief Mechanical Engineer, experimented in 1921 with rebuilding of No.126. It was rebuilt with a higher pitched boiler, extended smokebox with superheater, enlarged cylinders and stovepipe chimney. It was known at Nine Elms as the 'Coffeepot'. Despite its rebuilding, No.126 was not a great success, and was withdrawn in 1937.

Most of their days were spent on the former L. & S.W.R. system, although after grouping a few examples were sent for trials to depots in Kent, but soon returned to their native ground. Under B.R. ownership, a few were again sent to work in Kent and Sussex.

Major withdrawal commenced in 1958 as a result of branch line closures, and following publication of the Beeching Report, many more were made redundant. The start of 1964 saw them confined to the Swanage and Lymington branches. These duties were then handed over to the ex LMS Ivatt 2-6-2 Ts and the newer B.R. Standard Class 4MT 2-6-4 tanks.

In L. & S.W.R. days they carried lined green livery. Under Southern ownership they were finished in unlined black, and after Nationalisation B.R. lined black. British Railways in full or either crest was carried according to the period.

Hornby L & SWR Class M7

> Tri-ang Hornby introduced a ready to run OO gauge model in 1967. It passed to Hornby in 1972 following the collapse of the Tri-ang group. It was last produced in 1986.
>
> Hornby announced in 2006 that they were to produce a new model of the class which is currently available.

Class E2 0-6-0 T
London, Brighton & South Coast Railway

Introduced:	1913
Designed By:	L B Billington
Allocation:	London, Brighton & South Coast Railway, later Southern Railway, later British Railways Southern Region.
Locomotive Nos:	100 - 109, L.B. & S.C.R numbers, then 2100 - 2109, S.R. numbers.
	B.R. added 3xxxx to S.R. numbers.
Last of Class Withdrawn:	1963
Number Built:	10
Preserved Examples:	None
Duties:	Shunting and Pilot work. Initially envisaged as Passenger locos (see text).

Technical Data:

Tractive Effort:	(85%) - 21,305 lb
Loco Weight:	52 tons 15 cwt (Nos.32100-32104); 53 tons 10 cwt (Nos.32105-32109)
Driving Wheels:	4' 6" dia
Cylinders:	(2 inside) - 17½" x 26"
Valve Gear:	Stephenson.

LB&SCR Class E2 *Photograph courtesy of Colour Rail*

The first five E2 tank locomotives, Nos. 100-104, were built at the L.B. & S.C.R.'s Brighton Works during 1913/1914. A further batch, differing slightly from the first (Nos. 105-109), was ordered in 1914, but due to wartime conditions delivery was slow, with the last entering service in 1916.

The E2's were allocated to depots at Brighton, Eastbourne and London (New Cross). Nos. 103 and 104 were put to work on passenger push/pull trains between London Bridge and Crystal Palace. They were not particularly suitable for passenger working and were relegated to shunting duties, which the other members of the class had been performing since introduction. The New Cross locos also undertook pilot and empty stock workings at London Bridge, whilst others worked on local goods trains.

In 1923, the L.B. & S.C.R. became part of the Southern Railway, and the E2's became part of the Southern stock. After grouping, some of the class found their way to the former South Eastern & Chatham Railway lines around Victoria and Dover. At Dover, they were employed on pilot and shunting duties in the docks. With the advance of electrification and the transfer of steam to other areas, The E2's were allocated to Eastleigh for shunting in Southampton Docks.

Several modifications were carried out over the years, including the fitting of Ashford injectors and the removal of water heating equipment. Nos. 100-103 were fitted with lever reverse, other members of the Class had the normal screw reversing. The last five locos, Nos. 105-109, also had slightly longer tanks which increased the overall length by 3½ inches, and the weight to 53 tons 10 cwt.

Withdrawals commenced in 1961, and by 1963 all ten locos had been scrapped.

In L.B. & S.C.R. days, Nos. 103 and 104 carried lined umber (passenger) livery, whilst the remainder of the Class were painted black. Southern Railways lined black (goods) livery was later applied. Following an economy drive in the 1930's, the lining was not renewed as locos passed through works, and they carried plain black livery throught the rest of their working lives. British Railways in full or either crest was carried according to the period.

Hornby LB & SCR Class E2

Trix introduced a ready to run model manufactured to 3.8mm (midway between HO and OO scale) but running on OO track. This model was produced only between 1961 and 1972.

Hornby introduced a ready to run OO version in 1979. It was withdrawn in 1985 and adapted to become Thomas in the Thomas the Tank engine range. It remains available only as Thomas

Class 700 0-6-0
London & South Western Railway

Introduced:	1897
Designed By:	D Drummond
Allocation:	London & South Western Railway, later Southern Railway, later British Railways Southern Region.
Locomotive Nos:	687 - 716, built by Dübs & Co 1897.

NB: Nos. 702-715 were renumbered 306, 308, 309, 315, 317, 325-327, 339, 346, 350, 352, 355 and 368 during 1898.
No.716 was renumbered 459 during 1898, and further renumbered 316 during 1912.

BR added 30xxx to the running numbers.

Last of Class Withdrawn:	1963
Duties:	Generally Freight services, occasionally used for Passenger duties.
Technical Data:	**Tractive Effort:** (85%) - 21,698 lb; 23,540 lb Rebuilt
	Loco Weight: 42 tons 15 cwt; 46 tons 14 cwt Rebuilt
	Loco Driving Wheels: 5' 1" dia.
	Cylinders: (2 inside) - 18½" x 26"; 19" x 26" Rebuilt
	Valve Gear: Stephenson with slide valves.

L & SWR Class 700 *Photograph courtesy of Colour Rail*

This class of engines came about when William Adams (who was the Chief Mechanical Engineer of the LSWR) was suffering ill health, and Douglas Drummond, almost by default, circulated drawings of a similar locomotive to those he had recently designed for the Caledonian Railway. He received quotes from various contractors, the lowest being from Robert Stephenson for £2,675 per loco for delivery in 1898, however, Dübs & Co could deliver 30 locos within 1897 for £2,695 per loco.

Many parts of the new locomotives used the boiler, cylinders and motion that were also used on the Class M7 0-4-4 Tanks. Lever reverse was used rather than steam reversing (as it was deemed quicker when shunting), and steam brakes were applied to both loco and tender. Problems were found in the driving axles of some of the locos, and troubles with regulators which if opened suddenly failed to close properly. One accident is recorded at Yeovil Junction where No.690 struck the six coaches it was to haul.

In 1898, the locomotives were spread as follows: 11 at Nine Elms, 7 at Strawberry Hill, 1 at Guildford, 5 at Northam, 2 at Salisbury and 4 at Exmouth Junction.

Around 1903/1904, the class gained the nickname of 'Black Motors', although no reason has ever been found for this. The locomotives were generally used for freight duties to the Southampton or Exeter areas, although they were occasionally diagrammed as passenger specials, seaside excursions or Boer War troop trains. Instances during the 1914-1918 War record these locos at Oxford, Gloucester (Eastgate) and Peterborough North. In 1920, after the end of the War, Robert Urie (who succeeded Drummond as the CME in 1912) concluded that by modernising the locos, improvements could be achieved at a reasonable cost, hence No.316 went to Eastleigh for rebuilding. It received an extended smokebox, capuchon capped stove pipe chimney, Eastleigh pattern superheater, higher boiler pressure (raised from 175 to 180 lbs psi), new firebox and the boiler was pitched 9" higher. It was released into traffic in December 1920 at a cost of less than £315 if the normal shopping charges are ignored. Reports from the Eastleigh and later Nine Elms sheds, quickly proved the value of this rebuilding, so in 1921 orders were placed for a further 10 locos to be similarly treated when shopped as routine. Therefore, Nos. 308, 350, 368 and 694 were dealt with during 1922; Nos. 326, 346, 687, 689 and 700 were dealt with during 1923; and No.339 was dealt with during 1924. Superheating was also fitted to those locos not so treated using Maunsell superheaters, therefore Nos. 309, 315, 317, 325, 697 and 698 were modified during 1925; Nos. 327, 690-693, 695 and 696 were modified during 1926; Nos. 352, 688, 699 and 701 were modified during 1927; and Nos. 306 and 355 were modified during 1929.

In 1936, an attempt was made to reclassify the Class to Class C, but this caused confusion with the SE & CRs Class C which was built by Wainwright, and so the idea was dropped.

The locomotives did a lot of hard work during the Second World War when the Southern Railway loaned some of its 4-6-0 goods and passenger locos to the Great Western and London & North Eastern Railways. The locos continued to work either to Southampton or Exeter, although they also began to appear at Neasden and Cricklewood on cross London goods duties. The locos that continued in service during the late 1950s were based at Nine Elms, Feltham, Guildford, Basingstoke, Eastleigh, Bournemouth, Exmouth Junction and Salisbury.

As the BR Modernisation Plan began, and with the Beeching closures and increased use of road transport, this Class of locos were withdrawn in 1962. However, No.30316 was retained for snow plough works until February 1963, and Nos. 30689 and 30700 were similarly resurrected at Exmouth Junction until the end of the adverse weather.

These locomotives, when delivered, were in lined dark green livery with oval brass numberplates, also the tenders were lettered SWR, the green edged with brown. Later, numbers were applied to the cab sides with the full LSWR on the tender. At Grouping, the locos were repainted in lined black livery with Southern on the tender. In BR days, the class was in black livery with British Railways in full or either crest according to the period.

Union Mills have announced that they will be adding an N Gauge model to their range during 2007.

OO Works also produced a ready to run model during 2007.

V Class 4-4-0 (Schools)
Southern Railway

Introduced:	1930
Designed By:	R E Maunsell
Allocation:	Southern Railway, later British Railways Southern Region.
Locomotive Nos:	900 - 939, built at Eastleigh 1930-1935.
	B.R. added 30xxx to these numbers.
Last of Class Withdrawn:	1963
Number Built:	40
Preserved Examples:	30925 Cheltenham 926 Repton 928 Stowe
Duties:	Express Passenger trains on secondary main lines.
Technical Data:	**Tractive Effort:** (85%) - 25,135 lb **Loco Weight:** 67 tons 2 cwt **Loco Driving Wheels:** 6' 7" dia **Cylinders:** (3) - 16½" x 26" **Valve Gear:** Walschaerts with piston valves.

SR V Class (Schools) *Photograph courtesy of Colour Rail*

The V Class (Schools) locomotives were to become the last and most successful of a long line of British 4-4-0 locomotives.

At the time, the 4-4-0 wheel arrangement was being dropped by designers, in favour of the six coupled arrangement (4-6-0 and 4-6-2). The Southern was in need of a light weight locomotive, mainly for secondary main line work on the Eastern section. This section had a restricted loading gauge and a limited axle loading of around 21 tons.

The Schools made use of standard parts, where possible, from the King Arthur and Lord Nelson classes. The locomotives were fitted with a high degree of superheat, and an excellent boiler which worked on 220 lbs p.s.i..

Nos. 30900, 30901, 30907, 30909, 30914, 30915, 30917-30921, 30924, 30929-30931, 30933 and 30934 were fitted with multiple jet blast-pipes and large diameter chimneys.

Bullied experimented by fitting half of the class with double chimneys and Lemaitre blast pipes, and deflectors were fitted from 1932 onwards to improve the drivers vision.

The Class was designed primarily for express work over secondary routes. It was not long however, before they were undertaking heavier work. Most of their working lives were spent on the Eastern section, although in their earlier days Portsmouth and Bournemouth held an allocation. During the 1950's, they were all in use on the Eastern section, until electrification of lines in Kent made them redundant. Some were used on the Charing Cross to Hastings service, before the introduction of diesel multiple units. A few were sent to Salisbury and Exeter on the Western section. The bulk of the Class was withdrawn between 1959 and 1961, and the remaining few on the Western section survived until 1963.

On introduction, Southern Railways passenger green livery with Sunshine lettering was used. After Nationalisation, B.R. lined black was carried and lined green livery with British Railways in full and either crest was carried according to the period.

Hornby SR V Class (Schools)

Trix Twin were due to introduce a ready to run model in 3.8mm scale half way between HO and OO scale in 1939. The model was delayed by the second world war and did not appear until 1959. It was only available until 1960.

Hornby introduced a ready to run OO gauge model in 1981. It was last available in 2001.

N Class 2-6-0
South Eastern & Chatham Railway

Introduced:	1917
Designed By:	R E Maunsell
Allocation:	South Eastern & Chatham Railway, later Southern Railway, later British Railways Southern and Western Regions.

Locomotive Nos:

810 - 821
823 - 824
A825 - A875   See text for building details.
1400 - 1414

Southern Railway prefixed the letter A, later increased numbers by 1000.

B.R. prefixed 30xxx to the numbers.

Last of Class Withdrawn:	1966
Number Built:	80
Preserved Examples:	31874 Brian Fisk
Duties:	Mixed Traffic.

Technical Data:

Tractive Effort: (85%) - 26,035 lb
Loco Weight: 61 tons 4 cwt
Loco Driving Wheels: 5' 6" dia
Cylinders: (2) - 19" x 28"
Valve Gear: Walschaerts with piston valves.

Shortly after his appointment as Chief Mechanical Engineer of the South Eastern & Chatham Railway, Maunsell began design work on a 2-6-0 for heavy freight work, for which the company was in dire need. The locomotive was designed, to enable it to be used for passenger duties if required, thus making it a mixed traffic type.

The first locomotive to be built, No.810, entered service in 1917, and after the initial minor problems had been ironed out, proved to be a great success. Fourteen further locos, Nos. 811-821 and 823-825, were ordered in 1917. Recovery from the First World War was slow, and it was not until 1920 that the first of these entered service, the last of them not appearing until after grouping in 1923.

At the Grouping, numbers were prefixed by the letter A, a practise which continued until the early 1930's, when the letter was removed and the numbers increased by 1000.

Initially, Lambert wet sanding equipment was fitted, but it was later discovered that this ruined the tyres of the driving wheels, and the conventional steam system replaced it.

Another problem concerned rough riding when working passenger trains. It was found, after consultation with the G.W.R., that the balancing required modification. This was duly done on all locos at Ashford, the first wheel sets being balanced correctly at Swindon (G.W.R.).

The blastpipe was also causing loss of steam, and drivers carried a special tool for dealing with this problem. Often made by the shed blacksmith, it was much frowned upon by shed foremen and senior management. At Bricklayers Arms they resolved the problem unofficially, by modifying the blastpipe and chimney on a loco which had a reputation for being a poor steamer. The effect was dramatic, and word eventually got to Maunsell who summoned the loco to Ashford for inspection. Eventually, after consulting the G.W.R., blastpipes from the G.W.R.'s 43xx Class 2-6-0's were fitted, along with different chimneys.

SE & CR N Class *Photograph courtesy of Colour Rail*

At the end of the First World War, the Ministry of Munitions found it necessary to find work for its large work force, which were no longer required to manufacture items for war. Ashford was asked for drawings of the N Class, 100 of which were to be manufactured at Woolwich Arsenal. Boilers were sub-contracted, 80 being supplied by the North British Locomotive Co., and 20 by Robert Stephenson & Co. Limited. The South Eastern & Chatham and the Great Eastern Railway were both keen to purchase, but progress was slow and costs were far in excess of estimates, and construction was sloppy. Both companies lost interest, which left Woolwich with the problem of not having prospective customers.

After Grouping, the Southern Railway became interested in 20 locos and tenders at a very competitive price, the Ministry having decided to cut its losses and dispose of the various bits and pieces as best it could. Ashford was responsible for getting them ready for service, a considerable feat which involved almost total reconstruction of the nearly completed locos, and assembly of the remainder. They became Nos. A826-A845.

A further 30 locos, Nos. A846-A875, were purchased soon after in kit form. One of these, No.A866, was exhibited at the Wembley Exhibition in 1925.

The Southern ordered 15 additional locomotives, which entered service between 1932 and 1934, bringing the Class total to 80. This batch incorporated several modifications and detail differences, over the earlier batch. They became Nos. 1400-1414. Nos. 1407-1414 entered service with smoke deflectors, which the rest of the Class received in due course.

The class were well spread around the Southern network, working from Ashford, Eastleigh, Bricklayers Arms, Exmouth Junction, Redhill, Salisbury, Eastbourne, Norwood Junction, Battersea, Dover, New Cross Gate, Barnstaple and Okehampton, on both freight and passenger services.

During the Second World War, the class were used almost exclusively on heavy freight work destined for the Channel ports. Some re-allocation took place to cope with changes in traffic, and workings to Banbury and Oxford (G.W.R.) were regular occurances.

By the early 1960's, electrification work was progressing well, and the first of the Class 33 diesels had also been delivered. This resulted in a major re-allocation of locos from the South Eastern division to the Western and Central division depots, Brighton and Weymouth receiving examples. The end of steam working was, however, not far away, and the first withdrawals took place in 1962. Following boundary changes in 1963, several Southern Region depots in the West Country were acquired by the Western Region. Several N's were transferred into W.R. stock, but were quickly withdrawn.

Remaining locomotives worked out their days on works trains, empty stock working, and on occasional local passenger duties. The final locos, Nos. 31405 and 31408, were withdrawn in 1966.

Initially, early members of the Class carried S.E. & C.R. austerity grey. The Southern repainted them in lined green. During the Second World War, the lining was not replaced, and from 1941 unlined black was applied. From 1946, malachite green livery was used. After Nationalisation, B.R. lined black became standard, British Railways in full or either crest was carried according to the period.

Bachmann SE & CR N Class

Bachmann introduced a ready to run OO model in 1995. This is not currently available.

N Brass introduced a ready to run N gauge version in 1996.

King Arthur Class 4-6-0
Southern Railway

Introduced:	1923, developed from Uries design of 1914.
Designed By:	R. E. Maunsell
Allocation:	Southern Railway, later British Railways Southern Region.
Locomotive Nos:	448 - 457, built at Eastleigh 1923.

Maunsell modifications to Urie design:
736 - 755, built at Eastleigh 1925 with Maunsell cab.
763 - 792 built by North British Locomotive Co., Glasgow 1925.
793 - 806, built at Eastleigh 1926/1927, fitted with 3,500 gallon six wheel tenders.

BR increased numbers by 30,000.

Last of Class Withdrawn:	1962
Number Built:	55
Preserved Example:	777 Sir Lamiel
Duties:	Express Passenger.

Technical Data:

Tractive Effort:	(85%) - 25,320 lb Nos.448-457, 763-806; No.735 26,245 lb; Nos.736-754 23,915 lb
Loco Weight:	Nos.448-452 & 763-792 80 tons 19 cwt; Nos.453-457 79 tons 18cwt; Nos.736-755 80 tons 7cwt; Nos.793-806 81 tons 19 cwt
Driving Wheels:	6' 7" dia.
Cylinders:	(2) - Nos.448-457 and 763-806 20½" x 28"; Nos.736-754 21" x 28"; No.755 22" x 28"
Valve Gear:	Walschaerts with piston valves.

The Southern Railway's King Arthur Class owes its existence to Uries H15 Class 4-6-0, the first batch of which were built at Eastleigh in 1914 for the London & South Western Railway. The class eventually numbered ten locomotives before the shortage of materials, caused by World War I, brought production to an end.

At the grouping in 1923, the L&SWR became part of the Southern Railway to which R. E. Maunsell was appointed C.M.E.. The urgent priority was the need to build an express locomotive for use on all three sections (Central, Eastern and Western) of the newly formed company. It was decided to order ten more H15s, and work commenced at Eastleigh. They were, however, different from the first batch, being fitted with a new front end, smaller cylinders, longer valve travel and redesigned outside steam pipes. The boiler pressure was increased from 180 lbs to 200 lbs per square inch, and the superheater size was also increased. The locos retained their Drummond type cab, which therefore limited them to the former L&SWR lines out of Waterloo. These locos were also paired with eight wheeled bogie 5,000 gallon tenders known as Drummond Watercarts, or similar Urie tenders.

SR King Arthur Class *Photograph courtesy of Colour Rail*

A further batch of locomotives were built at Eastleigh in 1925, and these were fitted with redesigned cabs to allow them to be used on other sections of the Southern Railway. More locos were required, but Eastleigh did not have the capacity and was unable to supply further examples. Southern looked to an outside contractor to build a further 30 locos, and the North British Locomotive Company of Glasgow was given the job.

During 1926, Nos.737-739 were converted to oil fired, but many problems surfaced and they were re-converted back to coal fired within the same year.

In 1926/1927 the final batch of 14 locomotives was built at Eastleigh. These were for use on the Central section, and were paired with six wheel tenders of Maunsell design.

By now, the H15 Class had become the N15 Class, and as they were all named after characters etc. from the King Arthur legends, they were collectively known as the King Arthur Class.

In 1942, the LNER were acutely short of mixed traffic locomotives, and Nos.739, 740, 742, 744, 747-751 and 754 were sent to Heaton (Newcastle) via the ex Great Central Line. The locos were generally used on fast goods to Hull, Edinburgh and Starbeck (Harrogate), also appearing on secondary passenger services around York, Selby, Leeds and Newcastle-Darlington. No.742 probably achieved the most fame when following a failure of the booked engine, took over the 10pm Edinburgh to Kings Cross at Berwick, loaded to 20 coaches, and starting with a boiler pressure of 120 lbs psi, worked to Newcastle losing only 9 minutes. However, with the USA pattern Class 2-8-0s becoming more plentiful, the locos were returned to the Southern in July 1942.

Further experiments with oil burning took place during 1946/1947, and Nos. 740, 745, 748, 749 and 752 were so converted, again short lived, as all had been re-converted to coal fired before the end of 1948.

The King Arthurs were found on express passenger duties until the last of the Class was withdrawn in 1962. They earned their place in history by becoming the first British locomotive to be fitted with smoke deflectors, which improved drivers vision when drifting exhaust caused problems. This became a standard practice on many classes over the next few years.

In Southern Railway days the class were painted in lined Malachite green with sunshine lettering. Under BR ownership they carried standard lined Brunswick green, British Railways in full or either crest according to the period.

Hornby SR King Arthur Class

Hornby introduced a ready to run model in 1976, and this was last produced in 1978. An upgraded version was released by Hornby during 2007.

Class Q1 0-6-0
Southern Railway

Introduced:	1942
Designed By:	O V Bullied
Allocation:	Southern Railway, later British Railways Southern Region.
Locomotive Nos:	C1 - C40, built at Ashford and Brighton 1942.
	B.R. added 330xx to these numbers.
Last of Class Withdrawn:	1965
Number Built:	40
Preserved Examples:	33001 Part of the National Collection at York
Duties:	Freight and occasional Passenger.
Technical Data:	**Tractive Effort:** (85%) - 30,080 lb
	Loco Weight: 51 tons 5 cwt
	Loco Driving Wheels: 5' 1" dia
	Cylinders: (2 inside) - 19" x 26"
	Valve Gear: Stephenson with piston valves.

Despite the arrival of the Q Class 0-6-0's in 1938, the Southern Railway found itself desperately short of modern freight locomotives at the outbreak of the Second World War. Bullied had arrived on the Southern Railway just as the Q Class were being completed, and he soon realised that additional freight locos would be required.

SR Class Q1 *Photograph courtesy of Milepost 92½*

The outbreak of the war saw a large increase in the number of freight trains bound for the Channel ports. This required locomotives capable of hauling heavy trains, yet still keeping within the maximum axle load of 18 tons, and a total weight limit of 54 tons.

The Q1's were designed around the largest possible firebox, which was based on the Lord Nelson type, suitably modified. Multiple Jet blastpipes were also fitted. The need to keep weight to a minimum, and the restrictions regarding supply of construction materials, led to many conventional locomotive features, such as running plates and splashers being omitted. The boiler casing was in three sections, and made of lightweight materials. Other notable features were the 'bucket' shaped chimney, flat topped dome and box-pok type wheels, similar to those fitted to his Pacific Class locos.

The Q1's found themselves working over most parts of the Southern system, occasionally hauling passenger trains on the Reading to Tonbridge and Eastleigh to Portsmouth routes. During the 1960's, all were allocated to Feltham, Guildford and Eastleigh depots. These locos were used by the Southern Railway to head many of their cross London freight services, and it was not unusual to see examples of the class at Willesden, Cricklewood or Neasden. At the time of withdrawal, all were allocated to Guildford.

Hornby SR Class Q1

Under Southern Railway ownership, the locomotives were painted unlined black with 'Southern' on the tenders. In B.R. days, the locos retained this livery with both British Railways in full or either crest being carried according to the period.

Hornby introduced a ready to run OO model in 2003. It remains available.

West Country/Battle of Britain Class 4-6-2 Southern Railway

Introduced:	1945, rebuilt from 1957
Designed By:	O V Bullied, rebuilt by R G Jarvis
Allocation:	Southern Railway, later British Railways Southern Region.
Locomotive Nos:	21C101 - 21C120, built at Brighton 1945. 21C121 - 21C152, built at Brighton 1946. 21C153 - 21C170, built at Brighton 1947. 34071 - 34089, built at Brighton 1948. 34090 - 34094, 34096, 34098 and 34100, built at Brighton 1949. 34095, 34097 and 34099, built at Eastleigh 1949. 34103 and 34105 - 34109, built at Brighton 1950. 34101, 34102 and 34104, built at Eastleigh 1950. 34110, built at Brighton 1951.

Nos. 21C101-21C170 were built for Southern Railway and were later renumbered 34001-34070.
Nos. 34071-34110 were built and numbered in BR days.

West Country Class: 34001 - 34048 and 34091 - 34108.
Battle of Britain Class: 34049 - 34090 and 34109 - 34110.

West Country Class Rebuilding took place between June 1957 and May 1961. They were Nos:
34001, 34003-34005, 34008-34010, 34012-34014, 34016-34018, 34021, 34022, 34024-34029, 34031, 34032, 34034, 34036, 34037, 34039, 34040, 34042, 34044-34048, 34093, 34095-34098, 34100, 34101, 34104 and 34108.
Battle of Britain Class Rebuilding took place between August 1958 and March 1961. They were Nos:
34050, 34052, 34053, 34056, 34058-34060, 34062, 34071, 34077, 34082, 34085, 34087-34090 and 34109.

Last of Class Withdrawn:	1967
Number Built:	110

Preserved Examples:	34007 Wadebridge	34059* Sir Archibald Sinclair
	34010 Sidmouth	34067 Tangmere
	34016 Bodmin	34070 Manston
	34023 Blackmore Vale	34072 257 Squadron
	34027* Taw Valley	34073 249 Squadron
	34028* Eddystone	34081 92 Squadron
	34039* Boscastle	34092 City of Wells
	34046* Braunton	34101 Hartland
	34051 Winston Churchill	34105 Swanage
	34053* Sir Keith Park	*Denotes rebuilt
	34058* Sir Frederick Pile	locomotives.

Duties: Express Passenger and Mixed Traffic.

Technical Data:
Tractive Effort: (85%) - 27,715 lb
Loco Weight: 86 tons as built; 90 tons 1 cwt as rebuilt.
Loco Driving Wheels: 6' 2" dia
Cylinders: (3) - 16 3/8" x 24"
Valve Gear: Bullied or Walschaerts piston valves, as rebuilt.

SR Battle of Britain Class as built *Photograph courtesy of Colour Rail*

The West Country and Battle of Britain Class locomotives were almost identical in appearance to Bullied's earlier larger Merchant Navy Class, which was introduced in 1941. They were, however, smaller and lighter and hence had a wider route availability weighing in at 86 tons, compared with the 97 ton 18 cwts of the larger locos. However, they retained many of the features of the larger locos, including patterned box-pok driving wheels, electric generators for headlights, steam reversing gear and a chain drive encased in an oil bath (which was prone to catch fire), as well as the air smoothed casing (streamlining).

As initially shaped, the drivers vision was often impeded by drifting smoke, and several attempts were made to clear this by changing the draughting around the chimney and modifying the size of the smoke deflectors. During the BR Locomotive Exchange Trials, Nos 34004, 34005 and 34006 received extra long smoke deflectors.

SR Rebuilt Battle of Britain Class *Photograph courtesy of Colour Rail*

When delivered in July 1947, No.34064, after trials, was taken back into Brighton Works and was fitted with a wedge shaped (or Vee) cab with two side windows. From No.34066 onwards, three windows were fitted and retrospectively fitted as the new cabs were applied the class. Also, from No.34071 onwards, cabs were made 9' 0" wide as opposed to the original 8' 6", and those locos destreamlined were similarly modified. Tenders stayed at 8' 6" wide and were shuffled to get 9' 0" wide locos with 9' 0" wide tenders. The wedge shaped cabs took until March 1957 to complete, almost 10 years!

As built, the locomotives had 3 safety valves set in a triangle, approximately at the longitudinal midpoint of the boiler. However, as modifications to the locos took place, they were reduced to 2 safety valves which were positioned nearer the cab.

Generally speaking, the West Country Class locomotives tended to be used on services from Waterloo to the West Country, as they were named after towns and locations there. The Battle of Britain Class were used from Victoria, Charing Cross and Cannon Street to Kent and Sussex, and were named after the Squadrons and personalities who served in the R.A.F..

Two attempts were made by British Rail to send some of these locomotives to the Great Eastern section of the Eastern Region. Initially, No.34059 went to Stratford for some 5 months early in 1949. Lack of maintenance facilities and staff shortages at Stratford was the excuse this time.

A further attempt was made by BR in 1959 to strengthen the stud of the Great Eastern Sections Thompson B1 Class 4-6-0s, still being delivered until 1952. Hence, Nos. 34039, 34057 and 34065 were sent initially, then Nos. 34076 and 34089 followed, to be used between Liverpool Street and Norwich (direct or via Cambridge) to Clacton or Parkestone Quay. However, the BR Britannia's were coming, and they were preferred and indeed highly successful, transforming the Great Eastern line services.

In the 1948 Interchange Trials, No.34004 worked between Inverness and Perth, No.34006 was sent to work on the ex Great Central Main line between Manchester and London (Marylebone), and No.34005 was also involved. To enable the locos to work on these lines, they were coupled to ex LMS tenders fitted with water pick-up apparatus (the Southern Railway had no water troughs).

Problems continued to show themselves with the chain drive and steam operated valve gear, it was not unknown for a driver to be doing 90 mph forwards with the valve gear set in full reverse!

In 1955, R.G. Jarvis (Chief Technical Assistant at Brighton Works), under the direction of Bullied's successor H.H. Swift, produced plans ro rebuild the Merchant Navy Class locos commencing with No.35018 which was outshopped from Eastleigh in February 1956. The whole 30 locos were so treated, whilst the West Country and Battle of Britain Classes were next considered with No.34005 released into traffic from Eastleigh in June 1957. Changes included removal of air smoothed casing, elimination of oil bath, and provision of Walschaerts valve gear, screw reversing, new smoke boxes with superheater elements, together with modifications to the tenders which involved removing the high sides making them similar to those fitted to the BR standard Pacifics (BR1). Tenders still varied from 4,500 to 5,500 gallons of water and 5 tons of coal. The modified locos proved more successful than the un-rebuilt versions, and 60 locos duly rebuilt, No.34104 being the last in May 1961.

By this time, British Railways were experimenting with other forms of traction, and it rapidly became evident that steam traction was no longer acceptable. Thus, the remaining 50 locos remained un-rebuilt, although several remained in service until the cessation of S.R. steam in 1967.

In Southern days, the Class were painted in Malachite Green with 3 yellow bands along the locomotive and tender side. A cast Southern ring surrounded the smoke box door handles, Southern in full was applied to the tender sides, and the loco number was applied to the cab sides and cover plate above the buffer beam between the main frames.

In early BR days, several experimental liveries were tried. Nos. 34011, 34056, 34064, 34065 and 34086-34088 had a test apple green livery applied with 2 horizontal yellow lines, by now with British Railways in full on the tender sides (the latter 3 from new between March and December 1948).

Application of the lined BR Brunswick Green livery occurred between October 1949 and March 1953, and many photos show the locos with no ownership title on their tenders, although the Southern label has gone from the smoke box door and been replaced by a cast number plate. In early BR days, the revised BR number was also placed on the front cover plate where the former Southern number was carried. Nos. 34091-34110 were delivered in BR lined Brunswick Green livery, and later both BR crests were carried according to the period.

Hornby SR West Country Class as built

Hornby SR Rebuilt West Country Class

Hornby Dublo introduced a ready to run OO gauge model of the rebuilt locomotive in 1961. After the closure of the Meccano operation in 1964, the tools passed to Tri-ang and it was re-released under the Tri-ang Wrenn label in 1968. After the collapse of the Tri-ang empire in 1971, Wrenn then became independent again in 1972 and continued to produce the model until retirement resulted in the sale of the company to Dapol in 1993. The model did not reappear under Dapol ownership and despite the sale of the Wrenn tooling to G & R Wrenn (Mordvale) in 2001, it has not reappeared.

Tri-ang introduced a ready to run OO model of the streamlined locomotive in 1961. It became part of the Tri-ang Hornby range in 1965 and to Hornby in 1971. The model was upgraded in both 1981 and 1995 before being replaced by a completely new model manufactured in China during 2001. Hornby introduced a rebuilt West Country Class model during 2006.

Graham Farish introduced a streamlined N gauge ready to run model in 1974. The tooling became damaged and was not available from 1985 until new tooling was produced in 1999. This tooling passed to Bachmann when they acquired the company in 2000 and an upgraded model was released in the Graham Farish range in 2004, which is still available.

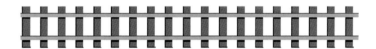

Merchant Navy Class 4-6-2
Southern Railway

Introduced:	1941. Rebuilt from 1956.
Designed By:	O V Bullied. Modified by R G Jarvis
Allocation:	Southern Railway, later British Railways Southern Region.
Locomotive Nos:	21C1 - 21C20, built at Eastleigh between 1941 and 1945. Later British Railways Nos. 35001 - 35020. 35021 - 35030, built at Eastleigh 1948/1949.
Last of Class Withdrawn:	1967
Number Built:	30
Preserved Examples:	35005 Canadian Pacific
	35006 Peninsular & Oriental Steam Navigation Company
	35009 Shaw Savill
	35010 Blue Star
	35011 General Steam Navigation
	35018 British India Line
	35022 Holland-America Line
	35025 Brocklebank Line
	35027 Port Line
	35028 Clan Line
	35029 Ellerman Line
Duties:	Express Passenger.

Technical Data: **Tractive Effort:** (85%) - 33,493 lb
Loco Weight: 97 tons 18 cwt
Loco Driving Wheels: 6' 2" dia
Cylinders: (3) - 18" x 24"
Valve Gear: Bullied, rebuilt as Walschaerts with piston valves.

The arrival of Bullied's first Pacifics caused something of a sensation when they made their debut in 1941. Despite the conflict then casting shadows over Britain and the rest of Europe, the Southern Railway somehow managed to gain maximum publicity for its new locomotive class, when 21C1 Channel Packet was named in Eastleigh in March 1941.

SR Merchant Navy Class as built *Photograph courtesy of Colour Rail*

The Merchant Navy's were first conceived in 1938, shortly after the arrival of Bullied, who had succeeded Maunsell as Chief Mechanical Engineer in November 1937. Prior to joining Southern Railway, Bullied had been Chief Assistant to Sir Nigel Gresley on the London & North Eastern Railway. Before Bullied's arrival, the Southern Railway had been pressing forward with its electrification programme, and as a result, few steam locos had been built in the preceeding years.

SR Rebuilt Merchant Navy Class *Photograph courtesy of Colour Rail*

In March 1938, the construction of ten new locomotives was authorised, but at that time no design details were available, but this was soon underway at the company's Brighton Works. When the Second World War broke out in September 1939, all the materials had been ordered. Eastleigh did not have the capacity to build the boilers, so this work was sub-contracted to the North British Locomotive Company.

The Merchant Navy's were the first of the Bullied Pacifics and were fitted with air smoothed casing. This was also applied to the later smaller and lighter West Country and Battle of Britain Classes. The first of the Merchant Navy's had a front end best described as being vaguely triangular in design. This was soon modified due to problems caused by drifting smoke. This modification later became the standard design. Another new innovation was the valve gear, which was steam operated and enclosed in an oil bath. This in turn led to maintenance problems and failures were not uncommon, but despite these problems two further batches, each consisting of ten locos, were built in 1944/1945 and 1948/1949 respectively. The last batch was not delivered until after Nationalisation, and were never allocated numbers in the 21C series. The numbering system adopted by Bullied was devised from the continental descriptions used for wheel arrangements. A Pacific 4-6-2 was classified 21C on continental railways. This system was abandoned under the new regime.

The Merchant Navy's were not particularly successful in their orginal form, and it was obvious that before long something would have to be done by British Railways. Once design work on the Class 9F 2-10-0's had been completed at Brighton, plans for rebuilding the Merchant Navy's commenced. It was decided to rebuild the locos on more conventional lines, and they were rebuilt between 1956 and 1958. The main modifications were centred around the removal of the air smoothed casing, and the replacing of the Bullied valve gear with Walschaerts. These, and other smaller modifications, completely transformed the locos, and a few of the class remained in service until the end of steam on the Southern Region in 1967.

On delivery, the first five locomotives were finished in Southern Railway malachite green with yellow lining. The second five locos of the first batch were painted in wartime black. After the cessation of hostilities they were repainted in green. After Nationalisation, most of the Class were turned out in the experimental blue livery. The Class completed their service in the lined brunswick green with 'British Railways' in full and both B.R. crests were carried, although only the latter crest on rebuilt locos.

Hornby SR Rebuilt Merchant Navy Class

Graham Farish introduced a ready to run OO model of the streamlined version in 1951. It was last produced in 1953.

Tri-ang produced a TT ready to run version in 1959 which remained until the demise of the range in 1964.

Wrenn introduced a OO ready to run model of the rebuilt locomotive in 1986 which was produced from the old Hornby Dublo West Country / Battle of Britain tooling. The tooling passed to Dapol in 1992 and to G & R Wrenn (Mordvale) in 2002, but has not been produced by either of them.

Model information continues on the next page

Graham Farish introduced a streamlined N gauge ready to run model in 1980. The tooling became damaged and was not available from 1985 until new tooling was produced in 1999. This tooling passed to Bachmann when they acquired the company in 2000 and an upgraded model was released in the Graham Farish range in 2004, which is still available.

Graham Farish also introduced an N gauge ready to run model of the rebuilt locomotive in 1997. When Bachmann took over Graham Farish in 2000 the tooling passed to them and an upgraded model was released in 2004.

Hornby chose the rebuilt Merchant Navy as the subject for the relaunch of their OO ready to run products in 2000.Whilst not in the current Hornby catalogue, it remains available.

Lord Nelson Class 4-6-0
Southern Railway

Introduced:	1926
Designed By:	R E Maunsell
Allocation:	Southern Railway, later British Railways Southern Region.
Locomotive Nos:	850 - 865, built at Eastleigh 1926-1929.
	B.R. added 30xxx to these numbers.
Last of Class Withdrawn:	1962
Number Built:	16
Preserved Example:	850 Lord Nelson
Duties:	Express Passenger.
Technical Data:	**Tractive Effort:** (85%) - 33,510 lb; 33,300 lb (No.859) **Loco Weight:** 83 tons 10 cwt; 84 tons 16 cwt (No.860) **Loco Driving Wheels:** 6' 7" dia. No.859 Lord Hood with 6' 3" dia **Cylinders:** (4) - 16½" x 26" **Valve Gear:** Walschaerts with piston valves.

SR Lord Nelson Class *Photograph courtesy of Milepost 92½*

In 1924, the recently formed Southern Railway began preliminary work on a new express locomotive. Following trips behind a G.W.R. Castle Class and a Gresley Pacific of the L.N.E.R., it was decided that a four cylinder loco would be able to cope admirably with the traffic departments requirements.

Work on the new design began in earnest in 1925, and delivery of the first locomotive took place in the late summer of 1926. Some six months of trial working followed before No.850 was available for normal service. Once sufficient experience had been gained with this loco, ten more locos were constructed in 1928, and a further five in 1929.

Originally, the class were fitted with 6' 7" dia wheels, however, during 1939 Bullied experimented by reducing the driving wheels of No.859 Lord Hood to 6' 3" dia, whilst No.860 Lord Hawke was fitted with a large boiler which was retained throughout its life. Other changes throughout the class was redesigned cylinders and the fitting of Lemaitre blast-pipes, which improved the locos dramatically.

The Lord Nelson's saw service on many of Southern Railways principal passenger trains, including the 'Atlantic Coast Express' and 'The Golden Arrow'. The arrival of the Bullied Pacifics from 1941, heralded the end of the Lord Nelson's superiority on Southern passenger services. The class then worked mainly over the former L. & S.W.R. line to Bournemouth.

In Southern Railways days, the Lord Nelson's were in fully lined malachite green. Under B.R. ownership, they carried B.R. lined brunswick green livery. 'British Railways' in full and either crest was carried according to the period.

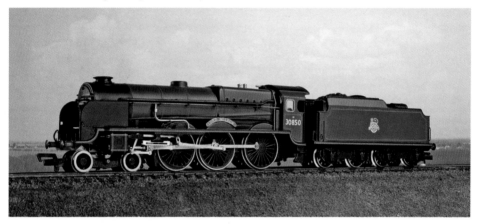

Bachmann SR Lord Nelson Class

Bachmann introduced a ready to run OO model in 1992. It is no longer available and last appeared in 2006.

Class B7 0-4-0 ST (Pug)
Lancashire & Yorkshire Railway

Introduced:	1886
Designed By:	J A F Aspinall
Allocation:	Lancashire & Yorkshire Railway, later London Midland & Scottish Railway, and British Railways Eastern, London Midland and Southern Regions.
Locomotive Nos:	L.M.S. Nos.: 11201 - 11257, built at Horwich from 1891 to 1920.

Sample L&Y Nos.:

11207	(504)	11243	(19)
11218	(68)	11247	(64)
11220	(139)	11249	(76)
11230	(814)	11254	(481)
11238	(2)	11257	(614)

Nos. 11210 & 11218 (1163 & 654) were withdrawn in 1926 without being re-numbered.

Nos. 11224, 11225, 11243, 11251 and 11255-11257 were sold by the L.M.S. to private owners between 1931 and 1937.

B.R. added 4xxxx to all L.M.S. numbers, e.g. 51202 etc..

23 numbers survived into B.R. days, they were Nos. 51202, 51204, 51206, 51207, 51212, 51216-51218, 51221, 51222, 51227, 51229, 51230, 51231, 51232, 51234, 51235, 51237, 51240, 51241, 51244, 51246 and 51253.

Last of Class Withdrawn:	1963
Number Built:	60
Preserved Examples:	11243 51218
Duties:	Shunting, usually dock areas or where short wheel based locos were required.
Technical Data:	**Tractive Effort:** (85%) - 10,060 lb (boiler pressure 140 p.s.i.), and 11,492 lb (boiler pressure 160 p.s.i.) **Loco Weight:** 21 tons 5 cwt **Loco Driving Wheels:** 3' 0" dia **Cylinders**: (2) - 13" x 18" **Valve Gear**: Stephenson with slide valves.

These locomotives were a development of a previous Aspinall design for three locos built by Vulcan Foundry in 1886, the last survivor allocated L.M.S. No.11200 (916), but withdrawn in 1925 without re-numbering. Although designed by John Aspinall, the locos were built in six batches, approximately

Lancashire & Yorkshire Railway Class B7 *Photograph Courtesy of Colour Rail*

half under Aspinall between 1891 and 1899, and after George Hughes became Chief Mechanical Engineer in 1904, additional locomotives were built through to 1910.

These locomotives were one of the few on any British Railway company which had dumb buffers. They also had very open cabs, although from photographic evidence several were provided with additional steel slide sheets, which provided some protection against the elements.

Only having a 5' 9" wheelbase, these diminutive little locomotives were used mainly in dock areas where sharp curves limited larger locomotives usage.

These locomotives were allocated to Bank Hall (for the Liverpool Docks), Preston and Goole. Others were allocated to Bath Green Park (S&DJ), and sub shedded to Radstock for working the colliery sidings alongside an L.M.S. pattern Sentinel Shunter.

Hornby Lancashire & Yorkshire Railway Class B7

The locomotives were unusual in having protective covers to the slide bars and cross heads to prevent sand being spilt onto these parts while filling the sandbox located above. Several of the Bank

Hall locos (including Nos. 11212, 11216 and 11232), were fitted with a swivelling smoke hood to deflect the blast from the chimney in low headroom areas.
The locomotives were always in unlined black livery, and British Railways in full or either B.R. crests were carried according to the period.

Dapol introduced a OO gauge ready to run model in 1984. It subsequently passed to Hornby who reintroduced it in 1998. Whilst it is not in the current Hornby catalogue, it is available.

Class 264/611 0-4-0 ST
Caledonian Railway

Introduced:	1885. Derived from standard Neilson 0-4-0 ST of 1875.
Designed By:	Dugald Drummond. Further examples by J F McIntosh.
Allocation:	Caledonian Railway, later London Midland & Scottish Railway, later British Railways Scottish & London Midland Regions.
Locomotive Nos:	264 & 265, LMS Nos. 16012 & 16013, built 1885.

264 & 265, LMS Nos. 16012 & 16013, built 1885.
266 - 268, LMS Nos. 16008 - 16010, built 1885.
269, Withdrawn before grouping, built 1885.
270, LMS No. 16011, built 1885.
271, LMS No. 16014, built 1885.
431, LMS No. 16039, built 1908.
463, LMS No. 16038, built 1908.
510 - 515, LMS Nos. 16020 - 16025, built 1890.
611 - 614, LMS Nos. 16026 - 16029, built 1895.
615 - 618, LMS Nos. 16015 - 16018, built 1889.
619, Withdrawn before grouping, built 1889.
620, LMS No.16019, built 1889.
621 - 626, LMS Nos. 16030 - 16035, built 1900.
627 & 628, LMS Nos. 16036 & 16037, built 1902.
All built at St. Rollox.

Nos. 514 & 515 and remainder fitted with steam brakes when new.

First digit (1) altered to 5 in B.R. days.
Nos. 56010, 56011, 56020, 56025-56032, 56035, 56038 and 56039 entered B.R. stock at Nationalisation.

Last of Class Withdrawn:	1962
Number Built:	39
Preserved Examples:	None
Duties:	Mainly Shunting in dock areas.
Technical Data:	**Tractive Effort:** (85%) - as built 10,601 lb (boiler pressure 140 psi), Modified 12,115 lb (boiler pressure 160 psi). **Loco Weight:** 27 tons 7½ cwt **Loco Driving Wheels:** 3' 8" dia **Cylinders:** (2) - 14" x 20" **Valve Gear:** Stephenson with slide valves.

Caledonian Railway 264/611 Class *Photograph Courtesy of Milepost 92½*

These locomotives were intended for shunting in dock areas, with their short wheel base of only 7', they were able to negotiate curves down to 1½ chains radius (99'). The first order was initially for ten locomotives, but the first two were built as 0-4-2 ST's and used on the Killin Branch (known as 'Killin Pugs'), being fitted with Westinghouse brakes to operate this steeply graded branch.

The 0-4-0 ST's, which cost £720 to build, were very spartan locomotives having no back to the cab, no coal bunkers, eight spoke cast iron wheels, dumb buffers and reversing lever on the right hand side of the loco, despite being left hand drive. The cab side sheets were extended to provide some coal storage space, and later (in LMS days) four wheel wooden bodied trucks were provided, some locos received round shank buffers on the front of dumb buffers, full depth back cab sheets and spark arrester chimneys.

The Caledonian Railway also built several 0-6-0 ST's of similar design, with outside cylinders, and larger water and coal capacity. When McIntosh took over as Chief Mechanical Engineer in 1895, his first locos were more 0-4-0 ST's, almost identical to the Drummond locomotives, except they had twelve spoke cast iron wheels.

These locomotives were shedded mainly around the Glasgow and Edinburgh areas for working in the dockland areas. They were also used as works pilots at St. Rollox and Lochgorm (Inverness).

Sheds which had allocations of the 264 Class included Airdrie, Balornock, Dalry Road, Grangemouth, Greenock and Yoker. No.56032 finished its life at Crewe Works, whilst No.56027 spent its final days at Preston working in the docks. The final locomotive to be withdrawn, No.56025, was used as a works shunter at St. Rollox Works.

No.56025 received B.R. white/grey/red lining, carrying British Railways in full or either crest according to the period. It is uncertain whether any other examples were so treated, although all locos were in black livery through their service lives, losing their Caledonian Railway brass numberplates at grouping in 1923. None of the class carried Caledonian blue livery as far as can be ascertained.

Hornby 264/611 Class

Hornby introduced a OO ready to run model in 1980. It has also appeared in a number of fictitious industrial liveries over the years. It is currently available.

Class 2P 4-4-0
London Midland & Scottish Railway

Introduced: 1928

Designed By: Sir Henry Fowler

Allocation: London Midland & Scottish Railway, later British Railways
                         London Midland, Southern and Scottish Regions.

Locomotive Nos: 563 - 571, built at Derby 1928.
                         572, became 601 shortly after entering service. Built at Derby 1928.
                         573 & 574, built at Derby 1928.
                         575 & 576, became Somerset & Dorset Joint Committee Nos. 44 & 45
                         in 1928, and L.M.S. Nos. 633 & 634 in 1930. Built at Derby 1928.
                         575 & 576*, built at Derby 1929.
                         577 - 579, built at Derby 1928.
                         580, became SDJC No.46 in 1928, and L.M.S. No.635 in 1930. Built
                         at Derby 1928.
                         580*, built at Derby 1929.
                         581 - 600, built at Derby 1928.
                         602 - 612, built at Derby 1928.
                         613 - 628, built at Derby 1929.
                         629 - 632, built at Derby 1930.
                         636 - 660, built at Crewe 1931.
                         661 - 665, built at Derby 1931.
                         666 - 685, built at Derby 1932.
                         686 - 700, built at Crewe 1932.
                         * Replacement locos for those transferred to SDJC

                         Note that No.601 was fitted with Owens double port exhaust valves.

B.R. prefixed all numbers with 40xxx.

Last of Class Withdrawn: 1962

Number Built: 135

Preserved Examples: None

Duties: Light Suburban Passenger or Pilot Work.

Technical Data: **Tractive Effort:** (85%) - 17,730 lb
Loco Weight: 54 tons 1 cwt
Loco Driving Wheels: 6' 9" dia
Cylinders: (2 inside) - 19" x 26"
Valve Gear: Stephenson with piston valves.

LMS Class 2P *Photograph Courtesy of Colour Rail*

These locomotives were a derivative of a Midland Railway design from which Fowler, by rebuilding Johnson's 7' 4-4-0's, produced almost a new engine. This embodied a standard L.M.S. pattern boiler with reduced driving wheel diameter, boiler mountings, cylinder diameter and increased boiler pressure from 160 psi to 180 psi. This produced a more sprightly locomotive.

In 1933 Nos. 633 & 653 were fitted with Dabeg feed water heater apparatus, which was retained until both were withdrawn in 1959. Some of the tenders were fitted with coal rails to increase their coal carrying capacity.

In Scotland, the class were mostly allocated to the sheds to the South West of Glasgow at Hurlford, Ayr, Ardrossan and Dumfries. They worked trains on the Glasgow and Ayrshire suburban services alongside Fairburn 2-6-4 tanks. Several were allocated to sheds along the North Wales coast for local services, whilst ten of the class were allocated to Bath (Green Park) and Templecombe on the Somerset & Dorset line. They were often used for double heading the heavy holiday trains on the steeply graded route between Bath and Evercreech Junction. Most of these locomotives were fitted with automatic tablet exchange equipment, on the front left hand side of the tender, for working on single line sections.

Some locomotives were allocated to the Carlisle area, and were used for piloting duties on the Settle to Carlisle line (known as the 'Long Drag').

The introduction of cross country diesel multiple units, and the closure of many local lines in the early 1960's, saw the rapid withdrawal of virtually the entire class of the locos within the period of 1959 to 1962.

When introduced, the locomotives were painted in L.M.S. black livery lined in red. During the war unlined black was applied. Early B.R. livery was unlined black with lettered 'British Railways' in full, but later the red/grey/white lining was applied. It is probable that only the first B.R. crest was carried.

Hornby Class 2P

Hornby produced a ready to run OO model in 1973. The model was withdrawn in 1974 and has not been available since.

Airfix tooled a ready to run OO model prior to the model railway company being taken over by Palitoy in 1981, and it was incorporated into the Mainline Railways range. It did not appear until 1984 and then few were released before the company closed and the former Airfix assets were acquired by Dapol in 1986. The tools then passed to Hornby in 1996 and the model reintroduced in 1999. It is currently available.

Union Mills introduced a ready to run N gauge model in 2004. It is still available.

Class 2F (Later 2MT) 2-6-0
London Midland & Scottish Railway

Introduced:	1946
Designed By:	H G Ivatt
Allocation:	London, Midland & Scottish Railway, later British Railways London Midland, Eastern, Scottish and Western Regions.
Locomotive Nos:	6400 - 6409, built at Crewe 1946. 6410 - 6419, built at Crewe 1947. 46420 - 46434, built at Crewe 1948. 46435 - 46464, built at Crewe 1950. 46465 - 46494, built at Darlington 1951. 46495 - 46502, built at Darlington 1952. 46503 - 46514, built at Swindon 1952. 46519 - 46527, built at Swindon 1953. B.R. added 4 to all pre-1948 built locomotives.
Last of Class Withdrawn:	1967
Number Built:	128
Preserved Examples:	46428 46464 46441 46512 46443 46521 46447
Duties:	Light Branch Passenger and Freight.

Technical Data: **Tractive Effort:** (85%) - 17,120 lb (Crewe Locos), 18,510 lb (Others)
Loco Weight: Crewe Locos 47 tons 2 cwt, others 48 tons 9 cwt
Loco Driving Wheels: 5' dia
Cylinders: (2) - Crewe Locos 16" x 24", others 16½ x 24"
Valve Gear: Walschaerts motion with piston valves.

LMS Class 2F (Later 2MT) *Photograph Courtesy of Colour Rail*

These locomotives were designed for light branch line passenger and freight duties, and with very light axle loads had a wide route availability. With their almost enclosed cabs, the locos were ideal for working tender first, thus making it unnecessary for turntables to be provided at each end of their journey. Many of these locomotives had a very short life of only 15 years, due to branch line closures and dieselisation. The locos were spread around all regions except the Southern Region, and a further development was the B.R. Standard 78xxx class, which was an almost identical locomotive built at Darlington from 1953.

Initially the locomotives were in plain L.M.S. black livery, and later locos were outshopped in B.R. black livery. Swindon turned out their locos in lined green livery, and as most of these were maintained at Swindon, they consequently retained this livery throughout their service life. No.6441 was initially preserved in L.M.S. maroon livery, although this was not carried by L.M.S. locos prior to Nationalisation. British Railways in full could have been carried by the locos up to No.46434, then either BR crest according to the period.

Bachmann Class 2F (Later 2MT)

Minitrix introduced a ready to run N gauge model in 1975. It has not been produced since 1997.

In OO gauge Hornby introduced a OO ready to run version in 1975. This model last appeared in 1979.

Bachmann announced in 2006 that they are producing a OO gauge ready to run locomotive which will be available during 2007.

Class 2MT 2-6-2 T
London Midland & Scottish Railway

Introduced:	1946
Designed By:	H G Ivatt
Allocation:	London Midland & Scottish Railway, later British Railways London Midland, Eastern, Western and Southern Regions.
Locomotive Nos:	1200 - 1209, built at Crewe 1946/1947. (a)
	41210 - 41229, built at Crewe 1948, push/pull fitted. (a)
	41230 - 41259, built at Crewe 1949. (a)
	41260 - 41289, built at Crewe 1950, Nos. 41270 - 41289 push/pull fitted. (a)
	41290 - 41299, built at Crewe 1951. (b)
	41300 - 41319, built at Crewe 1952. (b)
	41320 - 41329, built at Derby 1952, push/pull fitted. (b)
	B.R. added 4xxxxx to above numbers of pre-1948 locomotives.
Last of Class Withdrawn:	1967
Number Built:	130
Preserved Examples:	41241
	41298
	41312
	41313
Duties:	Light Branch Passenger and Freight.
Technical Data:	**Tractive Effort:** (a) 17,410 lb; (b) 18,510 lb
	Loco Weight: (a) 63 tons 5 cwt; (b) 65 tons 4 cwt
	Loco Driving Wheels: 5' dia
	Cylinders: (2) - (a) 16" x 24"; (b) 16½" x 24"
	Valve Gear: Walschaerts with piston valves.

These locomotives were the tank version of the Ivatt L.M.S. 2MT 2-6-0 Class, which were also introduced in 1946. The design was perpetuated in B.R. days, and with slight modifications became the B.R. Standard 84xxx 2-6-2 T Class.

Early examples were spread around the Midland Region working many of the branch lines, and replacing older L.N.W.R. 2-4-2 T's, 0-6-2 T's and Midland Railway 0-4-4 T's. Fleetwood's allocation was used on services to Poulton-le-Fylde and Kirkham. Bristol (Barrow Road) used their examples on services to Mangotsfield and Bath (Green Park), whilst other examples were used on local S&DJ

LMS Class 2MT *Photograph Courtesy of Colour Rail*

services to Highbridge and Burnham-on-Sea. In the London area examples were allocated to Neasden, where they replaced the ex G.C.R. Class C13's on the Chesham branch until electrification. Bletchley locomotives were used on the Wolverton to Newport Pagnell, and Leighton Buzzard to Dunstable branches. Bedford locomotives were used on the Bedford to Hitchin line. Watford locomotives worked the services to St. Albans (Abbey) and from Harrow & Wealdstone to Stanmore. Locomotives from Rugby were used on the local services to Leamington and Coventry, as well as the Weedon to Leamington branch. Llandudno Junction and Bangor locomotives were used on local services in the area, including the branch to Blaenau Ffestiniog.

Most of the locomotives in the middle of the class were allocated to ex L.M.S. sheds around the Leeds and Bradford area, which on Nationalisation became part of the Eastern Region. Nos. 41290-41319 were allocated to the Southern Region being spread between Stewarts Lane, Eastleigh, Barnstaple, Faversham and Plymouth (Friary). The locomotives were very light and had wide route availability. Those fitted for push/pull working being used with a variety of pre-Nationalisation coaching vehicles. This was particularly the case on the Southern Region, where some old L.S.W.R. vehicles were still in use on the Turnchapel branch from Plymouth (Friary).

With the introduction of diesel multiple units, and together with widespread closures of branch lines, the locos lost most of their work. Many finished up working pick-up freight services and other menial tasks, including station pilot work at Waterloo.

When introduced, the locos were painted in L.M.S. black unlined livery. After Nationalisation they appeared in lined black with red, cream and grey lining. At first, 'British Railways' in full appeared on the tank sides, but later both types of B.R. crests were carried according to the period.

Bachmann LMS Class 2MT

Minitrix introduced a ready to run N gauge model in 1973. It has not been available since 1997. Dapol announced that they would be producing a new N gauge ready to run model during 2006. Bachmann introduced a ready to run OO model in 1995. It remains available.

Class 3F (Jinty) 0-6-0 T
London Midland & Scottish Railway

Introduced:	1924
Designed By:	Sir Henry Fowler
Allocation:	London Midland & Scottish Railway, later British Railways London Midland Region.

Locomotive Nos:

Pre 1934	Post 1934
7100 – 7119	7260 - 7279 built by Vulcan Foundry 1924.
7120 – 7134	7280 - 7294 built by North British 1924.
7135 – 7149	7295 - 7309 built by Hunslet 1924/1925.
16400 – 16459	7317 - 7376 built by North British 1926.
16460 – 16509	7377 - 7426 built by Vulcan Foundry 1926.
16510 – 16534	7427 - 7451 built by Hunslet 1926/1927.
16535 – 16549	7452 - 7466 built by Bagnall 1926/1927.
16550 – 16599	7467 - 7516 built by Vulcan Foundry 1927/1928.
16600 – 16624	7517 - 7541 built by Beardmore 1928.
16625 – 16674	7542 - 7591 built by Hunslet 1927-1929.
16675 – 16684	7592 - 7601 built by Bagnall 1928.
16685 – 16749	7602 - 7666 built by Beardmore 1928/1929.
16750 - 16764	7667 - 7681 built by Horwich 1931.

Nos. 7150 - 7156 are ex Somerset & Dorset Joint Railway Nos. 19 - 25, built by Bagnall 1929, subsequently re-numbered 7310 - 7316.

In B.R. days all post 1934 numbers were prefixed by 4xxxx.

Last of Class Withdrawn:	1967
Number Built:	422

Preserved Examples:

47279	47383
47298	47406
47324	47445
47327	47493
47357 (16440 number carried)	47564

Duties:	Mainly Shunting and Station Pilot duties, occasional Branch working.
Technical Data:	**Tractive Effort:** (85%) - 20,835 lb
	Loco Weight: 49 tons 10 cwt
	Loco Driving Wheels: 4' 7" dia
	Cylinders: (2 inside) - 18" x 26"
	Valve Gear: Stephenson with piston valves.

LMS Class 3F (Jinty) *Photograph Courtesy of Milepost 92½*

These locomotives, like the 4F 0-6-0's, were based on earlier designs stemming from S.W. Johnson's first design, which was introduced in 1874. Built by outside contractors and at Derby, some of the 180 locos had been built by 1899.

Subsequently, between 1899 and 1902, Vulcan Foundry produced 60 slightly larger locomotives, some of which were fitted with condensing gear for working over the City Widened Lines. These locomotives had round top fire boxes and Salter safety valves. From 1919, as this batch of locos were shopped, Belpaire type boilers were fitted, and from this Fowler designed the 3F, a slightly larger locomotive with extended smokebox and other differences.

Some of these locomotives were loaned to the War Department during the Second World War, and not all returned. During 1944, two examples had their gauge altered to 5' 3" to run on the Northern Counties Committee lines in Northern Ireland.

The 'Jinties' were frequently used for banking duties, and up to three at a time would often be seen assisting expresses up the Lickey Incline (near Bromsgrove) on the Bristol to Birmingham line. They frequently banked trains out of Euston up to Camden, which was usually hard going. With the widespread introduction of diesel shunters, and the lower powered main line diesels being used for empty stock working, these locomotives were all withdrawn by 1967.

Bachmann Class 3F (Jinty)

The 'Jinties' were always painted in unlined black livery. On the tank sides the initials L.M.S., British Railways in full or the appropriate B.R. crest (from 1948) was carried according to the period. The numberplate was carried on the coal bunker.

Tri-ang introduced a ready to run model in OO gauge in 1953. It passed to Tri-ang Hornby in 1965 and to Hornby in 1972 before the model was withdrawn the same year. It was replaced by a new model in 1978 and continued in production until 1991. This model is due to be reintroduced during 2006.

Tri-ang also produced a TT gauge model for its short lived system in 1957. It remained available well after production stopped in 1964 with stocks remaining until 1968.

Graham Farish introduced a ready to run N gauge version in 1996. Following the takeover by Bachmann in 2000 the model was upgraded and was reintroduced in 2003.

Bachmann introduced a ready to run OO gauge version in 2004. It remains available.

Class 4P Fowler 2-6-4 T
London Midland & Scottish Railway

Introduced:	1927
Designed By:	Sir Henry Fowler
Allocation:	London Midland & Scottish Railway, later British Railways London Midland Region.
Locomotive Nos:	2300 - 2303, built 1927.
	2304 - 2324, built 1928.
	2325 - 2374, built 1929.
	2375 - 2384, built 1932.
	2385 - 2423, built 1933.
	2424, built 1934.
	All built in Derby.
	Nos. 2395 - 2424 had side window cabs and doors.
	No. 2313 was named 'The Prince' (hand lettered), the name was removed in 1933.
	B.R. added the number 4xxxx.
Last of Class Withdrawn:	1966
Number Built:	125
Preserved Examples:	None
Duties:	Mixed Traffic.
Technical Data:	**Tractive Effort:** (85%) - 23,125 lb
	Loco Weight: 86 tons 5 cwt
	Loco Driving Wheels: 5' 9" dia
	Cylinders: (2) - 19" x 26"
	Valve Gear: Walschaerts with piston valves.

LMS Class 4P Fowler 2-6-4T *Photograph Courtesy of Colour Rail*

When George Hughes, the first Chief Mechanical Engineer of the L.M.S. from the grouping in 1923, retired towards the end of 1925, Sir Henry Fowler became the new CME. He immediately set to work on several standard designs, and to reduce the large number of odd classes of locos absorbed from the constituent companies. One of the new designs, as opposed to modifications to earlier locomotives, was for the Class 4 Tank for suburban duties to displace ageing tank locomotives.

The locomotives used as many standard L.M.S. parts as possible, and had the usual 8' + 8' 6" coupled wheelbase. A large parallel boiler was provided, but one drawback was the very open cab which many of the enginemen disliked. It was particularly uncomfortable running bunker first with a load of dusty coal flying about.

It should be noted that the Stanier 2-6-4 T's were almost identical locomotives mechanically, but had a tapered boiler and more enclosed cab. The design was perpetuated by Fairburn with an amended wheelbase, and then by Riddles, with the Standard Class 4 (80xxx) tanks.

The locomotives were spread fairly widely around the country. Some were used on the St. Pancras, Euston and Clydeside suburban services, others worked in the Birmingham area. Several were shedded at Swansea (Paxton Street) and Shrewsbury for working the very difficult Central Wales line, which was hard work for a tank locomotive. Another arduous route regularly worked, was that from Manchester to Buxton (just over 1000 ft above sea level) via Stockport, which was a steady gradient for some twelve miles from Hazel Grove to beyond Dove Holes. Other locos were shedded at Tebay for banking trains up to Shap summit, and these locos had their cabs modified to provide additional protection against the elements.

Hornby Fowler Class 4P

The first twelve locomotives, when built, were in maroon lined livery for a short time, but the remainder appeared in black with red lining. In wartime plain black appeared, and after Nationalisation black livery with red/grey/white lining was applied. British Railways in full or either crest would have been carried according to the period.

> Hornby introduced a ready to run OO model in 1980. This model was withdrawn in 1995 and replaced by a new model in 2003. It is currently available.

Class 4F 2-6-0 (Later 4MT)
London Midland & Scottish Railway

Introduced:	1947
Designed By:	H G Ivatt
Allocation:	London Midland & Scottish Railway, later British Railways Eastern, London Midland, Southern and Scottish Regions.
Locomotive Nos:	3000 - 3002, built at Horwich 1947.
	3003 - 3010, built at Horwich 1948.
	43011 - 43022, built at Horwich 1948.
	43023 - 43049, built at Horwich 1949.
	43050 - 43069, built at Doncaster 1950.
	43070 - 43096, built at Darlington 1950.
	43097 - 43106, built at Darlington 1951.
	43107 - 43111, built at Doncaster 1951.
	43112 - 43125, buitl at Horwich 1951.
	43136, built at Horwich 1952.
	43137 - 43155, built at Doncaster 1951.
	43156 - 43161, built at Doncaster 1952.
	Nos. 3000-3010 received prefix 4xxxx at Nationalisation in 1948.
	Nos. 3000-43049 were all initially fitted with large double chimney, but all were removed by 1952.
Last of Class Withdrawn:	1968
Number Built:	162
Preserved Example:	43106
Duties:	Mixed Traffic.
Technical Data:	**Tractive Effort:** (85%) - 24,170 lb
	Loco Weight: 59 tons 2 cwt
	Loco Driving Wheels: 5' 3" dia
	Cylinders: (2) - 17½" x 26"
	Valve Gear: Walschaerts with piston valves.

These locomotives were the last new design to be introduced by the L.M.S.. Although building of the ubiquitous Fowler 4F had continued up to 1941, many proposals had been tabled to find a suitable replacement.

LMS Class 4f (Later 4MT) *Photograph Courtesy of Colour Rail*

Thus, these locomotives were introduced, incorporating features of the large American S160 Class 2-8-0's, many of which were used in this country during the Second World War. Whilst in transit to Europe they earned the nickname of 'Mucky Duck', with their very high running plate and exposed pipe work, although this made them very easy to maintain having easy access to all parts. The class was developed with B.R. standard fittings into the successful 76xxx Class 4MT 2-6-0 later, giving a sum total of the two Classes of some 277 locomotives.

Initially, the first 50 locomotives were fitted with an ugly double chimney which, due to the relatively small size of the smoke box, meant that the exhaust was not truly vertical. Following the fitting of a Derby designed single chimney, and tests at Swindon to improve draughting in 1951, a very satisfactory loco emerged, and further examples were ordered from Doncaster and Darlington for work on the Eastern Region. During 1953, No.43027 was tested with a small stovepipe chimney, but this was not retained.

The locomotives were fitted with a cut down tender, but with almost enclosed cab, to enable them to work tender first with good rear vision, and yet provide protection for the footplate crew.

The locomotives were of mixed traffic design, and therefore used for both passenger and freight services. When delivered, the L.M.S. locos were fairly evenly spread around the country at Leeds, Sheffield, Workington, Saltley, Nuneaton, Bletchley, Bristol (Barrow Road) and Bath (Green Park).

When deliveries commenced to the Eastern Region, examples were sent to New England (Peterborough), Neasden, Middlesbrough, Darlington, Boston and Hull (Dairycoates).

It was not unknown for the Neasden locomotives to work passenger services on the Marylebone to to High Wycombe/Aylesbury services, which, because there was no turntable at either country station, meant the locos worked tender first in one direction. With the building of the aforementioned B.R. Standard Class 76xxx, Neasden lost its allocation of these locos.

Later, a number of locomotives went to South Lynn and Melton Constable, where they became the mainstay of the Midland & Great Northern system until its closure. Some of the Eastern Region built locos also went to Scotland, they were allocated to Eastfield (Glasgow) and Polmont. The Eastfield locos regularly worked stopping passenger services to Perth. Others were allocated to Carlisle (Canal) for use on the Waverley Route (Carlisle/Hawick/Edinburgh).

Towards the end of their service lives, several of the class were transferred to Tebay for banking duties on Shap, where no doubt their enclosed cabs were useful on this exposed section of track.

The class lasted right until the end of steam on the London Midland Region, and outlasted many of the similar Standard Class 4 2-6-0's.

Bachmann Class 4F (Later 4MT)

In L.M.S. days the locomotives were in plain black livery. Following Nationalisation, the locos first appeared with M prefix and later 'British Railways' in full. Later, the lined B.R. black livery was applied, and either crest carried according to the period.

Bachmann introduced a OO ready to run model in 2005. It remains available.

Class 4F 0-6-0
London Midland & Scottish Railway

Introduced:	1924
Designed By:	Sir Henry Fowler
Allocation:	London Midland & Scottish Railway, later British Railways London Midland Region.
Locomotive Nos:	4027 - 4056, built at Derby 1924/1925.
	4057 - 4081, built by North British 1925.
	4082 - 4106, built Kerr Stuart 1925.
	4107 - 4176, built at Crewe 1924-1926.
	4177 - 4206, built at St. Rollox 1924/1925.
	4207 - 4301, built at Derby 1925-1927.
	4302 - 4311, built at Crewe 1926.
	4312 - 4331, built at St. Rollox 1927/1928.
	4332 - 4356, built Kerr Stuart 1926/1927.
	4357 - 4381, built at Andrew Barclay 1926/1927.
	4382 - 4406, built by North British 1926/1927.
	4407 - 4436, built at Derby 1927.
	4437 - 4456, built at Crewe 1927/1928.
	4457 - 4466, built at Horwich 1928.
	4467 - 4476, built at St. Rollox 1928.
	4477 - 4506, built by North British 1927.
	4507 - 4556, built at Crewe 1928.
	4562 - 4576, built at Crewe 1937.
	4577 - 4606, built at Derby 1939-1941.

N.B.: Nos. 4557-4561, ex Somerset & Dorset Joint Railway Nos. 57-61, were built to a Midland Railway design of 1911, although not constructed until 1930.

B.R. added the number 4xxxx.

Last of Class Withdrawn: 1966

Number Built: 575

Preserved Examples: 4027
44123
44422

Duties: Freight and occasional Branch Passenger trains.

Technical Data:
Tractive Effort: (85%) - 24,555 lb
Loco Weight: 48 tons 15 cwt
Loco Driving Wheels: 5' 3" dia
Cylinders: (2 inside) - 20" x 26"
Valve Gear: Stephenson with piston valves.

LMS Class 4F *Photograph Courtesy of Colour Rail*

Like the Class 3F 0-6-0 tanks ('Jinties'), these locomotives were developed from S.W.Johnson's earlier designed 0-6-0, built for the Midland Railway from 1875 up to 1902. No less than 921 locos were built for the Midland Railway, Somerset & Dorset Joint Railway and the Midland & Great Northern Joint Railway. R.M.Deeley commenced rebuilding in 1903, with Belpaire fireboxes and Ross pop safety valves being used.

Later, in 1911, Sir Henry Fowler introduced a larger 0-6-0 which was developed from the earlier designs, and 772 of these locomotives were produced between 1911 and 1941.

A variety of chimneys and domes were carried by the locos, and during 1947 a few were temporarily converted to oil burners. All were re-converted to coal firing during 1948. Some also received tender cabs for running tender first, and for working over some of the exposed lines in the North. Some locomotives also received high sided tenders.

Although classed as freight locomotives, they often performed passenger duties on branch lines, and were often turned out to haul excursion and holiday relief trains - particularly over the S&DJR and M&GN lines.

Hornby Class 4F

The class spent their entire working lives, in L.M.S. and B.R. days, in unlined black livery with British Railways in full or either crest according to the period.

When Lima entered the British market in 1975 they chose the 4F as their first steam locomotive. They opted for the European HO scale and did not sell as well as they should have done. Although the company quickly abandoned HO in favour of OO in 1976, the 4F did not reappear in this scale. The HO 4F continued to be produced for other markets (Ireland and Australia) until 1983.

Lima also produced a ready to run N gauge model in 1975. Again there was a scale problem as the model was too big for the British market. This model was withdrawn around 1985. Although Lima tools passed to Hornby in 2005 it is unlikely that the HO or N gauge models will be reintroduced.

Airix introuded a OO ready to run model in 1979. The tooling passed to Mainline in 1981 who did not reissue it. When Dapol acquired the stock and former Airfix tooling in 1986, they continued to sell unsold Airfix stock until 1994. The tooling was sold to Hornby in 1996. An upgraded Hornby model was released in 1998 and remains available.

Graham Farish introduced a ready to run N gauge model in 1993. After the company was sold to Bachmann in 2000, an upgraded model was released in 2004. It remains available.

Stanier Class 4P 2-6-4T
London Midland & Scottish Railway

Introduced:	1935
Designed By:	Sir William Stanier
Allocation:	London Midland & Scottish Railways, later British Railways London Midland and North Eastern Regions.
Locomotive Nos:	2425 - 2475, built at Derby 1936.
	2476 - 2494, built at Derby 1937.
	2537 - 2544*, built at Derby 1935.
	2545 - 2609, built by North British Co. 1936.
	2610 - 2617, built by North British Co. 1937.
	2618 - 2651, built at Derby 1938.
	2652, built at Derby 1939.
	2653, built at Derby 1940.
	2654 - 2662, built at Derby 1941.
	2663 - 2670, built at Derby 1942.
	2671 & 2672, built at Derby 1943.

* Originally authorised as 3 cylinder locomotives similar to Nos. 2500 - 2536, but the order was revised to a 2 cylinder version.

BR added 4xxxx to these numbers post 1948.

Last of Class Withdrawn: 1967

Number Built: 206

Preserved Examples: None

Duties: Mixed Traffic.

Technical Data: **Tractive Effort**: (85%) - 24,670 lb
Loco Weight: 87 tons 17 cwt
Loco Driving Wheels: 5' 9" dia
Cylinders: (2) - 19 5/8th" x 26"
Valve Gear: Walschaerts with piston valves.

LMS Stanier Class 4P *Photograph Courtesy of Colour Rail*

Sir Henry Fowler had introduced his parallel boilered 2-6-4T locomotives in 1927 before handing over to Sir William Stanier in 1932. By 1934, a 3 cylinder design with tapered boiler and Belpaire firebox was designed, which was tried around the LMS system before the 37 locos (Nos. 2500-2536) were utilised on the London Tilbury and Southend section, often heading up to 13 suburban coach trains.

Following, in 1935, Stanier introduced the first of 206 locomotives with 2 cylinders, still using the tapered boiler. Being an ex GWR Swindon man, he preferred tapered boilers and Belpaire fireboxes as opposed to the parallel boilers used by Fowler, and indeed would later modify many of the Patriots and all of the Royal Scots in such a manner.

All of these tank locomotives used the identical coupled wheelbase (8' 0" + 8' 6"), a Derby trademark and similar to those used on the earlier 4F 0-6-0s, Fowler and Stanier 2-6-2Ts, 3F 0-6-0Ts, Hughes and Stanier 2-6-0s and the Fowler Garratts 2-6-0 + 0-6-2 locos. This was to achieve considerable standardisation of parts followed by Fowler and Stanier, totalling nearly 1900 locos.

When Stanier was moved to a governmental post in 1942, he was succeeded by C.E. Fairburn (previously with the English Electric Company and not a steam man, who died in 1945) and H.G. Ivatt, son of H.A. Ivatt the former GNR C.M.E. The outcome of the change was the development of a 2-6-4T with a slightly reduced wheelbase of 7' 7" + 7' 9". Ultimately, a further 277 locos were designed by Fairburn, and were produced together with 162 Class 4MT (43000) 2-6-0 Ivatt design locos, again building on the standardisation theme then pursued by Riddles in the British Railways era.

The Stanier locomotives were spread around the LMS system in England and Wales, but no examples appear to have been used in Scotland. Most of the main sheds adjacent to terminals (e.g.

Willesden, Edge Hill and Longsight) all had examples for either empty stock working or local suburban passenger services, as were other regional centres (e.g. Crewe, Preston, Birmingham, Stoke, Rugby, Chester, Accrington and Rose Grove).

With Regional boundary changes, examples of these locomotives were ultimately to be found on the former Great Central Line from Marylebone to Aylesbury/High Wycombe local services, also the former Metropolitan Line services from Aylesbury to Rickmansworth. On the North Eastern Region, examples shedded at Starbeck (near Harrogate) and Low Moor (near Bradford).

When built, livery would have been black, lined red. The wartime period would have been unlined black and then in BR days lined black livery with 'British Railways' in full and either crest was carried according to the period.

> Hornby have announced they will be introducing a OO Gauge ready to run model during 2007.

Fairburn Class 4P (Later 4) 2-6-4 T
London Midland & Scottish Railway

Introduced:	1945
Designed By:	C E Fairburn
Allocation:	London Midland & Scottish Railway, later British Railways London Midland, Eastern, Southern and Scottish Regions.
Locomotive Nos:	42050 - 42065, built at Derby 1950. 42066 - 42078, built at Brighton 1950. 42079 - 42095, built at Brighton 1951. 42096 - 42106, built at Brighton 1950. 42107 - 42132, built at Derby 1949. 42133 - 42146, built at Derby 1950. 42147 - 42182, built at Derby 1948. 42183 - 42186, built at Derby 1949. 2187 - 2189, built at Derby 1947. 2190 - 2199, built at Derby 1948. 2200 - 2217, built at Derby 1945. 2218 - 2222, built at Derby 1946. 2223 - 2264, built at Derby 1946. 2265 - 2272, built at Derby 1947. 2273 - 2299, built at Derby 1947. 2673 - 2699, built at Derby 1945. Numbers not already prefixed 4xxx were increased at Nationalisation in 1948.
Last of Class Withdrawn:	1967
Number Built:	277
Preserved Examples:	2073 2085
Duties:	Mixed Traffic.

Technical Data: **Tractive Effort:** (85%) - 24,670 lb
Loco Weight: Nos. 2050-2146 were 84 tons 14 cwt (1875 gallons of water); Nos. 2147-2299 and 2613-2699 were 85 tons 5 cwt (2000 gallons of water).
Loco Driving Wheels: 5' 9" dia
Cylinders: (2) - 19 5/8th" x 26"
Valve Gear: Walschaerts with piston valves.

LMS Fairburn Class 4P *Photograph Courtesy of Milepost 92½*

Following Sir William Staniers promotion to working for the government during the Second World War, his place as C.M.E. for LMS was filled by Charles Fairburn. Initially, in 1942, this was a temporary appointment, but he was fully elevated to the post in 1944. Sadly, he suffered a fatal heart attack in 1945, and was succeeded by H.G. Ivatt (son of the former GNR Chief Mechanical Engineer H.A. Ivatt).

Fairburn evaluated many of the standard LMS designs and concluded with a slightly shorter wheelbase than 8' 0" and 8' 6", lighter locos would be an advantage, and so these locos were designed, and construction was able to commence at Derby at the closure of the War in 1945. The Class 4 MT 2-6-0 locos (Mucky Ducks or Flying Pigs) also used the same wheelbase (7' 7" and 7' 9") allowing for standardisation of many parts, as was always the LMS policy. The locos carried the LMS standard Type 4C boiler, as used for the Stanier 2-6-4 Ts (both 2 and 3 cylinder versions).

Following Nationalisation in 1948, a series of locomotive exchanges took place to attempt to determine which were the most satisfactory designs of the Grouping railways, to develop further standard designs under the R.A. Riddles British Railways banner, as generally things were pretty bad after the Second World War, with many locos in excess of 60 years old and getting more difficult to maintain.

The locomotives generally worked alongside their previous Fowler and Stanier counterparts, although some 34 Icocos of the Class were allocated to the Brighton area for working the non-electrified lines in the Sussex and Kent area, replacing much older former LBSCR and SECR tank locos. One area where previous examples had not been sent was around the Glasgow, Edinburgh and Dundee areas in Scotland, working suburban passenger services as well as empty coaching stock working into the former LMS Glasgow and Edinburgh termini. Likewise, they were seen on the southern end of the former Great Central Main Line into Marylebone from Aylesbury and High Wycombe, where they displaced the Eastern Regions Thompson Class L1 2-6-4Ts following the Regional Boundary changes on February 1st 1958. Also, of course, the Metropolitan Line services from Aylesbury to Baker Street/Liverpool Street as far as Rickmansworth (where they were replaced by Met. Electric locos), until extension of the electrification was completed to Amersham in September 1961.

As with most Tank locomotives, their lives were curtailed by the widespread advent of the diesel multiple unit and the Beeching cuts which reduced their work, and these locos were all withdrawn by 1967.

Bachmann Fairburn Class 4P

Standard LMS black livery was applied when they were introduced in 1945. Subsequently, they carried British Railways in full and either BR crest according to the period. In BR days red, cream and grey lining was applied to tank and bunker sides.

Bachmann introduced a ready to run OO Gauge model in 2006.

Class 5 (Black 5) 4-6-0
London Midland & Scottish Railway

Introduced:	1934
Designed By:	Sir William Stanier
Allocation:	London Midland & Scottish Railway, later British Railways London Midland and Scottish Regions.
Locomotive Nos:	44658 - 44667, built at Crewe in 1949.
	44668 - 44717, built at Horwich in 1948-1951.
	44718 - 44747, built at Crewe from 1947 to 1949.
	4748 - 4753, built at Crewe from 1947 to 1949.
	44754 - 44757, built at Crewe from 1947 to 1949.
	4758 - 4782, built at Crewe from 1947 to 1949.
	4783 - 4799, built at Horwich in 1947.
	4800 - 4825, built at Derby in 1944.
	4826 - 4931, built at Crewe from 1944 to 1946.
	4932 - 4966, built at Horwich in 1945/1946.
	4967 - 4981, built at Crewe in 1946.
	4982 - 4999, built at Horwich in 1946/1947.
	5000 - 5019, built at Crewe in 1935.
	5020 - 5069, built at Vulcan Foundry in 1934/1935.
	5070 - 5074, built at Crewe in 1935.
	5075 - 5124, built at Vulcan Foundry in 1935.
	5125 - 5451 built by Armstrong Whitworth from 1935 to 1937.
	5452 - 5471, built at Crewe in 1938.
	5472 - 5499, built at Derby in 1943/1944.
	B.R. added 4xxxx to all pre 1948 built locomotives.

Last of Class Withdrawn:	1968
Number Built:	842
Preserved Examples:	4767 George Stephenson
	44806 Magpie
	44871 Sovereign
	44901
	44932
	45000
	45025
	45110 RAF Biggin Hill
	45163
	45212
	45231 The Sherwood Forester
	45293
	5305 Alderman A.E. Draper
	45337
	45379
	5407
	5428 Eric Treacy
	45491
Duties:	Mixed Traffic.

Technical Data: **Tractive Effort:** (85%) - 25,445 lb
Loco Weight: Generally 72 tons 12 cwt. Heaviest 75 tons 6 cwt
Loco Driving Wheels: 6' 0" dia
Cylinders: (2) - 18½" x 28"
Valve Gear: Walschaerts with piston valves, unless noted otherwise (see text).

LMS Class 5 (Black 5) *Photograph Courtesy of Colour Rail*

These were highly successful mixed traffic locomotives, of which no less than 842 were built, and from which the standard 73xxx Class 5 locomotives were largely designed, the main modification being the higher running place and standard B.R. cab. They were designed soon after Stanier took over as Chief Mechanical Engineer and incorporated several G.W.R. features.

The Black 5's were probably the most widely used steam locomotives ever to run on Britain's railways, being in use on the old S&DJR line from Bath to Bournemouth; shedded at Bristol (Barrow

Road) for working the Bristol/Gloucester/Birmingham line, the remainder of the L.M.S. system and also on the former Great North of Scotland lines up to Wick and Thurso.

Probably some of their most important and arduous work was carried out on the old Highland Railway main line between Perth and Inverness, and also on Glasgow to Oban/Fort William and Mallaig services, often double heading the heavy trains handled over these severely graded routes. They also ran on the more austere routes from Inverness to Kyle of Lochalsh and Wick. Development took place throughout the period of construction, with variations from 14 to finally 28 sets of superheater elements, and those locomotives fitted with roller bearings and Caprotti valve gear had a 4" longer coupled wheelbase.

Several of the locomotives were non-standard. Amongst these, No.4767 had Stephenson link motion (outside the frames), Nos. 44686, 44687, 44738-44747, 4748-4753 and 44754-44757 had Caprotti valve gear, and Nos. 44755-44757 and 4765-4767 (No.44767 altered to single chimney in 1953) had double chimneys when built. Also Nos. 44658, 44659, 44755 and 4865-4867 were built with electric headlamps etc., but these were removed in 1952.

The locomotives were always in black livery. During L.M.S. days a thin straw coloured lining was used. In B.R. days red/white/grey lining was applied and the locos carried British Railways in full or either crest according to the period.

Hornby Class 5 (Black 5)

Graham Farish produced the first ever commercially produced 2 rail OO locomotive with their Black 5 model manufactured in 1949. It has not been produced since 1951.

It was not until 1972 that the next OO version arrived from Hornby. This model was subsequently replaced with a new model from Hornby in 2001. The original tooling remains in use however, as it is now No. 3 Henry in the Thomas series produced by Hornby. Both versions remain in the catalogue.

Graham Farish introduced a ready to run N gauge version in 1978. Following the take over of Farish by Bachmann in 2000, the model was upgraded and reintroduced in 2004. It is currently available.

Class 4 (Later 5P 4F, 5P 5F, 6P 5F) 2-6-0
London Midland & Scottish Railway

Introduced:	1926
Designed By:	G Hughes & Sir Henry Fowler
Allocation:	London Midland & Scottish Railway, later British Railways London Midland and Scottish Regions.

Locomotive Nos:	Pre 1934	Post 1934
	13000 – 13029	2700 - 2729 built at Horwich 1926/1927.
	13030 – 13109	2730 - 2809 built at Crewe 1926-1929.
	13110 – 13149	2810 - 2849 built at Horwich 1929/1930.
	13150 - 13244	2850 - 2944 built at Crewe 1930.

B.R. added number 4xxxx to 1934 numbers.

Last of Class Withdrawn: 1967

Number Built: 245

Preserved Examples: 2700
42765
42859

Duties: Express or normal Freight, occasional Passenger work.

Technical Data: **Tractive Effort:** (85%) - 26,580 lb
Loco Weight: 66 tons
Loco Driving Wheels: 5' 6" dia
Cylinders: (2) - 21" x 26"
Valve Gear: Walschaerts with piston valves. Nos. 13118, 13122, 13124, 13125 and 13129 fitted Lentz rotary cam poppet valves in 1931, altered to Reidinger R.R. poppet valve gear in 1953.

LMS Class 4 (Later 5P 4F, 5P 5F, 6P 5F) *Photograph Courtesy of Colour Rail*

These locomotives (which were nicknamed 'Crabs') were originally designed by George Hughes when he was the first L.M.S.R. Chief Mechanical Engineer working from Horwich. Hughes retired in 1925 and Sir Henry Fowler altered some details before the Class was introduced in 1926, by which time Fowler had transferred all main L.M.S.R. locomotive deisgn work to Derby.

The Crabs were especially designed for express freight and excursion passenger duties, and with their large boiler and fairly large driving wheels were capable of running at considerable speed.

The design was to some extent a forerunner, by almost forty years, of the B.R. standard designs with very high running plates, making access to the valve gear easy for maintenance. The whole design was one of great utility, and in accordance with the L.M.S. plans of standardisation which Fowler was attempting to achieve.

The locomotives certainly lived up to Fowler's expectations and were very active on the fast freight services, although they were slightly displaced by the introduction of the Stanier Class 5.

A notable duty for some of the Ayr based locomotives was to remove heavy coal trains from a nearby colliery, and the sight and sound of a pair of Crabs on the heavily graded start produced a fine spectacle.

The first 100 locomotives built were turned out in the pre 1928 Crimson Lake lined livery. From 1927 to 1934 many locos were in lined black livery, but after 1934 were generally unlined until Nationalisation. In B.R. days black livery with red/grey/white lining was applied, British Railways in full and both types of crest were carried according to the period.

Bachmann Class 4 (Crab)

Lima introduced the first OO gauge ready to run model in 1980. Following the demise of Lima, the tools have passed to Hornby but there is no indication as yet that it will be reintroduced.

Bachmann introduced a ready to run OO model in 2004 which remains available,

In N gauge Graham Farish introduced a ready to run model in 1992. Following the takeover by Bachmann in 2000, the model was reintroduced in 2004 and remains available from Graham Farish.

Class G1, G2 & G2a 0-8-0
London & North Western Railway

Introduced:	1892
Designed By:	F W Webb. Rebuilt and modified by G Whale, C J Bowen-Cooke, Capt. H P M Beames & G Hughes.
Allocation:	London & North Western Railway, later London Midland & Scottish Railway, later British Railways London Midland and Western Regions.
Locomotive Nos:	Due to the LNWR numbering, locos are in no chronological order. Only the first and last numbers of batches will be quoted. All locos were built at Crewe.

	LMS Nos.	**LNWR Nos.**

Webb 4 Cylinder
Compound – Class E: 9600 - 9609   1888 & 1585.
Built 1901-1904, rebuilt to 2-8-0s 1904-1907.
Nos. 9600, 9604, 9607 & 9609 were rebuilt to 0-8-0 simple locos as
Nos. 3892 - 3895. The remainder were withdrawn by 1928.

Whale 4 Cylinder
Compound - Class F: 9610 – 9615   899 & 647.
Built 1901-1904, rebuilt to 2-8-0s 1904-1907.
Nos. 9610, 9612, 9613 & 9615 were rebuilt to 0-8-0 simple locos as
Nos. 8896 - 8899. The remainder were withdrawn by 1928.

Webb 4 Cylinder
Compound - Class B: 8900 - 8952   1881 & 1543.
Built 1901-1904, rebuilt 1923-1927.
N.B.: Nos. 8900, 8916, 8918, 8919, 8923, 8928, 8937, 8938, 8946,
8947 & 8949 were withdrawn, unrebuilt, by 1926.

Webb 3 Cylinder:
Compound - Class C
(ex Class A) 8953 - 8967   2541 & 1803.
Built 1894-1899, rebuilt as 2 cylinder simple locos 1904-1906.

Webb 3 Cylinder:
Compound - Class C1 8968 – 9001   1862 & 1835.
Built 1896-1899, rebuilt with small boiler 1909. All withdrawn by 1933.

Webb 3 Cylinder
Compound - Class D: 9002 - 9010 and 9012 – 9064 1866 & 1821.
Built 1893-1900, rebuilt as 2 cylinder simple locos 1906-1909.

Webb 2 Cylinder
Simple Loco: 9011   2524.
Built 1892. Original member of the Class.

Webb 2 Cylinder:
Simple Locos - Class G 9065 - 9153   1900 & 2566.
Built 1910, includes 32 locos rebuilt from Webb Class B Nos. 9065 -
9076, 9085, 9090, 9099, 9100, 9120, 9122, 9132, 9133 & 9142
(between 1906 and 1910), and Nos. 9145 - 9153 (between 1910 and
1917).

Bowen-Cooke Class G1: 9154   2635.
Built 1910. This loco was the first Class G1 having been rebuilt and
superheated in 1912.

LMS Nos.	LNWR Nos.
9155 – 9200	1329 & 2421. Built 1912.
9201 – 9224	326 & 2452. Built 1913.
9225 – 9254	20 & 2224. Built 1914.
9255 – 9264	170 & 2288. Built 1916.
9265 - 9267, 9272, 7273 & 9292	1884 & 2118. Rebuilt 1917/1918.
9268 - 9271 & 9274 – 9279	94 & 2423. Built 1917.
9280 - 9291, 9293 - 9299, 9300 - 9303, 9305 - 9320, 9323, 9325 - 9330 & 9332 - 9334,	83 & 2497. Built 1918.
9304, 9319, 9324 & 9331	1043 & 410. Rebuilt 1917/1918.
9335 - 9346	1353 & 1241. Rebuilt 1918-1920.
9347 & 9348	1286 & 1891. Rebuilt 1907/1908, then 1920-1921.
9349 – 9394	1038 & 2575. Rebuilt 1921-1923.

Locos listed as rebuilt were from Webb 4 Cylinder Compounds
Class B.

Several ran as 2-8-0s between 1904 and 1925, as rebuilt by Whale, and these included Nos. 9266, 9267, 9319, 9340, 9343, 9345, 9349, 9351, 9353, 9359, 9363, 9367, 9372-9374, 9386 & 9393.

Beames Class G2:	9395 - 9454	485 & 2178. Built 1921/1922.

BR added 4xxxx to LMS numbers.

Last of Class Withdrawn: 1964

Number Built: 836

Preserved Examples: 9395 (485)

Duties: Heavy Goods.

Technical Data:

Tractive Effort:	(80%) - 17,406 lb Classes E & B; 15,221 lb Class F. (85%) - 25,440 lb Classes C, C1 & D; 29,015 lb Classes G, G2 & G2a; 24,705 lb Class G1
Loco Weight:	56 tons 10 cwt Classes E & F; 53 tons 10 cwt Classes B & G; 49 tons 5 cwt Classes C & D; 49 tons Class C1; 60 tons 5 cwt Classes G1, G2 & G2a.
Driving Wheels:	4' 5½" dia.
Cylinders:	(2) - HP(2) 15" X 24" LP(2) 20½" x 24" Classes E, F & B. 19½" x 24" Classes C, C1 & D. 20½" x 24" Classes G, G1, G2 & G2a.
Valve Gear:	Joys with piston valves.

LNWR Class G2 *Photograph Courtesy of Colour Rail*

The LNWR 0-8-0s, of which no less than 478 passed into BR ownership, present a very complex picture of locomotive history. They were modified by probably seven or eight different Chief Mechanical Engineers from Webb to Stanier, and alterations were still being carried out in BR days.

Webbs original locomotive, No.9011 (ex2524), was built in 1892 as a simple loco, but he was very keen to test the compound working theory. So, between 1894 and 1899, Webb produced 111 three cylinder compound locos, followed by further four cylinder examples. Whilst these locos seem to have been as successful as any of Webbs compounds, George Whale (when he became C.M.E), set about converting all the locos to two cylinder simple engines. On some locos the original boiler was retained, whilst others received the large Class G boiler, which was to be a standard for the classes until the superheated boiler was introduced in 1912. After this, development continued until the Class G2 was introduced in 1921.

Some of the locomotives originally built as 0-8-0s were rebuilt to 2-8-0s, whilst some 2-8-0s and those rebuilt to 2-8-0s, were all subsequently rebuilt to 0-8-0s.

From this mixture of locomotives, the LMS narrowed down the series to three basic types: Class G1 with 160 lbs psi boilers; Class G2 with 175 lbs psi boilers (built 1921/1922); Class G2a with 175 lbs psi boilers, originally G1, but either reboilered or the existing boiler raised to a higher pressure.

In LMS days, and continuing into BR days, a programme was developed of fitting Belpaire fireboxes to all of the Class, also continuing the process of conversion of Class G1s to the more powerful Class G2a. The locos all ran with 3000 gallon tenders, and some had tender cabs for working over exposed lines.

The locomotives worked over all the ex LNWR portions of the LMS, working much of that systems heavy freight traffic. Being 0-8-0s, the adhesive weight was all used, and the Class was particularly active on the steeply graded lines in the Buxton area, whilst those shedded at Shrewsbury and Swansea (Paxton St) worked the arduous Central Wales line. Examples shedded at Abergavenny worked across the route to Brecon and Merthyr. Examples were also at Carnforth which were used over Shap, whilst others from Bletchley (sub-shedded to Leighton Buzzard) were used for hauling sand trains originating on the steeply graded Dunstable branch.

Whilst displaced to a certain extent by the Stanier Class 8F 2-8-0s (introduced in 1935), most of the Class lasted well into BR days. Withdrawal of the 8Fs had commenced by the time the last of the 0-8-0s was withdrawn.

The locomotives have always run in unlined black livery. Initially they carried LNWR cast number plates. Subsequently, LMS painted numbers and lettering were applied, and later British Railways in full was applied. Both BR crests were carried according to the period. None of the Class ever carried BR or LMS cast smokebox numberplates.

Union Mills LNWR Class G2

Bachmann have announced they will be producing a ready to run OO Guage model during 2008.

Union Mills introduced a ready to run N Guage model in 2004.

Jubilee Class 4-6-0 5XP
London Midland & Scottish Railway

Introduced:	1934
Designed By:	Sir William A Stanier
Allocation:	London Midland & Scottish Railway, later British Railways London Midland, North Eastern and Scottish Regions.
Locomotive Nos:	5552 - 5556, built at Crewe 1934.
	5557 - 5606, built by North British 1934/1935.
	5607 - 5654, built at Crewe 1934/1935.
	5655 - 5664, built at Derby 1934/1935.
	5665 - 5742, built at Crewe 1935/1936.
	N.B.: In 1942 Nos. 5735 & 5736 were rebuilt with an L.M.S. standard 2A tapered boiler with double chimney, as a forerunner to rebuilding the Royal Scots.
	Nos. 5553, 5596, 5684 and 5742 were fitted with double chimneys, only No.45596 retained this.
	B.R. added 4xxxx to all numbers.
Last of Class Withdrawn:	1967
Number Built:	191
Preserved Examples:	5593 Kolhapur
	5596 Bahamas
	5690 Leander
	5699 Galatea
Duties:	Express Passenger, Parcels or fitted Freight.
Technical Data:	**Tractive Effort:** (85%) - 26,610 lb as built; 29,570 lb reboilered
	Loco Weight: 79 tons 11 cwt as built; 82 tons reboilered
	Loco Driving Wheels: 6' 9" dia
	Cylinders: (3) - 17" x 26"
	Valve Gear: Walschaerts with piston valves.

LMS Jubilee Class 5XP *Photograph Courtesy of Colour Rail*

The Jubilees were introduced in the same year as the Black 5's but had three cylinders, larger wheels and a slightly larger boiler. They were basically an un-rebuilt Patriot fitted with a taper boiler, which Stanier had introduced to L.M.S. following his appointment as Chief Mechanical Engineer from the G.W.R. at Swindon. Early locomotives had domeless boilers, but all later received domes with top feed located in front of the dome.

The Jubilees were intended for intermediate express duties less arduous than those the early Stanier Pacifics and Royal Scots were performing. Many were shedded on the Midland Division running on the lighter loaded trains of this route. They also frequently worked the two hour Birmingham to London expresses, occasionally double-heading with a Compound 4-4-0. Several were at Bristol for working the South West-North East route through to York, where they were frequent visitors. When built, the Jubilees were not named, and ran for almost a year until 1935, when during King George V's Silver Jubilee Year, it was decided to name a locomotive 'Silver Jubilee'. It was at this time that the original No.5552 and No.5642, which had been running for only four months, exchanged identities permanently. The new No.5552 was repainted in glossy black livery, and had all boiler fittings, handrails and special cut-out numbers chromium plated. This locomotive was never painted maroon, despite the remainder of the Class all being this colour, and was repainted only in B.R. days to green livery.

When it was decided to name the locomotives, the names were chosen from countries of the British Empire, former Admirals and Warships, together with some older names from withdrawn locomotives.

Many of these locomotives exchanged tenders frequently, and both Stanier 3,500 and 4,000 gallon tenders were used, together with 3,500 gallon flat sided tenders. In 1958 it was decided that the whole Class should have 4,000 gallon tenders, swapping with 8F's. It was 1964 before this happened, and some of these came from withdrawals which commenced in 1962.

Apart from the special livery applied to No.5552 Silver Jubilee, as already explained (an additional chromium plated number 4 was provided in B.R. days, although the remaining chrome embellishments were removed), the remainder of the Class were all painted in maroon livery. During 1946 the L.M.S. experimented with new liveries. No.5573 was painted slate blue-grey with yellow lining/red edged, and No.5594 in a darker maroon. After Nationalisation, three locomotives were turned out in a light green livery and ten in lined black livery (similar to the L.N.W.R.), before the lined brunswick green livery was adopted, British Railways in full or either crest was carried according to the period.

Mainline Jubilee Class

Peco produced a ready to run N gauge model in 1969. This was made for them by Rivarossi in Italy and has not been available since 1985. It was sold outside the UK under the Rivarossi name.

Mainline introduced a ready to run model in OO in 1980. Following the setting up of Bachmann in the UK in 1989 it was one of the first models to be reintroduced in 1990. A new Jubilee from Bachmann is due to be released during 2007.

Graham Farish announced a new N gauge ready to run Jubilee which will become available during 2007.

Patriot Class 4-6-0
London Midland & Scottish Railway

Introduced:	1930
Designed By:	Sir Henry Fowler, rebuilt by H G Ivatt.
Allocation:	London Midland & Scottish Railway, later British Railways London Midland Region.

Locomotive Nos:	**As Built**	**Post 1934**
	5971 & 5972	5500 & 5501 built at Derby 1930.
	5959, 5985, 5987,	
	5949 & 5974	5502 - 5506 built at Crewe 1932.
	5936, 6010, 6005, 6012	
	& 5942	5507 - 5511built at Crewe 1932.
	5966, 5958, 5983, 5992	
	& 5982	5512 - 5516 built at Crewe 1932.
	5952, 6006 & 6008	5517 - 5519 built at Crewe 1933.
	5954, 5933 & 5973	5520 - 5522 built at Derby 1933.
	6026 & 5907	5523 & 5524 built at Crewe 1933.
	5916, 5963, 5944 & 5996	5525 - 5528 built at Derby 1933.
	5926, 6022, 6027 & 6011	5529 - 5532 built at Crewe 1933.
	5905, 5935 & 5997	5533 - 5535 built at Derby 1933.
	6018, 6015, 6000, 5925,	
	5901 & 5903	5536 – 5541 built at Crewe 1933.
		5542 - 5551, built at Crewe 1934.

B.R. added 4xxxx to Post 1934 numbers.

Nos. 5500 & 5501 were rebuilt from earlier L.N.W.R. Claughton Class 4-6-0's.

Nos. 5502-5541 replaced other Claughton Class locos of the same numbers, but were virtually new locos.

Nos. 5542-5551 were built new.

The following locomotives were rebuilt similar to the Royal Scots Class with L.M.S. Standard 2A tapered boiler with double chimney:
5521 & 5530 were rebuilt in 1946.
5514, 5526, 5528, 5529, 5531 & 5540 were rebuilt in 1947.
45512, 45523, 45525, 45527, 45532, 45534-45536 & 45545 were rebuilt in 1948.
45522 was rebuilt in 1949.

Last of Class Withdrawn:	1965
Number Built:	52
Preserved Examples:	None
Duties:	Express Passenger, Parcels/Express freight.

Technical Data: **Tractive Effort:** (85%) - 26,520 lb as built; 29,570 lb rebuilt
Loco Weight: 80 tons 15 cwt as built; 82 tons rebuilt
Loco Driving Wheels: 6' 9" dia
Cylinders: (3) - 18" x 26" as built; 17" x 26" rebuilt
Valve Gear: Walschaerts with piston valves.

LMS Patriot Class (as built) *Photograph Courtesy of Colour Rail*

Hornby Patriot Class (as built)

These locomotives were used alongside the Royal Scots, and due to their similar appearance were nicknamed the 'Baby Scots'.

It should be noted that most of the original locomotives retained their 3500 gallon tenders, whilst the rebuilt locomotives received Stanier 4000 gallon high sided tenders. Most of the locos carried names, although a few remained un-named throughout their service life. The rebuilding of the Class was carried out with larger tapered boilers, new cylinders and double chimneys. An easy way to distinguish between a rebuilt Patriot and a rebuilt Royal Scot, was that the Patriots received a Jubilee pattern cab, whereas the Royal Scots retained their Fowler cabs (except for No.6170).

The Patriots tended to wander during their life, and several found service on the former Midland and Great Central main lines. The locos remained in main line service alongside the Royal Scots, the final examples of both Classes being withdrawn in the same year.

When built, the locomotives were turned out in L.M.S. maroon lined livery. During and after the war, L.M.S. black unlined and lined livery was carried, and in B.R. days the locos were turned out in the brunswick green livery with orange/black lining, British Railways in full or either crest according to the period.

LMS Rebuilt Patriot Class *Photograph courtesy of Colour Rail*

Mainline Rebuilt Patriot Class

During 1979, Hornby introduced their OO Gauge model of an un-rebuilt example of the class in LMS livery. Mainline also produced a rebuilt version in both BR and LMS liveries. Hornby have announced they are to introduce a new rebuilt version during 2007.

Class 7F 0-8-0
London Midland & Scottish Railway

Introduced:	1929
Designed By:	Sir Henry Fowler
Allocation:	London Midland & Scottish Railway, later British Railways London Midland Region.

Locomotive Nos:	9500 - 9599, built at Crewe 1929.
	9600 - 9602, built at Crewe 1930.
	9603 - 9619, built at Crewe 1931.
	9620 - 9632, built at Crewe 1931.
	9633, built at Crewe 1932.
	9634 & 9635, built at Crewe 1931.
	9636 - 9659, built at Crewe 1932.
	9660 - 9674, built at Crewe 1932.

BR added 4xxxx to these numbers.

NB: Numbers 9504, 9507, 9512, 9514, 9517, 9518, 9521, 9522, 9527-9530, 9533, 9534, 9542, 9546, 9549, 9550, 9559, 9565, 9572, 9573, 9576, 9577, 9588, 9597, 9599,9601, 9604, 9606, 9613, 9614, 9616, 9619, 9621, 9626, 9629, 9632, 9633, 9639, 9642, 9644-9646, 9652, 9654, 9656, 9658, 9669 and 9670 were withdrawn between 1948 and 1950 so were not renumbered.

Numbers 9511, 9533, 9613, 9642 and 9670 were converted to oil burning in 1947. No.9511 reverted to coal. The remainder were not used and were withdrawn following the cessation of oil burning in 1948.

Nos. 9672-9674 were fitted with ACFI feed water heaters as constructed, but these were removed in 1943/1944.

Last of Class Withdrawn: 1962

Number Built: 175

Duties: Heavy Freight.

Technical Data: **Tractive Effort:** (85%) - 29,745 lb
Loco Weight: 60 tons 15 cwt
Loco Driving Wheels: 4' 8½" dia.
Cylinders: (2 inside) - 19½" x 26"
Valve Gear: Stephenson with piston valves.

LMS Class 7F *Photograph courtesy of Colour Rail*

Having been Chief Mechanical Engineer of the Midland Railway from 1909 to 1923, Sir Henry Fowler became C.M.E. of the LMS in 1925 until 1931, and was very aware of the problems in moving freight traffic on the former Midland Main Line from Sheffield, Nottingham, Leicester and Derby to London. Midland Railways practice was to double two of their small 0-6-0 locomotives (the Class 4Fs dating from 1911), but of course double heading required two loco crews and increased the overheads against profitability. Thus, Fowler designed a stretched 4F to produce an 8 coupled loco, which was new for the Midland despite the fact that the North Western side had some 478 similar locos from the likes of Bowen-Cooke, Whale, Webb, Beames and Hughes. The boiler was slightly bigger, 4 foot longer and rolled to a pressure of 200 lbs psi, but retained the Belpaire firebox etc. of the earlier Class 4F, likewise a standard LMS 3,500 gallon tender with 4 tons of coal was supplied.

The locomotives were constructed at a time when the LMS was rebuilding much of its loco stock as the Garratts were being introduced in 1927, with more produced in 1930 and the Stanier 8F 2-8-0s to come in the near future. It is interesting to note that in trials between these locos, a borrowed S & DJ 2-8-0, an LNWR 0-8-0, a Garratt, the Lickey Banker and a Stanier 8F, the outstanding machine was the 7F. The route, of course, became the domain of the Garratts and 8Fs, and ultimately the BR standard 9Fs replaced all of those mentioned.

After the Second World War, it will be noted that a considerable number of this Class were withdrawn due to the increased use of road transport. Those remaining were basically allocated to the Liverpool to Manchester corridor at Agecroft, Aintree, Bolton, Bury, Lees, Mirfield, Newton Heath, Sowerby Bridge and Wigan, where they lasted until the widespread use of the developed diesel locos.

These locomotives were seen in unlined black livery throughout their lives, carrying either L.M.S., British Railways in full or both BR crests (as appropriate to the period) on the tender sides.

Union Mills Class 7F

Union Mills have a Class 7F ready to run N Gauge model in their range.

8F Class 2-8-0
London Midland & Scottish Rlwy/Ministry of Supply

Introduced:	1935
Designed By:	Sir William A Stanier
Allocation:	London Midland & Scottish Railway, later British Railways London Midland Region.

Locomotive Nos:

8000 - 8011, built at Crewe 1935.
8012 - 8026, built at Crewe 1936/1937.
8027 - 8095, built at Vulcan Foundry 1938-1943.
8096 - 8175, built at Crewe 1938-1943.
8176 - 8225, built by North British 1943/1944.
8226 - 8285, built by North British 1940-1942.
8286 - 8300, built by Beyer Peacock 1940.
8301 - 8330, built at Crewe 1943/1944.
8331 - 8399, built at Horwich 1943-1945.
8400 - 8479, built at Swindon 1943-1945.
8490 - 8495, built at Horwich 1943-1945.
8500 - 8509, built at Darlington 1944.
8510 - 8539, built at Doncaster 1943-1945.
8540 - 8559, built at Darlington 1944/1945.
8600 - 8609, built at Eastleigh 1943.
8610 - 8612, built at Ashford 1943.
8613 - 8617, built at Brighton 1943.
8618 - 8624, built at Ashford 1943.
8625 - 8649, built at Brighton 1943.
8650 - 8662, built at Eastleigh 1943/1944.
8663 - 8670, built at Brighton 1944.
8671 - 8674, built at Ashford 1943/1944.
8675 - 8704, built at Brighton 1943/1944.

For other locos (Nos. 8705-8772) constructed at Brighton, Darlington and Doncaster between 1944 and 1946, see LNER Class 06.

The following 8F's were requisitioned by the War Department in 1941 (51 Numbers):
8012-8016, 8018-8025, 8028, 8030-8032, 8034, 8038-8049, 8051, 8052, 8058, 8059, 8061, 8066, 8068, 8069, 8071, 8072, 8077, 8079, 8080, 8085-8088, 8091, 8093 and 8094.
War Department Nos. 572-622 were applied but not in chronological order.

Only Nos. 8024, 8069, 8078-8080, 8085, 8088 and 8093 were returned to the L.M.S. in 1943.

Sample War Department No.583 (ex L.M.S. No.8025) was returned to B.R. (L.M.R.) numbered 48775 in 1957.

B.R. added 4xxxx to these numbers - gaps do occur due to locos lost during the war.

It should be noted that these numbers were the only locos actually ordered by the L.M.S.R. (331 in total); other locos were ordered by the War Department, the Ministry of Supply, Wartime Railway Executive Committee and also the L.N.E.R. (see Class 06). Many were subsequently taken into B.R. stock (total of 666).

Last of Class Withdrawn: 1968

Number Built: 852

Preserved Examples:

48151	8233
48305	8624
48431	

Duties: Heavy Freight, occasional Passenger work.

Technical Data: **Tractive Effort:** (85%) - 32,440 lb
                                   Loco Weight: 72 tons 2 cwt
                                   Loco Driving Wheels: 4' 8½" dia
                                   Cylinders: (2) - 18½" x 28"
                                   Valve Gear: Walschaerts with 10" piston valves.

LMS Class 8F *Photograph courtesy of Colour Rail*

Designed by Stanier for heavy freight duties, with a boiler of very similar dimensions to his Black 5, these locomotives were ordered in large numbers by the Ministry of Supply, and it was perhaps unique that locos of this Class were being built by all four grouping companies (prior to Nationalisation), as well as outside contractors at the same time.

During the war, locomotives from this Class built for the M.O.S. saw service in Egypt, Iraq, Israel, Italy, Persia and Turkey, and some remained in service in Turkey until the mid 1980's.

These locomotives were used throughout the L.M.S. to haul heavy freight trains, as well as hauling excursions on occasions (particularly to Blackpool and Morecambe on Bank Holidays when almost anything capable of moving was utilized), and more regularly on passenger trains across the ex Somerset & Dorset Joint Railway between Bath and Bournemouth.

Some of these locomotives ran with flat sided 3500 gallon tenders, in place of the more normal 4000 gallon tenders.

These locomotives were always painted in unlined black livery. In B.R. days, British Railways in full or both crests were carried according to the period.

Hornby Class 8F

Hornby Dublo introduced the first OO ready to run locomotive in 1958. Following the collapse of the Meccano company in 1964 the tooling passed to Tri-ang Wrenn who reintroduced it in 1967. Following another financial collapse, this time within the Tri-ang group, Wrenn became an independent company again and continued manufacturing this model until 1992. Despite the sale of the company to Dapol in 1993 and to G & R Wrenn (Mordvale) in 2001, the model has not reappeared.

Hornby produced a ready to run OO model in their own right in 1989. This model was replaced with a new version in 2003, which remains available.

Graham Farish introduced a N gauge ready to run model in 1986. Following the takeover by Bachmann in 2000, the model was upgraded and reintroduced in 2004. It remains available in the Graham Farish range.

Royal Scot Class 4-6-0
London Midland & Scottish Railway

Introduced:	1927
Designed By:	Sir Henry Fowler, rebuilt by Sir William A Stanier
Allocation:	London Midland & Scottish Railway, later British Railways London Midland Region.
Locomotive Nos:	6100 - 6149, built by North British 1927. 6150 - 6169, built at Derby 1930.
	No.6399 Fury was built by North British in 1929 as a high pressure compound experimental locomotive, and in 1935 was subsequently rebuilt with a standard No.2 tapered boiler. It was initially fitted with single chimney, but was later changed to double chimney. It had a Jubilee style cab, which was replaced by a Fowler cab, and this loco became the first rebuilt Royal Scot, and was re-numbered 6170.
	B.R. added 4xxxx to the numbers.
	Nos. 6100-6169 were rebuilt with standard No.2A tapered boilers and double chimneys between 1943 and 1955.
Last of Class Withdrawn:	1965
Number Built:	71
Preserved Examples:	6100 Royal Scot 6115 Scots Guardsman
Duties:	Express Passenger.
Technical Data:	**Tractive Effort:** (85%) - 33,150 lb **Loco Weight:** 83 tons as built; 84 tons 18 cwt as rebuilt **Loco Driving Wheels:** 6' 9" dia **Cylinders:** (3) - 18" x 26" **Valve Gear:** Walschaerts with piston valves.

LMS Royal Scot Class (as built) *Photograph courtesy of Colour Rail*

The Royal Scots were turned out shortly after Fowler took over as Chief Mechanical Engineer, and due to the L.M.S. works already being committed to a heavy building programme, the initial locomotives were turned out from North British Locomotive Works in Glasgow. These were built after North British had completed the Southern Railway King Arthurs and certain similarities exist between the two Classes.

The locomotives initially ran with a 3500 gallon tender, but received 4000 gallon tenders, swapped from Jubilee Class 4-6-0's, as they were built.

When built, the Royal Scots were immediately pushed into main line service, being expected to compete against the larger Gresley Pacifics in the East Coast/West Coast route battle, which hotted up during 1928 when both L.N.E.R. and L.M.S. introduced non-stop London to Edinburgh/Glasgow services respectively. The locomotives produced some outstanding performances on these services before Stanier was able to introduce his larger Princess Royal and Princess Coronation Class Pacifics.

Bachmann Royal Scot Class (as built)

In 1933, Nos. 6152 and 6100 exchanged numbers permanently, and the new No.6100 went to the World Fair in Chicago. A tour of the U.S.A. and Canada followed, where it received a bell for working on the railroads. In America, all locomotives were compelled to carry a warning bell, and No.6100 retained this feature on its return to Britain.

Many of the locomotives originally carried old London & North Western Railway names, but were renamed after famous regiments between 1929 and 1936.

Following the rebuilding of No.6399, as previously mentioned, it was found to steam more readily

LMS Rebuilt Royal Scot Class *Photograph courtesy of Colour Rail*

than the locos with parallel boilers, and consequently all the Royal Scots were rebuilt with tapered boilers and double chimneys, although they retained the Fowler cab.

During later years the locomotives moved from the West Coast main lines to work on other lines, including the Settle to Carlisle and Glasgow line, the Midland and Great Central main line (when that line was taken over by L.M.R.).

When built, the locomotives were turned out in L.M.S. maroon lined livery. During and after the war, L.M.S. black unlined and lined livery was carried, and then in B.R. days the locos were turned out in brunswick green livery with orange/black lining, with British Railways in full or either crest was carried according to the period.

Bachmann Rebuilt Royal Scot Class

Ironically in 1977, three new ready to run Royal Scot models were announced by Airfix, Mainline and Rivarossi, although the latter was something of a scale compromise.

Mainline introduced a rebuilt Royal Scot in 1978. Following the closure of Mainline, this model became part of the Bachmann range when they set up their UK operation in 1989. The model was reintroduced in 1996 and is still available. Mainline also went on to produce the Royal Scot in original condition in 1982. This too passed to Bachmann and reappeared in 1994.

The Airfix OO model also appeared in 1978 and again the rebuilt version was chosen. The tooling eventually passed to Mainline in 1981 following the collapse of Airfix. The model was not reintroduced as Mainline already had their own version in the catalogue.

Model information continues on following page

In 1979, Rivarossi introduced a model at 3.8mm scale in original condition, in an effort to appease both HO modellers (3.5mm to the foot) and OO (4mm to the foot). It proved somewhat of a disaster for the company and sold poorly in the UK and was only produced for a short period. Stocks took sometime to clear, but the model sold better abroad as part of the Rivarossi range.

G & R Wrenn introduced a OO ready to run in original condition in 1981 although it had been advertised from some years before it eventually appeared. This is one of the models that collectors find particularly difficult to obtain and some versions were made in short runs and attract high prices. This model passed to Dapol in 1993 and G & R Wrenn (Mordvale) in 2001 but has not reappeared.

Hornby announced in early 2007 that they would be introducing a OO model.

Princess Coronation Class 4-6-2
London Midland & Scottish Railway

Introduced:	1937
Designed By:	Sir William A Stanier
Allocation:	London Midland & Scottish Railway, later British Railways London Midland and Scottish Regions.
Locomotive Nos:	6220 - 6224, built 1937 - Streamlined, single chimney, replaced by double chimney.
	6225 - 6229, built 1938 - Streamlined, single chimney, replaced by double chimney.
	6230 - 6234, built 1938 - Non streamlined, single chimney, replaced by double chimney.
	6235 - 6239, built 1939 - Streamlined, built with double chimney.
	6240 - 6244, built 1940 - Streamlined, built with double chimney.
	6245 - 6248, built 1943 - Streamlined, built with double chimney.
	6249 - 6252, built 1944 - Non streamlined, built with double chimney.
	6253 - 6255, built 1946 - Non streamlined, built with double chimney.
	6256*, built 1947 - Non streamlined, built with double chimney.
	6257*, built 1948 - Non streamlined, built with double chimney.
	All built at Crewe.
	* Modifications by H.G. Ivatt
	Streamlining removed: In 1946 - Nos. 6220-6224, 6227, 6235, 6246 & 6248. In 1947 - Nos. 6255, 6228, 6236-6242, 6244, 6245 & 6247. In 1948 - Nos. 6226-6229. In 1949 - No. 6243.
	B.R. added 4xxxx to numbers.
Last of Class Withdrawn:	1964
Number Built:	38

Preserved Examples:	6229 Duchess of Hamilton
	6233 Duchess of Sutherland
	46235 City of Birmingham

Duties: Express Passenger.

Technical Data: **Tractive Effort:** (85%) - 40,000 lb
Loco Weight: 108 tons 2 cwt Streamlined;
105 tons 5 cwt Non Streamlined
Loco Driving Wheels: 6' 9" dia
Cylinders: (4) - 16½" x 28"
Valve Gear: Walschaerts with 9" piston valves. Inside valves worked
by rocking shafts from the outside valve-motion.

LMS Princess Coronation Class (Non streamlined) *Photograph courtesy of Colour Rail*

After Stanier had introduced the Princess Royal Class, the next development was the Princess Coronation Class. Following wind tunnel tests the streamlined front shape was established, and by raising the boiler centre line and altering the boiler size and slope, together with enlarged firebox, a more powerful locomotive evolved. Larger diameter wheels were also added to assist in sustained high speed runnning.

Hornby Princess Coronation Class (Non streamlined)

On 29th June, shortly after the emergence of the new 'Coronation Scot' train set from Crewe, a press run was made from Euston to Crewe, and on the descent to Crewe No.6220 'Coronation' achieved 114 mph, breaking the world record for steam traction (which was held by the L.N.E.R.'s No.2512 Silver Fox at 113 mph on 27th August 1936). Arrival through the crossovers at the south end of Crewe station at almost 60 mph was fortunately managed without mishap, other than broken crockery in the restaurant cars. On the return trip to Euston, the timing of 135 minutes was reduced to 119 minutes, the approximate time taken by the early batch of 25kv electric locos.

LMS Princess Coronation Class (Streamlined) *Photograph courtesy of Colour Rail*

In 1939, No.6229 'Duchess of Hamilton', dressed up as No.6220 'Coronation', was shipped to New York to represent Great Britain's railways at the World Fair, together with a new seven coach partly articulated train set for the 'Coronation Scot', and a twelve wheel sleeper. The locomotive was fitted with the necessary bell and electric headlamp for working on the American Railroads.

Following a tour of several American cities, and whilst in New York, the Second World War broke out, and it was not until 1943 that it was considered safe to bring the train home.

Following tests during 1939 with No.6234 Duchess of Abercorn, with and without a double chimney, the steaming ability with double chimney was much improved and consequently all locomotives were modified to double chimney as quickly as possible.

As some of the locomotives were never streamlined, comparison between the two types was easy, and it was discovered that the streamlining made little difference. However, Lord Stamp, President of the L.M.S.R. Executive, felt the streamliners were good for publicity. Unfortunately, Lord Stamp lost his life during the war, and following this the decision was made to build Nos. 6249-6257 unstreamlined. Problems with lack of maintenance and inaccessibility around the casing, and with streamlining only becoming effective above 80 mph, it was superfluous with a speed limit of only 75 mph. Thus the streamlined versions of this Class were rebuilt in the period from 1946 to 1949 with casing removed. Smoke deflectors were first introduced to the Class in 1945, and all locomotives were subsequently fitted. Locomotives originally streamlined were easily identified by the way the front of the smokebox curved forwards in front of the chimney, but as locos were reboilered this detail was lost.

During 1948, No.46234 worked on the B.R. Locomotive Interchange Trials, working between Waterloo and Exeter, Paddington and Plymouth, and Kings Cross and Leeds.

In conclusion, it can be said that the Princess Coronation was a fine locomotive, possibly only bettered in performance by the L.N.E.R. A4 Pacifics.

Currently, No.46229 is being re-streamlined at Tysley for display at the N.R.M. York.

Nos. 6220-6224 were originally painted in the blue/silver livery for working the 'Coronation Scot'. Nos. 6225-6229 and 6235-6244 were painted red/gold. Nos. 6245-6248 were outshopped in wartime black livery. In B.R. days most of the Class were painted in early blue livery, the brunswick green lined orange/black, and finally some were repainted in the maroon livery with black/straw lining, British Railways in full or either crest was carried according to the period.

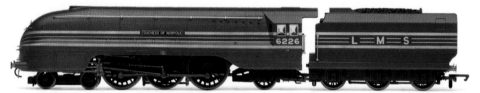

Hornby Princess Coronation Class (Streamlined)

Trix Twin introduced a OO ready to run streamlined version in 1939 which was only produced for a short period and not reintroduced after the war.

Hornby Dublo intended to introduce a OO ready to run non streamlined version also in 1939 but this was delayed by the Second World War and did not appear until 1948. The tools passed to the Tri-ang group after the collapse of the Meccano company in 1964 and was reintroduced by Tri-ang Wrenn in 1969. After Tri-ang had its own financial problems, G & R Wrenn became an independent company. Production continued until 1992 when the company closed. The tools passed to Dapol in 1993 and G & R Wrenn (Mordvale) in 2001 but have not been reintroduced.

Tri-ang Hornby produced a ready to run model in streamlined condition in 1970 which passed to Hornby in 1972. This was replaced by a scale length model in 2001. Whilst not in the current catalogue, it is available. Hornby produced a non-streamlined version in 1977, which was replaced by a retooled model in 2002. This version remains in the Hornby catalogue.

Graham Farish introduced a N gauge ready to run version in 1983 of the non streamlined version. Following the takeover by Bachmann in 2000 it was upgraded and reintroduced in 2003.

Princess Royal Class 4-6-2
London Midland & Scottish Railway

Introduced:	1933
Designed By:	Sir William A Stanier
Allocation:	London Midland & Scottish Railway, later British Railways London Midland and Scottish Regions.
Locomotive Nos:	6200 & 6201, built at Crewe 1933. 6203 - 6212, built at Crewe 1935. N.B.: B.R. added 4xxxx to the numbers. No.6202, later No.46202, was the ill-fated Turbomotive which was not included within this Class.
Last of Class Withdrawn:	1962
Number Built:	12

Preserved Examples: 6201 Princess Elizabeth
                            46203 Princess Margaret Rose

Duties: Express Passenger

Technical Data: **Tractive Effort:** (85%) - 40,300 lb
                            Loco Weight: 104 tons 10 cwt
                            Loco Driving Wheels: 6' 6" dia
                            Cylinders: (4) - 16¼" x 28"
                            Valve Gear: Walschaerts with 8" piston valves.

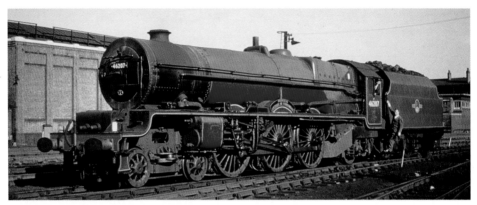

LMS Princess Royal Class *Photograph courtesy of Colour Rail*

In 1932 Stanier was appointed Chief Mechanical Engineer of the L.M.S. from being leading assistant to C.B. Collett, who was the CME of the Great Western Railway at Swindon.

Within 18 months, No.6200 The Princess Royal was delivered from Crewe with many Swindon features prominent. There were similarities to the G.W.R. King Class such as size of cylinders, wheel diameter, working pressure and tractive effort.

The Princess Royals had a much longer boiler and should have had an eight wheel tender. These would then have been too long for 70' diameter turntables then in use. When introduced Nos. 6200 & 6201 were fitted with a short six wheel tender with higher side sheets for additional capacity. But by the time Nos. 6203-6212 were delivered, the standard L.M.S. high sided tender with curved upper plates, carrying 9 tons of coal and 4000 gallons of water, became standard. Boiler modifications, following the test running of Nos. 6200 & 6201, were built into Nos. 6203-6212 and the other locomotives were altered to match.

In November 1936, No.6201 Princess Elizabeth was booked to run a special timing train from London to Glasgow, and back down the following day. Northbound, it took 5 hours 53 minutes and 38 seconds, whilst southbound the run only took 5 hours 44 minutes and 15 seconds, at an average speed of over 70 mph with eight coaches, including going over Shap and Beattock Summits. This run was the prelude to the introduction of the Coronation Scot in the summer of 1937.

During 1947, No.6205 Princess Victoria had the inner sets of Walschaerts valve gear removed and rocking levers (as on G.W.R. locos) fitted, (except the outside cylinders work the valves of the inside cylinders instead of vice-versa on G.W.R. locos). This locomotive was easily recognisable by the heavy brackets on each side of the valve gear.

Although only twelve Princess Royals were built, they were very impressive locomotives and worked side by side with the slightly larger Princess Coronation Class. They remained in service an equal number of years working the principal expresses between London, Glasgow and Perth.

From building, L.M.S. Crimson Lake livery was carried. They later acquired 1946 straw lined black livery. In B.R. days most were painted blue before changing to brunswick green. Several of the Class later acquired Crimson Lake maroon livery, British Railways in full or either crest was carried according to the period

Hornby Princess Royal Class

Trix Twin introduced a ready to run OO gauge model in 1938. As the chassis for this was made in Germany it did not appear again after the outbreak of the Second World War in 1939.

Rovex produced a OO gauge ready to run model in 1950, which passed to Tri-ang when they took over the company in 1952. The model passed to Tri-ang Hornby in 1965 and to Hornby in 1972. By 1974 the tooling was worn out and the model was withdrawn.

Hornby introduced a new version in 1984. This too was replaced with the current version in 2001. This remains available.

Class E1 0-6-0 T (LNER Class J72)
North Eastern Railway

Introduced:	1898
Designed By:	Wilson Worsdell
Allocation:	North Eastern Railway, later London & North Eastern Railway, later British Railways Eastern, Midland and Scottish Regions.
Locomotive Nos:	462, 1715, 1718, 1720-1722, 1728, 1732-1734, 1736, 1741, 1742, 1744, 1746, 1747, 1749, 1761, 1763, 1770, 2173-2192 and 2303-2317, built at Darlington 1898-1920. 2313-2337, built by Armstrong Whitworth & Co. 1922. 500, 512, 516, 524, 542, 566, 571, 574, 576 and 581, built at Doncaster in 1925. 69001-69028, built at Darlington from 1949 to 1951.
	In 1946 all locomotives then in existence were re-numbered 8670-8754 in sequence of building.
	B.R. added 6xxxx to these numbers.
Last of Class Withdrawn:	1964, two in departmental stock until 1967.
Number Built:	113
Preserved Example:	69023 Joem
Duties:	Goods Yard Shunting, later Station Pilot duties.
Technical Data:	**Tractive Effort:** (85%) - 16,760 lb **Loco Weight:** 38 tons 12 cwt **Loco Driving Wheels:** 4' 1¼" dia **Cylinders:** (2 inside) - 17" x 24" **Valve Gear:** Stephenson with slide valves.

NER Class E1 (LNER Class J72) *Photograph courtesy of Colour Rail*

These locomotives must be unique in all British Locomotive design, for no other locomotive built in quantity in the 1890's was still being produced, and required, fifty years later. The locomotives were a development of the earlier N.E.R. Class E 0-6-0 T, which was designed by Thomas William Worsdell (L.N.E.R. Class J71). Boiler, side tanks, cab and bunker were similar, but wheel size and a different front splasher, combined with sandboxes, made recognition of the two types easy.

Detail differences during their service life were the replacement of the Ramsbottom safety valve by the Ross pop safety valves, a breather pipe to each side tank, and altered smokebox door handle. When B.R. built the last member of the Class, group standard buffers and alternative sanding equipment were added to these modifications.

Four locomotives, shedded at Bidston, had their chimneys reduced in height by ten inches to work within Birkenhead Docks where a low bridge existed, whilst one of the class allocated to a Scottish shed, received a stove pipe chimney.

No.2331 featured in a novel experiment from 1939 to 1947, when it was fitted with a mechanical stoker.

Up until 1937, the J72's were concentrated solely on yard shunting and trip working, but with the withdrawal of the Class J71's they were fitted with vacuum ejectors, and then appeared on carriage shunting duties. Their diminutive appearance was deceptive for their power output.

Up until 1928, standard N.E.R. and L.N.E.R. lined black livery, then plain black livery was applied. Nos. 2313 and 1720 received lined livery again for station pilot duties at Newcastle Central, only to return to plain black during the Second World War. In 1947, No.8680 (ex 1720) was selected to be repainted in full L.N.E.R. green with black/white lining, and in 1949 it gained the B.R. emblem. Then, in 1952, it was repainted black with B.R. red/cream/grey lining, but quickly returned to B.R. plain black livery. However, in 1960 Nos. 68723 and 68736 were repainted N.E.R. green livery for duties at Newcastle Central and York stations respectively. Both carried the N.E.R. and the B.R. crest (lion clutching wheel) on either side of the number on the tank sides. Generally the class in BR days were unlined black livery with British Railways in full or either crest according to the period.

Bachmann NER Class E1 (LNER Class J72)

Mainline introduced a ready to run OO gauge model in 1976, the tools remained the property of Kader who made the models for Palitoy in Hong Kong. When Kader set up its British operation in 1989, an upgraded model was introduced in 1990. It remains available.

Class R 4-4-0 (LNER Class D20)
North Eastern Railway

Introduced:	1899
Designed By:	Wilson Worsdell
Allocation:	North Eastern Railway, later London & North Eastern Railway, later British Railways Eastern Region.
Locomotive Nos:	2011 - 2020 Pre 1946, 2340 - 2349 Post 1946, built 1899. 2021 - 2030 Pre 1946, 2350 - 2359 Post 1946, built 1900. 2101 - 2110 Pre 1946, 2360 - 2369 Post 1946, built 1900-1901. 476, 592, 707, 708, 711-713 & 723-725 Pre 1946, 2370 - 2379 Post 1946, built 1906. 1026, 1042, 1147, 1206, 1209, 1217, 1232, 1234, 1236, 1260, 1051, 1078 & 1184 Pre 1946, 2380-2385, 2387, 2389, 2391-2393 & 2395 Post 1946, built 1907. 1207, 1210, 1223, 1235, 1258, 1665 & 1672 Pre 1946, 2386, 2388, 2390, 2392, 2396 and 2397 Post 1946, built 1907. All built at Gateshead.

1147 and 1234 were withdrawn during 1943 and were not allocated 1946 numbers.

2346, 2356, 2361, 2368, 2385 and 2394 were withdrawn, again before renumbering. |
Last of Class Withdrawn:	1957
Number Built:	60
Preserved Examples:	None
Duties:	Mixed Traffic.
Technical Data:	**Tractive Effort:** (85%) - 17,026 lb **Loco Weight:** 54 tons 2 cwt (see text) **Loco Driving Wheels:** 6' 10" dia. **Cylinders:** (2 inside) - 19" x 26" **Valve Gear:** Stephenson with 8¾" piston valves.

These locomotives were designed by Worsdell for the North Eastern Railway, who were responsible for the East Coast Main Line workings between York and Edinburgh. Traffic and train weights had been increased gradually, and with the Great Northern introducing the Ivatt Atlantics for the southern end of the route, larger locos were needed for the northern end. The Class R proved to be the answer, which produced a speedy yet powerful locomotive.

NER Class R (LNER Class D20) *Photograph courtesy of Milepost 92½*

The class also featured in the advance of superheating. As built, No.1235 was fitted with a longer smokebox to incorporate a Sisterton superheater, but after a series of tests the experiment was not continued. However, when Raven became C.M.E., he soon started fitting locos with Robinson superheaters, No.2013 being the first so treated in 1912. Later, the Schmidt version was used in the class, and all were superheated by 1929/1930, but with Gresley as C.M.E., a return was made to the Robinson pattern. When the loco was superheated, the smokebox was increased by approximately 1 foot.

Tenders varied on these locomotives. Early examples had two coal rails, whilst during 1906/1907 three rails were placed around the tender with a fourth at the coal space. Water capacity varied from 3537 to 4125 gallons. During 1949/1950, several of the tenders were rebuilt with flush sides that were not unlike the group standard tenders.

Between 1912 and 1914, several of the Class received new main frames, which gave a convex profile to the frames infront of the smokebox, instead of the concave profile as on most of the Class.

During 1934, Darlington carried out a survey of boiler designs, and the D20 boilers were modified by increasing the number of tubes, thus giving additional heating surface. This new boiler was classified 59A.

In October 1936, No.2020 emerged from Darlington considerably rebuilt (as suggested by Edward Thompson who was in charge there), with similar cylinders, but with 10" piston valves above the cylinders. A diagram 59A boiler was fitted, the raised running plate was reshaped with reduced splashers, and an LNER pattern cab roof was fitted. Nos 592, 2101 and 62375 were the only other locomotives to be similarly rebuilt between 1942 and 1948. As a result, the loco weight was increased to 55 tons 9 cwt.

As built, the locomotives had a capuchon to their chimney, but from 1936 onwards this was removed from all the locos. By 1945 all locomotives had lost this detail, apart from No.62369 which retained this feature until withdrawal in 1951. The chimney originally carried a polished brass cap, but all were removed by 1934. Ramsbottom safety valves were originally fitted in a polished brass trumpet cover, but two Ross pop safety valves were applied from 1916, although not to every loco. As built, the locos had twin bell-shaped whistles mounted on the cab roof, but these were later moved to the top of the firebox, and some locos received organ whistles instead.

Most of the Class were fitted with NER pattern lubricators, although the rebuilt locos were fitted with the Wakefield pattern instead, driving linkage was off the leading right hand coupling rod pin.

The locomotives were dual braked having Westinghouse air brakes for engine and train, or vacuum ejector for an alternative train brake.

During their service lives, these locomotives were shedded at all the main NER sheds. They were initially used between Leeds, York, Newcastle and Edinburgh. Even with the introduction of the Raven Atlantics, the locos still remained at sheds along the East Coast Main Line.

By 1939, Gateshead and Darlington had lost their allocation, whilst Starbeck and Alnmouth had received examples, the latter shed being where the final locos completed their service lives. Although the locos continued to haul semi-fast trains over the main line, they were having to share duties with Gresley's D49 Class 4-4-0s.

No.2020, after its rebuilding, was shedded at Starbeck for hauling the 'Yorkshire Pullman' between Harrogate and Doncaster via York. During World War II the locos were used as pilots to the Class A3, V2 and Atlantics on the heavy trains. With the introduction of the Thompson B1 Class 4-6-0s and the K1 Class 2-6-0s, the locos lost much of their work, and the final six were withdrawn from Alnmouth in 1957, where they had been used on local trains from Alnmouth to Newcastle.

In NER days they were in lined green livery, which was modified to the LNER lined apple green after grouping. After 1928, LNER lined black livery was applied, initially with loco number and railway initials on the tender, but later the loco number was placed within the rear splasher. After the plain black of the wartime period, unlined black was applied in BR days, initially with 'British Railways' in full and an E prefix to the numbers. Later most locos had smokebox door number plates added and the first BR crest. Only three locos carried the second BR crest, they were Nos. 62381, 62395 (one side only for photographic purposes at withdrawal) and 62396.

Union Mills NER Class R (LNER D20)

Union Mills introduced a ready to run N Gauge model in 1996 which remains available.

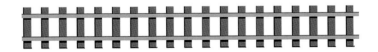

Class D 0-6-0 T (LNER Class J83)
North British Railway

Introduced:	1900
Designed By:	Matthew Holmes
Allocation:	North British Railway, later London & North Eastern Railway, later British Railways Scottish Region.
Locomotive Nos:	795 - 814, built by Neilson Reid & Co. 1900/1901. 815 - 834, built by Sharp Stewart & Co. 1901. At grouping numbers became 9795 - 9834. In 1946 they were renumbered 8442 - 8481. No.8462 was withdrawn in 1947. BR prefixed these numbers by 6xxxx.
Last of Class Withdrawn:	1962
Number Built:	40
Preserved Examples:	None
Duties:	Shunting and Branch Passenger Services.
Technical Data:	**Tractive Effort:** (85%) - 17,744 lb **Loco Weight:** 45 tons 5 cwt **Loco Driving Wheels:** 4' 6" dia. **Cylinders**: (2 inside) - 17" x 26" **Valve Gear:** Stephenson motion with slide valves.

NBR Class D (LNER Class J83) *Photograph courtesy of Colour Rail*

These locomotives worked around most of the Eastern side of Scotland from Berwick to Aberdeen, and also across to the Glasgow area from Eastfield, Kipps and Polmont.

They were used mainly for shunting duties and to transfer traffic between various yards, although for a time, two of (St Margarets) Edinburgh engines were used on the Musselburgh branch passenger service.

The entire class was completely rebuilt during 1924/1925, and all locos received new boilers, larger front sandboxes and different springs.

The whole class originally had steam brakes, but ten of the locos were soon fitted with Westinghouse brakes, and by 1916 with vacuum ejectors.

During and just after World War II, the locos lost their Westinghouse brakes for a combined steam/vacuum system. These locos were then used for carriage shunting at Glasgow, Edinburgh and Dundee.

During 1926, No.9806 was tested against other shunting locos at Leeds (Ardsley), and apart from two locos shedded at Carlisle (Canal), the locos did not venture outside Scotland.

Every locomotive of the class, except three shedded at Kipps (Glasgow), ran for one million miles, and No.9830 of St Margarets achieved over two million miles. This was very high mileage for locos doing only relatively light duties.

Until 1928 all the locomotives were lined black, except the Edinburgh Waverley station pilots. When the LNER reintroduced the lined green livery in 1946, six locos (Nos 8472-8474, 8477, 8478 and 8481) were quickly repainted for Waverley pilot duties, although only four were present at any one time. In BR days, Nos 68463, 68472, 68474, 68477, 68480 and 68481 all received fully lined black livery with British Railways in full or either crest according to the period.

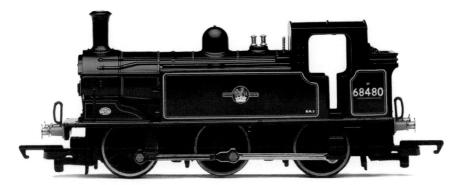

Hornby NBR Class D (LNER J83)

Hornby introduced a OO Gauge model in 1976, and this model was upgraded in 1994 and remains available.

Class N2 0-6-2 T (LNER Class N2)
Great Northern Railway

Introduced:	1920
Designed By:	Sir Nigel Gresley
Allocation:	Great Northern Railway, later London & North Eastern Railway, later British Railways Eastern and Scottish Regions.
Locomotive Nos:	GNR Nos. 1606 - 1615, built at Doncaster 1920/1921. Later became L.N.E.R. Nos. 4606 - 4615. G.N.R. Nos. 1721 - 1770, built by North British 1920/1921. Later became L.N.E.R. Nos. 4721 - 4770.
	2583 - 2594, built by Beyer Peacock & Co. 1925. 892 - 897, built at Doncaster 1925. 2685 - 2690, built by Yorkshire Engine Co. 1928/1929. 2662 - 2681, built by Hawthorn Leslie & Co. 1928/1929. 2682 - 2684, built by Yorkshire Engine Co. 1928.
	In 1946 re-numbering took place and the locomotives were re-numbered between No. 9490 and 9596.
	B.R. added 6xxxx to these numbers.
Last of Class Withdrawn:	1962
Number Built:	107
Preserved Example:	4744
Technical Data:	**Tractive Effort:** (85%) - 19,945 lb **Loco Weight:** 71 tons 9 cwt (max) **Loco Driving Wheels:** 5' 8" dia **Cylinders**: (2 inside) - 19" x 26" **Valve Gear**: Stephenson with 8" piston valves.

GNR Class N2 *Photograph courtesy of Milepost 92½*

The N2's were introduced as a development of the earlier Ivatt N1 Class locomotives with larger diameter cylinders, piston valves, super-heated boiler and increased water capacity. Other differences were a higher pitched boiler, necessitating the fitting of a smaller chimney to clear the Metropolitan loading gauge for working to Moorgate. The N2's were fitted with condensing gear that was removed from locomotives of the N1 Class (for working these trains to Moorgate), and remained on these and empty coaching stock duties in the Kings Cross area until dieselisation in 1958.

Some 40 of the Class were built without condensing gear (or it was removed on transfer), for working the Glasgow, Edinburgh and Dundee local services, and these had slightly taller chimneys. These locomotives also had Westinghouse brakes fitted. During 1930 the Class V1 2-6-2 tanks became available, and some of the N2's moved south from Scotland to Hatfield, Leeds and the former Great Eastern lines.

Following the dieselisation of the Kings Cross services, some of the locomotives were moved to Peterborough and Grantham and replaced the ex Great Central Railway N5 Class locos on station pilot duties. Due to prgressive dieselisation these locomotives did not last very long, although most of the locos had spent over 40 years in service. Many remained at Kings Cross (Top Shed) all their working life.

Before grouping in 1923, the locomotives built ran in the two-tone G.N.R. green livery. When the L.N.E.R. came into existence, the locomotives were painted black with red lining (omitted during the Second World War). In 1946, No.9522 was turned out in lined apple green livery, but this was the only example so treated. In B.R. days lined black livery was applied, British Railways in full or either crest was carried according to the period.

Hornby Class N2

Hornby Dublo introduced the first ready to run OO gauge model in 1938, which continued in production until the closure of Meccano in 1964 and its acquisition by the Tri-ang Group in 1965. The model reappeared in 1969 as part of the Tri-ang Wrenn range and passed to G&R Wrenn in 1971. Production continued until 1992 when retirement resulted in the sale of the company to Dapol in 1993, and from them to G&R Wrenn (Mordvale) Ltd in 2001. The model has not appeared since production ceased in 1992.

Trackmaster produced a clockwork OO ready to run model in 1949. This company was acquired by the fledgling Tri-ang Railways empire in 1951 mainly for its wagons. The locomotive continued to be produced until 1954, but was the only Tri-ang locomotive to have a die cast body.

In 1950, Gaiety introduced a ready to run OO gauge model, but this model has not been available for many years.

Model information continues on next page

Kirdon introduced a further OO ready to run model in 1955 which also disappeared many years ago.

Airfix intended to produce a OO gauge model but the tooling was not completed before the company was taken over by Mainline in 1981. Mainline produced the locomotive between 1982 and 1984 when it too closed down. The tools were acquired by Dapol in 1981 who sold the model with Mainline markings until 1996, when the tooling was sold to Hornby. An upgraded model was reintroduced by Hornby in 2000. Whilst not in the current Hornby catalogue, the locomotive remains available.

Class J13 0-6-0 T (L.N.E.R. Class J52)
Great Northern Railway

Introduced:	1897
Designed By:	H A Ivatt
Allocation:	Great Northern Railway, later London & North Eastern Railway, later British Railways Eastern Region.

Locomotive Nos:		**1924 Nos.**	**1946 Nos.**
1201 - 1210 built at Doncaster 1897		4201 - 4210	8805 - 8814
1216 - 1225 built by R Stephenson & Co. 1898/9		4216 - 4225	8815 – 8824
1226 - 1250 built by Sharp Stewart & Co. 1899		4226 - 4250	8825 – 8849
1251 - 1270 built at Doncaster 1901/1902		4251 - 4270	8850 - 8869
1271 - 1280 built at Doncaster 1905		4271 - 4280	8870 – 8879
1281 - 1290, built at Doncaster 1908/1909		4281 - 4290 I	8880 – 8889

B.R. added 6xxxx to all 1946 numbers.

Further to these locos, 51 Class J53's were rebuilt to Class J52's between 1922 and 1932 viz:

1924 Nos.	**1946 Nos.**
3921	
3922 & 3923	8757 & 8758
3924	
3925 - 3927	8759 - 8761
3929, 3930 & 3961-3963	8762 - 8766
3964	
3965 - 3979	8767 - 8781
3980	
4046 - 4060	8783 - 8797
4211 - 4215	8798 – 8802
3111 & 3155A	8803 & 8804

Nos. 8763 & 8801 did not receive B.R. numbers. All of the remainder had 6xxxx added to these numbers in 1946.

Last of Class Withdrawn: 1961

Number Built: 136

Preserved Example: 1247 (68846)

Duties: Shunting, Trip Freight working, and occasional Empty Stock working.

Technical Data:
Tractive Effort: 20,456 lb
Loco Weight: 51 tons 14 cwt
Loco Driving Wheels: 4' 8" dia
Cylinders: (2 inside) - 18" x 26"
Valve Gear: Stephenson with slide valves.

GNR Class J13 (LNER Class J52) *Photograph courtesy of Colour Rail*

These locomotives were introduced by Ivatt as a development of the earlier Stirling Class J53, which commencing in 1922 were rebuilt to match the Class J52. The principal difference between the Classes was that the J52's had a larger domed boiler, together with altered and wider cab. The final 20 locomotives of the Class J52 had a flared out top to their coal bunkers, and coal rails which were later plated, earlier locomotives being modified to match as they received overhauls. The final 10 locomotives received fluted coupling rods, in place of the plain type fitted to the remainder. Ross pop safety valves replaced the original Ramsbottom safety valves in L.N.E.R. days.

No.1260 was used for an experiment when it was fitted with a mechanical stoker between 1936 and 1938, although it was never released to revenue traffic during this period.

Many of the class received shorter chimneys to give clearance for working over the Metropolitan Widened Lines on through freight trains to the Southern Railway. Only some of the rebuilt class J53's had condensing gear, none of the J52's were so fitted. It was not unknown however, for non-condensing locos to work through the Widened Lines, and it was a magnificent sight and sound to hear one of these locos bring a long string of wagons round Hotel Curve and up through Platform 17 at Kings Cross.

Towards the end of their service lives, several J52's received chimneys only 2' 5" high, from the withdrawn Class C12 4-4-2 tanks. The bulk of the class at grouping were shedded at Kings Cross, Hornsey, New England (Peterborough), Doncaster, Ardsley (Leeds) and Bradford.

The Kings Cross locomotives looked after shunting at that yard, as well as working trains up to the Maiden Lane yard on the North London Line. Hornsey locos were used on transfer trips to the Great Eastern yards at Temple Mills (Stratford), as well as the aforementioned trips to the Southern and occasional trips into Kings Cross on empty stock workings. Those at Peterborough were used in the New England yards, as well as working transfer freights to the nearby Midland Railway Spital yard. Doncaster locos were used in Decoy yards and also as works pilots. One locomotive was frequently used on the staff train to Carr Wagon Works, hauling a train of old G.N.R. six wheel coaches, retained especially for this purpose. Those at Ardsley and Bradford were used in the yards, and for working the trip freights between the various companies yards. These locomotives later moved from the Leeds and Bradford area with the building of the Gresley Class J50 0-6-0 tanks, generally boosting the allocation at Kings Cross or Hornsey. With the construction of large numbers of diesel shunters, the class were quickly withdrawn at the end of the 1950's. Several of the locos from the class, when withdrawn in the 1930's, were retained at Doncaster as works shunters allocated to service stock.

In G.N.R. days the locomotives were painted in the lined two-tone green livery. Following grouping, L.N.E.R. black lined red livery was carried (from 1923 to 1928), later plain black was applied. During the Second World War, N.E. only was carried on the side tanks, and in B.R. days first 'British Railways' in full, then the first crest was applied. No.68846 was fully lined out by Kings Cross' shed in 1958, with the second B.R. crest (for exhibition purposes), but this would have probably been the only member of the Class so adorned.

Hornby Class J13 (LNER J52)

Hornby introduced a OO gauge ready to run model in 1981. It remains available.

Shire and Hunt Class D49 4-4-0
London & North Eastern Railway

Introduced: 1927

Designed By: Sir Nigel Gresley

Allocation: London & North Eastern Railway, later British Railways
                          Eastern and Scottish Regions.

Locomotive Nos:

As Built	Class Part	Year	1946 Nos.
234, 251, 256, 264, 236, 245, 246, 249 & 250	1	1927/1928	2700-2704, 2707, 2710, 2712-2714
265, 266, 270, 277, 281, 306, 307, 309, 310 & 311	1	1927/1928	2705 - 2709, 2711 & 2715 - 2719
318, 320, 322, 327, 329, 335, 336 & 352	3	1928	2720 - 2725
	2	1929	2726 & 2727
2753 – 2760	1	1929	2728 - 2735
201, 211, 220, 232, 235, 247, 255, 269, 273 and 282	2	1932	2736 - 2745
283, 288, 292, 297 & 298	2	1933	2746 - 2750
205, 214, 217, 222, 226, 230, 238, 258, 274 & 279	2	1934	2751 - 2760
353, 357, 359, 361 & 362	2	1934	2761 - 2765
363 - 366, 368, 370 & 374 - 377	2	1934/1935	2766 - 2775

All built at Darlington.

B.R. added 6xxxx to all 1946 numbers.

Last of Class Withdrawn: 1961

Number Built: 76

Preserved Examples: 246 Morayshire

Duties: Express Passenger and Mixed Traffic.

Technical Data:

Tractive Effort:	(85%) - 21,556 lb (No.365 19,890 lb)	
Loco Weight:	Part 1- 66 tons (max)	
	Part 2 - 64 tons 10 cwt	
	Part 3 - 65 tons 14 cwt (originally 64 tons 12 cwt)	
	Part 4 - 62 tons	
Driving Wheels:	6' 8" dia	
Cylinders:	Parts 1 - 3; (3) 17" x 26"	
	Part 4; 18" x 26" (2 inside)	
Valve Gear:	Part 1 with Walschaerts/Gresley valve gear with 8" piston valves.	
	Part 2 with rotary cam operated Lentz Poppet valves.	
	Part 3 with oscillating cam operated Lentz Poppet valves.	
	Part 4 with Stephenson with 8" piston valves.	

Part 3 locomotives did not prove successful and were all rebuilt to Part 1 in 1938.

Part 4 No.365 (later No.2768) was rebuilt with L.N.E.R. Class D11 type inside cylinders, hence reducing the tractive effort accordingly. Also classified L.N.E.R. Class D.

The D49's, together with the Class J38 and J39 0-6-0's, were the first Group Standard locomotives introduced by Gresley following his appointment as Chief Mechanical Engineer of the L.N.E.R.. He had previously continued to order locos which had proved successful from the constituent companies.

The D49's were intended for main line work on trains which did not justify a Pacific, but which were capable of hauling relatively heavy trains at a reasonable speed. Names were allotted to the whole

LNER Hunt Class D49/2 *Photograph courtesy of Colour Rail*

Class. Generally, the D49/1's and the D49/3's (which were rebuilt to D49/1's) were named after Counties, whilst the D49/2's were named after famous Hunts. Nos. 336 & 352 were named after Counties, but were renamed after Hunts after some three years in service.

Steam reversing gear was fitted as standard for Darlington built locomotives up to No.311, but this did not find favour in the Scottish area of the L.N.E.R., and Cowlairs Works altered the 14 Scottish examples to mechanical reversing in 1929/1930. It was 1935 before Darlington modified the six locomotives allocated to the North East.

After introduction, the D49's were always known for their rough riding, and it was not until 1934 after much experimentation and testing on the locomotive springs, that a reasonable ride was obtained.

Brakes also varied, the first 28 locomotives were dual fitted vacuum/Westinghouse, which were later converted to steam brake for the loco and vacuum for the train. The following 18 were built as latterly described, whilst the final 30 locos had vacuum brake only.

Tenders also varied, some had 4200 gallon Group Standard tenders of flared and slab sided (equal cut away back and front), Great Central pattern 4000 gallon tenders and also modified G.C. tenders with slab side as well as N.E.R. 4125 gallon tenders. Some of the Scottish areas D49's had automatic tablet exchange apparatus for work on the Aberdeen route.

The D49's allocated to the Scottish area, worked mainly in the Edinburgh/Glasgow area, although they also worked on the Waverley route to Carlisle, and to Perth, Dundee and Aberdeen. They also made occasional sorties on express freights up the East Coast Main Line to Newcastle.

Those in the North East worked mainly in the Leeds, York and Hull areas, hauling the principal trains between these centres. No.282 was transferred to Hull to cover the shed's hardest duty of working through to Sheffield (Victoria). Heaton gained some of the later built locomotives, one working was the 'Queen of Scots Pullman' from Newcastle to Leeds, whilst Leeds (Neville Hill) used D49's to haul the through Leeds to Glasgow service (later known as 'The North Briton') as far as Newcastle. At Nationalisation, and the increase of the number of Thompson Class B1 4-6-0's, the D49's tended to limit their operations and most of their final days were spent hauling local trains in the York area, including the Scarborough branch. Rapid dieselisation of these services sounded the death knell of this class.

Locomotives were originally in the lined L.N.E.R. apple green, although with the changes in allocation of tenders, several locos ran in green livery with black tenders. During the war, unlined black was applied, and in B.R. days the lined black livery was carried with 'British Railways' and either crest according to the period.

Hornby Shire Class D49

Trix Twin introduced a OO gauge ready to run model in 1939. The model produced for their 3 rail system has not been available since 1960.

Hornby introduced a ready to run OO model in 1981. It was last produced in 1998.

Class P1 0-6-0 (LNER Class J25)
North Eastern Railway

Introduced:	1898
Designed By:	Wilson Worsdell
Allocation:	North Eastern Railway, later London & North Eastern Railway, later British Railways North Eastern and Eastern Regions.
Locomotive Nos:	1961 - 1980, built at Gateshead 1898, became 5645 - 5655 in 1946. 1981 - 2000, built at Gateshead 1898/1899, became 5656 - 5670 in 1946. 536, 1724 - 1727 and 2031 - 2045, built at Darlington 1899, became 5671 - 5684 in 1946. 2046 - 2048, 2025, 463, 2049 - 2060, 29, 257 and 459, built at Darlington 1899/1900, became 5685 - 5714 in 1946. 2061 - 2080, built at Gateshead 1900, became 5690 - 5703 in 1946. 2126 - 2142, 1714, 1723 and 1743, built at Gateshead 1902, became 5715 - 5728 in 1946.
	NB: Numbers 1965, 1966, 1968, 1971, 1972, 1974, 1975, 1977, 1978, 1980, 1984, 1996-1999, 1724, 1727, 2031, 2035, 2036, 2039, 2049, 2050, 2052, 2054, 2058, 2060, 2062-2064, 2066, 2074, 2077, 2127,

2129, 2132, 2137, 1714 and 1743 were all withdrawn between 1933 and 1946, and hence were not renumbered in 1946.

Numbers 1967, 1970, 1973, 1983, 1991, 1994, 2032, 2051, 2056, 2080, 2126, 2135 and 2140, although renumbered in 1946 did not receive the prefix 6xxxx in BR days due to withdrawals between 1948 and 1951.

BR added 6xxxx to the 1946 numbers.

Numbers 29, 257, 536, 1725, 1963, 1964, 1967, 1969, 1970, 1973, 1981-1983, 1986, 1989, 1992, 1994, 2000, 2040, 2043, 2047, 2051, 2053, 2058, 2059, 2061, 2065, 2069, 2071-2073, 2075, 2076, 2126, 2134-2136, 2138, 2141 and 2142 were loaned to the GWR during the Second World War, periods varied between 1939 and 1946.

NB: Also, No.2000 was the selected number for Class D3 4-4-0 used for Directors tours etc, and hence the Class J25 received No.2050 (previously withdrawn loco), ultimately becoming No.5670 in 1946.

Last of Class Withdrawn: 1962

Number Built: 120

Technical Data: **Tractive Effort:** (85%) - 21,904 lb
Loco Weight: 41 tons 14 cwt
Loco Driving Wheels: 4' 7¼" dia
Cylinders: (2 inside) 18½" x 26"
Valve Gear: Stephenson with slide valves for saturated, Stephenson with 7½" piston valves for superheated.

NER Class P1 (LNER Class J25) *Photograph courtesy of Colour Rail*

Prior to the completion of Wilson Worsdells Class P (LNER Class J24), a larger engine had been designed using a boiler of the same diameter but 4 inches longer, and the firebox was some 6 inches longer. Consequently, the wheelbase was extended by 9 inches to 16' 6", identical to the Class C (LNER Class J21), with Stephenson valve gear again being adopted.

The first 100 members of the Class were built with 18¼" diameter cylinders, and the final 20 with 18½" diameter, commencing with No.2056 in 1906. 18½" diameter cylinders were fitted to most locomotives, the process lasting into LNER days, still retaining the slide valves. However, 28 of the Class were superheated between 1915 and 1918, and they received piston valves at the same time. They were numbers:
1976, 1980, 1985, 2037, 2038, 2044, 2045 and 2074 during 1915.
1714, 1726, 1727, 1962, 1971, 1972, 1997, 2039 and 2042 during 1916.
1961, 1968, 1975, 1988, 2055, 2079 and 2130 during 1917.
1977, 1985, 1991 and 2067 during 1918.

Schmidt Superheaters were used initially, but by 1932 the more standard Robinson Superheater was being used. The boilers used on this class were identical to those in use on Classes J21, N8, N9 and N10 locos. During the early 1930s, several of the above listed locos lost their superheated boilers as they were worn out, they were scrapped to be replaced in some instances by saturated boilers.

The locomotives fitted with superheaters tended to be fitted with a capuchon (or windjabber) chimney, and all locos as built carried the Ramsbottom style safety valves, which were later replaced with Ross Pop safety valves.

New boilers were developed in 1936 and 1938/1939, and several of the locomotives received examples. The new boilers had the dome located 7' 0" behind the smokebox, as compared with 5' 3" on the earlier boilers.

When introduced, the first 100 locomotives were fitted with a handbrake on both loco and tender. It would appear that the final 20 locos, built at Gateshead in 1902, were fitted with a steam brake, and the remainder were fitted as they were later shopped. They would have needed some very careful driving, particularly on unfitted wagons! In NER days, loco Nos. 1974, 2031, 2032, 2130, 2131 and 2132 were fitted with Westinghouse brakes, both for loco and train, whilst Nos. 459, 463, 1714, 1986, 2034, 2041 and 2133 were fitted with vacuum brakes for engine and train. All locos reverted to steam brake between 1920 and 1922.

As built, the locomotives received standard NER 3,038 gallon tenders fitted with water pick-up scoops. Two, three or four coal rails were fitted to the tenders, which could vary the amount of coal carried from 4 to 5 tons.

When built, the class was envisaged as a heavy mineral and general goods locomotive, but as the larger Classes Q6, J26 and J27 were built, the J25s were relegated to transfer freights and local goods workings. The locos were widely spread around the NER, and at Grouping in 1923, no less than 26 sheds shared the 120 locos. They were largely in and around Tyneside to Selby in the south, although Carlisle had two examples.

Withdrawals commenced in 1938 with 34 of the locomotives being cut up. A further 16 locos were withdrawn early in 1939, but these were stored (rather than cut up) because of the grave international situation. Almost coincidentally, a demand came from the War Department for the loan, from GWR, of their Dean goods locos, and hence the withdrawn locos were reinstated, ultimately some 40 locos of this class were loaned to the GWR. Most of the examples worked in the Wolverhampton and Worcester districts. No.2138 was initially allocated to Wolverhampton (Stafford Road), it was then passed to Worcester and Cheltenham, before moving to Reading in 1943. However, in 1944 it was noted at Old Oak Common (with PDN shed code), but whether it ever made it to Paddington (about 3 miles away) is unknown, but it was certainly the only J25 to visit the London area. Later, it moved to Kidderminster, the sole member of the class not to remain in the Wolverhampton or Worcester areas. Late in the 1940s, the Ivatt 2-6-0 Classes 2MT and 4MT were making their presence felt, and with the further standard class locos of similar size becoming available, the locos lost their work until finally being made redundant in 1962.

As built, the locomotives were painted in black livery with a small N.E. on the tender with larger numbers placed inbetween. In early LNER days, L & N.E.R. or L.N.E.R. was in about 7½" lettering, and the loco number was in 12" lettering carried on the from buffer beam. Later, the L.N.E.R. was placed on the tender side, and the loco number was placed on the cabside. In BR days, British Railways in full or either crest (as appropriate) was carried on the tender side with the loco number located on the cabside, a cast front numberplate was also carried on the smokebox door.

Union Mills NER Class B1 (LNER Class J25)

Union Mills have a ready to run N Gauge model in their range.

Class B12 4-6-0
Great Eastern Railway

Introduced:	1911
Designed By:	S D Holden
Allocation:	Great Eastern Railway, later London & North Eastern Railway, later British Railways Eastern and Scottish Regions.
Locomotive Nos:	1500 - 1504, built at Stratford 1911/1912.

1505 - 1519, built at Stratford 1913.
1520 - 1529, built at Stratford 1914.
1530 - 1535, built at Stratford 1914/1915.
1541 - 1560, built by W. Beardmore & Co. (Glasgow) 1920/1921.
1561 - 1570, built at Stratford 1920.
8571 - 8580, built by Beyer Peacock & Co. 1928.

Nos. 1500-1570 were re-numbered 8500-8571 at Grouping in 1923.

All locomotives were scheduled to be re-numbered in the 7415-7494 number series in 1942, but only seven were actually re-numbered. Consequently, in 1946, re-numbering returned to 1500-1580. No.1506 only lasted 7 months in 1913, and was withdrawn following a serious collision.

BR added 6xxxx to all 1946 numbers.

Last of Class Withdrawn:	1961	
Number Built:	81	
Preserved Examples:	61572	
Duties:	Express Passenger and secondary main line duties.	
Technical Data:	**Tractive Effort:** (85%) - 21,969 lb **Loco Weight:** 63 tons **Loco Driving Wheels:** 6' 6" dia **Cylinders:** (2 inside) - 20" x 28" **Valve Gear:** Stephenson with 10" piston valves.	

GER Class B12 *Photograph courtesy of Milepost 92½*

The B12's were a direct development from the James Holden 'Claud Hamilton' 4-4-0 locomotives, using smaller driving wheels but bigger inside cylinders. The locos built in 1928 by Beyer Peacock were modified by Gresley, and had several detail differences from the original locomotives. These included a longer smoke box, round topped firebox, cast iron chimney, Ross pop safety valves, less decorative splashers and Lentz Poppet valves driven by cams from the Stephenson motion (Lentz valves were all removed by 1933).

Locomotive Nos. 1500-1570 were all built initially with Westinghouse brakes. Once the L.N.E.R. had been formed, vacuum ejectors were added between 1924 and 1929. Locomotive Nos. 8571-8580 were built dual braked.

Between 1931 and 1933, 50 of the locomotives were fitted with the A.C.F.I. feed water heating apparatus, following earlier experiments with three of the class.This made a previously handsome engine appear somewhat continental with additional tanks, pipes and pumps on the boiler.

In 1932, a Gresley designed boiler (5' 6" diameter) was added to one of the Class, some 4 inches larger than the previous design. The piston valves were reduced to 9½" diameter, but the tractive effort remained unaltered. A larger superheater was fitted, and with other modifications the maximum axle weight rose to 17 tons.

After their initial years of main work on the Great Eastern Main Line, the B12's were replaced by the more modern Gresley B17 Sandringham Class. The B12's began to leave their home ground when some were transferred to the north of Scotland, and by 1942, 31 were in that area.

With their very light axle loads, the engines were used extensively during the Second World War (1939 to 1945), working ambulance trains far from their own grounds. They were based at Templecombe (S. & D.J.R.) and Westbury (G.W.R./S.R.).

The B12's were subsequently replaced by the Thompson B1 Class 4-6-0's, and most of the locomotives in Scotland were withdrawn, although a few did return to England. In 1948, most of the Class were concentrated at Stratford for working the Southend line trains.

Following electrification of the Southend line, the Class found themselves working from Yarmouth and South Lynn across the Midland & Great Northern Joint Line. Others worked from Grantham to Lincoln. The final area of activity was on the trains from Norwich to Cromer.

A few of the early locomotives were painted in the beautiful Great Eastern Railways dark blue with scarlet lining and polished brasswork etc.. This was replaced during World War I by plain grey livery. After grouping, the locos were turned out in L.N.E.R. apple green livery with white/black lining. During World War II, the locos received unlined black livery. Several of the locos were repainted in L.N.E.R. green livery after the war, but in B.R. days they were painted in lined black with British Railways in full or either crest according to the period.

Hornby GER Class B12

Tri-ang introduced a ready to run OO model in 1963. It passed to Tri-ang Hornby in 1965 and to Hornby Railways in 1972. After several years out of the catalogue it was reintroduced in 1999 after a 20 year gap, although it is not in the current Hornby catalogue, it is still available.

Union Mills introduced a ready to run N gauge model in 1999. It remains available.

Class J23 0-6-0 T (LNER Class J50)
Great Northern Railway

Introduced:	1922
Designed By:	Sir Nigel Gresley
Allocation:	Great Northern Railway, later London & North Eastern Railway, later British Railways North Eastern, Eastern and Scottish Regions.
Locomotive Nos:	3221 - 3230, built at Doncaster 1922.
	3231 - 3240, built at Doncaster 1924.

582, 586, 588, 589, 591, 593, 594, 596, 601, 603, 609, 610, 616 - 618, 621, 622, 635, 636, 1037, 1041, 1045, 1058, 1063 and 1068 - 1070, built at Doncaster 1926.
1074, 1079, 1081, 1082 and 1086, built at Doncaster 1927.
2789 - 2794, built at Doncaster 1930.
599, 600, 602, 605 and 606, built at Gorton 1938.
584, 585, 587, 590, 595, 598, 608, 611 and 615, built at Gorton 1939.

Later ex Class J51's were rebuilt with Class J50 boilers between 1929 and 1935, and reclassified as Class J50.

3157 - 3164, 3166 and 3167, orginally built 1913/1914.
3168 - 3176 and 3178, originally built 1914/1915.
3211 - 3220, originally built 1919.

Following re-numbering in 1943, locomotives were numbered 8890-8991.

B.R. added 6xxxx to these numbers.

Last of Class Withdrawn:	1965
Number Built:	102
Preserved Examples:	None
Duties:	Heavy Shunting, occasional Banking and Trip Freight trains. Worked Eastern Region Transfer Freight trains to Southern Region via City Widened Lines and Holborn Viaduct.
Technical Data:	**Tractive Effort:** (85%) - 23,636 lb **Loco Weight:** 58 tons 3 cwt **Loco Driving Wheels:** 4' 8" dia **Cylinders:** (2 inside) - 18½" x 26" **Valve Gear:** Stephenson with slide valves.

GNR Class J23 (LNER Class J50) *Photograph courtesy of Colour Rail*

Between 1914 and 1919, Gresley introduced new 0-6-0 tank locomotives GNR Class 23 (LNER Class J51), which were designed specially to work on the steeply graded lines in the West Riding area. These replaced the earlier Stirling 0-6-0 tender locos. The J51's used 4' 2" diameter boilers, displaced by reboilering the Ivatt 0-8-2 tanks (L.N.E.R. Class R1).

In 1922, further locomotives were built with 4' 5" diameter boilers, and the Great Northern Railway classified both sets of locos Class J23. After grouping, the L.N.E.R. split the Classes into J51 and J50 respectively. The L.N.E.R. selected the Class J50 as a standard locomotive, and a further 50 were built.

The early locomotives suffered from shortage of coal space, and several variations occurred within the Class, culminating in the hopper type bunkers of the Gorton built locomotives, which effectively doubled the capacity.

The first locomotives of the Class were all allocated to Ardsley (Leeds), and consequently earned the nickname of 'Ardsley Tanks'. More of the 1926/1927 batch went to Ardsley, but an interesting move was to send seven to Eastfield (Glasgow). When the 1938 batch was delivered, some went to East Anglia, whilst Hornsey and Hitchin received some in the London area. However, it was not until 1952, that a large allocation was made to the London area for cross-London trips to the Southern Region, although the locomotives were not fitted with condensing gear. With dieselisation, the locos spread their wings and appeared on Teeside and Humberside. By 1963 all locomotives had been condemned, apart from seven which were kept in Departmental stock at Doncaster which lasted until 1965.

The early Class J51's were painted a slate grey livery (some lined), and later the G.N.R. two-tone lined green livery. In L.N.E.R. days, first lined black, then unlined black livery was used. During 1946, No.8891 was turned out in full L.N.E.R. lined green livery, but soon returned to unlined black which all locomotives carried until withdrawal. British Railways in full or either crest was carried according to the period.

Lima GNR Class J23 (LNER J50)

Lima introduced a OO gauge model in 1976 but it has not been produced since 1982. The tools have now passed to Hornby but the model is not scheduled for early reintroduction.

N Brass introduced a ready to run N gauge version in 1996. It remains available.

Ex War Department Austerity Class 0-6-0 ST. (LNER Class J94) London & North Eastern Railway

Introduced:	1943
Designed By:	R A Riddles
Allocation:	London & North Eastern Railway, later British Railways Eastern and London Midland Regions. Also saw service with many industrial companies including the National Coal Board, The Army (Longmoor, Bicester, etc.) and other owners.
Locomotive Nos:	8006 & 8007, built by Hudswell Clarke & Co. 1944. 8008 - 8017, built by Hunslet Engine Co. 1944. 8018 - 8020, built by W.G. Bagnell & Co. 1944. 8025 & 8026, built by Hudswell Clarke & Co. 1944/1945. 8027 - 8030, built by Hunslet Engine Co. 1945. 8031 & 8032, built by R. Stephenson & Hawthorns 1945. 8033 - 8046, built at Vulcan Foundry 1945. 8047 - 8059, built by W.G. Bagnell & Co. 1945/1946. 8060 - 8069, built by Hudswell Clarke & Co. 1945/1946. 8070, built by R. Stephenson & Hawthorns 1945. 8071 - 8080, built by Andrew Barclay & Co. 1945-1947. Nos. 8006, 8009, 8012-8014, 8017, 8019, 8020, 8022-8025, 8029, 8030, 8035, 8036, 8038-8040, 8047, 8049-8051, 8053, 8054, 8058, 8062, 8071, 8073, 8075 and 8080 carried modified coal bunkers. 75 were purchased by the L.N.E.R.. B.R. added 6xxxx to these numbers. The following were sold upon withdrawal from B.R. for further use: 68020, 68067 and 68077 to the National Coal Board. 68070 to Glyn Neath Opencast Site in South Wales. 68078 to Widdrington Opencast Site in Northumberland.
Last of Class Withdrawn:	1967
Number Built:	377
Preserved Examples:	68077 68078
Duties:	Shunting and Trip working.
Technical Data:	**Tractive Effort:** (85%) - 23,860 lb **Loco Weight:** 48 tons 4 cwt; 49 tons 2 cwt with additional coal bunker detail. **Loco Driving Wheels:** 4' 3" dia **Cylinders:** (2 inside) - 18" x 26" **Valve Gear:** Stephenson with slide valves.

Ex War department Austerity Class (LNER Class J94) *Photograph courtesy of Milepost 92½*

These locomotives were designed for the British Government, and the first of the Class, No.50000, was turned out in January 1943. Over the following four years, 377 were outshopped from various contractors, and many were used by the Railway Operating Department (R.O.D.) in France, after the Normandy landings in 1944. After the end of the war, locos continued to be manufactured, and were placed in store at Longmoor.

Manufacture of this design continued for private use by the National Coal Board, and other users, until 1962.

During 1944, many of these stored locomotives were loaned to the Ministry of Fuel & Power for use at open-cast mining sites, and in October 1944 the various railway companies signed an agreement to undertake the six-monthly boiler inspections and necessary repairs. By January 1945, the L.N.E.R. had become responsible for the maintenance of 25 of the locos, and by November of that year No.71486 was loaned to the company for trials.

The simple yet rugged design resulted in the purchase of 75 of the locomotives, including the aforementioned No.71486 in May 1946, which was considered a cheaper option than building a further 50 Class J50 0-6-0 T's in their own workshops.

To suit the L.N.E.R., cab doors and seats were provided, together with standard lamp brackets, whilst after entry into service during 1948 the coal bunker capacity was increased by 15cwts, together with a rear ladder and altered rear cab windows. No.8006 was the first to be modified at Gorton, and most of these alterations to subsequent locos were also carried out here, the modification being similar to the bunkers provided on the Thompson Class L1 2-6-4 T's.

The locomotives were spread all round the L.N.E.R. system between Gateshead and Kings Cross, Hull (Dairycoates), and both Brunswick (Liverpool) and Bidston. By 1956 the Midland Region were having problems in maintaining the old North London Railway 0-6-0 T's on the Cromford and High Peak lines, particularly the No.8 section between Middleton Top and Parsley Hay. No.68006 was first hired, and further locomotives were transferred, basically to Rowsley for this work (viz. Nos. 68012, 68013, 68030, 68034, 68068 and 68079). By 1965 only the southern portion of the line was still open, and Nos. 68006, 68012 and 68068 were shedded at Burton for these duties. Many of the preserved railways in this country have examples of these locomotives running, mainly on passenger turns, but most were purchased for individual concerns and never saw B.R. service.

The locomotives in BR service were always in unlined black livery with British Railways in full or either crest according to the period.

Hornby Ex War Department Austerity Class (LNER Class J94)

Dapol introduced a ready to run OO model in 1985. The tools were taken over by Hornby in 1996 and an upgraded model introduced in 1998. The model remains available.

Graham Farish introduced a N gauge model in 1987. The tools passed to Bachmann in 2000 when they purchased the company and upgraded model reintroduced in 2002. It remains available.

Class P2 0-6-0 (LNER Class J26)
North Eastern Railway

Introduced:	1904
Designed By:	Wilson Worsdell
Allocation:	North Eastern Railway, later London & North Eastern Railway, later British Railways North Eastern and Eastern Regions.
Locomotive Nos:	132, 243, 342, 434, 442, 543, 554, 555, 1159, 1172, 1043, 1057, 1098, 1130, 1369, 1671, 1674, 1676, 1678 and 1773, built at Darlington 1904.
	835, 881, 1146, 1390, 1194, 1200, 1202, 1208, 1370 and 1781, built at Darlington 1905.
	1360, 1670, 816, 1673, 1698, 67, 233, 379, 406 and 1139, built at Gateshead 1905.
	412, 1366, 438, 517, 525, 765, 818, 831, 1131 and 1777, built at Gateshead 1905.
	Locomotives were renumbered in sequence to 5730 - 5779 in 1946.
	BR added 6xxxx to these numbers at Nationalisation post 1948.
Last of Class Withdrawn:	1962
Number Built:	50

Preserved Examples:	None
Duties:	Freight.
Technical Data:	**Tractive Effort:** (85%) - 24,642 lb
	Loco Weight: 46 tons 16 cwt
	Loco Driving Wheels: 4' 7¼" dia
	Cylinders: (2 inside) - 18½" x 26"
	Valve Gear: Stephenson with slide valves.

NER Class P2 (LNER Class J26) *Photograph courtesy of Colour Rail*

These locomotives were a development of the NER Class P1 (LNER Class J23) 0-6-0s, also designed by Worsdell and introduced in 1898. However, whilst the wheels, wheelbase and cylinders were identical, the boiler diameter was increased from 4' 3" to 5' 6", which appeared immense compared with the previous locos as the boiler was pitched 10" higher, with the longer firebox having a sloping grate to clear the rear driving axle.

By 1906, Worsdell had added the NER Class P3 (LNER Class J27), which were basically similar locos with slight differences to the sloping grate, and for economy no spare boilers were built, and Class P3 boilers (Diagram 57) were used also on this class between 1911 and 1922. No.1777 was the first to be so fitted, and only No.379 passed into Grouping with the original boiler, being modified in 1925. None of these boilers were superheated.

Further development work on the boilers took place, and during 1937 a redesigned boiler (Diagram 57A) became available, and No.1130 was the first to be changed during 1939. The most noticeable detail of the change was the dome being set back 13" and slightly lowered. No.1098 was the final loco to be converted in 1958.

Typical of NER locomotives, many of the chimneys fitted to the class had 2" high capuchons, or 'windjabbers', giving an overall height of 13' 3", and the LNER did not bother to change these to the Composite Rolling Stock Gauge. Many survived into BR days, although some ran with smaller chimneys by that period.

The standard NER smokebox wheel and handle were generally replaced by the twin handles by about 1935, whilst the twin whistles were generally changed from the cab roof to the more LNER standard boiler mounting position for only one organ type whistle.

As originally built, circular cab windows were provided to the front of the cab, but during LNER days, 22 of the class were modified with shaped spectacle windows. Group standard buffers replaced those of NER origin on several of the locos. Tenders for the class were originally NER 3038 gallon with oval frame slots, but changes did occur.

The class generally worked in the Teeside area hauling coal traffic. The exception was No.379 which was loaned to the Great Eastern Section for a brief period soon after Grouping. Widespread introduction of the Type 2 Diesel Electric locomotives brought about the elimination of this class in 1962.

Black livery was always carried, initially with NE split each side of the loco number on the tender, then LNER. During the War years just NE was again carried, and during BR days British Railways in full or both crests were carried according to the period.

Union Mills NER Class P2 (LNER Class J26)

Union Mills have an N Gauge model of the LNER Class J26 in their range.

V1 & V3 Class 2-6-2 T
London & North Eastern Railway

Introduced:	1930
Designed By:	Sir Nigel Gresley
Allocation:	London & North Eastern Railway, later British Railways Eastern, North Eastern and Scottish Regions.
Locomotive Nos:	2900 - 2933, built at Doncaster 1930-1935. 417, 446, 477, 479, 481, 484, 486, 487, 497 & 498, built at Doncaster 1935. 402, 414-416, 418 & 2897, built at Doncaster 1935. 419, 422, 423, 428, 440, 2898, 454, 455, 461, 465, 466 & 2899, built at Doncaster 1936. 404, 407, 420, 424, 425, 447, 448, 451, 467, 469, 472, 478, 480, 483 & 485, built at Doncaster 1938. 488-491, 496, 390-393, 395-399 & 401, built at Doncaster 1939/1940.
	The final locos (Nos. 390-393, 395-399 & 401), were classified as Class V3 as the boiler pressure, normally 180 lbs psi as on Class V1, was raised to 200 lbs psi (Boiler Diagram 102HP).
	Ultimately 59 Class V1s were further reclassified by this method between July 1952 and February 1961. These were Nos. 7600, 7604-7609, 7611-7621, 7623-7628, 7632-7636, 7638, 7640,

7642-7648, 7650-7654, 7656-7658, 7660-7663, 7666-7670, 7672, 7674-7679 & 7681.

Renumbered in 1946 to 7600 - 7691, in order from above.

BR added 6xxxx to the 1946 numbers.

Last of Class Withdrawn: 1964

Number Built: 92

Preserved Examples: None

Duties: General Suburban Passenger.

Technical Data: **Tractive Effort:** (85%) - V1 22,464 lb; V3 24,940 lb
Loco Weight: V1 84 tons; V3 86 tons 16 cwt
Loco Driving Wheels: 5' 8" dia.
Cylinders: (3) - 16" x 26"
Valve Gear: Walschaerts with 8" piston valves.

LNER V1 & V3 Class *Photograph courtesy of Colour Rail*

When first envisaged, the locomotives were based on Gresleys GNR designed H2 Class 2-6-0s (LNER Class K1), except that three cylinders were to be provided instead two. Initial thoughts also considered using the locos to work the Metropolitan widened line trains, so condensing gear was provided on initial drawings. However, this proposal was not pursued.

The locomotives were the heaviest 2-6-2 Ts to be built in Britain, with the leading driving wheel having an 18 ton axle load and the rear two driving wheels both having a 19 ton axle load. This required the Scottish Area Civil Engineers' approval before the design could be developed.

Early deliveries of the class were to the LNER sheds in the Edinburgh and Glasgow area for local suburban services. The North East Area received 26 locos which were allocated to the Newcastle area (Heaton, Blaydon and Gateshead), occasionally making journeys as far as Carlisle. Changes during 1939 brought transfers from Blaydon to Middlesbrough, where the NER Class A8 4-6-2 Ts often used to struggle on such workings. They were transferred to work the hourly fast service from Middlesbrough to Newcastle, usually carrrying express passenger headlamps.

During 1938 fifteen new locos were delivered to the Southern Area. The first three were vacuum braked only, and after starting in the Stratford area they finished up working in the Norwich area. The remaining twelve locos were allocated to Stratford (for working Clacton services) and Bishops Stortford. The locos originally at Norwich (Nos. 407, 420 and 424) moved to Neasden in 1943 for a short period, before returning to Norwich. The arrival of the Thompson Class L1 2-6-4 Ts allowed the concentration of the locos to go back to the North East and Scotland by 1951.

The locomotives had many former GNR features, including additional headlamp positions outside those normally placed over the buffers, and some locos had destination board brackets fitted to the smokebox doors and coal bunkers. NBR style clips for the destination boards were provided from construction.

During 1938 the elbow bend was amended on the combined cylinder block, which eliminated the need to provide hump shaped steam pipes to the outside cylinders, and a straight pipe was provided instead. Records show that some locos, having been modified, went back to the original position.

As built, the locomotives were provided with a coal bunker similar to the GNR Class N2 locos. Some modifications were necessary due to the problems coaling the locos at Bridgeton Cross, and the top rail was removed from Nos. 2900, 2901, 2902 and 2904. In 1931, backing plates were added to the coal rails to prevent spillage. Later, a hopper shaped coal bunker was designed which increased capacity by 10 cwts, but fitting eliminated the circular rear window and provided only a narrow vertical window which was slanted top and bottom.

As built, up to No.451, a curved opening was provided in the cab roof over the entry door, but this was stopped in 1938.

Several of the locomotives allocated to Eastfield (Glasgow) were equipped with apparatus to slip couplings after banking trains out of Queen Street Station up Cowlairs Bank, these were Nos 67600, 67601, 67603, 67608, 67628, 67671 and 67680. St Margarets (Edinburgh) also had a similar example, No.67666, which was fitted with a different type of bracket for banking purposes at Duddington.

Bachmann LNER Class V3

Maintenance for Scottish locomotives was undertaken at Cowlairs until 1943 when the locos travelled to Darlington, together with those from the North East Region. Doncaster maintained the Great Eastern Region, although Stratford undertook heavy repairs to Nos 478 and 447. As the locos migrated north, as previously mentioned, all maintenance became centred at Darlington.

Drivers glass side screens were fitted from new on No.2928 onwards, with a smaller version behind the cab opening for reverse running, and these were retrospectively fitted to earlier locos when shopped.

When introduced, the locomotives were in the standard LNER black livery with red lining. During the Austerity period of World War II, plain black livery was applied with NE on the side tanks. Post war, No.7684 was repainted in 1946 at Darlington, although the livery was retained when lettered British Railways in 1948, and it was the only member of the Class so treated. After appearing with E prefixes to the 1946 numbers, all locos received the standard BR red, cream and grey lining, with British Railways in full or either crest according to the period. The BR number was also applied to the bunker sides rather than the tank sides as in LNER days.

Bachmann introduced an OO Gauge ready to run model in 1992, it remains available.

Class 9J 0-6-0 (LNER Class J11)
Great Central Railway

Introduced:	1901
Designed By:	J G Robinson
Allocation:	Great Central Railway, later London & North Eastern Railway, later British Railways Eastern and London Midland Regions.
Locomotive Nos:	973 - 1012, built by Neilson, Reid & Co. 1901/1902, became 5973 - 6012 in 1924, then 4280 - 4319 in 1946.

973 - 1012, built by Neilson, Reid & Co. 1901/1902, became 5973 - 6012 in 1924, then 4280 - 4319 in 1946.
1043 - 1051, built by Neilson, Reid & Co. 1902, became 6043 - 6051 in 1924, then 4320 - 4328 in 1946.
198, 201, 203, 205, 206, 209 - 211, 214 and 215, built by Beyer, Peacock & Co. 1903, became 5198, 5201, 5203, 5205, 5206, 5209 - 5211, 5214 and 5215 in 1924, then 4329 - 4338 in 1946.
216, 218, 219, 221 - 231 and 234, built by Beyer, Peacock & Co. 1904, became 5216, 5218, 5219, 5221 - 5231 and 5234 in 1924, then 4339 - 4353 in 1946.
177, 197, 202, 204, 207, 208, 217, 220, 232, 233, 240 and 241, built at Gorton 1903/1904, became 5177, 5197, 5202, 5204, 5207, 5208, 5217, 5220, 5232, 5233, 5240 and 5241 in 1924, then 4354 - 4365 in 1946.
235 - 239, 242 - 250 and 252, built by Vulcan Foundry 1904, became 5235 - 5239, 5242 - 5250 and 5252 in 1924, then 4366 - 4380 in 1946.
253 - 257, built by Yorkshire Engine Co. 1904, became 5253 - 5257 in 1924, then 4381 - 4385 in 1946.
1078 - 1082, built by Yorkshire Engine Co. 1905, became 6078 - 6082 in 1924, then 4386 - 4390 in 1946.
1115 - 1119, built by Yorkshire Engine Co. 1906, became 6115 - 6119 in 1924, then 4391 - 4395 in 1946.
281 - 309, 311 - 320 and 322 - 330, built at Gorton 1906-1908, became 5281 - 5309, 5311 - 5320 and 5322 - 5330 in 1924, then 4396 - 4443 in 1946.
16, built at Gorton 1909, became 5016 in 1924, then 4444 in 1946.
947 - 955, built at Gorton 1910, became 5947 - 5955 in 1924, then 4445 - 4453 in 1946.

No.134 Class 9D (LNER Class J10) had its original 4' 4" diameter boiler replaced by a 5' 0" diameter boiler (as fitted to Class J11) during 1908, and was reclassified as Class 9M by the GCR. At Grouping, the

LNER classified No.(5)134 as Class J11, but during 1924 it was refitted with a smaller diameter boiler (as previously) and thus reverted back to Class J10.

No.16 was built with a Schmidt Superheater and piston valves, becoming the first GCR loco to be superheated. From 1913, superheating began to be fitted to these locos, but this was not completed until 1946, and many remained with the original slide valves.

During the First World War (1914-1918), the following locos saw service in France on loan to the Railway Operating Division: 204, 208, 211, 222, 248, 255, 256, 281, 288, 303, 306, 309, 326, 951, 952, 1043, 1046 and 1080.

The following locos were rebuilt by Thompson from 1942, and were reclassified Class J11/3:
6009 during 1942
5177, 5240, 5291 and 5302 during 1943
5246, 5326, 5328 and 6007 during 1943.
5206, 5208, 5231, 5287, 5303 and 5313 during 1945.
4332, 5952, 5977 and 6011 during 1946.
64317 and 64379 during 1948.
64323 and 64420 during 1949.
64393 during 1952.
64394 and 64395 in 1953.

Last of Class Withdrawn: 1962

Number Built: 175

Duties: Generally Freight services, but occasionally Passenger duties.

Technical Data: **Tractive Effort:** (85%) - 21,959 lb Saturated; 25,664 lb Superheated
Loco Weight: 52 tons 3 cwt Saturated; 52 tons 10 cwt Superheated
Loco Driving Wheels: 5' 2" dia.
Cylinders: (2 inside) - 18½" x 26" Saturated; 20" x 26" Superheated
Valve Gear: Stephenson with slide valves for saturated, Stephenson with 8" piston valves for superheated.

GCR Class 9J (LNER Class J11) *Photograph courtesy of Colour Rail*

The J11s were built in 1901 and were quickly nicknamed 'Pom-Poms' as the sharp staccato bark reminded those of the early type machine gun fire used during the Boer War. The class was a development of Parker and Pollits Classes 9D and 9H, which became Class J10.

The new locomotives had 5' 0" diameter boilers as opposed to 4' 4" diameter, the cylinder diameter increased to 18½", and the boiler and firebox were extended in length to produce a grate area of 19 square feet, with the boiler pressure also raised to 180 lbs per square inch.

When construction commenced, the first 40 locomotives were provided with 3,250 gallon tenders without water pick-up gear, whilst the next 66 locos had similar capacity tenders but had scoops. The remainder of the locos received 4,000 gallon tenders with scoop. On all these tenders the coal rails varied from 2 to 4, some subsequently being plated either internally or externally, or rails were removed and solid coal guards were fitted.

The locomotives were occasionally used for passenger work, more often on seaside excursions at the weekends, and were duly fitted to supply steam heating to the carriages. The J11s were used on stopping services across the Pennines between Manchester and Sheffield during the 1930s, and towards the end of steam Gorton shed (Manchester) had several suburban passenger duties in that area before being displaced by diesel multiple units.

These locomotives handled heavily loaded freight trains over the quite steeply graded ex Great Central Lines, as well as being used on the former Cheshire lines Committee routes between Manchester, Liverpool (Brunswick), Wrexham and Chester. In 1936 the LNER took control of the former Midland & Great Northern Line, and during 1937 six of the class were transferred to South Lynn, Melton Constable and Yarmouth (Beach), generally for only a short period. However, Nos. 5222 and 5323 remained at Melton Constable until 1942 and 1943 respectively. South Lynn also received Nos. 5235 and 5990 during 1941, but they moved away the following year.

From 1942, Thompson commenced rebuilding the class with new cylinders and long travel piston valves, which raised the boiler pitch by 4" which meant the chimney height had to be reduced by a similar amount to clear the LNER Composite Rolling Stock Gauge. As built, the locos had the standard Robinson flared chimney, tall dome and uncased Ramsbottom safety valves. Later, when superheating was added, a Gresley anti-vacuum valve was fitted behind the chimney, generally with a lower dome and machanical lubricator to lubricate the valve gear. Some locos were later fitted with the LNER pattern 'flowerpot' chimney. During the 1930s, Ross Pop safety valves became the norm and all were so fitted by 1939.

These locomotives were always painted in black livery, had cast numberplates, and had Great Central written on the tenders. In early LNER days, both L.N.E.R. and the loco number were carried on the tender, with the loco number on the front buffer beam. Later, L.N.E.R. was carried on the tender side and the loco number was on the cabside and front buffer beam. During the Second World War the LNER was shortened to N.E.. In BR days, unlined black livery was carried with British Railways in full or either crest carried according to the period.

Union Mills GCR Class 9j (LNER Class J11)

Class J39 0-6-0
London & North Eastern Railway

Introduced:	1926
Designed By:	Sir Nigel Gresley
Allocation:	London & North Eastern Railway, later British Railways Eastern Region.
Locomotive Nos:	(a) 1448 - 1452, 1454 - 1459, 1481, 1484, 1492 - 1498, 1233, 1255, 1259, 1263, 1265 - 1270, 1272 - 1275, 1277, 1281, 1282, 1286, 1287, 1289, 1290, 1295, 1296 and 1298, all built at Darlington 1926/1927.

(b) 2691 - 2742, built at Darlington 1928/1929.
(c) 2270 - 2288, 1418, 1425, 1429, 1466, 1470, 1487, 1489 and 1491, built at Darlington 1929/1930.
(d) 2962 - 2980, 1453, 1469, 1471, 1480, 1482 and 1483, built at Darlington 1931-1933.
(e) 1412, 1463, 1467, 1468, 1472, 1475 - 1479, 1488 and 1490, built at Darlington 1934.
(f) 2941 - 2953, 2981 - 2994, 1436, 1460, 1464, 1465, 1473, 1474, 1485 and 1486, built at Darlington 1935.
(g) 2995 - 3000, built at Darlington 1936.
(h) 1803, 1813, 1824, 1828, 1854, 1856, 1857, 1869 and 1870, built by Beyer Peacock 1936.
(i) 1532 - 1534, 1536, 1539, 1540, 1543 - 1545 and 1547, built by Beyer Peacock 1936.
(j) 1563, 1577, 1580, 1585 - 1587, 1875, 1880 and 1894, built by Beyer Peacock 1937.
(k) 1508, 1509, 1535, 1537, 1538, 1541, 1542, 1546, 1548, 1551, 1558, 1560, 1804, 1808, 1835, 1862, 1863, 1896, 1898, 1903, 1922, 1926 - 1928, 1930, 1933, 1940, 1942, 1943, 1952, 1965, 1971, 1974, 1977, 1980, 1984, 1996 and 1997, built at Darlington 1937/1938.
(l) 3081 - 3098, built at Darlington 1941.

L.N.E.R. Nos. (in order from above) in 1946:
(a) 4700 - 4716, 4718 - 4720, 4721, 4722, 4724, 4723, 4725 - 4727, 4730, 4731, 4717, 4728, 4729, 4732, 4734, 4733 and 4735 - 4743.
(b) 4744 - 4795
(c) 4796 - 4811, 4820 - 4822, 4812, 4813, 4815 and 4814 - 4819.
(d) 4823 - 4847
(e) 4848 - 4852, 4855 - 4859, 4853 and 4854.
(f) 4872 - 4884, 4885 - 4898 and 4860 - 4867.
(g) 4899 - 4904
(h) 4905 - 4913
(i) 4914 - 4923
(j) 4924 - 4932
(k) 4933 - 4970
(l) 4971 - 4988

B.R. added 6xxxx to all 1946 numbers.

Last of Class Withdrawn:	1962
Number Built:	289
Preserved Examples:	None
Duties:	Freight and some Branch Passenger services, occasional Excursion work.
Technical Data:	**Tractive Effort:** (85%) - 25,664 lb
	Loco Weight: 57 tons 17 cwt
	Loco Driving Wheels: 5' 2" dia
	Cylinders: (2 inside) - 20" x 26"
	Valve Gear: Stephenson with piston valves.

LNER Class J39 *Photograph courtesy of Colour Rail*

These locomotives, together with the very similar Class J38's (4' 8" driving wheels otherwise identical), were the first 0-6-0 tender locomotives to be built by the L.N.E.R. after grouping. They utilised the same boiler as Gresley used for the D49 Class, which were built at the same time. At grouping, the L.N.E.R. had collected over 800 various 0-6-0 locos from the constituent companies, many being nearly 50 years old and rapidly approaching their retirement. Hence, once in office, Gresley first sorted out the designs of an express passenger locomotive (Class A1, later A3) and for a mixed traffic locomotive (Class K3). With this work completed, he then set about designing a standard goods locomotive. Thus the J39's became the largest class of locos built by the L.N.E.R. until Thompson's Class B1 4-6-0's were completed. 289 locomotives were built, and several variations occurred within the class. A variety of tenders were used, including 3500 and 4200 gallon group standard tenders, with both flared and flat sides. The N.E.R. pattern 4124 gallon tenders from the Raven Pacifics, when they were replaced by eight wheel tenders, were also used, as were other N.E.R. 3940 gallon tenders from the withdrawn B13 and D17 Classes. Two surplus 4125 gallon tenders from Class C7, plus similar tenders from Class D21, were also utilised when the latter locos received surplus ex G.N.R. tenders in return.

The early J39's, as well as the early J38's and D49's, were fitted with N.E.R. steam operated reversing gear. It is probable that only those locos built up to the end of 1928 were so fitted. All locos were either then built with, or subsequently converted to, mechanical reversing.

Brake details also varied throughout the class, some initially appeared with steam brake only, some were vacuum fitted, whilst others had vacuum/Westinghouse brakes. The Westinghouse brakes were removed under B.R. ownership.

The locomotives ran over most of the English portion of the L.N.E.R. system, although they were seldom seen south of Leicester on the ex Great Central Main Line or south of Peterborough on the ex Great Northern Main Line. Post war, about six of the class were based at Dundee for working freight trains in that area. Carlisle (Canal) and St. Margarets (Edinburgh) had examples which worked across the Waverley route. The Carlisle locos based at Canal Depot, also worked on the

Silloth branch passenger services from Carlisle (Citadel). Another branch passenger service worked by the J39's in later years, was the ex North Eastern Railway branch to Alston from Haltwhistle. The Class also worked Race specials to Wetherby Racecourse from the Leeds/York area. The locos were frequently used on passenger services from London (Liverpool Street) to Southend, prior to that line being electrified.

The locos were mainly used on freight services, and a large number allocated to Gorton (Manchester) and Darnall (Sheffield) were used across the Woodhead Route alongside the ex G.C. 2-8-0's. Those in East Anglia worked services between Whitemoor (March) and Temple Mills (Stratford, London). They also appeared on local freights around the Norwich and Lincoln areas, as well as working trains from Nottingham to Lincoln with traffic from the local coalfields.

With the large scale introduction of diesel multiple units on local passenger services, and the lower horsepower diesel locos on freight work, the whole Class were withdrawn fairly quickly over the period from 1959 to 1962.

When introduced, locomotives were in L.N.E.R. unlined black livery. Some carried both numbers and initials on the tender, but later, numbers were affixed to the cab sides. During the Second World War, only N.E. was carried on the tender. In B.R. days they appeared in unlined black livery with 'British Railways' in full on the tender. Later both styles of B.R. crest were carried according to the period.

Bachmann LNER Class J39

Bachmann introduced a ready to run OO gauge model in 1993. It is currently available.

Union Mills introduced a ready to run N gauge version in 1994 which is still available.

Class B1 4-6-0
London & North Eastern Railway

Introduced:	1942
Designed By:	Edward Thompson
Allocation:	London & North Eastern Railway, later British Railways Eastern, London Midland and Scottish Regions.
Locomotive Nos:	8301 - 8310, built at Darlington 1942-1944. Re-numbered to 1000 - 1009 in 1946.

1010 - 1039, built at Darlington 1946/1947.
1040 - 1139, built by North British Locomotive Co. 1946/1947.
1140 - 1189, built at Vulcan Foundry 1947.
1190 - 1287, built by North British Locomotive Co. 1947/1948.
E1288 - E1303, built by North British Locomotive Co. 1947/1948.
61304 - 61339, built by North British Locomotive Co. 1947/1948.
61340 - 61349, built at Gorton 1948/1949.
61350 - 61359, built at Darlington 1949.
61360 - 61399, built by North British Locomotive Co. 1950-1952.
61400 - 61409, built at Darlington 1950.

E prefix added to all L.N.E.R. locomotives up to and including
No.E1303, the E prefix being later dropped.

B.R. added 6xxxx to these numbers.

Last of Class Withdrawn: 1967, some remained in Service Stock until 1968.

Number Built: 410

Preserved Examples: 61264
1306 Mayflower

Duties: Mixed Traffic.

Technical Data: **Tractive Effort:** (85%) - 26,878 lb
Loco Weight: 71 tons 3 cwt
Loco Driving Wheels: 6' 2" dia
Cylinders: (2) - 20" x 26"
Valve Gear: Walschaerts with 10" piston valves.

LNER Class B1 *Photograph courtesy of Milepost 92½*

When Edward Thompson became Chief Mechanical Engineer on Gresley's death in 1941, he quickly produced plans for standard locomotives in several part classifications.

The Class B1 design is basically a Gresley Class B17 'Sandringham', with slightly smaller driving wheels, only two cylinders and a higher pressure boiler, although many of the Gresley features such as the curved stepped running plates and shaped cab were omitted, making the design much simpler.

When the L.N.E.R. announced a Modernisation Plan in 1945, it included a further 400 Class B1's to supplement those already in service, thus becoming the largest class of that railways design, although building was not completed until after Nationalisation.

Although a newer design than the L.M.S. Stanier Class 5, the B1's can be likened in many respects to these locomotives. They were spread throughout the length of the L.N.E.R. system, and since the locos were relatively light, had a wide route availability.

Some of the locomotives were intended to have electric alternators fitted to the rear bogie, but this did not prove successful. Later a steam generator was fitted to some locos.

For work on the single line sections between Aberdeen and Inverness, and the branches around Elgin, automatic tablet exchange equipment was fitted to the front left hand side of the tender. The Class generally received 4200 gallon group standard flat sided tenders which varied, particularly in the early series. Also four coal weighing tenders were passed through the Class, as required for experimental purposes.

Only 59 of the 410 locomotives received names, the early locos being named after varieties of the Antelope, whilst 18 were named after the Directors of the L.N.E.R.. To celebrate the ties between Boston, England and Boston, Massachusetts, No.61379 was named Mayflower and also carried special plaques on its cab sides. This name has since been used on the preserved locomotive No.1306.

In the 1948 Locomotive Exchange Trials, the B1's were matched with the G.W.R. Modified Hall, the L.M.S. Stanier Class 5 and Bullied West Country Class.

As stated earlier, the B1's were widely spread around the former L.N.E.R. sections, including working alongside the Stanier Class 5's on the West Highland Line, and also across the Pennine routes in the North.

During 1953, due to problems with the Bullied Pacifics, the Eastern Region loaned 14 of the Class to the Southern Region, where they were allocated to Stewarts Lane (Battersea, London) for working trains to Dover and Ramsgate. In later days, the Class appeared frequently on the Southern Region, on through troop specials, working generally via the West London Line.

The B1's arrival sounded the death knell of the Ivatt Atlantics, particularly on the Kings Cross suburban services out to Letchworth. They worked in conjunction with Class B17's on the Cambridge Buffet Car Expresses. On the Great Eastern section, they took over the duties of the D16 and B12 Classes, working alongside the B17's. Both Classes lost out when the G.E. section received their allocation of B.R. Standard Class 7 'Britannia' Pacifics.

Bachmann LNER Class B1

In the North East, the Class replaced many of the older North Eastern 4-4-0's, whilst in Scotland similar North British and Great North of Scotland 4-4-0's were replaced.

The locos generally proved successful wherever they ran, and were only withdrawn as a result of the widespread introduction of medium range diesel locos, and a reduction of the rail network following the Beeching closures.

When introduced, the first ten locomotives were delivered in unlined black with wartime N.E. initials on the tender. Nos 1040 - 1093 were delivered in black lined red, whilst some of the locos received lined L.N.E.R. apple green, but a very complicated picture ensued. The subsequent deliveries of Nos. 1010-1039, 1094-1139, 1140-1189 and up to 1287 were in lined green with L.N.E.R. on the tender, but from No.1288 onwards 'British Railways' in full was applied to the tender, although they still carried L.N.E.R. lined green livery. From No.61340 the black lined B.R. livery was applied with 'British Railways' in full, whilst from No.61355 onwards the first B.R. crest was carried. Subsequently all locomotives, except No.1057 which was withdrawn following collision damage in 1950, would have carried the second B.R. crest.

> Airfix announced in 1981 that they were going to produce a OO ready to run model. It did not appear as the company were taken over by Mainline in the same year. The model was tooled by Kader (in Hong Kong) but the closure of Mainline resulted in the model not being released. It was eventually released by Replica in 1987 who had some models produced by Kader from the tooling that Kader owned. When Kader set up Bachmann in the UK in 1989 the arrangements with Replica ceased and an upgraded model was released by Bachmann in 1994. The model remains available.

Class J38 0-6-0
London & North Eastern Railway

Introduced:	1926
Designed By:	Sir Nigel Gresley
Allocation:	London & North Eastern Railway, later British Railways Scottish Region.
Locomotive Nos:	1400, 1401, 1403-1411, 1413-1417, 1419-1424, 1426-1428, 1434, 1437 and 1440-1447, built at Darlington 1926.
	Locos were renumbered in sequence 5900-5934 in 1946.
	B.R. added 6xxxx to the numbers after 1948.
Last of Class Withdrawn:	1967
Number Built:	35
Preserved Examples:	None
Duties:	Freight and occasional Excursion Traffic.
Technical Data:	**Tractive Effort:** (85%) - 28,414 lb **Loco Weight:** 58 tons 19 cwt **Loco Driving Wheels:** 4' 8" dia **Cylinders**: (2 inside) - 20" x 26" **Valve Gear**: Stephenson with 8" piston valves.

LNER Class J38 *Photograph courtesy of Colour Rail*

These locomotives were part of the 1925-1926 Joint Traffic & Locomotive Committees discussions during 1924, when 103 new goods locos were required for the Southern, North Eastern and Scottish Areas of the LNER. 1 month after the meeting it was possible to purchase 48 ex R.O.D. (Class 04) 2-8-0s, and hence the order for 0-6-0s was eventually trimmed to 35, all for the Scottish Area. They were deemed to be modified J27s, but were in fact quite different, the only similarity being the wheel arrangement. Although only a small class, they were the last LNER steam Class to remain intact until 1962, and Nos. 65901 and 65929 (withdrawn in 1967) were the last Gresley steam locos in service.

As was the case with many former NER Darlington locos, steam reversers were fitted, which were fine for quick reversal when shunting, but could cause problems when notching up when the loco could reverse (or try to). Between 1945 and 1948 the entire class was converted to screw reversers. The boilers originally fitted were classified Diagram 97A, but when the J39s were developed (being of similar proportions with only detail differences), these were classified Diagram 97 and became interchangable.

When built the whole class received group standard 4200 gallon tenders with stepped out copings. Between 1931 and 1933 the entire Class received new group standard 3500 gallon tenders (slab sided), but towards the end of their service lives the locos were seen with 4125 gallon NE type tenders, 3500 gallon high fronted group standard tenders (ex Class K4) and 4200 gallon group standard tenders (ex Class K3).

Unusually for Darlington built locos, a continuous boiler handrail encircled the top of the smokebox, whilst the smokebox fastening was a double handle, not the more usual NER wheel and handle, although No.1442 gained such a detail during a works visit in 1932. From about 1930, the upper lampiron was transferred to the smokebox, completed in 1949 when No.65929 was altered.

Spencer's double-case buffers, as fitted to Classes A1, K3 and 02, were fitted to the loco fronts, the drawgear was originally 3 link couplings, but evidence shows that most acquired the screw pattern during their life. Again, in common with Darlington built locos, the front vacuum pipe was hung below the front buffer beam, although during the life of the class, generally in the 1930s, the swan-neck vertical standpipe became standard.

Initially the locomotives were allocated to most sheds in the Fife and Lothian coalfields. During the Second World War several instances occurred of J38s being seen south of Newcastle, in 1940 No.1416 was seen at York, No.1403 at Doncaster and No.1423 at Retford heading north (which may have been to Grantham or more probably Peterborough). St Margarets (Edinburgh) locos appeared on the Waverley route with crews changing locos with Carlisle men on the journey. In March 1948, No.5931 headed a northbound East Coast Main Line train into Edinburgh Waverley, following the failure of a Class A2 Pacific at Drem.

These locomotives were strong engines and did very good work, once the problems with the pull out regulator, steam reversing and inadequate tender brakes were dealt with.

During 1960/1961, Nos. 65909, 65910, 65912, 65916-65918, 65920, 65922, 65926, 65929, 65930, 65931, 65933 and 65934 were fitted with British Railways A.W.S. equipment.

These locomotives were always in unlined black livery. Initially they carried LNER and the loco number on the tender, then the number was on the cabside, and during the Second World War just NE was on the tenders. In BR days British Railways in full or either crest was carried according to the period.

Union Mills LNER Class J38

Union Mills have a ready to run N Gauge model available.

Class B17 (Sandringham) 4-6-0
London & North Eastern Railway

Introduced:	1928
Designed By:	Sir Nigel Gresley
Allocation:	London & North Eastern Railway, later British Railways Eastern Region.
Locomotive Nos:	B17/1 2800 - 2809, built by North British Locomotive Co. 1928. B17/2 2810 - 2821, built at Darlington 1930, boilers supplied by Armstrong Whitworth & Co.. B17/2 2822 - 2836, built at Darlington 1931, boilers supplied by Armstrong Whitworth & Co.. B17/2 2837 - 2842, built at Darlington 1933. B17/3 2843 - 2847, built at Darlington 1935. B17/4 2848 - 2861, built at Darlington 1936. B17/4 2862 - 2872, built by R Stephenson & Co. 1937.
	Nos. 2800 - 2847 were fitted with Great Eastern Railway pattern 3700 gallon tenders. Nos. 2848 - 2872 were fitted with L.N.E.R. pattern 4200 gallon group standard tenders.

Re-numbered 1600 - 1672 in the 1946 scheme.

B.R. added 6xxxx to the numbers after Nationalisation.

In 1937, Nos. 2859 & 2870 were streamlined, similar to Class A4 profile, for hauling the 'East Anglian' and were reclassified Class B17/5. Group standard 4200 gallon tenders were fitted with higher side sheets for appearance. This streamlining was removed in 1951.

Nos. 2814 - 2816, 2839, 2871, 1603, 1607, 1617, 1632 and 61644 were rebuilt by Thompson at Darlington 1945-1949, and reclassified Class B2 by fitting diagram 100A Class B1 boiler, and providing only two cylinders instead of three.

Nos. 61601, 61624, 61625, 61629, 61660 and 61667 retained the original diagram 100 boiler, remainder of B17 Class was reclassified B17/6 with diagram 100A boiler.

Nos. 2800 - 2815 were fitted with Westinghouse brakes for engine and train with vacuum ejector for alternative train braking.

Nos. 2816 - 2872 had steam brakes with vacuum ejector for train.

Nos. 2848, 2854, 2856, 2860, 2861, 2863, 2865, 2868, 2871 and 2872 were intended to be fitted with Westinghouse brakes during 1941/1942, but not all were carried out, and with the reduction of Westinghouse brake stock, many lost the equipment after a relatively short period.

Last of Class Withdrawn:	1960
Number Built:	73
Preserved Examples:	None
Duties:	Express Passenger.
Technical Data:	**Tractive Effort**: (85%) - 25,380 lb, reduced to 22,842 lb in 1943. 28,553 lb B17/6.
	Loco Weight: 77 tons 5 cwt (max); B17/5, 80 tons 10 cwt
	Loco Driving Wheels: 6' 8" dia
	Cylinders: (3) - 17½" x 26"
	Valve Gear: Walschaerts/Gresley with 8" piston valves.

In 1926, due to increased loadings and the introduction of more modern vacuum braked stock in East Anglia, services were in a poor way, so Gresley was asked to design a larger 4-6-0 with relatively light axle loadings to supplement the Holden Class B12's.

A variety of attempts were made using details from the Class D49 4-4-0's and the Gresley Class A1 Pacifics. Finally a contract was let to North British Locomotive Co. who completed the final design, the inside cylinder being set forward as they had been on the L.M.S.R. 'Royal Scot' Class, which this company had produced previously.

When introduced, the early members of the class were spread around East Anglian area; they were better suited to the Cambridge line than the Norwich line as they were not particularly good hill climbers, and although one thinks of East Anglia as flat, some very severe banks occur on the

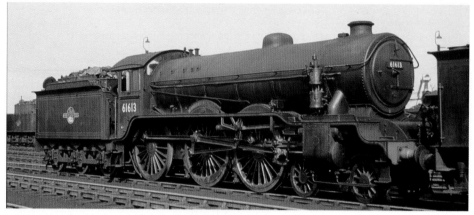

LNER Class B17 *Photograph courtesy of Colour Rail*

Norwich route including the difficult start up to Bethnal Green, Brentwood Bank, and the undulating stretch between Ipswich and Norwich. One of the jobs the B17's took over from the B12's, was the unofficially named 'North Country Continental' (Harwich to Liverpool), to which a B17 was diagrammed to undertake the 215 mile Ipswich to Manchester section (via the old Woodhead Tunnel), on a lodging turn diagram opposite a B17 from Gorton (Manchester). As special route knowledge was required for this working, only certain drivers undertook the duty and the locos were kept in excellent condition.

Further locomotives were sent to Doncaster and worked to York and Hull, as well as across to Banbury on cross country fish trains from Grimsby.

Once the Class B17/4's were being delivered with the heavier 4200 gallon tender, these were restricted to the G.C. section. And since these were weight restricted on the Great Eastern section, allocations were made in quantity to the ex Great Central Main Line sheds at Neasden, Leicester, Darnall (Sheffield), and further examples to Gorton to replace the earlier G.C. Atlantics and smaller 4-4-0's. These locos were diagrammed for some long distance workings, one Sheffield loco on a Swindon to York duty was timed well inside the G.W.R.'s crack 'Cheltenham Flyer' timings, when running between Swindon and Steventon.

The 'Sandringhams' were used for Royal Train workings in East Anglia, taking over from the Cambridge 'Royal Clauds' Nos. 8783 and 8787. First Class A3, then Class V2 ousted the B17's away from the G.C., and apart from occasional visits, few were seen on the G.C. line after Nationalisation, all the locos being concentrated on the G.E. section.

With the introduction of the B.R. Standard 'Britannias', together with electrification of the Southend and Clacton lines, this heralded the demise of the 'Sandringhams'. Many of the drivers preferred the B1 Class 4-6-0's, for as with all Gresley locos, unless maintenance was good, their performance was often poor.

Hornby LNER Class B17

When introduced, the locomotives were painted in standard L.N.E.R. lined apple green livery. During World War II, they only carried unlined black livery with N.E. initials. After Nationalisation, No.61661 was repainted in a very light green experimental livery with yellow lining. A few of the Class received L.N.E.R. green livery during 1948, and all subsequently received the B.R. standard brunswick green lined livery and carried British Railways in full or either crest according to the period.

Hornby introduced a OO ready to run version in 1980. It remains available.

Classes K1 & K2 0-8-0 (LNER Classes Q1, Q2 & Q3) Great Northern Railway

Introduced:	1901
Designed By:	H A Ivatt (K2 rebuilt by H N Gresley)
Allocation:	Great Northern Railway, later London & North Eastern Railway, later British Railways Eastern Region.
Locomotive Nos:	401, built at Doncaster 1901.
	402 - 411, built at Doncaster 1902.
	412 - 421, built at Doncaster 1902/1903.
	422 - 440, built at Doncaster 1903/1904.
	441 - 445, built at Doncaster 1906/1907.
	446 - 450, built at Doncaster 1909.
	451 - 455, built at Doncaster 1909.
	At Grouping the classes consisted of:
	Class Q1 - 3401, 3403, 3404, 3408, 3409, 3411-3415, 3418, 3419 and 3422-3449.
	Class Q2 - 3402, 3405-3407, 3410, 3416, 3417, 3421 and 3450-3455.
	Class Q3 - 3420, rebuilt in 1914.
Last of Class Withdrawn:	1937
Number Built:	54
Technical Data:	**Tractive Effort:** (85%) - 27,610 lb Saturated Q1; 26,835 lb Superheated; 29,580 lb Superheated Q2 & Q3
	Loco Weight: 54 tons 12 cwt Saturated Q1; 55 tons 14 cwt Superheated; 58 tons 5 cwt Superheated Q2; 60 tons 9 cwt Q3
	Loco Driving Wheels: 4' 8" dia
	Cylinders: (2 inside) - 20" x 26" Saturated Q1 & Superheated; 21" x 26" Superheated Q2 & Q3
	Valve Gear: Stephenson with slide valves on on Saturated Q1 & Superheated, Stephenson with 8" piston valves on Superheated Q2, and Stephenson with 8¾" piston valves on Q3.

These locomotives were needed as the Great Northern Railway was carrying more and more coal traffic, much destined for the London area from the Nottinghamshire/Derbyshire coalfield. The earlier Stirling and Ivatt Classes J3 and J4 0-6-0s could only manage about 50 loaded wagons, whereas 60 loaded wagons became the requirement for these locos to head traffic on the East Coast Main Line, either from the coalfield to Peterborough or thence forward to Ferme Park (in London, between Harringay and Hornsey).

Initially, all locomotives conformed with Class K1 (Nos. 401-445). During 1908, No.417 was fitted with a superheater and piston valves. Ten further locos were added in 1909 with Nos. 446-450 being basic Class K1, whilst Nos. 451-455 were superheated with piston valves being Class K2. On the final five locos, the boilers were pitched 2" higher, making them 8' 6¼" rather than the previous 8' 4¼". Further locos also acquired superheaters and piston valves, and at Grouping only Nos.413, 419, 428, 431, 433, 434, 437 and 439 remained in original condition.

No.420 was rebuilt in 1914 with a Class H3 5' 6" diameter boiler (LNER Class K2) pitched at 8' 9", and was classified Class K2 (becoming LNER Class Q3). The locos were nicknamed 'Long Toms' due to their long boilers, which reminded them of a term used for a long barrel naval gun.

A batch of 20 locomotives were ordered in 1902/1903, this was reduced to 19 (Nos. 422-440) and the remaining parts were used to construct a similar 0-8-2T.

No.116, which was the prototype GNR Class L1 (LNER Class R1), was initially proposed to work freight traffic over the City Widened Lines through to Blackfriars on the Southern Railway, which was steeply graded. However, Ivatt had got it wrong, and the Civil Engineer pronounced it as too heavy for the route, so the loco returned to Doncaster to be rebuilt with a smaller boiler and shorter side tanks, reducing the axle loading from 17 tons to 15 tons 5cwt.

Experiments continued with superheater elements and anti-vacuum valves, and ultimately a conventional Robinson 24 element example with a standard Gresley anti-vacuum valve was located behind the chimney at the forward end of the boiler.

A variety of chimneys were carried to meet loading gauge requirements. When built, the locomotives ran with Ivatt Class B tenders with 5 tons of coal and 3,670 gallons of water. This was later changed to a more modern pattern Class B tender with 6½ tons of coal and 3,500 gallons of water. As the Classes O1 and O2 were constructed, these locos duly lost these and were instead supplied with Ivatt Type A tenders with 6 tons of coal and 3,170 gallons of water.

When built, No.401 appeared in black lined red livery and polished brass trims to the splashers. However, by 1912, Gresley had written to the Locomotive Committee suggesting that goods and shunting engines shouuld be painted in dark grey, rather than the two tone GNR livery. In LNER days, lined black livery was adopted until it was abandoned in 1928 when plain black became the norm. Initially, just the initials GNR were carried on the tender with a number on the cabside, but after Grouping L. & N.E.R. and then L.N.E.R. in 7½" lettering, and the loco number in 12" lettering were both applied on the tender side, and the loco number was applied to the front buffer beam. In 1929 it became common practice for the initials LNER to be on the tender and the loco number being applied to the cabsides.

Union Mills have a ready to run N Gauge model in their range.

Union Mills LNER Class Q2

Class H4 2-6-0 (LNER Class K3)
Great Northern Railway

Introduced:	1920
Designed By:	Sir Nigel Gresley
Allocation:	London & North Eastern Railway, later British Railways Eastern, London Midland, North Eastern and Scottish Regions.
Locomotive Nos:	GN Locos:

GN Locos:
1000 - 1009, built at Doncaster 1920-1921.
Renumbered 4000 - 4009 in 1924.

17 Series:
17, 28, 32, 33, 36, 38, 39, 46, 52, 53, 58, 69, 73, 75, 80, 91, 92, 109, 111-114, 116, 118 and 120, built at Darlington 1924.
121, 125-127, 134, 135, 140, 141, 143, 146, 153, 156, 158, 159, 163, 167, 170, 178, 180, 184, 186, 188, 191, 195 and 200, built at Darlington 1925.
202-204, 206-208, 227-229 and 231, built at Darlington 1925.

1300 Series:
1300, 1312, 1318, 1331, 1345, 1364, 1365, 1367, 1368 and 1386, built at Doncaster 1929.
1387-1389, 1391, 1392 and 1394-1398, built at Doncaster 1929.

2761 Series:
2761-2769, built at Darlington 1930. Boilers supplied by N.B. Locomotive Co..

1100 Series:
1100-1102, 1106, 1108, 1117-1119, 1121, 1125, 1133, 1135, 1137, 1141, 1154, 1156, 1158, 1162, 1164 and 1166, built by Armstrong Whitworth 1931.

1302 Series:
1302, 1304, 1306, 1308, 1310, 1324 and 2934-2937, built by Armstrong Whitworth 1934/1935. Originally ordered from Darlington.
1307, 1322, 1325, 1332, 1333, 1339, 1399 and 2938-2940, built by R Stephenson 1934/1935.
2425-2428, 2438-2440, 2442, 2443, 2447-2451, 2459, 2461, 2463 and 2466-2468, built by N.B. Locomotive Co. (Hyde Park Works) 1935.
2470, 2473, 2498 and 2499, built at Darlington 1936.
3813-3832, built at Darlington 1936/1937.
2417, 2429, 2445, 2446, 2453, 2455, 2458, 2465, 2471 and 2472, built by Armstrong Whitworth 1936.

In 1946 the locos were renumbered sequentially from above to 1800-1992.

B.R. added 6xxxx to the numbers at Nationalisation in 1948.

N.B.: Thompson rebuilt No.206 (later (6)1863) to a 2 Cylinder loco in 1945. No other conversions took place.

Last of Class Withdrawn: 1962 (Please see text)

Number Built: 193

Preserved Examples: None

Duties: Mixed Traffic.

Technical Data: **Tractive Effort:** 30,031 lb
Loco Weight: 71 tons 14 cwt
Loco Driving Wheels: 5' 8" dia
Cylinders: (3) - 18½" x 26"
Valve Gear: Walschaerts with 8" piston valves.

GNR Class H4 (LNER Class K3) *Photograph courtesy of Colour Rail*

This class forms a very difficult subject to provide comment on as no less than 4 different chimneys were fitted, 6 different cabs, as well as 4 different tenders! The locos will be described as per the Series batches in the number tables.

During 1917, Gresley considered the need for a further express goods engine based on the GNR Class H3 2-6-0s (LNER Class K2). At this time the first 'Tango' (LNER Class 02) was being constructed, and Gresley incorporated his patented valve gear, and the 2:1 drive to the inside cylinder, which was found to be successful. Hence, he proceeded with the design incorporating a 6' dia boiler to provide plenty of steam, and a 32 element Robinson superheater. The locos became known as 'Jazzers' due to their syncopated exhaust beat and gyratory movement at the rear end.

G.N. Locos:
No.4000 entered service in 1920. The chimney, sitting on top of the 6' diameter boiler, was 13' 4" above rail level, despite squat boiler mountings. The cab, laid out for right hand drive, was the usual wrap-around detail as per most Ivatt locos, and there were no side windows. These locos were provided with GNR Class B tenders holding 3500 gallons of water and 6½ tons of coal. Later developments were to include the fitting of long lap valves (1929-1933), after the GWR Castle/LNER Class A1 interchanges, some received group standard 4200 gallon tenders and a GS cab. Some were revised to left hand drive and had a height reduction to clear the composite loco gauge of 13' 0".

17 Series:
The next batch were more familiar to NER standards with right hand drive, side window cab, horizontal handrails above and below cab windows, and a 9½" high chimney to sit within the composite load gauge. Group standard 4200 gallon tenders with stepped out coping plates were generally provided. No.141 was fitted with steam reversing gear rather than screw reverse. Nos. 202-231, delivered between August and December 1925, were similarly fitted. Again the long lap valves and group standard cabs were amended later.

1300 Series:
These locos were built with long lap valves, screw reversing and left hand drive, a cab based on that provided for the Class D49 4-4-0s, and Westinghouse brakes to work in the North Eastern area. Cab cut outs were different, and the 20 locos were modified by Doncaster between 1930 and 1932. The North Eastern loco men also complained about the loss of the upper handrail above the cab, so Gresley agreed to a short vertical handrail to the front of the cab. Problems were found with 'fatigue' cracks occuring in the cut outs for the hornblocks. It was often necessary to replace the rear portions of one or both side frames on these locos, and also, due to the rough riding, the cab often became unfixed from the running plate. Originally, folding or bucket seats were provided, but due to the rocking of the cab, pedestal seats (almost bar stools) were fitted throughout the class.

2761 Series:
These locomotives were also constructed at Darlington and received the same cab as the 1300 Series (which had become the standard for this Class). They were also fitted with left hand drive and flat sided group standard 4200 gallon tenders. A new improved regulator was introduced as the earlier slide version had drawn complaints from the North Eastern area drivers over its stiffness.

1100 Series:
These 20 locomotives were constructed by Armstrong Whitworth and were similar to the 2761 Series, but were supplied without axlebox wedges. Instead, solid hornblocks were used as Gresley was attempting to eliminate axlebox knock. No.1125 of this batch received a new pattern liner and cowl, and a slightly modified chimney, to improve blastpipe performance which became a standard for the entire class when they were next shopped.

1302 Series:
This batch covered the final 74 locos, produced by contractors as well as Darlington Works. The modifications already mentioned above were incorporated, together with roller bearings to some parts of the valve gear and front steps below the buffer beam.

Gresley always took an interest in these locomotives and advanced their development, and of course, many of the K3 details were incorporated in his mixed traffic locos such as the Class V2 2-6-2s which were introduced in 1936.

The K3s, however, left their mark whether hauling passengers or freight trains. So far as passenger work was concerned, they often hauled express passenger trains from Kings Cross to Leeds, and were turned out to head the Hull portion of the Yorkshire Pullman from Doncaster to Hull. Records also show that they worked at least as far as Swindon on what was part of the through train from Aberdeen to Penzance via the Great Central Main Line.

Freight wise, the locos were in use from London to Aberdeen working the Waverley route, as well as Carlisle to Newcastle freight traffic. Examples in East Anglia often featured on fish trains from the Great Yarmouth and Lowestoft ports, as well as in the Hull area. They were slightly knocked by the development of the Class V2s, which being newer locos actually outlived these locos by about 4 years (not counting those used as stationary boilers).

Although the Class were withdrawn in 1962, three locos, Nos. 61835, 61912 and 61943, survived as stationary boilers and were finally withdrawn in 1965.

These locomotives were originally painted black with red lining in LNER days. During the Second World War the locos were in unlined black livery with only NE on the tenders. After that period, No.1935 was repainted in full LNER lined apple green livery in 1946, but was the only one to be so treated until it was repainted to black in 1949. Post Nationalisation, they were lined out in red, cream and grey, and either British Railways in full or BR crests were carried as appropriate.

Bachmann LNER Class K3

Bachmann introduced a ready to run OO Gauge model in 2005 which remains available.

Class 06 2-8-0
London & North Eastern Railway

Introduced:	1935
Designed By:	Sir William Stanier. These locos were built and used by the L.N.E.R. during and after the Second World War (see also L.M.S.R. Stanier 8F).
Allocation:	London & North Eastern Railway, transferred back to British Railways London Midland Region.
Locomotive Nos:	3100 - 3124, built at Brighton 1944, originally Nos. 7651 - 7675. 3125 - 3134, built at Darlington 1945. 3135 - 3147, built at Darlington 1946. 3148 - 3155, built at Doncaster 1945. 3156 - 3167, built at Doncaster 1946.
	These locomotives were numbered 3500 - 3567 inclusive in the 1947 re-numbering. They were re-numbered 8705 - 8772 inclusive when taken into L.M.S. stock by January 1948.
Last of Class Withdrawn:	1968
Duties:	Heavy Freight.
Technical Data:	**Tractive Effort:** (85%) - 32,438 lb **Loco Weight:** 72 tons 2 cwt **Loco Driving Wheels:** 4' 8½" dia **Cylinders:** (2) - 18½" x 28" **Valve Gear:** Walschaerts with 10" slide valves.

LNER Class 06 *Photograph courtesy of Milepost 92½*

These locomotives remained with the L.N.E.R. for only a relatively short time. All were returned to the L.M.S. by January 1948, because the L.N.E.R. bought 200 of the W.D. Austerity 2-8-0 locos (Class 07), which were built by the North British Locomotive Co. and Vulcan Foundry. Some of these were shedded at March for working freight trains to London, and also northwards to Doncaster via the G.N./G.E. route.

These locomotives were delivered in black livery with the wartime shortened N.E. on the tender. Later locos were treated with the full L.N.E.R. lettering, before being renumbered in LMR range.

Hornby LNER Class 06

Wrenn introduced a ready to run OO gauge model in 1977 which used the old Hornby Dublo 8f tools. The model remained available until 1980.

Graham Farish introduced a ready to run model in 1987 which remained available until the company was taken over by Bachmann until 2000. An upgraded version was introduced in 2004 and is currently available.

Hornby introduced a ready to run OO gauge model in 2003. It is currently available.

Class A3 4-6-2
Great Northern Railway

Introduced:	1922
Designed By:	Sir Nigel Gresley
Allocation:	Great Northern Railway, then London & North Eastern Railway, later British Railways Eastern and Scottish Regions.
Locomotive Nos:	1470 - 1479, 1480N/1N, later 4470 - 4481, built at Doncaster 1922/1923. 2543 - 2562, built at Doncaster 1924/1925. 2563 - 2582, built by North British (Hyde Park Works, Glasgow) 1924. 2743 - 2752, built at Doncaster 1928/1929. 2500 - 2508 and 2595 - 2599, built at Doncaster 1930-1935. Later re-numbered 35 - 112 in 1946. B.R. numbers 60035 - 60113 (see below). No.1470 Great Northern, later No.4470, was rebuilt to Class A1/1 by Thompson in 1945. B.R. No.60113.
Last of Class Withdrawn:	1966
Number Built:	79
Preserved Example:	4472 Flying Scotsman
Duties:	Express Passenger.
Technical Data:	**Tractive Effort:** (85%) - 29,835 lb A1; 32,410 lb A3. **Loco Weight:** 92 tons 9 cwt A1; 96 tons 5 cwt A3. **Loco Driving Wheels:** 6' 8" dia **Cylinders:** (3) - 20" x 26" A1; 19" x 26" A3. **Valve Gear:** Walschaerts/Gresley with 8" piston valves.

Following the development of the large Ivatt Atlantics, Gresley became aware of the advantages of the wide bottom fire box, and by scaling down a boiler which had been successfully applied to the Pennsylvania Railroad Class K4 Pacific, to suit the British loading gauge, the Class A1 Pacific was developed with a boiler pressure of 180 lbs p.s.i.. Where the Ivatt Atlantics were capable of working 400 ton trains over the East Coast Main Line, Gresley designed the Pacifics to haul 600 ton trains.

Later, in 1927, Gresley increased the boiler pressure of Nos. 2544 and 4480 to 220 lbs p.s.i., and following trials of various cylinder diameters, settled for 19".

Consequently, the locomotive Nos. 2500-2508, 2595-2599, 2743-2752 and 2795-2797 were built as Class A3 (all with left hand drive). It was not until after 1948 that the other locomotives (reclassified A10 upon the introduction of Thompson's Class A1/1, rebuild of No.4470 in 1945) were converted to Class A3, and all these locomotives were modified to left hand drive after 1951.

Class A3 locomotives were built to the L.N.E.R. standard loading gauge, as opposed to the larger G.N.R. gauge. As the early locomotives were rebuilt, the boiler mountings and cabs were reduced in height, also modifications took place to the cab side sheets.

GNR Class A3 *Photograph courtesy of Colour Rail*

Tenders varied during the service lives of this class. Originally fitted with the G.N.R. eight wheel coal rail tender, then for the non-stop 'Flying Scotsman' working, some were fitted with eight wheel corridor tenders; then a new high sided eight wheel tender for later locos built as Class A3's, and finally some locos gained streamlined non-corridor tenders from the Class A4's, instead of the corridor type as the A4 Class took over the more important work.

Other alterations included the fitting of double chimneys to all locomotives by 1960, and following drivers' complaints, all but five of the Class appeared with the German type trough smoke deflectors.

No.4472, 'The Flying Scotsman', was the first steam locomotive to be officially recorded at 100 mph (whilst still an A1) on 30th November 1934, when working a timing special between Leeds and Kings Cross, and also set a Kings Cross to Leeds record time which stood for over 30 years.

On 5th March 1935, A3 No.2750 Papyrus, whilst working a Kings Cross to Newcastle to Kings Cross special, broke the record with 108 mph on Stoke Bank.

The A3's, during 43 years of work, were seen in service over all parts of the L.N.E.R. system, apart from the Great Eastern side, and many finished their days working the heavily graded Leeds-Settle-Carlisle-Glasgow run. The final loco, No.60052 Prince Palatine, was withdrawn from St. Margarets (Edinburgh) in January 1966. The record holder for mileage was No.60106 Flying Fox, which exceeded 2,600,000 miles.

Nos. 1470 and 1471 were initially delivered in G.N.R. passenger green livery, subsequently all locomotives were in standard L.N.E.R. green livery, and Nos. 1470 and 1471 were repainted by 1924.

During the Second World War (1939 to 1945), the locos were painted unlined black, which lasted until 1946 when L.N.E.R. green livery was once again applied. All, except Nos. 60070 and 60076, then gained the B.R. blue livery, before all the Class were painted B.R. brunswick green with orange/black lining, and carried British Railways in full or either crest according to the period.

Following preservation, Flying Scotsman has operated over British Rail, and more recently Network Rail. It has operated in both Australia and the USA during visits. Following a high profile campaign to secure the locomotive for the nation in 2004, it now forms part of the National Collection. It is currently being restored to operational condition at the National Railway Museum in York. It is likely to see regular use on York to Scarborough specials on completion.

Hornby GNR Class A3

Trix Twin introduced a ready to run model in 1938. The model ceased to be produced after 1958. British Trix developed a brand new model in 1968 which continued in production until the company closed in 1971. The tools passed to Liliput who continued to produce the model until 1987. In 1992 the company was acquired by Dapol but during Liliput days, the tooling remained with Liliput in Vienna and the components shipped to Wales for assembly. Liliput was purchased by Kader (the owners of Bachmann) in 1992 and the tooling sent to China for evaluation. The British models which passed to China were either the wrong scale (Trix used 3.8mm to the foot prior to 1968) or else worn out. The A3 tooling fell into the latter category and was not reintroduced.

Tri-ang Hornby introduced its own OO version at the same time as the British Trix model. It passed to Hornby after the collapse of the Tri-ang empire in 1971. From 1986 the initial tooling has been adapted and used for the production of Gordon in the Thomas the Tank engine range. In 1993, Hornby introduced an improved model and this again was replaced with an improved version in 1999 and another in 2005, which is the current model.

Hornby also introduced a OO ready to run live steam version in 2005, which became the second live steam locomotive to be introduced.

Graham Farish introduced a ready to run N gauge model in 1987. When Bachmann acquired the company in 2000, the model was upgraded and reintroduced in 2004.

Minitrix also introduced a ready to run N gauge model in 1988. The model has not been available since 1997.

In 1993 Precision Scale Models in Australia produced a ready to run HO model. No. 4472 'Flying Scotsman' visited Australia in 1988/9. The model was made for them by Samhongsa.

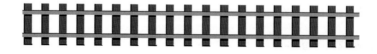

Class V2 2-6-2
London & North Eastern Railway

Introduced:	1936
Designed By:	Sir Nigel Gresley
Allocation:	London & North Eastern Railway, later British Railways Eastern Region.

Locomotive Nos:

As Built	1946 Nos.
4771 – 4775	800 - 804 built at Doncaster 1936.
4776 – 4842	805 - 871 built at Darlington 1937-1939.
4843 – 4852	872 - 881 built at Doncaster 1939/1940.
4853 – 4898	882 - 927 built at Darlington 1939-1941.
3655 – 3664	928 - 937 built at Doncaster 1941/1942.
4899 and 3641 - 3695	938 - 983 built at Darlington 1942-1944.

B.R. added 60xxx to 1946 numbers.

Last of Class Withdrawn:	1966
Number Built:	184
Preserved Example:	4471 Green Arrow
Duties:	Express Passenger or Freight.

Technical Data:
Tractive Effort: (85%) - 33,730 lb
Loco Weight: 93 tons 2 cwt
Loco Driving Wheels: 6' 2" dia
Cylinders: (3) - 18½" x 26"
Valve Gear: Walschaerts with derived motion and 9" piston valves.

LNER Class V2 *Photograph courtesy of Colour Rail*

The 'Green Arrows', as they were later known, were given this title after the first of the Class had been named after a new express freight service, which was introduced in 1936 with the same name. The first five locos built had different valve guides to the remainder of the Class. Locomotive Nos. 4804-4808 had multiple valve regulators when built, but these were removed in the early 1940's.

Other modifications carried out during their service life was the alterations to No.813 in 1947, with a rimless stovepipe chimney surrounded by a shovel shaped smoke deflector, which was retained until withdrawal.

Nos. 60817 and 60963 were fitted in 1960 with double chimneys without Kylchap cowls, and later during 1960/1961 Nos. 60850, 60862, 60880, 60881, 60902 and 60903 were converted complete with Kylchap cowls. Between May 1956 and March 1962, no less than 71 locomotives were fitted with cylinder casting and outside steampipes, they were Nos. 60802, 60803, 60806, 60808, 60809, 60814, 60816, 60821, 60822, 60824, 60825, 60828, 60830, 60831, 60833, 60835-60837, 60852, 60855, 60856, 60859, 60861, 60862, 60865, 60866, 60868, 60869, 60876, 60877, 60881, 60884, 60886, 60889, 60891, 60893, 60899, 60901, 60904-60906, 60910, 60912-60914, 60923, 60929, 60931-60932, 60935, 60936, 60940, 60942, 60943, 60945, 60948, 60950, 60956, 60957, 60964, 60967-60970 and 60976.

The locomotives ran with three different tenders, the 4200 gallon group standard with flared top, and flush sided with low and high front plates, and many exchanged tenders during their service lives.

The locomotives were a very important development by Gresley, some considered them a scaled down Class A3 Pacific, whilst others considered them a bigger Class K3 2-6-0.

As the construction of the locomotives continued almost throughout the Second World War, it was obvious that they were considered to be very important in assisting in hauling the additional traffic being handled by the L.N.E.R.. It was not unknown for them to haul 700 ton trains of up to 24 coaches unassisted over the East Coast Main Line. They also handled much of the E.C.M.L. fitted freight as well as expresses, and were active across the Waverley route (Edinburgh-Hawick-Carlisle), whilst several ran on the ex Great Central main line from Marylebone to Manchester. The locomotives were not permitted to run on the ex Great Eastern main line to Liverpool Street, although several were shedded at March for working over the G.N./G.E. joint line to Doncaster.

Towards the end of steam they had their swan song, performing on the tightly timed 3 hour expresses between Glasgow and Aberdeen, working alongside the Gresley Class A4's which had been displaced by diesels further south. One of the double chimney V2's was timed at 101.5 mph on Stoke Bank on a test train, which was exceptional for a mixed traffic locomotive with only 6' 2" diameter driving wheels.

Bachmann LNER Class V2

Locomotives were originally delivered in L.N.E.R. lined green livery, which was changed during the war to wartime black. In B.R. days, lined black livery was initially applied with British Railways in full on the tender sides, but happily all locos were repainted in the lined brunswick green livery, and appropriate B.R. crests were carried according to the period.

Hornby Dublo proposed building a OO ready to run locomotive and prepared drawings in 1961, but it was never produced.

Bachmann introduced their ready to run OO gauge model in 1991 which remains available.

Graham Farish produced a ready to run N gauge locomotive in 2004. It was tooled at the old Graham Farish factory and was the first new locomotive to be introduced following the company's sale to Bachmann in 2000.

Class A4 4-6-2
London & North Eastern Railway

Introduced:	1935
Designed By:	Sir Nigel Gresley
Allocation:	London & North Eastern Railway, later British Railways Eastern and Scottish Regions.
Locomotive Nos:	2509 - 2512, built at Doncaster 1935.
	4482 - 4498, built at Doncaster 1936/1937.
	4462 - 4464, built at Doncaster 1937.
	4465 - 4469, 4499, 4500 and 4900 - 4903, built at Doncaster 1937/1938.
	Nos. 4468 and 4901-4903 were built with Kylchap blast pipe and double chimney. Remainder of the class were fitted as such in 1957/1958.
	No.4469 was withdrawn in 1942 following bomb damage at York.
	Locomotives were re-numbered 1-34 in 1946.
	B.R. added 600xx to 1946 numbers.
Last of Class Withdrawn:	1966
Number Built:	35
Preserved Examples:	60007 Sir Nigel Gresley
	60008 Dwight D Eisenhower
	60009 Union of South Africa
	60010 Dominion of Canada
	60019 Bittern
	4468 Mallard
Duties:	Express Passenger
Technical Data:	**Tractive Effort:** (85%) - 35,455 lb
	Loco Weight: 102 tons 19 cwt

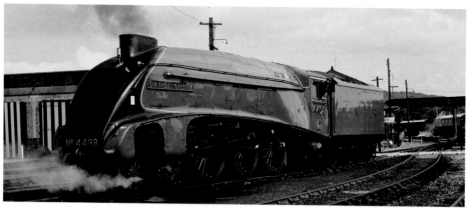

LNER Class A4 *Photograph courtesy of Milepost 92½*

Loco Driving Wheels: 6' 8" dia
Cylinders: (3) - 18½" x 26"
Valve Gear: Walschaerts/Gresley with 9" piston valves.

In 1935, the L.N.E.R. decided to introduce a new streamlined train to run between London and Edinburgh, and an order was placed in March with the complete train ready within six months. The locomotive was a streamlined development of the earlier Class A3 Pacifics, but with higher boiler pressure and slightly altered cylinder sizes. Much has been written about the exploits of the A4's, both before the Second World War on the 'Silver Jubilee', 'Coronation' and 'West Riding', and post war on the 'Flying Scotsman', 'Talisman' and 'Elizabethan' expresses. Silver Link No.2509 was the first to hit the headlines on its trial trip for the press during the Silver Jubilee year, when it ran 55 miles at an average speed of 100 mph, with a maximum of 112 mph at Sandy. On 3rd July 1938, No.4468 Mallard during brake trials, achieved 126 mph descending Stoke Bank between Grantham and Peterborough. A world speed record was created and still stands to this day for steam traction.

During the Second World War, the A4's often hauled trains weighing over 700 tons, so they were not only capable of running lightweight high speed trains. It was during the war that the side valancing was removed for easier maintenance. Very little outward changes occurred to the A4's during their working life, other than the adding of double chimneys and variations of three different tenders (two corridor and one non-corridor). The Flaman speed recorders were removed during 1940, and standard Smith-Stone speed indicators were added between 1959 and 1961.

During the 1948 Locomotive Exchange Trials, the A4's proved to be the most economical of the large engines they were being tested against.

Following their displacement on the E.C.M.L. by the Deltics, instead of withdrawal, most of the A4's went to Scotland, principally working the Glasgow to Aberdeen services where, upon their introduction, schedules were slashed dramatically and the locomotives finished their service lives in the exciting style which had followed them through the years.

The first four locomotives were painted in the two-tone grey livery for hauling the 'Silver Jubilee', followed by five locos painted in standard L.N.E.R. apple green livery. With the decision to introduce the 'Coronation', five locos (Nos. 4488-4492) were selected to be painted garter blue with dark red wheels and stainless steel numbers and letters. After this, a few more locos were painted green, but then the garter blue livery became standard for the class. In 1941, Doncaster commenced painting the locos in the wartime black livery. During 1946 full garter blue livery was re-applied. Following Nationalisation, an experimental almost purple livery was applied to some of the class, then the darker blue livery with black/white lining was applied to the complete class. Lastly, the B.R. standard green livery with orange/black lining was applied to all locomotives, initially with British Railways in full or either crest according to the period.

Hornby LNER Class A4

Hornby Dublo introduced a OO gauge ready to run model in 1938. After the takeover of Meccano by Tri-ang and the establishing of Tri-ang Hornby in 1965, the model was reintroduced by Tri-ang Wrenn in 1969. Following the collapse of the Tri-ang empire in 1971, the tooling passed to the newly independent G & R Wrenn company in 1972. The model continued in production until 1992 when retirement saw the closure of Wrenn and the sale of tools to Dapol in 1993. In 2001 these passed to G & R Wrenn (Mordvale) in 2001 but the model has not reappeared since closure of the original G & R Wrenn company in 1992.

British Trix introduced a ready to run model in 1970 but it was only available for a short time before the company closed in 1971. The tools passed to Liliput who continued to produce the model until 1987. In 1992 the company was acquired by Dapol but during Liliput days, the tooling remained with Liliput in Vienna and the components shipped to Wales for assembly. Liliput was purchased by Kader (the owners of Bachmann) in 1992 and the tooling sent to China for evaluation. The British models which passed to China were either the wrong scale (Trix used 3.8mm to the foot prior to 1968) or else worn out. The one exception was the A4 and in 1994 Bachmann reintroduced it, albeit with a brand new chassis and improved bodywork. The model remains available.

In 1979 Hornby introduced a ready to run OO model. Such was the importance of the model to the Hornby range that it was retooled in 1999, upgraded in 2001 and retooled as a new super detailed model in 2004. In 2003 Hornby introduced a ready to run OO live steam system and chose the A4 to launch it.

Minitrix introduced a ready to run N gauge model in 1983. This model ceased to appear after 1997 when the British range ceased production.

This led Graham Farish to introduce a ready to run N gauge model in 1999. After the company was acquired by Bachmann in 2000, the model was upgraded and reintroduced in 2002. It remains available.

Class A1 4-6-2
London & North Eastern Railway

Introduced:	1948
Designed By:	H A Peppercorn
Allocation:	London & North Eastern Railway, later British Railways Eastern and Scottish Regions.
Locomotive Nos:	60114 - 60123, built at Doncaster 1948/1949. 60124 - 60129, built at Doncaster 1949. 60130 - 60152, built at Darlington 1948/1949. 60153 - 60162, built at Doncaster 1949.

Last of Class Withdrawn:	1966
Number Built:	49
Preserved Examples:	One replica locomotive now under construction (No.60163 Tornado).
Duties:	Express Passenger and Mixed Traffic.
Technical Data:	**Tractive Effort:** (85%) - 37,397 lb **Loco Weight:** 105 tons 4 cwt (max) **Loco Driving Wheels:** 6' 8" dia **Cylinders**: (3) - 19" x 26" **Valve Gear:** Walschaerts with 10" piston valves.

LNER Class A1 *Photograph courtesy of Colour Rail*

When Edward Thompson became Chief Mechanical Engineer upon Gresley's death, one of his earliest and probably most unpopular tasks was to rebuild Gresley's first Pacific No.4470 'Great Northern'. This left Doncaster works, rebuilt, in September 1945, classified Class A1/1.

Many drawings of the Class A1's appeared before the actual locomotives were built. Design work commenced in 1944, but No.60114 did not enter service until August 1948.

Five of the Class, Nos. 60153-60157, were fitted throughout with Timken roller bearings, following several years of testing on Class A4 tenders. This experiment was to achieve greater mileages between heavy repairs, and proved highly successful. Normal locos averaged 100,000 miles, whilst the roller bearing fitted locos averaged 118,000 miles.

When introduced, the A1's were fitted with a plain double chimney, except No.60158 which had a full lip around the rim. The remainder of the Class were fitted with chimney lips from December 1950 onwards. Nos. 60114-60129, 60130, 60133, 60134 and 60136 were fitted with Flaman speed recorders when built, which were removed during 1950/1951, and later, all except No.60115 were fitted with Smith-Stone speed recorders between 1960 and 1963.

Tenders from Darlington had countersunk headed rivets, whilst the Doncaster tenders had snap-head rivets which were easily visible. The locos, when built, were initially un-named. They later took old names removed from the Class A4's when some were re-named, whilst others were named after previous Chief Mechanical Engineers and the constituent companies of the L.N.E.R..

When introduced, the A1's were allocated to the principal sheds between London and Edinburgh along the East Coast Main Line, and they worked many of the principal expresses. Locos from Haymarket (Edinburgh) often worked to Glasgow, Perth and Aberdeen. Between 1951 and 1953, Nos. 60153, 60160 and 60161 worked from Polmadie (Glasgow) on West Coast Main Line trains from Glasgow to Carlisle, and even to Crewe on accasions. Neville Hill (Leeds) acquired some A1's during 1963, and these regularly worked through to Glasgow via the Settle-Carlisle route. With the coming of the English Electric Class 40's and the 'Deltics', the A1's were soon withdrawn. This was a pity, for these locos were only 15 years old, and had been the least difficult Doncaster designed locos to maintain.

When built, Nos. 60114-60126 and 60130-60152 were delivered in L.N.E.R. lined green livery, and were lettered 'British Railways' in full. The remainder of the Class appeared in lined blue with the first B.R. crest, which by 1951 was carried by the entire class. By August 1951, the blue was replaced by the standard B.R. brunswick green livery, which had been applied to the whole class by mid 1953, later the second BR crest was carried as appropriate.

Bachmann LNER Class A1

Bachmann produced a ready to run OO gauge model in 2001. It remains available.

LMS Princess Coronation Class 'Duchess of Hamilton' *Photograph courtesy of Milepost 92½*

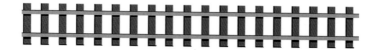

76xxx Standard Class 4 2-6-0
British Railways

Introduced:	1952
Designed By:	R. A. Riddles
Allocation: and Southern Regions.	British Railways Eastern, London Midland, North Eastern, Scottish
Locomotive Nos:	76000 - 76019, built at Horwich 1952/1953. 76020 - 76029, built at Doncaster 1952/1953. 76030 - 76044, built at Doncaster 1953/1954. 76045 - 76074, built at Doncaster 1955/1956. 76075 - 76099, built at Horwich 1956/1957. 76100 - 76114, built at Doncaster 1957.
Last of Class Withdrawn:	1967
Number Built:	115
Preserved Examples:	76017 76077 76079 76084
Duties:	Mixed Traffic.
Technical Data:	**Tractive Effort:** (85%) - 24,170 lb **Loco Weight:** 59 tons 2 cwt **Loco Driving Wheels:** 5' 3" dia. **Cylinders:** (2) - 17½" x 26" **Valve Gear:** Walschaerts with piston valves.

British Railways 76xxx Standard Class 4 *Photograph courtesy of Colour Rail*

The 76xxx Standard Class 2-6-0, introduced in 1952, was the Riddles version of H.G. Ivatts 'Mucky Duck' 2-6-0, which was introduced in 1947.

The Riddles version followed Ivatt's design very closely in terms of dimensions, cylinder sizes, wheelbase and boiler pressure etc., but it did, however, differ considerably in its appearance. The Ivatt design, which emerged after the war, followed wartime Austerity design. The Riddles locomotives on the other hand, were designed on more conventional lines, and incorporated modifications to the blastpipe arrangement. The BR standard chimney and cab was fitted.

Design work on the new class was undertaken at Doncaster, and construction was divided between there and Horwich.

Built for mixed traffic duties, the Class were well spread around the Eastern, North Eastern, London Midland, Scottish and Southern Regions. They performed regularly on secondary and cross country passenger duties. Examples allocated to Neasden worked on the ex-Great Central Main Line between Marylebone and Woodford Halse. Others allocated to the Southern Region worked between Reading and Tonbridge, Salisbury and Portsmouth, Eastleigh and Weymouth, etc.. Scottish Region locos worked stopping trains from Thornton Junction, on the Waverley route (Carlisle to Hawick), and on the Stranraer to Dumfries line via Newton Stewart. London Midland Region locos worked between Kirkby Stephen and Darlington (ER). Others were allocated to Heaton Mersey and Trafford Park for use on Manchester suburban services. On the Eastern Region, Stratford (London) had examples for use on cross London freight trains. Others were found at West Auckland for freight working.

All Southern locomotives had BR1B 4725 gallon tenders, which were high-sided and had 9 ton coal capacity. Other regions locos had BR2 and BR2A 3500 gallon tenders holding 6 tons of coal.

Due to the transition from steam to diesel traction, which took place in the early 1960s, the service life of these locos was considerably reduced. The first withdrawal took place in 1964, and the last locomotive of the Class (No.76084) was withdrawn in 1967.

British Railways lined black livery was carried throughout, and both crest types were carried according to the period.

Bachmann British Railways 76xxx Standard Class 4

Bachmann released a OO Gauge model in 2007.

80xxx Standard Class 4 2-6-4 T
British Railways

Introduced:	1951
Designed By:	R A Riddles
Allocation:	All Regions except Western Region.
Locomotive Nos:	80000 - 80009, built at Derby.
	80010 - 80053, built at Brighton.
	80054 - 80058, built at Derby.
	80059 - 80105, built at Brighton.
	80106 - 80115, built at Doncaster.
	80116 - 80154, built at Brighton.
	All built between 1951 to 1957.
Last of Class Withdrawn:	1967
Number Built:	155

Preserved Examples:

80002	80080	80105
80064	80097	80135
80072	80098	80136
80078	80100	80150
80079	80104	80151

Duties:	Mixed Traffic.
Technical Data:	**Tractive Effort:** (85%) - 25,100 lb
	Loco Weight: 88 tons 10 cwt
	Loco Driving Wheels: 5' 8" dia
	Cylinders: (2) - 18" x 28"
	Valve Gear: Walschaerts with piston valves.

The 80xxx tanks were a development of the L.M.S. Fairburn 2-6-4 tanks, many of which were built at Brighton prior to them commencing construction of the Standard Class 4 tanks.

Basically, the locomotive was identical to the B.R. Standard Class 4 4-6-0 (75xxx) with the same boiler, wheels and motion, but with side tanks and bunker instead of a tender.

These locomotives were introduced to replace older tank locos, including the 4-4-2 Tilbury tanks, the early Fowler 2-6-4 tanks, and some of the S.R. 0-6-2 tanks used on passenger services. When introduced, the locos were based in groups, and were found on Glasgow suburban services, St. Pancras to St. Albans/Bedford, Euston to Bletchley, Fenchurch Street to Shoeburyness and the Marylebone to High Wycombe/Aylesbury lines. The Southern Region used them between Victoria and Oxted, and other services on the Central Division.

They were free running locomotives, although they tended to have difficulty in raising steam on occasions. Some of the 75xxx Class were fitted with double chimneys to improve steaming, but this modification was never carried out on the 80xxx Class. During later years, with electrification of the Euston and Fenchurch Street suburban services and dieselisation of the other lines, these locos, being reasonably new, found work elsewhere and appeared on the old Somerset & Dorset Joint

British Railways 80xxx Standard Class 4 *Photograph courtesy of Colour Rail*

Line, as well as banking duties on Beattock. Other duties performed included ousting the ex L.S.W.R. Class M7 0-4-4 tanks from their carriage pilot duties at Waterloo, and heading the special Post Office staff trains from Clapham Junction to Kensington Olympia.

The 80xxx Class were always in B.R. lined black livery, and both crests were carried according to the period.

Bachmann British Railways 80xxx Standard Class 4

Hornby Dublo introduced the first ready to run OO gauge model in 1954. This passed to the Tri-ang Hornby organisation in 1964 and was reintroduced in the Tri-ang Wrenn range in 1967. When the Tri-ang company collapsed in 1971, G & R Wrenn became an independent company and continued to produce the model until the company closed on retirement of the owners in 1992. Despite the tooling passing to Dapol in 1993 and to G & R Wrenn (Mordvale) it has not been available since.

It was left to Graham Farish to introduce a ready to run N gauge locomotive in 1991 which continued in production until 2000 when the company was sold to Bachmann. An upgraded model was reintroduced in 2004 which is still available.

Bachmann introduced a ready to run OO gauge model in 2001 which remains available.

75xxx Standard Class 4 4-6-0
British Railways

Introduced:	1951
Designed By:	R A Riddles
Allocation:	Southern, Western and London Midland Regions.
Locomotive Nos:	75000 - 75079, built at Swindon 1951-1957.

Nos. 75000 - 75064 were fitted with BR2/2A 3500 gallon tenders.
Nos. 75065 - 75079 were fitted with BR1B 4725 gallon tenders.
Nos. 75003, 75005, 75006, 75008, 75020, 75026, 75029 and 75065-75079 were fitted with double chimneys from 1957.

Last of Class Withdrawn:	1968
Number Built:	80
Preserved Examples:	75014
	75027
	75029 The Green Knight
	75069
	75078
	75079
Duties:	Mixed Traffic, generally off main lines.
Technical Data:	**Tractive Effort:** (85%) - 25,100 lb
	Loco Weight: 69 tons
	Loco Driving Wheels: 5' 8" dia
	Cylinders: (2) - 18" x 28"
	Valve Gear: Walschaerts with piston valves.

British Railways 75xxx Standard Class 4 *Photograph courtesy of Colour Rail*

These locomotives were built using a boiler that was originally used on the earlier L.M.S./L.M.R. Fairburn 2-6-4 T locomotives, the last of which was built at Brighton in the 1950's. The 75xxx Class was designed at Brighton, although Doncaster, Derby and Swindon were responsible for certain details.

The early locomotives had a very wide route availability, and only Nos. 75065-75079 were slightly restricted due to their larger tenders having heavier axle loads than the rest of the locos (increased water capacity as S.R. had no water troughs). The loco is basically a tender version of the B.R. Standard 80xxx Class 2-6-4 T.

The early locomotives were used widely on secondary route services such as Oxford-Bletchley-Cambridge and the Cambrian services (Shrewsbury to Aberystwyth/Pwllheli). On the S.R., locos ran on the cross country Reading to Tonbridge and Reading to Portsmouth services, and also across the Somerset & Dorset Line from Bath to Bournemouth. With the withdrawal of the Fowler 2-6-4 tanks, some of the 75xxx Class were shedded at Tebay for banking freight or passenger trains up to Shap summit, and no doubt the tenders cabs proved extremely useful owing to the erratic weather experienced in that part of the country.

Although, when announced, it was difficult to understand the need for the Standard Class 4 4-6-0's, the locos were successful in handling quite substantial trains, and provision of the double chimney produced a better steaming locomotive.

The 75xxx Class were originally turned out in B.R. lined black livery, but many on the W.R. subsequently received B.R. lined green livery upon later visits to Swindon Works. Both B.R. crests were carried according to the period.

Mainline British Railways 75xxx Standard Class 4

Mainline introduced a ready to run OO model in 1977, the tooling for which was owned by Kader, the company which made the models in Hong Kong. For a period after the closure of the Mainline operation 1983, the tooling was used by Replica. When Kader set up its own Bachmann operation in 1989, the 75xxx reappeared in 1990 and remained available until 2002. Bachmann announced in July 2007 that it is retooling the 4MT which will be available in late 2008.

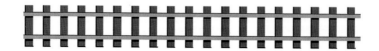

73xxx Standard Class 5 4-6-0
British Railways

Introduced:	1951
Designed By:	R A Riddles
Allocation:	All British Railways Regions.

Locomotive Nos:

	Regional Allocation When Built	Tender Type
73000 - 73004, built Derby 1951	LMR	BR1
73005 - 73009, built Derby 1951	SCR	BR1
73010 - 73029, built Derby 1951/52	LMR	BR1
73030 - 73039, built Derby 1952/53	SCR	BR1
73040 - 73049, built Derby 1953	LMR	BR1
73050 - 73052, built Derby 1954	SR (S&DJR)	BR1A
73053 - 73054, built Derby 1954	LMR	BR1H
73055 - 73064, built Derby 1954	SCR	BR1H
73065 - 73074, built Derby 1954	LMR	BR1C
73075 - 73079, built Derby 1955	SCR	BR1C
73080 - 73089, built Derby 1955	SR	BR1B
73090 - 73099, built Derby 1955	LMR	BR1C
73100 - 73109, built Doncaster 1955/6	SCR	BR1B
73110 - 73119, built Doncaster 1955	SR	BR1F
73120 - 73124, built Doncaster 1956	SCT	BR1B
73125 - 73134, built Derby 1956	WR	BR1B
73135 - 73144, built Derby 1956	LMR	BR1C
73145 - 73154, built Derby 1957	SCR	BR1B
73155 - 73159, built Doncaster 1956/7	ER	BR1B
73160 - 73171, built Doncaster 1957	ER	BR1B

Tenders:

BR1 - Stepped sides, 4250 gallons, 7 tons of coal.
BR1A - Stepped sides, 5000 gallons, 7 tons of coal.
BR1B - Flush sided, 4725 gallons, 9 tons of coal.
BR1C - Flush sided, 4725 gallons, 9 tons of coal.
BR1F - Stepped sides, 4250 gallons, 7 tons of coal.
BR1H - Stepped sides, 4250 gallons, 7 tons of coal.

Last of Class Withdrawn:	1968
Number Built:	172

Preserved Examples:

73050 City of Peterborough	73129
73082 Camelot	73156
73096	

Technical Data:

Tractive Effort: (85%) - 26,120 lb
Loco Weight: 76 tons 4 cwt
Loco Driving Wheels: 6' 2" dia
Cylinders: (2) - 19" x 28"
Valve Gear: Walschaerts with 11" piston valves, or Caprotti.

British Railways 73xxx Standard Class 5 *Photograph courtesy of Colour Rail*

The Standard Class 5's are basically a development of the L.M.S. Stanier Class 5. Doncaster produced the drawings, and initially the design proposed a two cylinder light Pacific locomotive with an 18 ton maximum axle load. The final design used the same cylinders, valve gear and driving wheels as the Standard Class 6 ('Clan') Pacifics. The boiler developed for the last L.M.S. Class 5's, as modified by H.G. Ivatt, was used for these locos, along with the Standard B.R. cab.

Tenders varied according to allocation. Those locos allocated to the Southern Region had the greatest water capacity as that Region had no water troughs. These also carried two additional lamp brackets for the headcode route discs used on the Southern Region.

The first 30 members of the Class were initially fitted with 'chime' whistles, located immediately behind the chimney. These were replaced by the more usual 'bell' type, and all the remainder of the Class carried whistles located just in front of the cab, adjacent to the safety valves.

Following the successful trials with the B.R. Caprotti valve gear on Standard Class 8 (No.71000 Duke of Gloucester), it was decided to fix this valve gear to 30 members of the Class, and Nos. 73125-73154 were so built, and were proved extremely powerful locos for their size. It is unfortunate that, as with so many of the Standard Classes, only a limited working life was achieved, some running for only nine or ten years.

Following withdrawal of Southern Railways King Arthur Class 4-6-0's, Nos. 73080-73089 and 73110-73119 all received names from these locos. New nameplates were cast and affixed to the straight running plate, but unlike the previous nameplates carried by the Urie and Maunsell locomotives for the Southern Railway, these did not carry the words 'King Arthur Class'.

Nos. 73030 and 73031, when built, were fitted with Westinghouse brakes, the pumps being fitted on the front right hand side of the smokebox. These were used, together with Britannia Class 7 Nos. 70043 and 70044, to haul special test trains of air braked goods stock, when consideration was being given to this form of braking. This is now universal on British Railways.

From the table of Regional allocations, it will be seen that these locomotives were spread all over the B.R. system. They were often substituted for larger Pacific locos at short notice during the later days of steam.

These locomotives, apart from the period towards the end of steam when those which survived ended their service lives in the North West of England, had tended to stay at the shed to which they were first allocated.

After the initial batch were originally allocated to Derby or the nearby Nottingham shed, the next batch went to Perth for working trains to Glasgow, and alongside their Stanier counterparts over the gruelling Highland route to Inverness. Shrewsbury and Canton (Cardiff) received the next batch, and these locos were used over the route between these centres via Hereford, and also on Cardiff to Bristol services. After further examples had been delivered to the Midlands, Bath (Green Park) received some locos for work over the ex S. & D.J.R. route. Polmadie (Glasgow) received the next batch and these were used on services over the Caledonian route via Beattock to Carlisle. The first Southern Region locos were allocated to Stewarts Lane (London) for work on the Kent Coast route until this was electrified. A further batch went to Shrewsbury. The next Scottish allocation was split between Corkerhill and Eastfield (both Glasgow), whilst further examples were sent to Perth. The Corkerhill locos were used on services to Stranraer and Ayr, whilst the Eastfield locos were used on the West Highland Line to Fort William. The locos often double headed trains with Stanier Class 5's or Eastern Region Class B1's. The next batch allocated to the Southern Region went to Nine Elms (London), and were used on semi-fast trains on the ex L.S.W.R. routes to Bournemouth and Salisbury.

The Caprotti valve gear locomotives were split between three sheds - Patricroft (Manchester) for work over the Midland route to Derby; Derby, where they were used on services to London (St. Pancras) and Birmingham; and St. Rollox (Glasgow) where they were used on Perth and Aberdeen services, often hauling the named trains ('Saint Mungo' and 'Granite City') over this route.

The final batch went to the Eastern Region. The first five initially went to Neasden (London) for work on the G.C. section, occasionally hauling the 'Master Cutler' when the train travelled via this route. The final examples went to Bradford and Scarborough, where they were used on services to Leeds from these centres.

When delivered, these locomotives were in lined black livery, with the early crest, and later the second crest was also carried. Several of the locos allocated to the Western Region acquired the lined brunswick green livery.

Bachmann British Railways 73xxx Standard Class 5

Trix Twin introduced a ready to run model in 1959 which was produced in 3.8mm scale almost half way between HO and OO scales.

Bachmann released a OO gauge model in 2002, which remains available.

Britannia Class 4-6-2
British Railways

Introduced:	1951
Designed By:	R A Riddles
Allocation:	All British Railways Regions.
Locomotive Nos:	70000 - 70024, built at Crewe 1951. Tender Type BR1. 70025 - 70029, built at Crewe 1952. Tender Type BR1A. 70030, built at Crewe 1952. Tender Type BR1. 70031 - 70044, built at Crewe 1952/1953. Tender Type BR1. 70045 - 70054, built at Crewe 1954. Tender Type BR1D.
Last of Class Withdrawn:	1968
Number Built:	55
Preserved Examples:	70000 Britannia 70013 Oliver Cromwell
Duties:	Express Passenger.
Technical Data:	**Tractive Effort:** (85%) - 32,150 lb **Loco Weight:** 94 tons **Loco Driving Wheels:** 6' 2" dia **Cylinders:** (2) - 20" x 28" **Valve Gear:** Walschaerts with piston valves.

British Railways Britannia Class *Photograph courtesy of Colour Rail*

Following the 1948 Locomotive Trials and analysis of results, the first British Railways standard design locomotive to appear was No.70000 'Britannia' in 1951.

Surprise was expressed as locomotives only had two cylinders, and was expected to be able to work alongside W.R. Castles, L.M.R. Royal Scots, E.R. V2's and S.R. West Country Pacifics, all of which had either 3 or 4 cylinders.

The first 24 Britannias emerged from Crewe in 1951 and found their way to Eastern, Western and Southern Regions. The Eastern locos were put into service on the former Great Eastern Line between Liverpool Street and Norwich/Clacton before these lines were electrified. Here, the timetables were completely rewritten to use the power capabilities of these locos to their fullest. Having replaced the ageing Sandringham 4-6-0's, they put in some excellent performances and were an instant success with the train crews. The Southern Region received three locos, Nos.70004 William Shakespeare, 70009 Alfred the Great and 70014 Iron Duke, which were allocated to Stewarts Lane (London) for working the heavy 'Golden Arrow' boat trains.

During 1952/1953, a further 20 locomotives were delivered, and Cardiff Canton Depot (W.R.) received five of them. The remainder were allocated to the London Midland Region, and were shedded mostly at Longsight (Manchester) and Holyhead. The Western Region locos at Old Oak Common (London) and Laira (Plymouth) were not well received due to their wide fireboxes, when compared with those of the Castle Class. These Britannias were quickly transferred to Canton, where the crews got on well with them. It was unfortunate that No.70026 Polar Star was involved in the Milton (near Didcot) accident in 1955, when it was diverted from the main line to the goods line at excessive speed. Blame was placed on the handrails attached to the smoke deflectors, obscuring the drivers vision of signals, and these were subsequently removed and replaced with handholds.

In 1954, a final batch of ten locomotives was built at Crewe. Most were sent to the Scottish Region and shedded at Polmadie (Glasgow).

Following the dieselisation of the G.E. and West of England main lines, and the re-allocation of W.R. King Class locos to Canton, the Britannias found themselves transferred to other lines. These included Leeds-Settle-Carlisle, the ex Great Central line to Nottingham, and St. Pancras to Derby/Sheffield/Leeds.

The life of the Britannias was cut drastically short by the publication of the Modernisation Plan in 1955, and the change of attitude towards steam traction. The last of the Class, No.70013 Oliver Cromwell, was withdrawn in August 1968 after taking part in the last weekend of steam activities. The depot at Lostock Hall (near Preston) became the last B.R. depot to house a Britannia. After servicing, the loco ran light to Norwich for road transfer to Bressingham Museum at Diss in Norfolk, where it was originally preserved.

British Rail originally intended to preserve No.70000 Britannia, and because of this, the locomotive was stored at Preston Park (near Brighton) for some considerable time. No.70013 Oliver Cromwell was the last loco to be shopped at Crewe, and therefore in better condition, and thus selected to preservation. No.70000 Britannia was preserved privately.

Hornby British Railways Britannia Class

The prototype locomotives were officially mixed traffic types, but were mainly found on express passenger duties (as previously outlined). As the decline set in, they were often relegated to more mundane tasks which included parcels and occasional freight workings.

The Britannias initially appeared in B.R. mixed traffic lined black, but was quickly repainted in lined green livery, as was the remainder of the Class. Either crest was carried according to the period.

Trix Twin introduced a ready to run locomotive in 1959 which was produced to a scale of 3.8mm approximately half way between HO and OO. It was withdrawn in the mid 1960s.

Tri-ang produced a ready to run OO model in 1960. This passed to Tri-ang Hornby in 1965 and to Hornby in 1971. The model was withdrawn in 1972 and replaced by a new version in 1981 and by another in 2001. A brand new model was introduced in 2006.

Tri-ang also produced a TT version in 1960 but the model was shortlived as production ceased in 1964.

In 1970, Minitrix introduced a ready to run N gauge version. It has not been available since 1997.

Austerity Class 2-8-0
War Department

Introduced:	1943
Designed By:	R A Riddles
Allocation:	Initially all Railways, later all Regions except Southern.
Locomotive Nos:	7000 - 7049, built by North British in 1943.
	7050 - 7149, built at Vulcan Foundry in 1943.
	7450 - 7459, built at Vulcan Foundry in 1943.
	7150 - 7449, built by North British in 1943/1944.
	7460 - 7509, built at Vulcan Foundry in 1943/1944.
	800 - 879, built by North British in 1944.
	8510 - 8624, built by North British in 1944/1945.
	8625 - 8718, built at Vulcan Foundry in 1944.
	9177 - 9219, built at Vulcan Foundry in 1944.
	9220 - 9262, built at Vulcan Foundry in 1944/1945.
	9263 - 9312, built at Vulcan Foundry in 1945.

During 1944, it was decided to increase the W.D. numbers by 7xxxx to avoid duplication with other railway companies locos, and from No.78715 the locos were delivered so prefixed. The L.N.E.R. took delivery of 200 of these locos after the Second World War in 1946, classified 07 and re-numbered 3000-3199. At Nationalisation, Nos. 3000-3100 became Nos. 90000-90100, and Nos. 3101-3199 became Nos. 90422-90520. It is obviously difficult to tabulate which W.D. number became any specific B.R. number. A further 533 locos of this Class were purchased by the Railway Executive in 1948, making a total of 733 locos running on British Railways, they were Nos. 90000-90732. No.90732 carried a small nameplate ('Vulcan') on the cabside.

Last of Class Withdrawn:	1967

Number Built:	935
Preserved Example:	90733
Duties:	Heavy Freight.
Technical Data:	**Tractive Effort:** (85%) - 34,215 lb **Loco Weight:** 70 tons 5 cwt **Loco Driving Wheels:** 4' 8½" dia **Cylinders:** (2) - 19" x 28" **Valve Gear:** Walschaerts with piston valves.

WD Austerity Class *Photograph courtesy of Milepost 92½*

Following the outbreak of the Second World War, an immediate demand was made on the railway companies to provide locomotives for use in Europe. Amongst locos requisitioned were 100 G.W.R. Dean Goods Class 2301 0-6-0's, whilst over 200 Stanier Class 8F's were built for the War Department, as well as the transfer of some L.M.S. owned locos (although these did not see service in France).

Consideration was also given to using the Robinson Great Central design 2-8-0's, as had been used during the 1914-1918 war, but many of these locos had been rebuilt to become a non-standard class, and clearance problems also existed.

Whilst the Stanier Class 8F's would have proved satisfactory, the design used over 20 tons of steel castings, which in wartime were difficult to obtain, and hence the decision was made to design an entirely new loco ready for the invasion of Europe. So urgent was the need for locos, that orders were placed with American firms (Baldwins, Alco and Lima) for a similar 2-8-0 loco, and some 390 locos came to this country before passing into Europe. These were somewhat similar to the W.D. locos, but had an eight wheel double bogie tender as well as other typical American fittings.

Many of the American features were reproduced in this Class, although a rigid wheelbase eight wheel tender was provided, which had a capacity of 5000 gallons of water and 9 tons of coal.

The first locomotive appeared five months after the initial order was placed, and once all the parts had been collected together, the first loco was fabricated in ten days, a record by the North British Locomotive Company, and impressive for a loco containing some 95 tons of material.

Westinghouse air pumps, as well as vacuum brakes, were fitted to the locos, although this was removed generally as the locos were taken back into ownership of the various railway companies. Other examples of the locomotives were sold to the Kowloon-Canton Railway (12 engines, final withdrawal in 1963), whilst other examples ran in Holland and Sweden. Nos. 77337 and 79250 were retained by the War Department and were used on the Longmoor Military Railway.

Of the 935 examples built, only three locos did not see service on the European mainland. Having a light axle loading, the locos had wide route availability and were used throughout the country both before shipping to Europe and on their return. After Nationalisation, no representative remained on the Southern Region, nor tended to work in Scotland North of Perth or Aberdeen. Many of the locos allocated to the Western Region acquired shaped covers over the top feed, as well as a fairing on the right hand side running plate for fire irons, instead of using the space provided on top of the tank on the right hand side of the tender. Also, these locos had the G.W.R. style lamp brackets, fitted 90 degrees to normal for that railways pattern headlamps.

The locomotives were used for heavy freight workings, particularly on the Peterborough to Ferme Park coal trains, alongside the ex G.N.R. Class 02 2-8-0's, and also for banking up the steep grades to Consett Iron Works. One feature that was not appreciated by drivers, was the fact that from full forward to reverse gear was 30 turns on the reversing wheel, and if they worked a pick-up freight involving sorting wagons in various sidings, this proved quite tiring.

The locomotives were displaced from some of their longer runs (particularly on the Eastern and Western Regions) with the building of the Standard Class 9F, but examples of the Class survived almost to the end of steam on B.R..

In W.D. days, the locomotives were in khaki green, brown, or the brighter Army green livery. After purchase by the L.N.E.R. and B.R., they were in unlined black, lettered either L.N.E.R. or British Railways in full, or carried either crest according to the period.

Bachmann WD Austerity Class

Bachmann introduced a ready to run model in 1999 and it remains available.

Class 9F 2-10-0
British Railways

Introduced:	1954
Designed By:	R A Riddles
Allocation:	British Railways Eastern, London Midland and Western Regions.

Locomotive Nos:

92000 - 92009 BR1G
92010 - 92014 BR1F
92015 - 92019 BR1C
92020 - 92029 BR1B
92030 - 92044 BR1F
92045 - 92059 BR1C
92060 - 92066 BR1B   *See Text for all Building Details*
92067 - 92076 BR1F
92077 - 92086 BR1C
92087 - 92096 BR1F
92097 - 92099 BR1B
92100 - 92139 BR1C
92140 - 92149 BR1F
92150 - 92167 BR1C
92168 - 92202 BR1F
92203 - 92250 BR1G

No.92178 onwards were built with a double chimney.
No.92250 was fitted with Gisel ejector.

Last of Class Withdrawn:	1968
Number Built:	251

Preserved Examples:

92134	92219
92203 Black Prince	92220 Evening Star
92207 Morning Star	92240
92212	92245
92214	

Duties:	Heavy Freight.

Technical Data:

Tractive Effort:	(85%) - 39,667 lb
Loco Weight:	86 tons 14 cwt;
	90 tons 4 cwt Nos.92020-92029 Crosti Boilers
Loco Driving Wheels:	5' 0" dia
Cylinders:	(2) - 20" x 28"
Valve Gear:	Walschaerts with piston valves.

The last of the British Railways Standard Class locomotives to be designed by Riddles and his team, was the 9F heavy freight loco. Design work on the 9F's was undertaken mainly at Brighton and Derby, and work commenced on the drawings in the summer of 1951. By the end of 1953, the first of the Class had left Crewe Works.

In all, 251 locomotives were constructed, Crewe building 198 and Swindon 53. Most of the later locos were fitted with double chimneys and double blastpipes. Nos. 92020-92029 were based on 9F

British Railways Class 9F *Photograph courtesy of Colour Rail*

locos, but were fitted with Franco Crosti boilers. This altered their external appearances greatly, having two smokebox doors. They were not initially fitted with smoke deflectors. The only other loco to have different details was No.92250, which was fitted with a Gisel ejector. Nos. 92060-92066 and 92097-92099 were fitted with dual Westinghouse pumps, which provided air to operate doors on the Consett iron ore train workings in the North East. Nos. 92165-92167 were fitted with mechanical stokers for heavy Washwood Heath (Birmingham) to Kingmoor (Carlisle) overnight freight trains, which saved having to provide two firemen to work the train.

The 2-10-0 was chosen as the arrangement for the heavy freight locomotive, following the designers success with the Austerity 2-10-0's. These were built during the Second World War when Riddles was Director of Royal Engineering Equipment at the Ministry of Supply.

At the time the 9F's were being built, British Railways was in the transition from steam to diesel traction. As they had decided to go diesel, it is difficult to understand the reasoning behind the British Railway Board's decision to continue construction of the last of these locos. Nevertheless, construction continued after 1957. The 9F's were the last steam locos to be built by B.R., and as a result, No.92220 was given preferential treatment. The Class had all been outshopped in B.R. unlined black livery, but this was considered too undignified for a locomotive involved in such an important phase of British locomotive history. The final loco was duly named Evening Star during a special ceremony at Swindon Works in March 1960. It was turned out in the old Swindon tradition in fully lined B.R. green livery with a copper capped chimney. The loco carried a small commemorative plaque underneath the nameplate.

The last steam locomotives ran on B.R. in August 1968, thus the life of many 9F's was drastically cut short as construction was not completed until 1960.

It is a pity that these magnificent locomotives should have been withdrawn from the service a few years after delivery, for they were excellent steamers and extremely powerful. The Class were often seen running on summer passenger trains over the Somerset & Dorset and other lines. No.92220 Evening Star was allocated to Bath Green Park shed for this type of work. The 9F's were not fitted with steam heating equipment, and consequently could not be used on passenger work during the winter.

The 9F's were always at their best hauling heavy mineral or freight trains. They were extremely popular with the crews, and could often reach 60 mph with a heavy train, and one was recorded at 90 mph on a passenger train descending Stoke Bank between Grantham and Peterborough!

Other than No.92220, the remainder of the class were in unlined black livery with either crest carried according to the period.

Bachmann British Railways Class 9F

Tri-ang Hornby introduced a ready to run OO gauge model in 1971 just before the collapse of the Tri-ang empire. It passed into the Hornby range and was improved in 1988 and again in 1999. It remains available.

British Railways Class 24 *Photograph courtesy of Milepost 92½*

Class 03 0-6-0 Diesel Mechanical Locomotive British Railways

Introduced:	1957
Allocation:	All Regions.
Locomotive Nos:	D2000 - D2199 D2372 - D2399 Re-numbered in 03 series from October 1968.
Last of Class Withdrawn:	1993
Number Built:	228

Preserved Examples:

D2022 (03022)	D2084 (03084)	03152
D2023	Helen Louise	03157
D2024	D2089 (03089)	D2158 (03158) Margaret Ann
D2027 (03027)	D2090 (03090)	D2162 (03162)
03037	D2094 (03094)	D2170 (03170)
D2041	03099	D2178
D2051	D2112 (03112)	D2180 (03180)
D2059 (03059)	D2113 (03113)	D2182
D2062 (03062)	D2117	D2184
D2063 (03063)	D2119 (03119)	D2189 (03189)
D2066 (03066)	D2120 (03120)	D2192 Ardent/Titan
D2069 (03069)	D2128, D2133	D2196 (03196)
D2070	D2134 (03134)	D2197 (03197)
D2072 (03072)	D2138	D2199
D2073 (03073)	D2139	03371
D2078 (03078)	03141	D2381
D2079 (03079)	D2148 (03148)	D2399 (03399)

Duties:	Shunting and Pilot.
Technical Data:	**Tractive Effort:** 15,650 lb **Loco Weight:** 30 tons 16 cwt **Transmission:** Mechanical **Engine:** Gardner 8L3 of 204 bhp at 1200 rpm

The 03 Class diesel shunters were introduced in 1957, and were the second largest diesel shunter class in the B.R. locomotive fleet. At one time, the Class totalled 228 examples. All have now been withdrawn.

The 03's were built by British Railways, mostly at Doncaster and Swindon. Initially, allocation was spread around all regions.

The Western Region, locomotives were mostly found in South Wales, although one or two operated in the Bristol area. Of special note were the eight locos (Nos. 03119, 03130, 03141, 03142, 03144, 03145, 03151 and 03152) allocated to Landore, which have modified low cabs for working the Burry Port to Cwmmawr Line in Dyfed, where they were ultimately replaced by Class 08's with modified cabs.

British Railways Class 03 *Photograph courtesy of Colour Rail*

On the Eastern Region, examples were allocated to principal depots in Tyne & Wear, Cleveland, Yorkshire, Humberside, Lincolnshire, Norfolk, Cambridgeshire and Suffolk.

The Class 03 locomotives survived to work over some lines with limited weight restrictions. They weighed just 30 tons, as opposed to the 48 tons of Class 08.

The first locomotive was withdrawn in 1968, and the last in 1993. 52 have been preserved for use on Heritage Railways, and a number remain in industrial use in Belgium, Italy and the UK.

At first, the 03's carried B.R. green, before the blue/yellow livery was adopted, only the final BR crest or arrow symbol would have been carried.

Replica British Railways Class 03

Mainline introduced a ready to run OO gauge model in 1983. When Mainline closed down in 1985, the tooling remained the property of Kader who produced the model for Replica in 1987. When Kader set up Bachmann in the UK in 1989, the model passed to Bachmann who released it in 1991. The tooling was altered to make the Class 04 (see separate entry) which was released in 1997.

Graham Farish introduced an N Gauge version during 2007.

Class 04 0-6-0 Diesel Shunter
British Railways

Introduced:	1952
Allocation:	British Railways Eastern, North Eastern and Southern Regions.
Locomotive Nos:	11100 - 11239, built by Drewry Car Co., Vulcan Foundry and Robert Stephenson & Hawthorn (Darlington & Newcastle).
	Later became D2200 - D2339
	D2340, built as a Drewry loan loco in 1956.
	D2341, built for the LNER in 1947, becoming a departmental loco (DS1173) until being reclassified as a BR Class 04 loco.
Last of Class Withdrawn:	1972
Number Built:	142

Preserved Examples:		
	D2203 (11103)	D2280
	D2205 (11106)	D2284
	D2207 (11108)	D2298 Lord Wenlock
	D2229 (11135)	D2302
	11104	D2310
	D2245 (11215)	D2324
	D2246 (11216)	D2325
	D2267	D2334
	D2271	D2337 Dorothy
	D2279	

Duties:	Shunting.	
Technical Data:	**Tractive Effort:**	16,850 lb D2200-D2214 & D2274-D2340; 15,650 lb D2215-D2273
	Loco Weight:	29 tons 15 cwt
	Transmission:	Mechanical
	Engine:	Gardner 8L3
	Horsepower:	204

The decision to replace steam shunting locomotives with diesel equivalents gained momentum after Nationalisation in 1948. Attention turned to the Drewry Car Company, who had built a prototype loco for the LNER in 1947.

British Railways Class 04 *Photograph courtesy of Colour Rail*

An order for the locomotives was placed with Drewry in 1952. As Drewry had no manufacturing capability at the time, construction was subcontracted to Vulcan Foundry at Newton-le-Willows. The first loco entered service on the Wisbech & Upwell Tramway in May 1952, which together with the next three, had side skirts and cowcatchers fitted. British legislation relating to tramways and unfenced railway lines, required these to be fitted to protect pedestrians and other users.

Later, locomotives were subcontracted to Robert Stephenson & Hawthorn, and were built at their works in Darlington and Newcastle-upon-Tyne.

Bachmann British Railways Class 04

These locomotives were used on shunting and trip duties, and could be found at use in yards and docks across the Eastern, North Eastern and Southern Regions.

When delivered, the exhaust was released through a hole in the bonnet top. This proved unsatisfactory, and the class were then fitted with either conical or flowerpot chimneys.

In addition to the 140 locomotives constructed, the earlier LNER demonstrator became one of the Class (No.D2341), together with a loan loco supplied by Drewry (No.D2340), which made the final Class total 142.

The reduction in duties, and the closure of many lines, resulted in the first locomotive being withdrawn in 1968. By 1972, all had been withdrawn with many passing into industrial use. Two locos were sold to an Italian industrial company, and 19 locos passed into preservation.

The class were allocated 04 under the British Rail TOPS numbering system, but none of the locos survived long enough to carry five digit numbers.

The first 61 locomotives emerged in BR black livery, whilst those delivered later emerged in green livery. After 1967, a small number received BR corporate blue livery with yellow and black warning stripes, and either the second BR crest or arrows symbol would have been carried.

> Bachmann introduced a ready to run OO Gauge model in 1997, having altered the Class 03 tooling to produce the new loco. It still remains available.
>
> Graham Farish introduced an N Gauge version during 2007.

Class 06 0-4-0 Diesel Shunter
British Railways

Introduced:	1956
Allocation:	British Railways Scottish Region.
Locomotive Nos:	D2400 - D2444
	Due to withdrawals, only 10 locomotives survived to be renumbered 06001 - 06010.
Last of Class Withdrawn:	1981 (Departmental 1986)
Number Built:	45
Preserved Examples:	06003 (Previously D2420/97804)
Duties:	Shunting.
Technical Data:	**Tractive Effort:** 15,340 lb D2400-D2409; 20,000 lb D2410-D2444 **Loco Weight:** 32 tons D2400-D2409; 35 tons D2410-D2444 **Transmission:** Mechanical **Engine:** Gardner 8LE **Horsepower:** 204

45 locomotives were built by Andrew Barclay of Kilmarnock between June 1956 and October 1960 for the Scottish Region of British Railways. Two batches were built, and the first ten locos (Nos. D2400-D2409) had two windows in the rear of the cab, whilst the remaining 35 had three windows.

British Railways Class 06 *Photograph courtesy of Colour Rail*

The locomotives were somewhat unusual in that the fuel tank was located in front of the cab, and was reached by a ladder on the left hand side only. This affected the view of the crew.

The 7' wheelbase allowed them to work on lines down to a minimum radius of two chains, ideal for shunting in restricted locations such as dockyards. Initially they saw service around Glasgow, Ayr, Inverness and Aberdeen. Later the Aberdeen and Inverness examples were relocated to the Edinburgh, Dunfermline and Dundee areas.

The first locomotive was withdrawn in June 1968 after many line closures, and freight traffic had been lost. Only ten survived to receive TOPS numbers in the 06001-06010 series as members of Class 06.

The last locomotives worked around Dunfermline and Dundee, with the last being withdrawn in September 1981. After withdrawal, one loco entered Departmental service as No.97804 working at Reading Signalling Works. This loco was withdrawn in September 1986 and was subsequently preserved.

Initially the class were painted in BR green livery, but surviving locos later carried blue livery. Wasp stripes were later applied, only the second BR crest or arrow symbol would have been carried.

> Hornby introduced a ready to run OO Gauge model in 1991,whilst not in the current Hornby catalogue, it is still available.

Class 08 0-6-0 Diesel Electric Locomotive
British Railways

Introduced: 1953. (Developed from an L.M.S. standard design of 1945).

Allocation: All Regions.

Locomotive Nos:	D3000 - D3116	D3672 - D3718
	D3127 - D3136	D3722 - D4048
	D3167 - D3438	D4095 - D4098
	D3454 - D3472	D4115 - D4186
	D3503 - D3611	D4191
	D3652 - D3664	D4192

Re-numbered 08004-08958 from October 1968 (numbers do not run consecutively).

Gaps in numbers are due to withdrawals, and sales to industrial companies and preservation societies.

Number Built: 996

Preserved Examples:

D3000
D3002 (13002) Dulcote
D3014 (13014) Volunteer/Samson
D3018 (08011 & 13018) Haversham
D3019
D3022 (08015 & 13033)
D3023 (08016) Geoff L Wright
D3029 (08021 & 13029)
D3030 (08022 & 13030) Lion
D3059 (08046 & 13059) Brechin City
D3074 (08060 & 13074) Unicorn
D3079 (08064 & 13079)
D3101 (13101)
08133
D3167 (08102 & 13167)
D3174 (08108 & 13174)
D3180 (08114 & 13180)
D3190 (08123 & 13190) George Mason
08216
D3232
D3236
D3255 (13255)
D3261 (13261)
D3265 (08195 & 13265) Mark
08288
D3290 (08220 & 13290)
D3308
08238 & 13308)
08308

03336 (08266 & 13336)
08375
D3420 (08350)
D3429 (08359)
08436 Beigton
08445
D3462 (08377)
08479
08507
D3558 (08443)
D3559 (08444)
08576
D3586 (08471)
08590
D3591 (08476)
08604 (604) Phantom
D3605 (08490)
08704 Port of Boston
D3723 (08556)
08788
08850
08868
08870
D3935 (08767)
08936
D3940 (08772)
08944
D4115 (08885)
D4167 (08937)

In addition, there have been many locos sold by B.R. for service with industrial companies.

Duties: Shunting and Pilot.

Technical Data:
Tractive Effort: 35,000 lb
Loco Weight: 48 tons
Transmission: Electric
Engine: English Electric 6KT (6 Cylinder)
Horsepower: 350

The London Midland & Scottish Railway first experimented with diesel shunting locomotives in 1932. Within a very short time it became abundantly clear that, for shunting purposes, this form of traction

British Railways Class 08 *Photograph courtesy of Milepost 92½*

offered considerable savings in both cash and manpower. Prior to this, it was necessary to keep steam locos at the ready, even when they were not required for actual shunting, and train crews remained on the locos during long pauses in operations. The diesel-shunters had one major advantage in this respect, they could be shut down and 'parked' allowing the train crews to be used in other ways.

By 1945, L.M.S. had developed a standard design of 0-6-0 diesel shunter. After Nationalisation, the design was made standard by B.R. following further developments. The 08 Class (as they became known after October 1968) totalled 996 units, although many have been subsequently withdrawn due to reduction in freight traffic. Initially, there were variations in that three different engines were fitted, and were either of English Electric, Crossley or Blackstone manufacture. All locos are now fitted with the English Electric 6 cylinder 6KT engine. Construction of the 08 Class locos took place between

Bachmann British Railways Class 08

1953 and 1962. Locos are fitted with either vacuum, air or dual brakes. Locos are currently numbered in the series 08004-08958, although not consecutively due to withdrawals, etc..

The 08 Class were found throughout the B.R. system on shunting and station pilot duties. Some of the class have been in for special treatment. At first, locos were finished in black then green livery, then in B.R. blue. In both cases, each was painted with yellow and black warning stripes.

Three locomotives, Nos. 08993-08995 (allocated to Landore in South Wales), had their cabs reduced in height, headlights were attached, and they were fitted with special cast numberplates, and in one case nameplates (to work the Burry Port & Gwendraeth Valley Line where they took over from the 03's), most of which have been subsequently withdrawn. Many more locos have now been named, and locos have been turned out in Inter City, Network South East and freight sector liveries, as well as L.N.W.R. and L.M.S. black, and G.W.R. brunswick green livery (with G.W. pattern numberplates), and more recently to the various train operating companies.

Many have been sold to industrial users and/or preserved lines. As a result, the Class can be found in a wide variety of liveries.

Lone Star produced a OOO (now N gauge) non motorised model in 1957. It has not been available since 1965.

The first ready to run OO model was introduced by Tri-ang in 1956. It passed to Tri-ang Hornby in 1965 and to Hornby Railways but was withdrawn in 1975. It was replaced by a new model in 1976, although the tooling was used for 'Devious Diesel' in the Thomas the tank engine series in 1987 which is still available. The 1976 version was withdrawn in 2003. A new Hornby model was introduced in 2005 and this still forms part of the range.

Tri-ang introduced a ready to run TT gauge model in 1959 but this was short lived and the model was last produced in 1967.

Hornby Dublo introduced a ready to run OO gauge model in 1960. When the range was taken over by Tri-ang in 1965 the tooling passed to the Wrenn division of the Tri-ang company. The model was not reintroduced until 1977, when Wrenn was again an independent company. When Wrenn closed due to retirement of the owners in 1992, the tooling passed to Dapol and again to G & R Wrenn (Mordvale) in 2001. The model has not been produced since 1992.

Graham Farish produced a ready to run N gauge model in 1979. It was reintroduced in 2002 following the takeover of the company by Bachmann in 2000. It is not currently available.

Roco produced a ready to run HO model in 1982. This was a model of the locomotive as operating on the Dutch railway system (NS). It is currently available in the Dutch livery.

Bachmann introduce a ready to run OO model in 2000. It remains available.

Class 09 0-6-0 Diesel Electric Locomotive British Railways

Introduced:	1959
Allocation:	Southern Region.
Locomotive Nos:	D3665 - D3771 D3719 - D3721 D4099 - D4114 Re-numbered 09001-09026 from October 1968.

Number Built:	26
Preserved Examples:	D3666 (09002)
	D3668 (09004)
Duties:	Shunting.
Technical Data:	**Tractive Effort:** 25,000 lb
	Loco Weight: 50 tons
	Transmission: Electric
	Engine: English Electric 6 Cylinder 6KT
	Horsepower: 400

The 09 Class 0-6-0 diesel shunters were built between 1959 and 1962, and were uprated versions of the 08 Class. They are fitted with the same English Electric 6 Cylinder 6KT engine as the 08's, which has been uprated to 298 kw (as opposed to 261 kw). They are slightly faster with a maximum speed of 27 mph (the 08's have a maximum speed of 15-20 mph), and all locos have air brakes.

They were originally numbered with the other standard 0-6-0 shunters, but on re-organisation of the B.R. fleet in October 1968, they were given a separate classification of Class 09. A further 12 Class 08 diesel shunters were converted to Class 09 during 1992/1993, and some remain in service, whilst two have so far been preserved.

The 09's were originally painted in black livery, then green livery, but were then altered to the standard blue livery, later crest and arrow symbol would have been carried before TOC liveries were applied.

Hornby British Railways Class 09

Lima introduced a ready to run OO model in 1977. It remained available until 2000. The tooling has now passed to Hornby but the model is unlikely to be reintroduced due to the superiority of the Hornby model (see below).

Hornby introduced a ready to run OO model in 2005 which remains available.

Class 17 Bo-Bo Diesel
British Railways

Introduced:	1962
Allocation:	Eastern, London Midland and Scottish Regions.
Locomotive Nos:	D8500 - D8616
Last of Class Withdrawn:	1971
Number Built:	117
Preserved Examples:	D8568
Duties:	Mixed Traffic.
Technical Data:	**Tractive Effort:** 40,000 lb **Loco Weight:** 68 tons **Transmission:** Electric **Engine:** 2 x Paxman 6ZHXL; D8586 & D8587 2 x Rolls Royce D **Horsepower:** 900

British Railways Class 17 *Photograph courtesy of Colour Rail*

Built by Clayton Equipment and Beyer Peacock between 1962 and 1965, these locomotives were visually attractive but mechanically inept. This, without doubt, resulted in their early demise, and all had been removed from the national network in under 10 years.

Mechanical problems were widespread and the Paxman power units suffered a number of faults. To try and remedy this, two locomotives (Nos. D8586 and D8587) were fitted with Rolls Royce D engines. To accommodate them, the centre section of each bonnet was raised. On all others the bonnets were at the same height.

Although the class are usually associated with Scotland, not all the class worked there. Fifteen of them saw service in the North East and were allocated to Gateshead and Thornaby depots. Eleven were initially allocated to Tinsley in Sheffield and Staveley in Derbyshire. Carlisle also had an allocation and these worked on the Cumbrian Coast line around Workington and Whitehaven.

It was in Scotland that the Class found most work. Polmadie (Glasgow) examples worked lines to the south of the city, particularly in the coal mining areas of Lanarkshire and Ayrshire. They could also be found on passenger workings. Haymarket (Edinburgh) examples worked in Fife and south to Carlisle over the Waverley route via Hawick.

Mechanically these were poor locomotives and often worked in multiple. Failures were numerous, and this led to the transfer of the English based locos to Scotland. The Derbyshire and Yorkshire locos were in Scotland from 1966, and the North East examples followed a year or so later. The first loco was withdrawn in October 1968, and by December 1971 all had been removed from the British Rail fleet.

On delivery, the class were painted green and had small yellow warning panels from the onset, with the later BR crest being carried. About 50% survived long enough to receive blue livery with arrow symbols, but none carried TOPS numbering.

All but one locomotive were eventually scrapped. Two locos, Nos. D8521 and D8598, were retained for use by the Railway Technical Centre (Research Department) in Derby, but both were scrapped in the late 1970s. The remaining survivor, No.D8568, saw service as an industrial loco on the former Harpenden to Hemel Hempstead branch with Hemelite. It later worked at Ribblesdale Cement Works in Clitheroe, and was subsequently purchased for preservation.

> Heljan are due to release a OO Gauge model in 2008.

Class 20 Bo Bo Diesel Electric Locomotive British Railways

Introduced:	1957
Allocation:	Eastern, London Midland and Scottish Regions.
Locomotive Nos:	D8000 - D8199 D8300 - D8327 Re-numbered 20001-20228. Some gaps occur due to withdrawals.
Number Built:	228

Preserved Examples:

D8000 (20050)	D8110 (20110)
D8001 (20001)	D8118 (20118)
20007	20135
D8020 (20020)	D8137 (20137)
D8031 (20031)	D8142 (20142)
D8048 (20048)	20154
D8056 (20056)	D8166 (20166) River Fowey
D8069 (20069)	D8188 (20188) River Yeo
D8087 (20087)	20189
20094	D8197 (20197)
20096	20205
D8098 (20098)	D8310
20105	20214
D8107 (20107)	D8327 (20227)

Duties: Freight and Passenger (summer only).

Technical Data: **Tractive Effort:** 42,000 lb
Loco Weight: 72 tons 15 cwt
Transmission: Electric
Engine: English Electric 8 SVT MKII
Horsepower: 1,000

British Railways Class 20 *Photograph courtesy of Milepost 92½*

Amongst the first locomotives ordered as part of the 1955 Modernisation Plan was an order for 20
Type 1 locomotives, Nos. D8000-D8019 of 1000 bhp. These were to be built by English Electric
Company's Vulcan Foundry. The first locos entered service in the London area of the London
Midland Region in 1957, and were allocated to Devons Road (Bow) Depot.

When working in multiple, they are usually coupled nose to nose (thus a cab at each end), for when
being used as a single unit the drivers visibility is restricted by the long engine compartment.

A further batch was constructed between 1959 and 1960 at the works of Robert Stephenson &
Hawthorns Limited (part of English Electric group), and these entered service as Nos. D8020-D8034.
Construction continued with further batches until 1962, when D8127 was delivered.

This locomotive was not destined to be the last of the class, however, when following a change of
policy, construction re-commenced in 1966 with the building of No. D8128. A further 99 locos were
built between 1966 and 1968 when the final loco, No. D8327, was delivered. By now, the class had
become the standard 1000 bhp loco of British Railways, and all other pilot scheme Type 1 designs
have been withdrawn. In accordance with B.R. policy, the locos were classified Class 20, and were
re-numbered between 20001 and 20228 from October 1968 onwards.

The locomotives saw service on the Eastern, London Midland and Scottish Regions, and were used
principally on freight trains. They occasionally haul summer passenger trains, for example trains from
the Midlands to Skegness, but were not found on passenger trains during the winter due to lack of
train heating equipment.

Approximately one quarter of the class have air/vacuum brakes, the remainder being vacuum braked only.

The first locomotive was withdrawn in March 1976, and four saw service with CFD in France (now returned to the UK for preservation). Most have now been withdrawn, although Direct Rail Services (DRS) continue to operate a fleet of Class 20s on the National Network from its Carlisle base in their distinctive blue livery.

In the period up to the mid 1960's, the locomotives were finished in B.R. green livery with a grey roof and the later crest. All locos have since been painted in the blue/yellow scheme with arrow symbol. The last 100 locos, Nos. D8128-D8327, were fitted with headcode boxes, earlier locos used the disc system for identification.

Bachmann British Railways Class 20

Hornby Dublo introduced a ready to run OO gauge model in 1958. When the range was taken over by Tri-ang in 1965 the tooling passed to the Wrenn division of the Tri-ang company. The model was not reintroduced until 1977, when Wrenn was again an independent company. When Wrenn closed due to retirement of the owners in 1992, the tooling passed to Dapol and again to G & R Wrenn (Mordvale) in 2001. The model has not been produced since 1992.

Graham Farish introduced a ready to run N gauge model in 1982. After the company was taken over by Bachmann in 2000, the model was upgraded and reintroduced in 2004. It remains available.

Lima introduced a ready to run OO gauge model in 1984. The model has not appeared since 2001 and the tools have now passed to Hornby. The model has not yet been scheduled for reintroduction.

Bachmann introduced a ready to run OO gauge model in 2004. This model was upgraded in 2005 and remains available.

Class 24/25 Bo Bo Diesel Electric Locomotive British Railways

Introduced:	1961
Allocation:	Eastern, London Midland, Western and Scottish Regions.
Locomotive Nos:	Class 24: D5000 - D5150 Following renumbering became 24001 – 24150
	Class 25: D5151 - D5199 D7500 - D7599 D5200 - D5299 D7600 - D7677
	Following re-numbering in the series to 25001-25327, the Class were sub divided into five categories; Class 25/0, Class 25/1, Class 25/2, Class 25/3 and Class 25/9.
Last of Class Withdrawn:	1987
Number Built:	478
Preserved Examples:	D5032 (24032) D5054 (24054) D5061 (24061) D5081 (24081) D5185 (25035 & 25735) Castell Dinas Bran D5207 (25057) D5209 (25059) D5217 (25067) D5222 (25072) D5233 (25083) D7523 (25173) John F Kennedy D7535 (25185) Mercury/Hercules D7541 (25191) The Diana D7585 (25235) D7594 (25244) D7612 (25262 & 25901) D7615 (25265) Harlech Castle D7628 (25278) Powis Castle/Sybbilla, D7629 (25279) D7633 (25283 & 25904) D7659 (25309 & 25909) D7663 (25313) Chirk Castle/Castell Y Waun D7671 (25321) D7672 (25322 & 25912) Tamworth Castle
Duties:	Mixed Traffic.
Technical Data:	**Tractive Effort:** 40,000 lb Class 24; 45,000 lb Class 25 **Loco Weight:** 75 tons Class 24; 71-76 tons Class 25 **Transmission:** Electric **Engine:** Sulzer 6LDA 28 Class 24; Sulzer 6LDA 28B Class 25 **Horsepower:** 1,160 Class 24; 1,250 Class 25

British Railways Class 24 *Photograph courtesy of Milepost 92½*

The Class 24 locomotives, from which the Class 25's were developed, were first introduced in 1958 as part of the 1955 Modernisation Plan.

The Class 25's entered service in 1961 and were more powerful than the Class 24's, being fitted with uprated Sulzer engines of 1250 hp compared with the 1160 hp of the Class 24's. Most of the class were fitted with four A.E.I. traction motors, whereas Nos. D5151-D5175 were fitted with the British Thompson Houston motors as found on Class 24's.

Variations occur in body style, particularly the cab windows which fall into two designs. Early locos had two main windows (left and right hand side) and a small central window, with double doors beneath, for multiple working.

Locomotives delivered to this design were Nos. D5151-D5175 (Class 25/0), Nos. D5176-D5232 (Class 25/1), and Nos. D7568-D7597 (part of Class 25/2). The remaining locomotives did not require the communicating door, and it was therefore possible to enlarge the central window to the same depth as the other windows. Locos built to this design were Nos. D5233-D5299 (Class 25/2), D7500-D7567 (Class 25/2), and Nos. D7598-D7677 (Class 25/3). Those fitted with doors were welded up or re-panelled in time, but the small central window has been retained.

British Railways Class 25 *Photograph courtesy of Colour Rail*

Construction of the Class 25's was shared between British Railways workshops at Darlington and Derby. Outside contractors, Beyer Peacock of Gorton (near Manchester), were responsible for the construction of Nos. D7624-D7659.

Initially, locomotives were painted in the standard B.R. green livery. Later examples were finished in the two-tone green scheme (as applied to Class 47's) carrying the second BR crest. All were later finished in the blue/yellow livery with the arrow symbol.

The Class 25's were very versatile units and were found on all regions on a wide variety of duties. Two locos were repainted in Inter City livery to provide electric train heating for steam hauled specials. Twelve locos were selected at random and re-numbered to 25901-25912 in 1985, especially for freight working. The remainder of the class were allowed to run down with the fall off in freight traffic. Revised allocations, plus better availability of more powerful locomotives, resulted in all locos being withdrawn by early 1987.

Bachmann British Railways Class 24

Bachmann British Railways Class 25

Hornby introduced a ready to run Class 25 OO gauge model in 1977. The model was upgraded in 1999 and although it is not in the current catalogue, it remains available.

Graham Farish introduced a N gauge ready to run model of the Class 25 in 1983. This remained available until 2000 when the company was taken over by Bachmann. Following an upgrade the model reappeared in 2004 and remains currently available.

Bachmann introduced ready to run OO models of both Classes in 2001 which are still available.

Class 26 Bo Bo Diesel
British Railways

Introduced:	1958
Allocation:	Eastern, London Midland and Scottish Regions. All were allocated to the Scottish Region in 1970.
Locomotive Nos:	Class 26/0 Nos. 26001 - 26020 (Originally Nos. D5300 - D5319).
	Class 26/1 Nos. 26021 - 26046 (Originally Nos. D5320 - D5346).
Last of Class Withdrawn:	1993
Number Built:	47
Preserved Examples:	D5300 26011 D5301 26024 D5302 26035 D5310 26038 D5314 26040 D5325 26043 26004
Duties:	Mixed Traffic.
Technical Data:	**Tractive Effort:** 42,000 lb **Loco Weight:** Between 73 & 79 tons **Transmission:** Electric **Engine:** Sulzer 6 Cylinder 6LDA 28 or 6LDA 28-B **Horsepower:** 1,160 or 1,250

British Railways Class 26 *Photograph courtesy of Milepost 92½*

222

Built by the Birmingham Railway Carriage & Wagon Company, the Class 26 locomotives were sub divided into two categories. Class 26/0 comprised of 16 vacuum braked locos, of which 9 were fitted with steam heating. The Class 26/1 fleet totalled 26 units, all of which were fitted with vacuum brakes and steam heating.

The Class 26 locomotives, when delivered, had inter-connecting doors fitted to the cab fronts for multiple working. This allowed the crew access between the locos.

The first 20 locomotives were initially based at Hornsey for use on Great Northern suburban workings to and from London Kings Cross, with the remainder being allocated to Scotland. By late 1960 they were all at work in Scotland allocated to Haymarket (Edinburgh) or Inverness, from which they worked Inverness to Thurso/Wick and Inverness to Kyle of Lochalsh trains. The Haymarket locos regularly worked over the Waverley route from Edinburgh to Carlisle, and also on duties in Fife. They were used on both passenger and freight services, and as multiple units took over many of the passenger trains, the Class were relegated to freight working. Towards the end of their working life they became associated with Eastfield depot in northern Glasgow.

Initially the locomotives were painted in green livery with second BR crest, with the cab window surrounds being painted white. Small yellow warning panels were added later. The class subsequently carried BR corporate blue livery with yellow ends and arrow symbols were carried. Towards their latter days some of the Class appeared in Railfreight grey livery carrying coal sector markings. These worked coal trains out of the remaining collieries in the Lothian coalfield, all of which have subsequently closed.

A number of modifications were made over the years. Some received air brakes for working merry-go-round (mgr) coal trains, some had tablet catchers for working single line sections, the recesses remaining after the original equipment had been removed. Some locomotives had the cab door windows plated over.

The first locomotive (No.D5328) was withdrawn in July 1972, and the last was withdrawn from Inverness in October 1993. Thirteen members of the Class have survived for use on Heritage Railways.

Heljan British Railways Class 26 *Photograph courtesy of Hattons of Liverpool*

Lima introduced a ready to run OO model in 1989, but it has not been available since 2000. The tools passed to Hornby in 2005, but the model has not yet been scheduled for reintroduction.

Heljan introduced a ready to run OO Gauge model in 2006.

Class 27 Bo-Bo Diesel
British Railways

Introduced:	1961
Allocation:	Eastern, London Midland and Scottish Regions. From 1970 all were allocated to the Scottish Region.
Locomotive Nos:	Class 27/0 Nos. 27001 - 27066 (Originally Nos. D5347 - D5415).
	Class 27/1 Nos. 27101 - 27124 (Originally part of Class 27/0 series).
	Class 27/2 Nos. 27201 - 27212 (Originally part of Class 27/1 series).
Last of Class Withdrawn:	1987
Number Built:	102

Preserved Examples:

D5347 (27001)
D5351 (27005)
D5353 (27007)
D5370 (27024 & ADB968028)

D5386 (27103, 27212 & 27066)
D5394 (27106 & 27050)
D5401 (27112 & 27056)
D5410 (27123, 27205 & 27059)

Duties: Mixed Traffic.

Technical Data:
Tractive Effort: 40,000 lb
Loco Weight: Between 71 & 76 tons
Transmission: Electric
Engine: Sulzer 6 Cylinder 6LDA 28B
Horsepower: 1,250

British Railways Class 27 *Photograph courtesy of Colour Rail*

Like the Class 26 locomotives, from which the Class 27s were developed, they were built by the Birmingham Railway Carriage & Wagon Company. The engine was an upgraded version of that fitted to the earlier Class 26 locos. GEC (General Electric Company) electrical equipment replaced the Compton-Parkinson equipment fitted to the Class 26s.

The body work also differed from the Class 26 version. No inter-connecting doors were fitted to the cab ends, and four digit route indicators were fitted to the cab ends. Most Class 27 locomotives were fitted vacuum braked and had steam heating, although 4 were later converted to dual braking.

The Class 27/1 versions were converted at Glasgow Works from 1970 to push-pull working for use on Glasgow Queen Street to Edinburgh Waverley services. At the same time the Class 27/2 sub class was formed, these locos providing the steam heating. This work was also carried out at Glasgow in 1974/1975. They replaced the Class 126 diesel multiple units on these services. Trains on this route were worked with a Class 27/1 loco at one end, and a rake of Mark 2A coaches, with a Class 27/2 at the other end to provide the steam heating for the train. The locomotives worked in multiple. These services eventually went over to Class 47 haulage with a Driving Van Trailer provided at one end.

Initially they saw service in England working on both the Eastern and London Midland Regions. These duties included workings from Londons Kings Cross, St Pancras and Marylebone.

In Scotland they could be found on the Waverley route working between Edinburgh and Carlisle via Hawick until the line closed in 1969. They also worked the West Highland routes to Oban and Mallaig, between Aberdeen and Edinburgh/Glasgow, and on the former Highland lines north of Inverness. By 1970, following standardisation of the locomotive fleet, the whole Class were at work in Scotland. By August 1987 the whole Class had been withdrawn, but 8 have been preserved for use on Heritage lines.

Like their Class 26 counterparts, the Class 27s were delivered in green livery with second BR crest, with white cab window surrounds. They subsequently received BR corporate blue livery and carried arrow symbols and full yellow ends.

Heljan British Railways Class 27 *Photograph courtesy of Hattons of Liverpool*

Minitrix introduced a ready to run N Gauge model in 1967. It has not been available since 1997.

Lima introduced a ready to run OO model in 1989, and it was last produced in 1999. The company was acquired by Hornby in 2005, but this model has not yet been scheduled for reintroduction.

Heljan introduced a ready to run OO model in 2006.

Class 29 Bo Bo Diesel Electric Locomotive
British Railways

Introduced:	1959
Allocation:	Eastern Region in the early days, later all found on Scottish Region.
Locomotive Nos:	D6100 - D6157
Last of Class Withdrawn:	1971
Number Built:	58
Preserved Examples:	None
Duties:	Mixed Traffic.
Technical Data:	**Tractive Effort:** 45,000 lb **Loco Weight:** 72 tons 10 cwt **Transmission:** Electric **Engine:** N.B.L./MAN. 20 locos were later re-engined with Paxman. **Horsepower:** D6100-D6109 1,100; Rest of Class 1,160.

British Railways Class 29 *Photograph courtesy of Colour Rail*

The Class 29 locomotives were built by the North British Locomotive Company, and the first entered service in 1959. They were very similar in external appearance to the Western Region Class 22 diesel hydraulic locos, which had been supplied (also in 1959) by the same manufacturer. There were small differences to the bodywork, but the mechanical components differed considerably between the two Classes.

The Class 29's were fitted with N.B.L./MAN engines and four G.E.C. nose suspended traction motors. Paxman engines were fitted during 1968 to 20 of the Class, locos not re-engined were early candidates for withdrawal.

Although designated Class 29 under the 1968 re-organisation, the locomotives carried their original numbers throughout their working lives, and were not re-numbered in the 29xxx series. The 'D' prefix was later dropped.

The Class 29's entered service on the Eastern Region, working local trains to and from Kings Cross. They were soon transferred to the Scottish Region, and most of the Class were allocated to Eastfield Depot (Glasgow). In 1963, the Class was divided between Eastfield and Kittybrewster Depot (Aberdeen). By 1969 numbers had been reduced, and all except one loco (allocated to Fort William) were shedded at Eastfield. The Class 29's were particularly associated with Glasgow (Queen Street) to Oban/Mallaig services, until replaced by Class 25 or Class 26 locos.

By 1971, only four locomotives remained in service (Nos. 6112, 6116, 6119 and 6133), and the class became extinct in December of that year.

Locomotives were delivered in B.R. green livery with second BR crest, with a grey roof and yellow warning panel. The blue/yellow livery was later applied with arrow symbol.

Hornby British Railways Class 29

Hornby introduced a OO ready to run model in 1978, it still remains available.

Class 31 AIA-AIA Diesel Electric Locomotive British Railways

Introduced: 1957

Allocation: Originally all Eastern Region, later spread to London Midland and Western Regions.

Locomotive Nos: Originally D5500 - D5699 and D5800 - D5862, built from 1957 to 1962.

Class 31/0 fitted with electro-magnetic control equipment and vacuum brake only. Re-numbered 31001-31018. All now withdrawn.

Class 31/1 were a development of Class 31/0, some dual braked (air/vacuum) retaining steam heating. Now re-numbered 31101-31327.

Class 31/4 were a development of Class 31/1, electric train heating. Now re-numbered 31401-31469

Number Built: 263

Preserved Examples:

D5500 (31018)
D5518 (31101)
D5522 (31418)
          Boadicea
31106
31107
D5526 (31108)
D5531 (31113)
D5537 (31119)
D5541 (31123)
31128
D5548 (31130)
D5557 (31139, 31438 & 31538)
D5562 (31144)
D5580 (31162)
D5581 (31163)
D5584 (31166)

D5600 (31179 & 31435)
D5611 (31188), D5634 (31210)
D5641 (31216 & 31647)
D5662 (31235)
D5679 (31251 & 31442)
D5683 (31255)
D5695 (31265, 31430 & 31530)
          Sister Dora
D5800 (31270)
D5801 (31271)
D5814 (31514 & 31414)
31289
D5823 (31291, 31456 & 31556)
D5830 (31297, 31463 & 31563)
D5862 (31327)
31524
33019 Griffin

Duties: Mixed Traffic.

Technical Data: **Tractive Effort:** 42,800 lb
Loco Weight: 113 tons max.
Transmission: Electric
Engine: English Electric 12SV (see text)
Horsepower: 1,470

British Railways Class 31 *Photograph courtesy of Colour Rail*

When introduced, the Class 31 (or Brush Type 2 as they were previously known) were the first main line diesels to be produced in the dieselisation programme. Originally, all locomotives were powered by a Mirlees Bickerton Day 12 Cylinder JVS 12T engine of 1250 hp, which was uprated to 1365 hp after the first 20 locos. Subsequently, a few locos (Nos. D5655-D5670) were supplied at 1600 hp, and No.D5545 was further uprated experimentally to 2000 hp. However, cracks developed in the engine castings, and No.D5677 was re-engined with the English Electric 12SV engine of 1470 hp, and this modification was then carried out to the entire class.

The Eastern Region received all of the locomotives, but as the larger diesels were delivered, some locos were transferred to the London Midland and Western Regions. Initially they were put to work from Stratford on the Great Eastern section working the Norwich Line. As the larger Class 40's were delivered, the Class 31's moved to the less glamorous mixed traffic and empty stock duties. The next batch went to Finsbury Park, and were used on the Kings Cross outer suburban trains and 'Cambridge Buffet Car Expresses'. They worked these trains until the electrification of the line to Royston, and the withdrawal of the Kings Cross to Cambridge services. Darnall (Sheffield) received a large allocation for freight work in the area, and these were then transferred to Tinsley when Darnall was closed.

Although not allocated to the Southern Region, the locomotives frequently appeared on inter regional workings. With a relatively light axle load, these locomotives had a wide route availability, and worked many of the secondary lines which existed on the Eastern, London Midland and Western Regions.

A small number of locomotives remain in service with FM Rail. The rest have been withdrawn, the first loco having been withdrawn as early as July 1976. 30 locos have been preserved.

When delivered, the locomotives were in brunswick green livery with a grey roof and white bands around the middle of the body, and they carried the second B.R. totem. One of the Class appeared in an experimental orange livery, another in experimental light blue. The first 50 locos were fitted with disc indicators, but the remainder of the Class had four digit indicators above the cab windows. The yellow warning panels were added, later the standard blue livery with full yellow ends and arrow symbols was applied. More recently, front marker lights (for greater visibility) were added, and many of the Class 31/1s appeared in freight sector grey livery. Several of the locos acquired official names.

Hornby British Railways Class 31

Tri-ang introduced a ready to run TT model in 1959. This remained in the catalogue until 1967. This was followed by a OO gauge model in 1962 which passed to Tri-ang Hornby in 1965 and to Hornby in 1972. The model was last produced in 1976.

Airfix launched its ready to run railway system in 1976 with the Class 31. It was last produced by Airfix in 1981.When the Airfix range passed to Mainline in 1981 the model was not reintroducted. After Dapol acquired the tools in 1986 the model was available until 1994. The tools passed to Hornby in 1996 but the model was not reintroduced.

Lima introduced a ready to run N gauge model in 1977 which remained in the catalogue until 1983.

Lima also introduced a ready to run OO gauge version in 1989 which remained available until 2002. Although Hornby acquired the Lima range in 2005 and are now incorporating into their own range, this model is unlilkely to reappear as Hornby developed their own model prior to the takeover (see below).

Graham Farish introduced their ready to run N gauge model in 1995. Following the takeover in 2000 by Bachmann, the model was upgraded and was reintroduced to the catalogue in 2004. It remains available.

Hornby introduced a new OO gauge ready to run model in 2005. It remains available.

Class 33 Bo Bo Diesel Electric Locomotive British Railways

Introduced:	1960
Allocation:	Southern Region.
Locomotive Nos:	Class 33/0 Nos. D6500 - D6585, re-numbered 33001 - 33065.
	Class 33/1 Nos. D6511 - D6580, re-numbered 33101 - 33119.
	Class 33/2 Nos. D6586 - D6597, re-numbered 33201 - 33212.
	Class 33/3 Nos. 33303, 33305 and 33306, modified for train ferry loading at Dover.
	N.B.: They were not re-numbered in numerical building order.
Number Built:	98

Preserved Examples:

D6501 (33002) Seaking	33056 Burma Star
D6514 (33103)	D6583 (33063) R J Mitchell
D6515 (33012)	D6585 (33065) Sealion
D6525 (33109) Captain Bill Smith RNR	33102
D6552 (33034)	33108
33035	33117
D6566 (33048)	33201
D6570 (33052) Ashford	D6593 (33208)
33053	

Duties:	Mixed Traffic.

Technical Data:

Tractive Effort:	45,000 lb
Loco Weight:	Class 33/0 77 tons;
	Class 33/1 77 tons 10 cwt;
	Class 33/2 76 tons 10 cwt.
Transmission:	Electric
Engine: Sulzer	8 Cylinder LDA 28
Horsepower:	1,550

The Class 33's were built by the Birmingham Railway, Carriage & Wagon Company exclusively for the Southern Region. They were based on the same firms Class 26/7 locomotives which had been supplied to the Eastern, London Midland and Scottish Regions. They were fitted with larger Sulzer engines providing 300 additional horse power.

The first Class 33 locomotives were delivered in 1960. The final 12 units (Class 33/2) were built with much narrower bodies (8' 8" wide), for working the Tonbridge to Hastings line which had a very restricted loading gauge, but most of the tunnels were singled for the electrification scheme which has removed all clearance restrictions, releasing the Class 33/2 to general traffic. Nos. 33303, 33305 and 33306 were selected to perform pilot duties on the new roll-on/roll-off ferries at Dover, where the loads exceeded the capabilities of the Class 09 shunters within the boats limited turn around time, these were designated Class 33/3.

British Railways Class 33 *Photograph courtesy of Milepost 92½*

The locomotives were sub divided into three categories, Class 33/0, Class 33/1 and Class 33/2. The Class 33/0 locos were found on passenger and freight workings on all sections of the Southern Region, and were also seen on other regions on inter-regional trains. Some Class 33/0 locos were fitted with electric bells and flashing amber lights, for working Channel Island boat trains between Weymouth Town and Weymouth Quay, where the trains worked through the streets enroute for the boats. The Class 33/1 locos were fitted for push/pull working with multiple units (non powered) between Bournemouth and Weymouth Town. Although electrification of this route during 1988 rendered most of these locos surplus to requirements, allowing withdrawal to commence. Some of the class were allocated to the Railfreight sector for Channel Tunnel construction trains.

Heljan British Railways Class 33 *Photograph courtesy of Hattons of Liverpool*

Traction was supplied by a Sulzer 8 Cylinder turbo charged diesel-electric engine, which drives four Crompton-Parkinson motors. The locos were unusual in that they offered the driver the choice of right or left hand drive, each loco had four consoles (two at each end) which was particularly useful for shunting or other difficult movements.

A few locomotives remain in use with Direct Rail Services (DRS) and FM Rail, in the livery of their respective owners.

On delivery, the class were finished in standard B.R. green livery and carried the second BR rest with a white line along the waist and white edging around the cab windows. Later, small yellow warning panels were added to the front ends. Later B.R. blue livery was applied with full yellow front ends with arrow symbol. Several of the Class received names, and No.33008 (named Eastleigh) was repainted in the original green livery for appearances at open days and other exhibition purposes.

Lima appeared on the British market in 1974. Unfortunately they chose the accurate HO scale rather than the accepted OO scale and sales suffered. Lima abandoned its strategy and adopted OO scale in line with all the other manufacturers and the OO Class 33 locomotive appeared in 1977.

Graham Farish introduced a ready to run N gauge model in 1987. After the company was taken over by Bachmann in 2000, it reappeared much improved in 2004 and remains available.

Heljan introduced a ready to run OO gauge model in 2005 which is still available.

Class 35 Bo Bo Diesel Hydraulic Locomotive British Railways

Introduced:	1961
Allocation:	Western Region.
Locomotive Nos:	D7000 - D7100, built 1961-1964.
Last of Class Withdrawn:	1973
Number Built:	101
Preserved Examples:	D7017
	D7018
	D7029
	D7076
Duties:	Mixed Traffic.
Technical Data:	**Tractive Effort:** 49,700 lb
	Loco Weight: 74 tons
	Transmission: Hydraulic
	Engine: Bristol-Siddeley/Maybach MD870
	Horsepower: 1,700 (some were downrated to 1,350)

The Class 35 locomotives were amongst the last to be produced by Beyer Peacock, who had been building locos for many years, including many of the larger Beyer Garratt type steam locos from their works in Gorton (Manchester).

British Railways Class 35 *Photograph courtesy of Colour Rail*

When the Hymeks were introduced, they were immediately drafted onto the South Wales Main Line services from Paddington, replacing the King Class steam locos. These trains were often loaded to 13 vehicles, and a Hymek with only 1700 hp was really underpowered to haul this size of train. As the Western Region received its more powerful diesels, subsequently the Hymeks moved on to less arduous duties such as Paddington-Worcester-Hereford, Cardiff to Portsmouth and Bristol to Weymouth trains, as well as local commuter services to London from Oxford, Didcot or Westbury on which they were more able to hold their own.

As well as passenger work, there were to be seen frequently working freight trains on many of the Western Region branches, as well as across London freights to Willesden (L.M.R.), Stratford (E.R.) and Norwood Junction (S.R.).

The Hymeks sphere of operations changed in 1966, when most of the class were allocated to South Wales to replace the Class 37's, which were required to displace steam traction in the Sunderland/Newcastle area, as well as in Scotland.

Heljan British Railways Class 35 *Photograph courtesy of Hattons of Liverpool*

Being unable to electrically train heat or operate air conditioned coaching stock, and following a further reshuffle of locos inter-regionally due to the fall off in goods traffic, spare Class 25's and 31's, together with some of the previously mentioned Class 37's, were drafted back to South Wales, which, as with all the Western Regions hydraulics, sounded the death knell of the class after a very short service life.

When introduced, the Hymeks were in a very attractive two-tone green livery with the second B.R. totem. Later, the blue livery with full yellow ends and B.R. arrow symbol was applied. None of the locos were re-numbered into the 35xxx series, the only modification to the numbers being the removal of the 'D' prefix after 1968.

Tri-ang Hornby introduced a ready to run OO model in 1967. This passed to Hornby in 1972 and remained in the catalogue until 1982 when it was withdrawn. It reappeared in 2004 and remains available.

Tri-ang Wrenn worked together on a joint project where the Tri-ang OO model was fitted with the Wrenn horn sound system and sold under the Wrenn label.

Heljan introduced a ready to run OO model in 2003. It remains available.

Class 37 Co-Co Diesel Electric Locomotive
British Railways

Introduced: 1960

Allocation: Eastern, Western and Scottish Regions.

Locomotive Nos: D6700 - D6768, built by Vulcan Foundry at Newton-le-Willows 1960-1962.
D6769 - D6795, built by Robert Stephenson & Hawthorn at Darlington 1962/1963.
D6796 - D6818, D6829 - D6858, D6869 - D6878, D6899 - D6999 and D6600 - D6608, built by Vulcan Foundry 1962-1965.
D6819 - D6828, D6859 - D6868 and D6879 - D6898, built by Robert Stephenson & Hawthorn 1963/1964.

No.D6700 was re-numbered 37119.
Nos. D6701-D6818 were re-numbered 37001-37118.
All had split two digit indicators above the buffers with central doors.

No.D6819 was re-numbered 37283.
Nos. D6820-D6982 were re-numbered 37120-37282.
No.D6983 was withdrawn in 1965.
Nos. D6984-D6999 and D6600-D6608 were re-numbered 37284-37308.
All had combined four digit indicators and no nose door.

Class is now sub divided as follows:
Class 37/0 - Unrefurbished locos, approx. 175.
Class 37/3 - Unrefurbished locos, 12 originally allocated to Motherwell for use on British Steel air braked traffic.
Class 37/4 - Refurbished locos fitted with electric train heating, main generator replaced by alternator.

Class 37/5 - Refurbished locos with main generator replaced by alternator.

Class 37/7 - Refurbished locos with main generator replaced by alternator, with additional ballast weight added to increase weight to 120 tons.

Class 37/9 - Refurbished locos fitted with alternative power unit, also generator replaced by alternator, with additional ballast to increase weight to 120 tons.

Number Built: 309

Preserved Examples:

D6703 (37003) The First East Anglian Regiment
D6725 (37025)
37029
D6732 (37032)
D6737 (37037 & 37321) Gartcosh
37038
D6775 (37075)
37097
D6799 (37099 & 37324) Clydebridge
37111
6842 (37142)
D6907 (37207) William Cookworthy

37190 Dalzell
37197 Dalzell
37214
D6915 (37215)
37217
37219
D6927 (37227)
D6940 (37240)
D6964 (37264)
37358
37901

Duties: Mixed Traffic.

Technical Data:

Tractive Effort: 55,500 lb
Loco Weight: 105 tons 13 cwt max.
Transmission: Electric
Engine: English Electric 12 CSVT (see above).
Horsepower: 1,750

British Railways Class 37 *Photograph courtesy of Milepost 92½*

When the initial 1955 dieselisation plan was announced, no locomotives were envisaged in the 1700 hp range. Consequently these locos, together with the W.R. Hymeks (Class 35), came about as an intermediate loco between the 1250 hp Type 2's and the 2000 hp Type 4's. Due to the high cost of maintaining the W.R. diesel hydraulics, extra Class 37's were built to permit the withdrawal of the Hymeks.

Apart from a variation of bogies (changing from castings to fabricated sections), removal of steam heating boilers from some locos, conversion of water tank to extra fuel tanks on some W.R. units, and fitting of dual vacuum/air brakes, few alterations have occurred outwardly to the locos since introduction.

When initially introduced, the E.R. put them on Norwich to Liverpool Street and other Great Eastern line services, and ran them alongside their stablemate Class 40's. The next batch went to Hull and Tinsley (Sheffield) for working passenger and freight duties, including the Hull to Doncaster portion of the 'Yorkshire Pullman'. Some of these locos went on trial to Thornaby and Cardiff, and as a result extra locos were ordered, and the Class 37's almost took over the South Wales coal and steel traffic. In 1964, four locos were allocated to Bristol (Bath Road) to be used for banking on the Lickey Incline at Bromsgrove.

Mid 1965 saw pairs of Class 37's working experimental high speed runs from Paddington to Plymouth, including exceeding 100 mph on several occasions. Nothing came from this experiment, other than the W.R. for a short time using Warships, double heading the principal W.R. expresses until displaced by the more powerful Class 47's and Class 52's. In 1966, massive motive power changes were made to eliminate steam in the Sunderland/Newcastle area and around Edinburgh, and the Hymeks were drafted into the South Wales area, thus allowing release of some Class 37's to depots in the North East. These locos have often been selected for special duties; during 1968 one loco was used to test the Westinghouse air brake system, hauling 99 B.R. Ferry vans, the longest train ever to run on B.R.. In pairs they were used on molten metal trains between Cargo Fleet and Consett, but these services did not last very long.

Another heavy train worked in pairs was the A.R.C. aggregate train of some 35 G.L.W. Wagons (each weighing 50 tons) from Westbury to Wolverton, and three locos were used to work the 27 G.L.W. iron ore wagon trains (each weighing 100 tons) between Port Talbot and Llanwern steelworks, which operated six trains a day. Following trials in July 1979, most of these workings were handed over to Class 56 locos.

A small number of Class 37 locomotives remain in service with EWS and DRS (Direct Rail Services). Some EWS locos have been transferred abroad for service in France, Italy and Spain on infrastructure work. These locos carried contractors liveries. Some have now returned to the UK for storage.

VI Trains British Railways Class 37

When introduced, the locomotives were finished in B.R. green livery with a grey roof, with small yellow nose panel, subsequently covering the full nose, and the second B.R. symbol and full yellow end was applied. Later, freight sector grey livery was applied to allocated locos, including appropriate logo for traffic conveyed. Some passenger locos carried Intercity Swallow livery. They also appeared in Loadhaul, Mainline and Transrail liveries in the lead up to Privatisation. Since 1997 they have carried a number of liveries including EWS.

Tri-ang Hornby introduced a ready to run OO model in 1966. It passed to Hornby in 1972. It remains available.

Graham Farish introduced a ready to run N gauge model in 1981. It remained available until Bachmann acquired the company in 2000. An upgraded model reappeared in 2003, it remains available. New retooled versions are currently under development for release In late 2007.

Lima introduced a ready to run OO model in 1986. It remained in production until 2002. The company was acquired by Hornby in 2005 but no plans have been announced so far regarding the reintroduction of this model as part of the Hornby range.

Bachmann introduced a ready to run OO model in 2003. It was upgraded during 2006 and remains available.

ViTrains introduced their version during 2007.

Class 40 1 Co-Co 1 Diesel Electric Locomotive British Railways

Introduced:	1958
Allocation:	Eastern, London Midland and Scottish Regions.
Locomotive Nos:	D200 - D209, built at Vulcan Foundry 1958.
	D210 - D339, built at Vulcan Foundry 1959-1962.
	D200 was re-numbered 40122
	D201-D321 were re-numbered 40001-40121
	D322 was withdrawn
	D323-D399 were re-numbered 40123-40199
Last of Class Withdrawn:	1988
Number Built:	200

Preserved Examples:

40012	40122 (D200)
40013	40135
40106	40145
40118	

Duties:	Mixed Traffic.
Technical Data:	**Tractive Effort:** 52,000 lb max.
	Loco Weight: 134 tons max.
	Transmission: Electric
	Engine: English Electric 16SVT MKII
	Horsepower: 2,000

British Railways Class 40 *Photograph courtesy of Colour Rail*

The Class 40 was the first of British Rail's main line diesel locomotives to be introduced. The English Electric 16SVT engine installed, was identical to that used in the earlier L.M.S. diesel Nos. 10000-10001 and S.R. Nos. 10201-10203. This was uprated from its initial 1600 hp for Nos. 10000-10001, 1750 hp Nos. 10201-10202, and 2000 hp for No.10203. The Class 40's had identical bogies to those used on Nos. 10201-10203, giving an 18 ton maximum axle load, and consequently a fairly wide route availability.

When built, the first locomotives were fitted with small headlights and disc pattern train code indicators. Nos. D324-D344 carried divided two digit train reporting number indicators centred over each buffer, whilst from No.D345 onwards a combined four digit indicator was fitted centrally in the nose, thus eliminating the double doors. Many of these doors were sheeted over, and the indicators replaced by twin marker lights.

The Class 40's were first introduced onto the former Great Eastern and Great Northern lines of the Eastern Region. They ran an accelerated Norwich service, and on the E.C.M.L. careful diagrammiing meant they could be used on the 'Flying Scotsmans' London to Newcastle trip, and the 'Master Cutler' when this train was re-routed from the Great Central main line.

Further examples were delivered for running on the West Coast Main Line as a stop gap until its electrification. Nos. D210-D235 were all named after famous ocean liners during 1961, but many of these nameplates were removed, occasionally handpainted examples took their place. Further batches were delivered to the North East, North West and Scottish areas, as well as the London Midland Region.

With the introduction of the Deltics on the Eastern Region, and Classes 47 and 50 on the London Midland Region, the locos virtually ceased all main line work other than secondary duties such as Crewe to Holyhead, Kings Cross to Cleethorpes, York to Newcastle via Sunderland workings, and Glasgow to Aberdeen trains. Due to the flood of electrically heated air conditioned stock on these services, for which the Class 40's were not equipped to operate, the remaining locomotives were to be withdrawn in 1987. One example, No.D200 (40122), was retained for working enthusiasts specials until April 1988. During the Crewe remodelling, five of the Class were re-numbered 97400-97004 for ballast train workings (97xxx locos are classified such for engineers use only). All were subsequently withdrawn.

When introduced, the Class 40's were in B.R. green livery with grey roof and white line just below level between cab doors. Later, small and large front yellow warning panels were added. The second B.R. totem was applied to the locos as built. When the blue livery was introduced, initially the 'D' prefix was removed, but the re-numbering for computer classification meant the numbers were modified as listed. The new B.R. symbol was applied also with the blue livery. No.40106 was repainted in the full green livery having never received the blue livery, and was used for hauling some enthusiasts specials before withdrawal for preservation. No.40122 (D200) was painted in green livery during its later life on B.R..

Bachmann British Railways Class 40

Jouef chose the Class 40 to enter the British market with its one and only OO gauge model in 1977. By 1980 the models were being manufactured in the Republic of Ireland but by 1981, production had ceased. Eventually the tools passed to the Southern Model Railway Company (Eire) who produced a limited number of models in 1988. The model has not been available for many years.
A
Graham Farish introduced a ready to run N gauge model in 1986 which continued in production until the company was acquired by Bachmann in 2000. An upgraded model was reintroduced in 2004.

With the Jouef model becoming difficult to obtain, Lima introduced their OO gauge model in 1988. This continued in production until 2002. The company was acquired by Hornby in 2005 but no plans have been announced so far regarding the reintroduction of this model as part of the Hornby range.

Bachmann introduced a ready to run OO gauge model in 2004. It remains available.

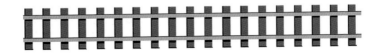

Class 42 Warship Bo Bo Diesel Hydraulic Locomotive British Railways

Introduced:	1958
Allocation:	Western Region, although later some were used on the Waterloo to Exeter services on the Southern Region.
Locomotive Nos:	D800 - D832 and D866-D870, built at Swindon. D833 - D865, built by North British, classified Class 43 with Paxman engines.
Last of Class Withdrawn:	1972
Number Built:	38
Preserved Examples:	D821 Greyhound D832 Onslaight
Duties:	Mixed Traffic.
Technical Data:	**Tractive Effort:** 52,400 lb **Loco Weight:** 78 tons 10 cwt **Transmission:** Hydraulic **Engine:** Two Bristol Siddeley/Maybach MD650V type of 1152 hp (D800-D802 only 1056 hp & D830 2400 hp). Two Paxman 12YJXL engines of 1200 hp. **Horsepower:** 2,000 to 2,400

British Railways Class 42 *Photograph courtesy of Milepost 92½*

When the Western Region began to design its diesel fleet, it looked to overseas railways for help and advice. Unlike the rest of B.R., the Western Region opted for diesel hydraulic transmission. Working in collaboration with Deutsche Bundesbahn (German Federal Railway) and Krauss-Maffei, they designed a second batch of Warships (later Class 42) whose ancestry can be easily traced to the D.B. V200 Class diesel (later classified Class V221).

The 38 locomotives which made the Class 42 Warships, built at Swindon, were preceded by an earlier form of Warship (Nos. D600-D604). These were built by the North British Locomotive Company and were of the A1A-A1A type. They were of different design and were not totally successful. This led to the developments already mentioned, which in turn resulted in the Class 42's being constructed, and the early demise of the five North British Locomotive Companys locos.

All the locomotives in Class 42 (and the five North British Locomotive Company locos) were named after famous Royal Navy Warships. Since the withdrawal of the Class, many of the names have reappeared on the Class 50's since their transfer from the London Midland Region.

With the other regions opting for diesel-electric traction, the Western Region hydraulics were destined for early withdrawal as neither electric train heating or air conditioning of trains was possible.

On introduction, they worked principal trains to and from Paddington, taking over from King and Castle class diagrams. During their later years, some were drafted to the Southern Region line to work between Waterloo (London) and Exeter via Salisbury.

The Warships proved to be very useful locomotives, particularly well suited for the Waterloo to Exeter services, where the loadings were light and they were able to make good use of their 90 mph top speed.

When introduced, the locomotives were finished in green livery, and some were later repainted maroon livery carrying the second BR crest. At the time of withdrawal, all were finished in the standard B.R. blue livery carrying the arrow symbol.

The Class 42 Warship has been well represented in model form. Because the British locomotive was derived from a German prototype, a number of models were produced using chassis from the manufacturers HO German ranges in an attempt to break into the British market. These products generally failed to prosper alongside British OO gauge.

Trix introduced a ready to run model in 1960. This was not a true OO model having been made between HO (3.5mm) and OO (4mm) at 3.8mm to the foot. This model was last produced in 1971 when the company closed and most of the tools passed to Liliput UK. The Warship was not reintroduced under Liliput.

Marklin introduced an HO model in 1967 for its 3 rail system. It was also released in 2 rail format under the Hamo label.

Minitrix introduced a ready to run N gauge model in 1970. It was last produced in 1997.

Fleischmann introduced an HO ready to run model in 1977. It has not been available since 2001.

Lima produced a ready to run OO model in 1980. The model remained in production until 1999. The tools have now passed to Hornby following their acquisition of the company in 2005, but no plans have been released regarding future production of this model.

Mainline also produced a ready to run OO model in 1980. This model remained in production until closure of the company in 1984. When Kader set up Bachmann in the UK in 1989, the tools passed to the new company who reintroduced an upgraded model in 1999. It remains available.

Graham Farish have an N gauge ready to run model under development. This model is scheduled for release in 2008.

Bachmann British Railways Class 42

Class 44/45/46 1 Co-Co 1 Diesel Electric Locomotives British Railways

Introduced:	1960
Allocation:	London Midland and Eastern Regions.
Locomotive Nos:	D1 - D10, built at Derby in 1959/1960.
	D11 - D49, built at Derby in 1960/1961.
	D50 - D137, built at Crewe from 1960 to 1963.
	D138 - D193, built at Derby.

With the introduction of numerical classification, re-numbering took place but not in building sequence - Hence, Class 45/0, Nos. 45001-45077, (No.45067 was withdrawn following collision damage) have steam heating boilers. Class 45/1, Nos. 45101-45150, are fitted with electric train heating.

Last of Class Withdrawn:	1988
Number Built:	193
Preserved Examples:	Class 44s:
	D4 (44004) Great Gable
	D8 Penyghent
	Class 45s:
	D100 (45060) Sherwood Forester
	D120 (45108)
	D123 (45125) Leicestershire & Derbyshire Yeomanry
	D61 (45112) Royal Army Ordnance Corps
	45401 Royal Tank Regiment
	45149
	D14 (45015)
	D22 (45132)
	D40 (45133)

D67 (45118) The Royal Artilleryman
D86 (45105)
D99 (45135) 3rd Carabinier

Class 46s:
46045
D147 (46010)
D172 Ixion

Duties: Mixed Traffic.

Technical Data: **Tractive Effort:** 55,000 lb max.
                                   Loco Weight: 135 tons 7 cwt
                                   Transmission: Electric
                                   Engine: Sulzer 12LDA 28B with intercooling of 2500 bhp at 750 rpm
                                   Horsepower: 2,300 Class 44; 2,500 Classes 45 & 46.

British Railways Class 45 *Photograph courtesy of Milepost 92½*

Class 44:
Under the 1955 Modernisation Plan, British Railways ordered in a number of pilot scheme locomotives from various manufacturers, to evaluate them before possible large scale production. The order for the ten Class 44 locos was placed with British Railways' own workshops in Derby in December 1955.

Design work took some 2½ years, with construction of the prototype loco taking a further year. In April 1959, the first locomotive (No.D1) was handed over and began trials on the London Midland Region.

The tenth locomotive was completed in February 1960, and joined its sisters on principal express services to and from London Euston. All were allocated to the Camden depot, one mile north of Euston.

As electrification of the West Coast Main Line progressed during the early 1960s, the Class was transferred to Toton depot near Nottingham to work mainly freight trains.

To enable multiple working, the Class was provided with connecting doors between cabs at each end, allowing the crew access between moving locos as necessary. This feature, however, proved unnecessary, and over the years the nose end doors were either plated over or locked out of use.

Initially, the class were in Brunswick green livery carrying the second BR crest and were relieved by a grey bodyside stripe, carried just above the solebar between the cab doors. With the advent of British Rails corporate livery, locos began to appear in BR Monastral blue with full yellow nose ends from 1967 with the arrows symbol. Under the TOPS renumbering programme, initiated in 1971, the Class was designated Class 44, with No.D1 becoming No.44001 and so on.

When BR re-evaluated its motive power requirements under the National Traction Plan in the mid 1970s, the Class was one of those scheduled for early elimination. The first withdrawal took place in 1976, and the last in 1980. Two locos were preserved for use on Heritage Railways; No.D4 'Great Gable' is currently at Nottingham Heritage Centre and No.D8 'Penyghent' is on the Peak Railway.

As the first ten were all named after mountain peaks, the name has been generically applied to all Class 44, 45 and 46 locomotives by rail enthusiasts.

Class 45:
First introduced in 1960, the Class 45 locomotives were a development of the original ten Class 44 locos that were introduced a year earlier.

The first batch (originally numbered D11-D49) was built at Derby in 1960/1961. The second order (originally numbered D50-D137) was constructed at Crewe between 1960 and 1963. After the adoption of the TOPS numbering system in 1971, locomotives originally numbered in the series D50-D137 became Class 45. Those with steam heat boilers were designated Class 45/0 (Nos. 45001-45077), and those with electric train heating became Class 45/1 (Nos. 45101-45150).

During the 1960s, the Peaks replaced steam traction on principal trains to and from London St Pancras over the Midland Main Line, on the Settle/Carlisle route and also on the Waverley route between Carlisle, Hawick, Galashiels and Edinburgh, which took its name from the Waverley novels of Sir Walter Scott who lived near Melrose on this line. At one time, St Pancras had both day and overnight trains to both Glasgow and Edinburgh, and the Peaks regularly worked the St Pancras to Edinburgh sleeper train which travelled over the Settle & Carlisle route, and also the Waverley route, until its closure in January 1969.

During the early 1980s, the Peaks were displaced from front line passenger work on the Midland Main Line by the arrival of the High Speed Trains (HSTs). The Class was then utilised on other workings including parcels and freight trains. Some were transferred onto Cross Country routes such as Newcastle to Plymouth.

By 1988, only one locomotive remained in traffic, that was No.45106, which had been repainted in green livery specifically for hauling enthusiasts trains. A major defect resulted in the rapid withdrawal of the loco, and extinction of its Class, after a long and distinguished career. Eleven locos have been preserved for service on Heritage Railways, and one other, No.45112, is operated by traction provider FM Rail and is available for use on main line services.

Class 46:
A final batch of 76 locomotives were ordered from British Railways Derby Works during 1959. By the time the first loco emerged in 1961, the order had been reduced to 56, and the electrical equipment supplied by Brush was used for the first 20 Brush Type 4 locos (today known as Class 47).

The design was almost identical to the final batch of Class 45 locomotives, but there were minor differences to the bodyside grilles and also the battery box.

On delivery, the first 28 locomotives went to Derby for use on the Midland Main Line, with the remainder going to the North Eastern Region's Gateshead depot for use on services out of Newcastle.

The first locomotive was withdrawn in 1977, and by 1984 all had been withdrawn from front line service. Four locos, however, passed to the BR Research Department at Derby for use on the Old Dalby test track, and these were numbered in the 97xxx series. No.97403 was named 'Ixion' and was the only one which carried the Research Division's distinctive red and blue livery. After withdrawal, No.46009 was used in a spectacular demonstration to the worlds media, to prove the safety of nuclear flasks in a collision. It was driven under remote control into a flask which remained intact despite the destruction of the locomotive and three coaches. The spare loco for this venture was No.46023.

Three locomotives have survived. No.46035 'Ixion' (formerly D172 then No.97403), owned by pop impresario Pete Waterman, was the first Heritage diesel to be certified for working over the national network. Preserved or heritage diesel and electric traction was not permitted to run on the British Rail network prior to privatisation.

Bachmann British Railways Class 45

The Class 45 locomotive was introduced by Mainline in 1977 to launch the new range. It remained available until 1984 when the company closed. The tooling was owned by Kader who manufactured the locomotives for Mainline and for a period in 1989 the models were available through Replica Railways. During 1989 Kader opened its own company, Bachmann Europe and production for Replica ceased. This model had the buffers fitted on to the bodyshells and not on the bogies as per the prototype.

Bachmann did not release the old Mainline Class 45 but instead opted for adapting the bodyshell to produce a Class 46 instead. This model was introduced in 1993 and remained available until 2002.

Bachmann retooled the Peak Class in 2003 to produce Class 44, 45 and 46 versions. These models have recently been upgraded and remain available.

Graham Farish introduced ready to run N gauge models of all three versions (Classes 44/ 45/ 46) in 2006. These remain available.

Class 47 Co-Co Diesel Electric Locomotive British Railways

Introduced:	1962
Allocation:	All Regions except Southern.
Locomotive Nos:	D1100 - D1111 D1500 - D1999
	Re-numbered as per text.
Number Built:	512

Preserved Examples: D1500 (47401) North Eastern
D1501 (47402) Gateshead
D1516 (47417)
D1643 (47059, 47631 & 47765) Ressaldar
D1693 (47105) Goldcrest
D1705 (47117) Sparrowhawk
D1842, D1884 (47365)
D1886 (47367) Kenny Cockbird
D1895 (47376) Freightliner 1995
D1933 (47255 & 47596) Aldeburgh Festival
47449
47640
D1946 (47771)
D1970 (47643)
D1997 (47295)

Duties: Mixed Traffic.

Technical Data: **Tractive Effort:** 55,000 lb
Loco Weight: 114 tons
Transmission: Electric
Engine: Sulzer 12 Cylinder 12LDA 28C
Horsepower: 2,750

British Railways Class 47 *Photograph courtesy of Milepost 92½*

The Class 47, (Brush Type 4) diesel electric locomotives, have proved to be one of the most reliable types of diesel loco in the fleet, and are available for all sorts of mixed traffic duties.

There were 512 Class 47 locomotives in service with British Rail, making them the largest Class of main line locos. Each loco is sub divided into one of five classifications. These are 47/0, 47/3, 47/4, 47/7 and 47/9. The Class 47/0 totals 272 units, which were dual braked and fitted with steam heating, and 15 of the Class carried names for use on the Western Region. The Class 47/3 totalled 81 units, which were not fitted with train heating apparatus, and were usually found on freight workings. The Class 47/4 totalled 265 units, which were fitted with steam/electric train heating equipment, although all steam heating boilers have been removed as steam heating of trains had ceased. Some of these locos were named for working services on the ex Great Eastern main line out of London (Liverpool Street), whilst several of the named Western Region locos also appeared in this group. The Class 47/9 consists of only one loco, No.47901, which has been fitted with a Ruston-Paxman 3250 hp engine. The Class 47/7 had appeared more recently, and they were former 47/4 units converted for push/pull working between Glasgow (Queen Street) and Edinburgh. The 16 locos carried a Scottish name.

At first, locomotives were allocated to the Eastern, London Midland and Western Regions. They have since ventured onto the Southern and Scottish Regions, and are found on most types of freight and passenger duties. Many of the Class 47/3 units are fitted with slow speed control for working merry-go-round trains, thus enabling them to crawl through loading/unloading installations without having to stop.

Construction of the locomotives was undertaken at the works of Brush Electrical Engineering at Loughborough, and by British Railways at Crewe Works. Locos are fitted with Brush electrical equipment and Sulzer 12 cylinder engines. Delivery took place between 1962 and 1967.

Following Privatisation, a number of Class 47s saw front line passenger service with Virgin Trains on cross country routes. These were replaced by Class 220 and Class 221 units in 2002. A small number remain in service with passenger and freight operators including DRS, FM Rail and Cotswold Rail.

The Class 47 was supplied in two-tone green livery with second BR crest and yellow warning panels. All locos were subsequently repainted in blue/yellow livery and carried the arrow symbol, and were re-numbered according to classification. More recently these locos have appeared in Inter City, Scotrail, Freight and Network South East liveries, as well as three examples being named after former GWR officers which appeared in lined brunswick green with cast brass name and numberplates, as part of the GWR celebrations of 1985. One loco (No.47552) was also in LNER apple green livery. The remaining locomotives carry or had carried a number of Post Privatisation liveries.

After 1998, 33 Class 47 locos were rebuilt into Class 57 locos (see separate entry).

Bachmann British Railways Class 47

Trix had been planning to produce this model and announced it in their 1968 catalogue but it never appeared. When financial difficulties arose and the company closed in 1973, it became clear that the model would not appear.

This left the door open for other manufacturers and Hornby introduced a ready to run OO gauge model in 1975. Initially this model had raised ribs on the bodyside to enable the two tone green livery to be applied. However, when examples in BR Blue appeared this did not suit and in 1982 the tooling was adapted to remove them. This model remains available today.

Model information continues on the next page

Graham Farish introduced a ready to run N gauge model in 1981. This model remained available until 2000 when the company was taken over by Bachmann and production switched from Poole to China. An upgraded model was released in 2002 and it remains available.

Minitrix introduced a ready to run N gauge model in 1982, no doubt making good use of the research carried out for the abandoned OO gauge project some 16 years previously. The model remained available until 1997 and has not been available since.

Lima introduced a ready to run OO gauge model in 1987. The model last appeared in 2002. Although the tooling passed to Hornby in 2005 there are no plans at present for the model to be reintroduced.

Heljan, the Danish manufacturer, chose the Class 47 for its entry into the British OO gauge ready to run market in 2001. The model is currently available.

Bachmann have a OO gauge ready to run model available which was released in 2007.

Class 50 Co-Co Diesel Electric Locomotive
British Railways

Introduced:	1967
Allocation:	London Midland, Scottish, Western and Southern Regions.
Locomotive Nos:	D400 - D449
	Re-numbered 50001 - 50050, No.D400 re-numbered 50050).
	N.B.: No.50149 ex 50049 was experimentally converted for freight use.
Last of Class Withdrawn:	1994
Number Built:	50

Preserved Examples:

D400 (50050) Fearless	D429 (50029) Renown
50001 Dreadnought	D430 (50030) Repulse
D402 (50002) Super	D431 (50031) Hood
50007 Sir Edward Elgar	50033 Glorious
50008 Thunder	D435 (50035) Ark Roya
50015 Valiant	50040 Leviathan
D417 (50017) Royal Oak	D442 (50042) Triumph
D419 (50019) Ramillies	D444 (50044) Exeter
50021 Rodney	50045 Achilles
50023 Howe	D449 (50049 & 50149) Defiance
50026 Indomitable	
D427 (50027) Lion	

Duties:	Mixed Traffic.
Technical Data:	**Tractive Effort:** 48,500 lb
	Loco Weight: 115 tons
	Transmission: Electric
	Engine: English Electric 16CSVT
	Horsepower: 2,700

Early in 1961, a prototype locomotive DP2 emerged from the English Electric Vulcan Foundry Works at Warrington. Built on similar lines to the Deltic (Class 55) locos with large noses in front of the cabs, DP2 was a very impressive and successful prototype. It continued in use until it was involved in a serious crash at Thirsk in 1967.

The Class 50's were the production run of the DP2 prototype, although in this case they differed considerably in appearance. British Rail were anxious for the new locos to have a flat fronted design with cab directly above the buffer beam. This resulted in English Electric having to re-design the body shape to meet these requirements. It is also worth noting that the engine fitted to the Class 50's, was a modified version of the same type that had been fitted to the L.M.S. prototype diesels (Nos. 10000 and 10001) some twenty years previously.

The Class 50's entered service at the end of 1967, for use on principal express trains, usually double headed, between Crewe and Glasgow. This released other diesel locos from these duties, which in 1968 resulted in the withdrawal of British Rail's last steam locos, which at that time were concentrated in a small pocket of depots in the North West (Carnforth, Rose Grove and Lostock Hall). It was intended to use these locos between Crewe and Glasgow as a stop gap, until electrification between Weaver Junction (North of Crewe) and Motherwell was completed. Once this work was finalised, the Class 50's were then to be transferred to the Western Region to allow the remaining diesel-hydraulic locos to be withdrawn. The first loco was transferred, in conjunction with this plan, to Bristol (Bath Road) in 1972 for crew training purposes. As electrification work progressed, more of the class were transferred, and by the mid 1970's all 50 were at work on the Western Region. They continued as front line motive power on the Western Region until the arrival of the H.S.T.'s (High Speed Trains). Since then they lost many of their duties and some were put to use on the former Southern Railway West of England Mainline between Exeters St Davids and London Waterloo. Because this class was maintained at Doncaster, they were frequently seen on the Eastern Region working via Birmingham and Sheffield.

British Railways Class 50 *Photograph courtesy of Milepost 92½*

When delivered, the Class 50's were leased to British Rail by a subsidiary of English Electric. They were later sold to the British Railways Board.

The first withdrawals took place in 1987, and the last was in March 1994, just before Privatisation began, 22 were purchased for use on Heritage Railways.

On entering service, the Class were painted in blue/yellow, and subsequently the Class appeared in the modified blue/yellow livery with black window surrounds, large arrow logo and large numbers. During the mid 1970's, all of the Class were named after warships. No.50007 was renamed 'Sir Edward Elgar' and appeared in G.W.R. brunswick green livery with brass numberplates, as part of the G.W.R.'s 150 Year celebrations in 1985. No.50149 also ran in freight livery for a short time before withdrawal. Network SouthEast were the main employers of the fleet in the 1980s, and they were in use on Waterloo to Exeter services in NSE livery. Later a modified livery has been used.

Hornby British Railways Class 50

Lima introduced a ready to run OO gauge model in 1982. It remained in the catalogue until 2002. Following the company's demise the tools were acquired by Hornby but are unlikely to see further use as the company had already introduced its own OO ready to run model in 2003.

Graham Farish introduced a ready to run N gauge version in 1984 which remained in the catalogue until 2000 when the company was acquired by Bachmann. This was reintroduced following upgrading in 2003 and remains available.

Class 52 Western Co-Co Diesel Hydraulic Locomotive British Railways

Introduced:	1962
Allocation:	Western Region.
Locomotive Nos:	D1000 - D1029, built at Swindon from 1962 to 1964. D1030 - D1073, built at Crewe in 1962/1963.
Last of Class Withdrawn:	1978
Number Built:	74

Preserved Examples:

D1013 Western Ranger	D1041 Western Prince
D1015 Western Champion	D1048 Western Lady
D1023 Western Fusilier	D1062 Western Courier
D1035* Western Yeoman	

* Ran in B.R. service as No.D1010 Western Campaigner, and took the name and number of scrapped locomotive after preservation.

Duties:	Mixed Traffic.
Technical Data:	**Tractive Effort:** 72,600 lb
	Loco Weight: 108 tons
	Transmission: Hydraulic containing Torque Converters
	Engine: Two Maybach MD655 V Type of 1350 hp at 1500 rpm

British Railways Class 52 *Photograph courtesy of Colour Rail*

The Westerns were designed after it became apparent that the smaller Warships (Class 42) were under-powered for the work expected of them. Thus, in 1959 the design work commenced, and No.D1000 was completed early in 1962. Due to the limited construction space at Swindon, some of the locos were built at Crewe.

The locomotives utilised the same engines as the Warships, which were uprated from 1150 to 1350 hp at the same engine speed. The Voight hydraulic transmission was also modified from that used on the earlier North British locos.

Few outward modifications occurred to the locomotives during their service lives, other than the fitting of air brakes. As with the other Classes of Western Region diesel-hydraulic, maintenance costs were high, and with the B.R.B. insisting on standardisation of locos, they were not to have a very long service life. Like the earlier D8xx Class, the Westerns were almost completely enclosed in a skirt down to rail level, apart from around the bogies, and had a very clean workmanlike appearance.

With their high tractive effort, they were ideal for hauling the heavy passenger and freight trains over the severely graded South Devon and Cornwall banks.

When first delivered, many of the Westerns were put on Paddington/Birmingham/Shrewsbury trains, as the West Coast Main Line electrification was underway, and most Birmingham trains routed into Paddington. If the diesel Pullman units were out of action, a Western often headed a locomotive hauled Pullman rake in umber and cream livery, kept especially for such failures.

As the locomotives could not be used on electrically heated or air conditioned trains, they were displaced on express work by the Class 47 and later Class 50 (displaced by the electrification from Weaver Junction to Glasgow), and finished their lives hauling many of the heavy aggregate trains originating from the Westbury area. The introduction of H.S.T.'s to the Western Region then displaced further locos, and the Westerns finished their short career hauling enthusiasts specials, which were as popular as the end of steam workings some nine years earlier.

When introduced, No.D1000 appeared in desert sand, No.D1001 in green, No.D1002 in maroon livery (then standard for W.R. diesels), and No.D1015 in golden ochre livery. The remainder appeared in maroon livery, and Nos. D1000, D1001 and D1015 were also repainted including yellow warning panels. When built, they carried an aluminium cast version of the second B.R. crest (as did the 25KV AC electric locos), although when repainted in the blue B.R. livery these were removed and the B.R. aroow symbol used instead.

Heljan British Railways Class 52 *Photograph courtesy of Hattons of Liverpool*

Trix introduced a ready to run model at 3.8mm to the foot (roughly half way between the HO and OO Gauges) in 1965. The tools passed to Liliput UK and was reintroduced in 1974. The model remained available until1987 and following acquisition of the company by Dapol in 1992, the model was not reintroduced. Some of the tooling for this model remained with Liliput and passed eventually to Bachmann.

Hornby and Lima both introduced ready to run OO gauge models in 1979. The Hornby model is still available but the Lima model last appeared in 2001. Ironically the tooling for the Lima model passed to Hornby in 2005, but the Lima version is unlikely to see the light of day again.

Graham Farish introduced a ready to run N gauge model in 1985 which remained available until 2000 when the company was acquired by Bachmann. An upgraded model was reintroduced in 2004 and remains available.

Heljan introduced a ready to run OO gauge model in 2004. It remains available.

Class 53 Co-Co Diesel Electric Locomotive (Falcon) Brush Traction/British Railways

Introduced: 1961 (BR Stock 1970)

Allocation: Eastern, London Midland and Western Regions.

Locomotive Nos: D0280, later D1200. Built by Brush Traction in Loughborough.

Last of Class Withdrawn:	1975
Number Built:	1
Preserved Examples:	None
Duties:	Royal Mail, Freight and Passenger.
Technical Data:	**Tractive Effort:** 60,000 lb
	Loco Weight: 115 tons
	Transmission: Electric
	Engine: 2 x Maybach MD655
	Horsepower: 2,700

Brush Traction/British Railways Class 53 *Photograph courtesy of Colour Rail*

Design for a prototype twin engine Type 5 locomotive commenced at Brush Traction in Loughborough in 1959, and two years later saw the emergence of a one-off prototype No.D0280. This loco remained in the ownership of its builders, who were keen to demonstrate the locos capability to British Railways in an effort to win further orders. It emerged from the factory bearing the name Falcon, and carried a non standard livery of green and brown.

In order to obtain the necessary power, twin engines were fitted as no single engine was considered powerful enough to meet the specification. Maybach MD655 engines were chosen, and these were the same as fitted to to the Western Class 52 diesel-hydraulic locomotives, although electric transmission was preferred over the hydraulic system.

Initially the locomotive undertook trials on the London Midland and Eastern Regions, before being transferred to the Western Region.

The locomotive returned to Brush at regular intervals, and it was during a visit in March 1962 that it emerged with a cast nameplate. After an extensive 6 month trial period in the Sheffield area in 1963, the loco returned again to Brush. It remained at Loughborough for over 12 months before being returned to British Rail, and this time it was carrying two tone BR green livery. By now, Brush was building Class 47 locos, and Falcon was destined to remain a one-off.

British Rail took over responsibility for day to day maintenance, and it was allocated to Bristol Bath Road to work passenger trains between Bristol and London Paddington, alongside the Westerns.

The locomotive was sold to British Rail at a knockdown price in 1970, and was extensively rebuilt at Swindon Works during that year. Work included the fitting of air brakes (and removal of vacuum brakes). It was re-numbered D1200 and painted in corporate blue livery. Although it was allocated TOPS Class 53, it retained its D1200 number until withdrawal.

The locomotive was later transferred to Newport Ebbw Junction where it was used mainly on freight to and from the steelworks. It was withdrawn in 1975, and was cut up at a Newport scrap yard the following year.

Heljan are to introduce a OO Gauge ready to run model late in 2007.

Class 55 Deltic Co-Co Diesel Electric Locomotives British Railways

Introduced: Prototype in 1955, Production in 1961.

Allocation: Production - Eastern and Scottish Regions.

Locomotive Nos: D9000 - D9021

                             Re-numbered 55001-55022, in sequence
                             except D9000 became 55022.

Last of Class Withdrawn: 1982

Number Built: 22

Preserved Examples: Prototype Loco Deltic
                             D9000 Royal Scots Grey
                             55002 The Kings Own Yorkshire Light Infantry
                             55009 Alycidon
                             55015 Tulyar
                             55016 Gordon Highlander
                             D9019 Royal Highland Fusilier

Duties: Express Passenger.

Technical Data: **Tractive Effort:** 60,000 lb
                             Loco Weight: 99 tons (Production)
                             Transmission: Electric
                             Engine: 2 Napier 'Deltics'
                             Horsepower: 3,300

British Railways Class 55 *Photograph courtesy of Milepost 92½*

After publication of the Modernisation Plan in the early 1950's, and the decision to change to alternative forms of traction, diesel manufacturers were anxious to display their products to the British Railways Board. The English Electric Company raised the capital from private sources to finance the building of a powerful diesel locomotive, which it was hoped would result in a full order book. This loco was named Deltic after the Napier Deltic engines with which the loco was fitted. It was finished in a distinctive light blue livery and lined in yellow, and the roof and underframes were painted silver/grey.

Deltic entered service on the London Midland Region on trial in 1955. It was set to work mainly on London (Euston) to Liverpool trains. After one or two minor teething troubles had been corrected, 'Deltic' put in some impressive performances. Following trials over the steeply graded Settle to Carlisle route, the loco was passed over to the Eastern Region for evaluation on trains in and out of Londons Kings Cross.

The Eastern Region was looking for a locomotive capable of replacing the Gresley Pacifics on top link work over the Kings Cross/Newcastle/Edinburgh route. Suitably impressed with 'Deltics' performance, an order for 22 locos was placed. Before construction commenced, it was necessary to make several modifications. The length was increased by 1' 9" and the weight reduced by 7 tons, the bogie wheelbase was also reduced, and alterations made to the body sides to avoid the clearance problems that had been experienced with 'Deltic'. To improve drivers visibility, the angle of the windows was changed and minor alterations were made to the front end.

The production locomotives were powered, as 'Deltic', by two Napier 'Deltic' engines. These were extremely powerful engines having been designed in 1947 for Admiralty use in ships.

Delivery of the 22 production units commenced in 1961, and they were used as the main motive power on major trains in and out of Kings Cross. With the introduction of Class 254 High Speed Trains on principal Kings Cross services in 1978, the Class 55's were no longer required on these services. This resulted in most of the class being allocated to York and being reduced to hauling less important trains from Hull/Newcastle to Liverpool, and with production of further high speed units, the class was withdrawn with most of the locos having performed over two million miles of high speed working. The last of the class was withdrawn in January 1982.

At first, all locomotives were finished in B.R. green livery with lime green bands carrying the second BR cest. Later, they were repainted in the blue/yellow livery with lime green bands, then repainted again in the blue/yellow livery carrying the arrow symbol and re-numbered in the series 55001-55022 when the locos were classified as Class 55. The prototype Deltic was retired in 1963 having almost run half a million miles, and is now part of the National Collection.

Bachmann British Railways Class 55

Hornby Dublo introduced the first ready to run OO gauge model in 1960 before the production units had entered service with British Railways. The model was far too short and lacked detail, even the livery was a compromise. Although a superb performer on the track, the model not surprisingly disappeared with the closure of the Meccano company in 1964. Despite its shortcomings, it remains a firm favourite with Hornby Dublo collectors.

Lima introduced their ready to run OO gauge model in 1976. Originally announced as an HO model, the company emerged as a OO product when the Lima company abandoned HO scale and moved into the OO market. The model remained in the catalogue until 2002. The tools have been owned by Hornby since 2005 but the model has not yet been scheduled for re-release.

Lima produced a N gauge model in 1978. It remained available until 1985 but has not been produced since. The Lima tools are now owned by Hornby.

In 1984 Graham Farish introduced their own N gauge ready to run model. It remained available until 2000. Following the acquisition of the company by Bachmann that year, the model was upgraded and reappeared in 2003.

Bachmann introduced a ready to run OO gauge model in 2003. This remains available.

Class 56 Co-Co Disel Electric Locomotive
British Railways

Introduced:	1976
Allocation:	Eastern, London Midland and Western Regions.
Locomotive Nos:	56001 - 56030, built by Electroputere, Craiova Works, Romania. 56031 - 56090, built by British Rail Engineering Ltd., Doncaster. 56091 - 56135, built by British Rail Engineering Ltd., Doncaster.
Last of Class Withdrawn:	2004. Some reinstated for Jarvis Fastline in 2007.
Number Built:	135
Preserved Examples:	56003 56040 Oystermouth 56057 British Fuels 56097 56098
Duties:	Heavy Freight.
Technical Data:	**Tractive Effort:** 49,456 lb **Loco Weight:** 126 tons **Transmission:** Electric **Engine:** G.E.C. 16 Cylinder 16RK3CT **Horsepower:** 3,250

The Class 56 locomotives were first introduced in 1976, and were built exclusively for heavy freight haulage. They were built to cope with a massive increase in coal traffic, which had become the most

British Railways Class 56 *Photograph courtesy of Milepost 92½*

suitable fuel for power stations etc. following the high increase in oil prices from 1973. As a result, an initial order was placed for 30 locos with Electroputere of Romania, and for 30 locos with British Rail Engineering Ltd. at Doncaster.

The Romanian locomotives were fitted with some 70% of equipment exported from Britain. Electrical equipment and traction motors were supplied by Brush of Loughborough, whilst the engine was supplied by the General Electric Company (G.E.C.). Bogies and running gear was supplied by the Romanians, the six wheel bogies are identical to those used widely on Romanian State Railways (C.F.R.). The same bogie was adopted for the British built locos.

The bodies were similar to those of the Class 47 locomotives, as were the driving cabs with the addition of air conditioning. Driving controls were identical to those of the Class 47's, thus eliminating the need for driver training. Unlike the Class 47's, only air brakes were fitted, and marker light clusters instead of the four digit route indicators were fitted to cab fronts.

Delivery of the Romanian built locomotives took place from mid 1976. Locos were hauled dead to Zeebrugge (Belgium) via Czechoslovakia, East Germany and West Germany for shipping to Harwich.

The class were used mainly for coal traffic between colleries and power stations, and were fitted with slow speed control for working merry-go-round trains. Several locos were allocated to Cardiff Canton Depot for use on the heavy Port Talbot to Llanwern iron ore trains. The class was not fitted with train heating, and with a maximum speed of 80 mph were not designed for use on passenger services, although they have been used on enthusiasts specials from time to time.

Some difficulties were experienced with the Romanian built locomotives, which required modifications before they could be used in revenue earning service. Most of the modifications were made at Stratford Depot (London) or Doncaster.

On delivery, the first examples were allocated to Tinsley (Sheffield), and those not at Cardiff (Canton) were allocated to Toton (Nottingham). The class were found on heavy freight trains and freightliner services on the Eastern, London Midland and Western Regions.

With the arrival of newer locomotives, the first was withdrawn in September 1991, and the last in March 2004. Some locos have recently returned to work having been purchased by Jarvis Fastline.

The class first appeared in blue/yellow livery and numbered in the TOPS system. No.56036 was the first loco to carry the modified blue/yellow with black windscreen surround, large numbers and large logo, and other members of the class have appeared likewise. Many of the class have appeared in freight sector grey livery with appropriate subsector symbol. Some arrived in EWS livery, the remaining members of the class being transferred to English, Welsh & Scottish Railway on Privatisation.

Hornby British Railways Class 56

Mainline introduced a ready to run OO gauge model in 1976. Following closure of the company, Dapol acquired the tooling which was not owned by Kader and reintroduced the model in 1986, although it still carried Mainline logos on the chassis. The tooling passed to Hornby in 1998 and the locomotive remains part of the Hornby range.

Graham Farish introduced a ready to run N gauge model in 1984 which remained available until 2000 when the company was acquired by Bachmann. An upgraded model was reintroduced in 2003 and remains available.

Class 57 Co-Co Diesel Electric Locomotive
Brush Traction/Porterbrook

Introduced:	1998
Allocation:	Freightliner, Virgin Trains, First Great Western and West Coast Railway Company.
Locomotive Nos:	Class 57/0: 57001 - 57012, rebuilt 1997-1999.
	Class 57/3: 57301 - 57316, rebuilt 2001-2005.
	Class 57/6: 57601 - 57605, rebuilt 2001-2005.
Number Built:	33
Preserved Examples:	None
Duties:	Heavy Freight, Express Passenger and Train Breakdown Recovery.
Technical Data:	**Tractive Effort:** 55,000 lb **Loco Weight:** 120 tons 57/0; 117 tons 57/3 & 57/6 **Transmission:** Electric **Engine:** General Motors 64512E3 57/0; General Motors 64512F3B 57/3; General Motors 645F3B-12 57/6

The Class 47 locomotives were one of Britains railway success stories. Brush (Loughborough) designed them and British Rails Crewe Works manufactured 512 of them between the period 1963 and 1967. By the middle of the 1990's they were starting to show their age and many had been withdrawn from main line service. Privatisation saw a number of them pass to passenger and freight operators and it was clear to them that major re-engineering or long-term replacement was the only solution.

Brush Traction/Porterbrook Class 57 *Photograph courtesy of Colour Rail*

Freightliner, established as an independent company in 1996, was soon aware of the Class 47 fleet's inadequacies. In 1997 it asked Brush, the manufacturer of the Class 47s, to rebuild six locomotives. The locomotives were stripped and all redundant equipment removed, including the vacuum brakes which were no longer required on today's air braked railway. The power unit was also removed, the former Sulzer 12LDA28C engine no longer able to give the required performance. Reconditioned General Motors 645-12E3 engines were purchased from a specialist supplier in the United States and shipped to Brush for fitting. The emergence of General Motors locomotives since the mid 1980s on to British metals has seen performance enhanced considerably. The fitting of reconditioned engines is common practice amongst railroad operators in the USA, and it offers a cost-effective alternative to buying brand new. The result was virtually a brand new locomotive with an increase in life expectancy of around 20 years. With the performance characteristics of a Type 5 locomotive, the rebuilt locos were designated Class 57/0 and were numbered 57001–57006. The first loco, No.57001, emerged from Brush on 21 July 1998. These were funded through Porterbrook (now part of Santander).

Impressed by the results, Freightliner ordered another six locomotives in a deal brokered by train leasing company, Porterbrook. These were delivered between Autumn 1999 and April 2000. Freightliner did plan to have 25 such locomotives in the fleet but it opted for purchasing new Class 66 locomotives from General Motors. All 12 Class 57/0 locomotives remain in service with Freightliner Intermodal Division.

Realising that time was running out for a number of Class 47/4 locomotives, Porterbrook funded in Autumn 1999, the rebuilding of a prototype passenger locomotive with Electric Train Supply (ETS), required for heating, air conditioning and powering ancillary equipment such as cookers and fridges in catering vehicles. Locomotive No.57601 emerged in spring 2001 with modified front ends complying with group standards on lights, and in the purple livery of its owners Porterbrook. This locomotive was fitted with an uprated version of the General Motors 645-12E engine. The locomotive went into service with Great Western Trains, where it could be evaluated on the few remaining locomotive hauled trains such as the overnight London Paddington to Penzance sleeper.

Meanwhile, Virgin Trains was looking for a number of locomotives to haul 9 car 460 ton Pendolino trains over non electrified lines on diversions caused by engineering works, and to provide a compatible locomotive for rescue purposes should the need arise. These latter duties have often been nicknamed 'Thunderbird' after the cult television series featuring The International Rescue Organisation. Aware of the power requirements being above the 2,500 hp provided by the prototype ETS fitted locomotive No.57601, a larger engine unit (645-F3B12) had to be specified to drive the ancillary equipment, much of it high powered catering equipment, air conditioning and the complex on board computer systems. This is often referred to as 'hotel' power using up to 500 hp from the engine at 2750 hp.

With confidence that the uprated engine could provide the necessary power, Virgin, through Porterbrook, ordered 12 locomotives initially. These were numbered in the series 57301–57312 and were delivered between June 2002 and September 2003. A further 4 locos were ordered in August 2003 and the last delivered in December 2004. All 16 locos are named under licence after the characters in the cult puppet television series "Thunderbirds".

Not all Class 57/3 Pendolino 'drags' are caused by engineering work. Indeed the four additional locomotives were required for use with Pendolinos on the daily London Euston to Holyhead trains. The line between Crewe and Holyhead is 'off the wires', so the Pendolino's run to Crewe under their own power where a Class 57 couples on to the train for the remainder of the journey to the Welsh port.

When delivered the Class 57/3 was fitted with conventional buffers and couplings. They have subsequently been fitted with Dellner couplings to enable smooth coupling and uncoupling to take place. To accommodate these, it was necessary to return each locomotive to Brush for major work to take place at each end of the locomotive. This enabled the Dellner couplings to recess when the locomotive was required to couple to conventional stock.

Having thoroughly evaluated the prototype locomotive No.57601, First Great Western ordered 4 Class 57/6 locomotives (Nos. 57602-57605) through Porterbrook Train Leasing, which were delivered during 2004. These are the same as Class 57/3 locomotives but only have conventional couplings. During September and October 2004, the four locomotives were officially named after Totnes, Restormel, Pendennis and Tintagel Castles. These locomotives are mainly used on the sleeper services to and from London Paddington.

No longer required by First Great Western, No.57601 was returned to Porterbrook during 2004 and was subsequently sold to West Coast Railway Company in Carnforth who are involved in both the charter train business and short term hire to the main train operating companies when required. This locomotive was soon repainted from Porterbrook purple into the maroon colours of its new owner in order to match its coaching stock.

The Class 57s carried the liveries of their respective operators. No.57601 initially carried Porterbrooks purple livery which has since been replaced by West Coast Railways maroon.

Bachmann Brush Traction/Porterbrook/Virgin Class 57

Graham Farish introduced a ready to run N Gauge model in 1999, this was purely a repainted Class 47 locomotive. Following the take-over by Bachmann in 2002, It was re-introduced with an upgraded chassis, and was withdrawn and replaced by a brand new model which is acurate to prototype in 2007.

Lima followed Farish and produced a repainted Class 47 locomotive as a ready to run OO Gauge model. It remained in the catalogue until 2000. The tools were acquired by Hornby in 2005, although the model is not yet scheduled to appear.

Heljan produced a more accurate OO Gauge model in 2004, but this has recently been withdrawn.

Bachmann introduced a ready to run OO Gauge model in 2006, and it remains available.

Class 58 Co-Co Diesel Electric Locomotive
British Railways

Introduced:	1982
Allocation:	London Midland Region.
Locomotive Nos:	58001 - 58050
Last of Class Withdrawn:	2002
Number Built:	50
Preserved Examples:	None
Duties:	Heavy Freight.
Technical Data:	**Tractive Effort:** 61,800 lb
	Loco Weight: 129 tons
	Transmission: Electric
	Engine: G.E.C. Ruston-Paxman RK3 ACT
	Horsepower: 3,300

The Class 58 Railfreight locomotives were constructed by British Rail Engineering Ltd. at its Doncaster works.

The Class 58's follow American practice, rather than conventional British designs. Locomotives constructed in the U.S.A. have a hood (bonnet) as the central feature. A cab is placed either at one end, or both ends if required. The hoods are provided with access doors to the mechanical equipment contained inside. Because the cabs are wider than the hoods, walkways are provided between cabs for the use of maintenance and train staff.

The Class 58's follow this concept closely. Previously, British built locos were of box type construction with integral underframes. With the Class 58's, the bodywork and mechanical

British Railways Class 58 *Photograph courtesy of Milepost 92½*

equipment was supported by two girders running the length of the loco, between the two buffer beams.

The drivers cabs were considerably improved. They were designed to be draught free, entry being gained from an outer access cab which is part of the hood. The cab itself has controls mounted on a pedestal next to the drivers seat.

These locomotives were used on freight workings, and were fitted with slow speed controls for working merry-go-round trains.

The locomotives were all based at Toton for maintenance, but also worked from Shirebrook, Doncaster and Saltley (amongst other sheds) on merry-go-round traffic from the Notts and Yorkshire coalfields to nearby power stations. They were also used on Toton to Didcot power station workings, until they were replaced by the widespread importation of Class 66s.

All passed to EWS upon Privatisation and the first was withdrawn in June 1999, the last in September 2002. Since withdrawal a number of locos have been hired by EWS to ACTS in Holland and GIF in Spain.

The locomotives first appeared in railfreight grey livery, and later they received the freight sector grey livery with appropriate sub sector insignia added. A number of the locos carried EWS livery. Several of the Class received names.

Hornby British Railways Class 58

Hornby introduced a ready to run OO gauge model in 1982. Whilst not in the current Hornby catalogue, it remains available.

Heljan are due to introduce a OO Gauge ready to run locomotive in 2007.

Class 59 Co-Co Diesel Electric Locomotive
General Motors

Introduced:	1986
Allocation:	Foster Yeoman, ARC (now Hanson) and National Power (now EWS).
Locomotive Nos:	Class 59/0 Foster Yeoman: 59001 - 59005, built at La Grange, USA 1985-1989. Class 59/1 ARC/Hanson: 59101 - 59104, built in Ontario, Canada 1990. Class 59/2 National Power/EWS: 59201 - 59206, built Ontario, Canada 1994/1995.
Number Built:	15
Duties:	Heavy Freight.
Technical Data:	**Tractive Effort:** 122,000 lb **Loco Weight:** 126 tons **Transmission:** Electric **Engine:** EMD 16-645E3C **Horsepower:** 3,300

The first General Motors locomotives to be built for Britain were manufactured for Foster Yeoman, the aggregates company. Concerned about the reliability of British Rail locos used on its high density stone trains, it approached General Motors, a prolific supplier of traction to American and other railways. They asked them to build a variation of one of its standard SD50 locos for the British market. Because of the vast differences between the American and British loading gauges, it was necessary to completely redesign the locomotive body, and to factor buffers and couplings in to the design drawing, based on experiences of supplying Irish Rail. This was the first time that a British Rail customer had been permitted to purchase its own motive power and operate it on its own trains.

The first four Foster Yeoman locomotives were designated Class 59 and were built at General Motors La Grange, the Illinois plant in the USA. They were delivered on 23rd January 1986 and entered service on 17th March of the same year. In traffic, these locomotives (although privately owned) were still driven on the main line by British Rail crews, and maintained to BR standards. A fifth loco was acquired in 1989. All five locos carried Foster Yeoman livery and worked trains from Merehead Quarry in Somerset.

In December 1996, Foster Yeoman prepared No.59003 for transfer to work stone trains in Germany. It appeared in a joint DB (Deutsche Bahn/German Railways) and Foster Yeoman livery. It entered service on 14th September 1997 after having gone through a complex acceptance process, and having German operating systems fitted. It is still at work in Germany.

263

General Motors Class 59 *Photograph courtesy of Milepost 92½*

Subsequent orders saw ARC (Amalgamated Roadstone Corporation) delivered four Class 59/1 locomotives in 1990, which subsequently passed to Hanson Quarry Products in 1999, the current operators. Initially, these locos carried ARC yellow and later Hanson livery, and worked trains originating from Whatley Quarry in Somerset. Both Foster Yeoman and ARC/Hanson locos now work under the Mendip Rail name, and are used on aggregate trains from Somerset to customers in London and elsewhere.

National Power also entered the rail market and purchased six Class 59/2 locomotives, these were delivered in 1994/1995 and carried National Power powder blue livery. These were used to transport limestone from the Peak Forest to Drax Power Station in Yorkshire. After its formation in 1996, English, Welsh & Scottish Railways, a subsidiary company of American Railroad Wisconsin Central (now Canadian National), decided to opt for motive power, with which it was acquainted on the other side of the Atlantic. Not surprisingly, EWS turned their attention to the products of General Motors and ordered 250 new locos (see Class 66). With the General Motors Class 59 locos already producing outstanding performances with the three British operators, the company acquired the National Power fleet of six locos on 1st April 1998. These were subsequently repainted from National Power to EWS livery.

All Class 59 locomotives remain at work in the UK, apart from No.59003 which remains in Germany.

Hornby General Motors Class 59

Lima introduced a ready to run OO Gauge model in 1994, and the model remained available until 2000. The tools were acquired by Hornby in 2005 and the model has been upgraded and is currently available.

Class 60 Co-Co Diesel Electric Locomotive British Railways

Introduced:	1989
Allocation:	Please see text.
Locomotive Nos:	60001 - 60100
Number Built:	100
Duties:	Heavy Freight.
Technical Data:	**Tractive Effort:** 106,500 lb **Loco Weight:** 129 tons **Transmission:** Diesel Electric **Engine:** Mirrlees 8MB275T **Horsepower:** 3,100

British Railways Class 60 *Photograph courtesy of Colour Rail*

The Railfreight sector of British Rail found itself short of powerful locomotives for hauling heavy freight trains. With the General Motors Class 59 locos putting in some impressive performances on aggregates work, the British Railways Board issued specifications for a new Type 5 loco for which it issued tenders in 1987.

The successful bid was received from Brush Traction of Loughborough, who subcontracted the building of the bodies to Procor at Horbury Junction in Wakefield. The body shells were delivered to Loughborough ready painted.

The first locomotive was delivered in June 1989, but early on difficulties were experienced in traffic. Computer software proved troublesome, whilst mechanical defects were commonplace. At one time the situation was so bad, that many stood unfinished on the production line whilst the other problems were resolved. As a result, the last of the class was not delivered until 1993. Eventually these problems were rectified, and the class settled down to put in some impressive performances.

In the lead up to Privatisation, the Railfreight Sector was split into three shadow companies, Loadhaul, Mainline and Transrail, ready for sale. All three were acquired by Wisconsin Central in February 1996, whose British operation became English, Welsh & Scottish Railway. It was not long before EWS purchased Class 66 locos from General Motors, and by 2003 were placing the first Class 60 locos in store, pending an upturn in freight traffic. Although more powerful than the Class 66s, they have been eclipsed by the General Motors locos. By early 2007, around half of the 100 strong fleet were in store.

The Class are seen operating on heavy coal, metal, aggregates and oil trains.

Initially the class were delivered in Railfreight grey livery, and all were named on delivery. With the set up of the shadow companies, the class were allocated to all three, and some carried Mainline blue livery and some Loadhaul black and orange livery. The Trainload examples retained their grey livery, but when they passed to Transrail they were subsequently fitted with Transrail stickers. Following their transfer to EWS, a number of them have acquired the companies distinctive maroon and yellow livery.

Hornby British Railways Class 60

Lima introduced a ready to run OO Gauge model in 1990. The remained available until 2003. In 2005 the tools were acquired by Hornby, but this model is unlikely to reappear as Hornby introduced their own ready to run OO model in 2005, before the takeover.

Graham Farish have an N Gauge ready to run model in their range.

Class 66 Co-Co Diesel Electric Locomotive
General Motors

Introduced:	1998
Allocation:	Over the whole network.
Locomotive Nos:	Class 66/0: 66001 - 66250, built 1998-2000 by General Motors, London, Canada for EWS.
	Class 66/4: 66402 - 66420, built 2003-2006 by General Motors, London, Canada for Direct Rail Services.

Class 66/5:
66501 - 66593, built 1999-2004 by General Motors, London, Canada
for Freightliner.
(No.66521 was scrapped following the Great Heck accident).

Class 66/6:
66601 - 66625, built 2000-2005 by General Motors, London, Canada
for Freightliner.
(Modified Locos).

Class 66/7:
66701 - 66727, built 2001-2006 by General Motors, London, Canada
for GB Railfreight.
(Nos. 66718-66727 were 5 door versions).

Class 66/9:
66951 - 66952, built 2004 by General Motors, London, Canada for
Freightliner.

On Order:
66421 - 66430 for Direct Rail Services, due 2007.
5 locomotives for Jarvis Fastline.
3 locomotives for Victa Westlink.

Number Built: 419

Preserved Examples: None

Duties: Heavy Freight.

Technical Data: **Tractive Effort:** 57,000 lb
Loco Weight: 126 tons
Transmission: Electric
Engine: General Motors 12N-710G3B-EC
Horsepower: 3,300

General Motors Class 66 *Photograph courtesy of Milepost 92½*

Shortly after its formation in February 1996, English, Welsh & Scottish Railway (EWS), owned by the American company Wisconsin Central, placed an order in June 1996 for 250 locomotives costing some £500m. Wisconsin Central's operations in the USA used second-hand locomotives, which were refurbished by the manufacturers prior to entering traffic with them. In order to capture new traffic and to win back that previously lost to the road hauliers, it was necessary for EWS to improve the reliability of the existing freight fleet or to replace them with a new build. They chose the latter option, breaking the USA company's tradition of buying secondhand.

Not surprisingly EWS turned their attention to the products of General Motors. The new build locomotives were initially classified Class 61. By the time they entered service they had become Class 66 and utilised the basic body and cab design of the Class 59 locomotives. The restricted fuel capacity on British locos bemused the American owners, so on the new Class 66s this was increased to 1,800 gallons, almost twice that of a Class 59. The newer 710 Series engine, which was much smaller than the 645 Series fitted to the 59's, was nonetheless able to deliver the required 3,300 hp. The use of this smaller engine allowed engine room access and an internal corridor to be provided between cabs in the revised design. The cab design is almost identical to those of the Class 59s but with increased external high density head light clusters to comply with the standards adopted after the Class 59s had entered traffic. Provision for the fitting of an American style coupling was also made, should future rolling stock be built with a buckeye rather than the more traditional British system be adopted as standard in the future.

It had been initially intended that these locomotives would have been constructed under license at a British factory, but this proved to be impracticable. Construction was undertaken at the GM plant in London, Ontario, Canada commencing in the Autumn of 1997.

On March 23rd 1998, EWS Chairman Ed Burkhardt took delivery of the first EWS Class 66 locomotive, No.66001 at London, Ontario. Extensive trials then followed before the class entered service with EWS on 2nd June 1998 working the 0400 Bentwick to Drayton service. Construction was rapid, and when Nos. 66006-66011 arrived on 3 October, the locos were prepared at Newport Docks off the ship and sent straight to the depots to enter service. A year later (October 1999) over 150 of them were in traffic. The final locomotive, No.66250, was delivered in June 2000. There are currently 250 locos in service with EWS.

The locomotives carry EWS maroon and gold livery, which follows the livery carried in the USA by Wisconsin Central. Wisconsin Central was sold to Canadian National on 9 October 2001, and EWS is now owned by Deutchse Bahn (German Railways).

Another former British Rail freight company, specialising in container traffic at the time of Privatisation, was Freightliner. This company subsequently diversified into bulk freight under the HeavyHaul arm of the company, in addition to retaining and developing its core container market.

On Privatisation in 1996, Freightliner acquired an ageing locomotive fleet and ordered five Class 66 locomotives (Nos. 66501-66505) on 21st June 1999. These were built in Canada alongside the final batch of locomotives for EWS. In 1999 the company diversified from its traditional intermodal (container) base and entered the heavy haulage market in competition from EWS. A total of 81 Class 66/5 locos have been delivered, the last, No.66581, arriving as recently as March 2005. The reason for the odd number can be found in the tragic circumstances that occurred at Great Heck in Yorkshire on 28th February 2001. A road vehicle crashed on to the East Coast Main Line, which unfortunately resulted in a fatal accident involving Freightliner No.66521 and a GNER express. The locomotive was subsequently written off and was replaced by No.66554. On 12th November 2004, Freightliners No.66522 was painted into Shanks livery for use on landfill trains between Dagenham and Calvert in Buckinghamshire.

In November 2000 Freightliner HeavyHaul division took delivery of 6 locomotives. Unlike the earlier locos, which had 75 mph capability, the new batch had a top speed of 65 mph and a revised gearing ratio of 83:18, giving greater hauling power. These were numbered in a different series and were classified Class 66/6 (Nos. 66601-66606). So far 22 of this type have been delivered, the last entering service in March 2005.

A third British freight operator was formed in 1999 by GB Rail, which also operated the Anglia franchise. This company became known as GB Railfreight (GBRF). GBRF ordered seven locomotives on 14th April 2001, after securing a Railtrack contract to move engineering trains, which began from 31 March 2001. When First Group acquired the Anglia franchise in August 2003 from GB Railways, it also acquired GBRF, and the company continues today to operate as part of First Group. GBRF currently has 22 locos in its fleet (Nos. 66701-66722). GBRF have recently ordered five Class 66/9 locos (low sulphur emission), taking the size of its fleet to 27 units. A new subclass (Class 66/9) has been built in order to comply with the latest low sulphur emission requirements that have been introduced since the earlier locomotives were built. These have an additional door on one side.

Direct Rail Services (DRS) was formed in February 1995 as a subsidiary company of British Nuclear Fuels Limited. It secured a number of contracts in conjunction with logistics companies, and relied initially on locomotives secured from former British Rail operators. In 2002 DRS ordered its own fleet of Class 66 locos (Nos. 66401-66420).

The success of the locomotives in Britain led to interest being shown in the General Motors locomotives by a number of new open access freight operators formed in Europe. European Union legislation opened up nationalised systems in Europe to new operators outside the control of the state owned railway administrations. These are in service with ACTS in Holland, Cargo Net in Norway, DLC in Belgium, ERS in Holland, Freightliner in Poland, Heavy Haul Power International in Germany, HGK in Germany, DLC in Belgium, Rail4Chem in Benelux, Railion Nederland in Holland, Shortlines in Holland (now part of Rail4Chem) and TGOJ in Sweden. EWS are also active, and during 2007 were in the process of setting up a new Paris based operation.

The Class 66 has now become the standard European freight locomotive, and a number of additional locomotives for operators are now on order. They carry a wide range of liveries both at home and abroad.

Bachmann General Motors Class 66

Lima introduced a ready to run OO Gauge model in 1999. This was last produced in 2003, and in 2005 the tools passed to Hornby following their acquisition of the Lima Group.

The Slovenian manufacturer Mehano released a ready to run HO Gauge model in 2004. This model carries the liveries of many of the operators found outside the UK. This range is distributed in the UK by Bachmann.

Bachmann introduced a ready to run OO Gauge model in 2005, which is still available. A model of the latest environmentally friendly versions, with the fifth door on one side of the body, is due for release in late 2007.

In N Gauge, Dapol and Graham Farish have both introduced ready to run versions. Both remain available.

Class 67 Bo-Bo Diesel Electric Locomotive
English, Welsh & Scottish Railway

Introduced:	1999
Allocation:	English, Welsh & Scottish Railway (EWS).
Locomotive Nos:	67001 - 67030. Built by Alstom in Valencia, Spain.
Number Built:	30
Duties:	Royal Mail, Freight and Passenger.
Technical Data:	**Tractive Effort:** 31,750 lb **Loco Weight:** 90 tons **Transmission:** Electric **Engine:** JT42HWHS **Horsepower:** 3,200

General Motors Class 67 *Photograph courtesy of Colour Rail*

The Class 67s were conceived as a high speed 125 mph locomotive for use initially on Royal Mail trains to and from the London hub at Willesden to the West Country and the North East. English, Welsh & Scottish Railway acquired Rail Express Systems (operators of parcels) and the Royal Mail trains following privatisation in 1996.

EWS placed the Class 67 order with General Motors, althought the company had no experience of providing high speed diesel traction. With its factories in Canada and the USA at full capacity (the Class 66s were in full production at that time), the decision was taken to subcontract the building to Alstom who built the 30 locos at their plant in Valencia in Spain. Early in the design process it was discovered that there were no high speed Co-Co bogies available, and it became necessary to revert to a Bo-Bo design.

Construction began in Summer 1999, and No.67002 was despatched to the Toledo area to undertake high speed testing on the AVE Line, one of the few standard gauge (4' 8½") lines in Spain, most of the RENFE (Spanish National Railways) network being built to broad gauge (5' 6"). Railtrack, at that time, did not recognise European Safety Certificates issued by UIC (International Union of Railways), and despite these trials insisted on carrying out its own safety assessment when the locos arived in the UK. This delayed the process considerably, and the first loco did not begin operation in revenue earning service until December 1999.

These locomotives were initially used on Royal Mail trains and Travelling Post Office services. They also work special charter trains for which EWS often supply the traction in conjunction with major sporting and other events. Some have also been used on additional Summer holiday specials for operators such as Virgin.

The loss of the Royal Mail contract in 2003 was a major blow to the Class, and since then they have been used on both passenger and freight workings. Some are used on 'Thunderbird' duties on the East Coast Main Line by GNER. The Class are now the preferred choice for use on the non electrified routes used by First Scotrail sleeper services, and to haul the Aberdeen, Fort William and Inverness portions to and from the electrified section where they are combined for the main haul to and from London Euston by electric traction.

All carry EWS maroon and gold livery with the exception of three locomotives. No.67005 (Queens Messenger) and No.67006 (Royal Sovereign) carry Royal Train livery and work that train as required. At other times they are allocated to other duties. No.67029 received a special silver livery in 2004 for working the EWS company train.

Hornby General Motors Class 67

Lima introduced a ready to run OO Gauge model shortly before the demise of the range in 2003. It was not available for very long. The tools were acquired by Hornby in 2005, and the model was upgraded and released during 2006.

British Railways Class 40 *Photograph courtesy of Milepost 92½*

A.E.C. Railcar
Great Western Railway

Introduced:	1940
Allocation:	Great Western Railway, later British Railways Western Region.
Locomotive Nos:	G.W.R. Nos. 19 - 32
	B.R. re-numbered W19W - W32W
Last of Class Withdrawn:	1962
Number Built:	14
Preserved Examples:	20
	22
Duties:	Branch Line Passenger.
Technical Data:	
	Transmission: Mechanical
	Engine: 2 x A.E.C. 105 bhp

GWR AEC Railcar *Photograph courtesy of Milepost 92½*

Associated Equiipment Company Limited (A.E.C.) of Southall, is better known for its major involvement in road transport, and for many years was the principal supplier of buses to London Transport and other operators.

The London & North Eastern Railway introduced diesel traction to British Railways in 1931. The G.W.R. soon followed with a diesel railcar in 1933, which was built by A.E.C. and Park Royal, an associated company who supplied the bodywork. This was a streamlined design, and a total of 18 railcars were built.

Work commenced on a further 15 units (Nos. 19-32) in 1940, which were built to a more angular design, razor edged. The bodywork, bogies, underframe and brake gear were constructed at Swindon Works, whilst the remaining equipment was supplied by A.E.C.. Each unit had seating accommodation for 48 passengers, as these later units were built for branch line use and entered service from 1941. Unlike the earlier railcars, the later versions had full buffing and draw gear, which enabled them to haul tail traffic (up to 80 tons tare weight) when required.

The last railcars survived until 1962, and were withdrawn following the introduction of B.R. procured single power cars.

The railcars entered service finished in the G.W.R. coach livery of chocolate and cream. After Nationalisation, the B.R. coach livery of Crimson Lake and cream was applied, and from 1958 the standard diesel railcar lined green livery was used.

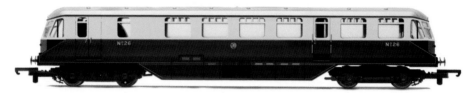

Hornby GWR AEC Railcar

Lima introduced a ready to run OO gauge model of the railcars in the number series 19 - 32 with the angular front end in 1981. It remained available until 2001. The tools passed to Hornby in 2005, the model has been re-introduced.

Graham Farish introduced an N gauge ready to run model of the19 - 32 series (angular front end) in 1985. This remained available until 2000 when the company was acquired by Bachmann. An upgraded model was reintroduced in 2005.

Express Parcels Railcar
Great Western Railway

Introduced:	1941
Allocation:	Great Western Railway, later British Railways Western Region.
Locomotive Nos:	G.W.R. No.34
	B.R. re-numbered W34W.
Last of Class Withdrawn:	1960
Number Built:	1
Preserved Examples:	None
Duties:	Express Parcels.

Technical Data: **Weight:** 34 tons 18 cwt
Transmission: Mechanical
Engine: 2 x A.E.C. 105 bhp
Load: 10 tons

GWR Express Parcels Railcar *Photograph courtesy of Colour Rail*

Following the success of the first railcars in 1934, and the building of the second batch, the G.W.R. authorised the construction of a second railcar, exclusively for the conveyance of express parcels traffic, and capable of hauling tail traffic up to 80 tons.

The first parcels railcar, No.17, was built to the original design, which were nicknamed 'Flying Bananas' due to their shape.

As with the previous batch of passenger carrying cars (Nos. 19-32), No.34 was built at Swindon. It had flush doors which opened to facilitate ease of loading/unloading, whilst No.17 had been fitted with recessed sliding doors. These modifications were no doubt made from operational experience gained on the earlier vehicle.

No.34 was allocated to Southall (London) for working between Paddington and Reading (General). This enabled No.17 to be transferred to the Birmingham area. No.34 continued work in the London area until withdrawal in September 1960.

Under G.W.R. ownership, No.34 was painted in the G.W.R. coach livery of chocolate and cream. It carried the words 'Express Parcels' on the upper panel, with the middle door separating the wording. Later it carried B.R. maroon livery.

Lima GWR Express Parcels Railcar

Lima introduced a ready to run OO gauge model in 1982. It was only available for a short period. The tools passed to Hornby in 2005 but the model has not yet been reintroduced.

Class 101 Metropolitan - Cammell 2/3/4 Car Diesel Multiple Units British Railways

Introduced: 1956

Allocation: Eastern, London Midland, Western and Scottish Regions.

Coach Nos:	Original Classification	Later Classification
MBS (2 Car) M50134-7	144	116/2 DTCL (2 Car) E56050-89
MCL (4 Car NE) E50138-51/234-45	147	101/1 DTCL (2 Car) M56090-3
MBS (2 Car) E50152-7/64-7	144	101/2 DTCL (2 Car) E56218-20
MCL (2 Car) E50158-63/68-71	144	101/1 DTCL (2 Car) M56332-61
MCL (4 Car) E50172-97	144	101/1 DTCL (2 Car) E56362-81
MBS (2 Car) E50198-233	144	101/2 DTCL (2 Car) SC56382-411
MBS (2 Car) E50246-8	162	101/2 TSL (4 Car) E59042-8/86-91
MBS (2 Car) E50250-9	168	101/2 TBSL (4 Car) E59049-55/92-97
MCL (2 Car) E50260-9	162	101/1 TSL (4 Car) E59060-72
MCL (3 Car) E50270-9	168	111/1 TBS (4 Car) E59073-85
MBS (3 Car) E50280-92	168	111/2 TBSL (4 Car) E59112/3
MBS (2 Car) E50293-6	171	101/2 TSL (3 Car) M59114-31
MBS (3 Car) M50303-20	162	101/2 TSL (3 Car) E59302-4
MCL (3 Car) M50321-38	162	101/1 TSL (4 Car) E59305/6
MCL (3 Car) E50745-7	171	101/1 TCL (4 Car) E59523-6
MCL (4 Car) E50748-51	Not Classified	101/1 DTSL (2 Car) E79263-91
MBS (2 Car) M51174-203	Not Classified	101/2 DTCL (2 Car) M79626-32
MBS (2 Car) E51204-23	Not Classified	101/2
MBS (2 Car) SC51224-53.	Not Classified	101/2
MBS (2x4 Car) E51425/6/35/6	Not Classified	101/2
MCL (2x4 Car) E51495/6/505/6	Not Classified	101/1
MBS (2 Car) E79047-75	Not Classified	Not Classified
M79076-82	Not Classified	Not Classified

Total Built: 153 x 2 Car, 54 x 3 Car and 38 x 4 Car.

All built between 1956 and 1960.

N.B.: No.M50136 had 203 hp Rolls Royce supercharged engines.

Last of Class Withdrawn: 2003

Preserved Examples: 40

Duties: Suburban and Cross Country Passenger.

Technical Data:	Weight:	Maximum: MCL 32 tons;
		MBS 33 tons; DTCL 24 tons 4 cwt;
		TS, TBS, TBSL & DTSL all 25 tons.
	Transmission:	Mechanical
	Engine:	2 x B.U.T. (A.E.C.) 6 Cylinders
		of 150 hp to each power car.

British Railways Class 101 *Photograph courtesy of Milepost 92½*

The units, run along with the Derby lightweight units numbered in the 79xxx series, were the first large quantity production of Diesel Multiple Units to be undertaken. The initial units in the 79xxx series were wired differently from the standard range of D.M.U.'s, and were all withdrawn after some ten or eleven years in service.

All the Metro-Cammell Units are 57' long and 9' 3" wide, all vehicles having vestibule connections to enable movement throughout the length of the unit.

As built, the first units were fitted with four indicator lights in the normal steam positions for headlamps. Later, two digit indicators, located centrally below the front windows, together with express pattern head/tail lamps were fitted. The four car units for the North East had four digit indicators located centrally above the cab windows, again with two head/tail lamps.

These units were found throughout British Rail and were used in the Edinburgh, Dundee, Perth and Glasgow areas. They were also found on non-electrictrified services on Tyneside, and the service via Blaydon to Carlisle, York, Leeds, Bradford and Scarborough areas, and occasionally they were used instead of the Trans Pennine Units on the Manchester to Hull services via Sheffield and Doncaster. Three trailer composites (Nos. 59528, 59538 and 59543) were transferred to the London Division of the Western Region, to strengthen the Pressed Steel three car units on the Paddington suburban services. The early units (79xxx series) were used in East Anglia and also in the Carlisle area of London Midland Region. Extensive use was made of these units in the Birmingham area, alongside Derby built units, on the busy services operated in this area. The Western Region units were generally found in the Plymouth area, and were often seen on the Par to Newquay line.

All of these units later ran with the first class accommodation declassified. Many of these units were replaced by the more modern Pacers and Sprinters.

Eight driving cars were converted into 4x2 Parcel Units in 1987, but all were withdrawn by 1989.

As built, the units were in green D.M.U. livery with the B.R. circular crest on power cars, together with cream lining and warning 'V' on the front ends. Small yellow warning panels were subsequently added. Later, units were painted in overall blue with yellow ends. Commencing in 1976, a refurbishing programme was started when all the units so treated were repainted in light grey livery with wide blue bands at waist level, and full yellow front ends. Owing to problems in keeping this livery clean, a further change gave the units the main line blue/grey paintwork with white lining. Those units which operated in Passenger Transport Executive areas (i.e. Glasgow, South Yorkshire and West Midlands etc.), all carried the P.T.E. insignia as well as the B.R. logo. After Sectionisation they carried both Network SouthEast or Regional Railways liveries.

One unit, No.101685, carried green livery until withdrawal, and was known as 'Daisy', it was named shortly before withdrawal by First North Western. 'Daisy featured in the Thomas the Tank Engine books by Rev. W. Audry.

Hornby British Railways Class 101

Tri-ang produced a ready to run OO gauge model in 1958. The tools passed to Tri-ang Hornby in 1965 and to Hornby in 1972. The model was last produced in 1978.

Graham Farish introduced a ready to run N gauge model in 1982 which remained available until the company was acquired by Bachmann in 2000.

Lima introduced a ready to run OO gauge model in 1997. This remained in production until 2001. The tools passed to Hornby in 2005 and it has since been reintroduced.

Class 108 Diesel Multiple Unit
British Railways

Introduced:	1958
Allocation:	Eastern, North Eastern and London Midland, later Southern and Western Regions.
Locomotive Nos:	DMBS Original Numbers: 50599-50629, 50924-50935, 50938-50987, 51416-51424 and 51901-51950. DMBS Revised Numbers: 53599-53629, 53924-53935, 53938-53987, 51416-51424 and 51901-51950.
	DMCL Original Numbers: 50630-50646, 51561-51572, 52037-52065 DMCL Revised Numbers: 53630-53646, 51561-51572 and 52037-52065
	DTCL Original Numbers: 56190-56215 DTCL Revised Numbers: 54114-54149 and 54412-54483
	TBSL Original Numbers: 59245-59250*
	TSL Original Numbers: 59380-59390*
	All built at Derby.
	* Withdrawn before re-numbering.
Last of Class Withdrawn:	1993

Number Built:	333
Preserved Examples:	51562
Duties:	Passenger.
Technical Data:	**Transmission:** Mechanical **Engine:** 2 x BUT (Leyland) 150 hp per vehicle **Horsepower:** 300

British Railways Class 108 *Photograph courtesy of Milepost 92½*

Built by British Railways at its Derby Works, 147 two car, 5 three car and 6 four car units were built between 1958 and 1961.Totalling 333 vehicles (210 powered and 123 trailer cars) they were generically known as 'Derby Lightweights', although they differed considerably from the earlier batch built from 1954. They were allocated to the Eastern, North Eastern and London Midland Regions, and saw service on a large number of routes around Bletchley, Carlisle, Chester, Crewe, Liverpool, Manchester, Newcastle, Nottingham, Preston and Sheffield. Each two car set could accommodate 117 passengers, and they were ideal for use on local services and branch lines. They later became more widespread in their travels, some seeing service on the Southern and Western Regions.

No.51562 was the 1000th diesel multiple unit vehicle to be built at Derby Works. This vehicle has been preserved by the National Railway Museum at York.

The first vehicle was withdrawn in 1964 as a result of accident damage. Most survived until the early 1990s when major withdrawal took place with the arrival of second generation units for Regional Railways. A number carried Network SouthEast colours and were used latterly on the Chiltern Lines (prior to the arrival of the Network Turbo units) and the Bletchley to Bedford line. The last unit was withdrawn in October 1993. Over 50 vehicles have passed into preservation for use on Heritage Railways.

Bachmann British Railways Class 108

Bachmann introduced a ready to run OO Gauge model in 2006.

Class 110 Birmingham R.C. & W. Co.
3 Car Diesel Multiple Units
British Railways

Introduced:	1961
Allocation:	British Railways, shared originally by London Midland and Eastern Regions, later all Eastern Region.

Caoch Nos.	Originally Classified	Now Classified
E51829 - E51848	110/1 MCL	110
M52076 - M52085	110/1 MCL	110
E51809 - E51828	110/2 MBC	110
M52066 - M52075	110/2 MBC	110
E56963 - E56712	163 TSL	110
M59808 - M59817	163 TSL	110

Number Built:	30 x 3 Car Units.
	All built in 1961/1962.
Last of Class Withdrawn:	1991
Duties:	Suburban and Cross Country Passenger.
Technical Data:	**Weight:** MCL 33 tons max; MBC 33½ tons max; TSL 25½ tons max. **Transmission:** Mechanical **Engine:** 2 x Rolls Royce 180 hp to each power car.

British Railways Class 110 *Photograph courtesy of Milepost 92½*

These units were a development of the earlier B.R.C.W. 3 Car Class 104 units, which were built between 1957 and 1959, but were of a more modern appearance with different shaped front windows, and incorporated a roof level four digit indicator box. Furthermore, Rolls Royce engines of increased power were fitted as opposed to the more usual Leyland 150 hp engines.

When built, the units were divided between the Eastern and London Midland Regions, and were allocated to Newton Heath (Manchester) and Hammerton Street (Bradford) for use on the Calder Valley route between Manchester and Bradford/Leeds (via Rochdale and Todmorden). With the concentration of units at one depot, all were maintained at Bradford, apart from two units at Neville Hill (Leeds).

The units covered services between Manchester, Bradford and Leeds, although they also cover trips from Leeds to Harrogate, York and Scarborough. These were later curtailed by the extension of some Liverpool to York Inter City loco hauled trains through to Scarborough.

The units were also used on the through Leeds to Southport service, via Manchester and Wigan (Wallgate). Although some of the multiple units operating in the North West later lost their first class accommodation, these units retained theirs. With the setting up of the Regional P.T.E.'s, these units later carried the West Yorkshire insignia.

When built, the units were in the green lined yellow standard D.M.U. livery with 'V' shaped from warning flash. The circular coaching crest was applied to power cars, and white front to roof around route indicator. Later, the overall blue livery (first with small yellow warning panel and later all over yellow front end) was carried, together with the B.R. arrow symbol. Some units were later refurbished in the overall white livery with broad blue waist band, again with overall yellow front ends. Vehicles treated thus included Nos. 51810, 51815, 51824, 51832, 51839, 51841, 51843, 51845, 52073, 59693, 59700, 59703, 59704, 59707, 59811 and 59816. The adoption of the blue/grey standard coaching stock livery was applied to all passenger vehicles.

Hornby British Railways Class 110

Hornby introduced a ready to run OO gauge model in 1982. Whilst not in the current Hornby catalogue, the model remains available.

Class 117 Pressed Steel Company
3 Car Diesel Multiple Unit
British Railways

Introduced:	1959
Allocation:	Western Region.
Coach Nos:	Class 117/2, Motor Brake Second, W51332 - W51373. Seats: 2nd 65. Class 117/1, Motor Second, W51374 - W51415. Seats: 2nd 89. Class 176, Trailer Composite (L), W59484 - W59522. Seats: 1st 22, 2nd 48.
	39 3 Car Units built and 6 spare driving motors.
Last of Class Withdrawn:	1999
Preserved Examples:	59
Duties:	Suburban Passenger.

Technical Data: **Weight:** Motor Brake Second & Motor Second 36 tons; Trailer Composite 30 tons.
Transmission: Mechanical
Engine: 2 x B.U.T. (Leyland) 6 Cylinder of 150 hp to each power car.

British Railways Class 117 *Photograph courtesy of Milepost 92½*

On introduction, the Pressed Steel units replaced Class 61xx 2-6-2 T locomotives on the Paddington suburban trains in the London commuter area. Working alongside single power car and drive end trailer units, they also took over all branch line services including Ealing Broadway to Greenford, Slough to Windsor, Maidenhead to Bourne End/Marlow/High Wycombe/Aylesbury, Twyford to Henley and Reading to Newbury/Bedwyn. These units also worked to Worcester from Oxford and Westbury from Reading, as well as more recently assisting with the through Reading to Tonbridge services. They are also found in the Birmingham, Bristol and Plymouth areas.

As originally built, the units had no gangway connections between cars, but these were added in the late 1960's, thus enabling Conductor Guards to move through the train on 'bus stop' services to collect fares. Some units ran as four car units with spare Metro-Cammell composite trailer vehicles.

Before withdrawl, several units appeared in they Perth area, working services to Edinburgh/Stirling and Dundee

The units were delivered in D.M.U. lined green livery with a yellow 'V' warning panel and a white cab roof. A yellow rectangular warning panel was later added. The B.R. coaching stock crest was applied to the power cars only. B.R. blue livery was subsequently used with full yellow cab ends. Some of the units were later refurbished, and the white/blue livery applied, retaining yellow ends. Due to cleaning problems, this refurbished livery was replaced by the standard blue/grey coaching stock livery with white lining, again the yellow ends being retained. Subsequently, the units appeared in Network South East red/blue/grey livery.

Lima British Railways Class 117

Lima introduced a ready to run OO gauge model in 1980. It remained available until 1994. In 2005 the tools passed to Hornby but no plans to reintroduce it have been announced.

Class 121 Diesel Multiple Unit
British Railways

Introduced:	1960
Allocation:	British Railways Western Region, later Network SouthEast. One remains in traffic with Chiltern Railways and another with Arriva Trains Wales. Others are in departmental service with Network Rail.
Coach Nos:	55020 - 55035 DMBS
	56280 - 56289, later became 54280 - 54289 DTS (Unpowered)
	16 single car units plus 10 identical trailer vehicles were built by Pressed Steel at Linwood.
Preserved Examples:	5 plus 3 trailers
Duties:	Branch Line Passenger.
Technical Data:	**Weight:** 37 tons DMBS; 29 tons DTS.
	Transmission: Mechanical
	Engine: 2 x Leyland 1595
	Horsepower: 300

British Railways Class 121 *Photograph courtesy of Colour Rail*

The Western Region of British Railways operated a large number of short branch or feeder lines prior to the publication of the Beeching Report in 1963 (The Reshaping of British Railways), which led to many of them being closed.

To replace steam on these lines, 16 single car units were ordered, together with 10 trailer cars (unpowered) from Pressed Steel at Linwood. They were virtually identical to the same company's Class 117 units, also favoured by the Western Region.

They saw service on a number of lines including Bristol Temple Meads to Avonmouth, Didcot to Newbury and Barnstaple to Taunton.

After the British Rail Sectors were set up, most of the remaining units became part of the Network SouthEast fleet where they were used on branch lines around London, Reading and Oxford. They could be seen at London Paddington on Greenford branch services. Later they were transferred to other Network SouthEast routes including the Bletchley to Bedford and Marks Tey to Sudbury lines. In 1992, the last of the unpowered trailers was withdrawn. All were withdrawn from passenger use after Privatisation, the last units giving way to Class 150 units on the Silverlink operated Bletchley to Bedford line during 2001. The first unit had been withdrawn as early as 1969. Those not in service with Network SouthEast were used on the former Western Region lines around Birmingham, operating out of Tyseley on West Midlands Passenger Transport Executive Services. These operated mainly on the very short line from Stourbridge Junction to Stourbridge, for which they carried for a time the short lived Midline Route, part of Provincial Services (later Regional Railways) operations.

The remaining units entered service with Railtrack (later Network Rail) who used them in departmental service including route learning, sandite, video surveying and emergency train duties for the Severn Tunnel.

Chiltern Railways received dispensation in 2003 for operating a rebuilt unit on the lightly used Aylesbury to Princes Risborough services outside the peak hours, when demand warrants through trains from London Marylebone. The unit No.121020 was purchased from the Network Rail departmental fleet, and after heavy rebuilding, together with the fitting of all necessary safety equipment, it was allowed to continue in service beyond November 30th 2005, when all Mark I based vehicles (slam doors) had to be withdrawn.

During 2006 Arriva Trains Wales purchased unit No.121032 for use on the short Cardiff Bay branch. This unit carries Arriva colours.

A number of units have been preserved for use on Heritage Railways.

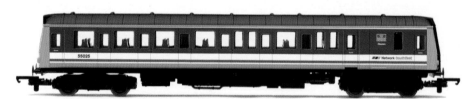

Hornby British Railways Class 121

Lima introduced a ready to run OO Gauge model in 1998, which remained available until 2001. The tools passed to Hornby in 2005, and the model has since been reintroduced.

Class 124 Trans-Pennine 6 Car Diesel Multiple Unit British Railways

Introduced:	1960	
Allocation:	Eastern Region.	
Coach Nos:	Class 124/1,	Motor Composite, E51951 - E51967. Seats: 1st 21, 2nd 36.
	Class 124/2,	Motor Brake Second (Non-driving), E51968 - E51984. Seats: 2nd 48.
	Class 180,	Trailer Second, E59765 - E59773. Seats: 2nd 64. Trailer Biffet First, E59774 - E59781. Seats: 1st 18, Buffet 8.

Total Built: 8 x 6 Car Units and 3 spare vehicles, built at Swindon.

Last of Class Withdrawn:	1984
Duties:	Express Passenger.
Technical Data:	**Weight:** Driving Motor Composite 40 tons; Motor Brake Second 41 tons; Trailer Second 32 tons; Trailer Buffet First 43 tons. **Transmission:** Mechanical **Engine:** 2 x B.U.T. (Leyland) 6 Cylinder Horizontal Type of 230 hp to each motor coach.

British Railways Class 124 *Photograph courtesy of Colour Rail*

Design wise, these units were probably the most characteristic diesel multiple units, other than the Diesel Pullmans, to run on B.R.. Their very curved nose and wrap-around windows have no comparisons, and with a total of 1840 hp for six cars, were the most powerful multiple units, other than the six car Midland Pullman units and eight car Western Region Pullman units.

All vehicles were basically 64' 6" long and 9' 3" wide, running on standard British Railways D.M.U. bogies.

The units were designed for the Trans-Pennine route from Liverpool to Hull (via Manchester, Stalybridge and Leeds), and as the name implies is a severely graded line with many sharp curves, requiring all the inbuilt power provided. The intention with the eight sets built, was to improve the timings across this route by introducing through services (instead of a series of cross country hops) with connections, thus making the journey less tedious.

Due to maintenance and other problems, the sets seldom ran at full strength, or had alternative vehicles of other pedigrees attached to provide accommodation, the buffet vehicles were often missing.

Latterly, with the delivery of the high speed train sets, it was possible to cascade newer loco-hauled coaching stock to the Trans-Pennine route, and the multiple units were used on less important work than that for which they were intended, and all were withdrawn in 1984.

When introduced, they were finished in the green with yellow lined livery for D.M.U.'s used at that time, with the circular coach crest applied to the vehicles. Later, the blue/grey rolling stock livery with full yellow ends and new B.R. symbol was applied.

Trix British Railways Class 124

Trix introduced a 3.8mm scale model, half way between HO and OO gauges in 1966. The tools passed to Liliput in 1973 and it remained available until 1988. After Dapol acquired the tools in 1993, they produced a limited run of 300 models in 2000. It has not been available since and the tools passed to Hornby in 1996, although reintroduction because of the scale issue is considered unlikely.

Class 142 Pacer (or Skipper) Diesel Multiple Units British Rail

Introduced:	1985
Designed By:	Associated Rail Technologies (Leyland/B.R.E.L. Derby).
Allocation:	Eastern, London Midland and Western Regions. For post Privatisation please see text.

Unit Nos:

	Class	DMS	DMS (L)
142.001 - 142.050	142/0	55542-91	55892-641
142.051 - 142.096	142/1	55701-46	53747-92

Number Built:	Only minor differences exist between Classes 142/0 and 142/1. 96 Units
Preserved Examples:	None
Duties:	Local Stopping Passenger services.
Technical Data:	

Weight: DMS 23 tons 26 cwt; DMS (L) 24 tons 96 cwt.
Transmission: Mechanical
Engine: Leyland TL of 200 hp per car turbo charged.

British Rail Class 142 *Photograph courtesy of Milepost 92½*

These units, which are built as a consortium effort by British Leyland for the bus type bodies and B.R.E.L. for the running gear, have been introduced on many branch and secondary lines since 1985, to replace many of the older style D.M.U.'s which were life expired. It has been developed as a wider bodied vehicle for the original Class 140 units. Unlike most of the earlier fleet of D.M.U.'s, which usually had two motors on one vehicle and the trailer being non-powered, each vehicle has one motor. The units are compatable with other classes of Pacer or Sprinter, having the B.S.I. Standard couplers, and can be frequently seen working in tandem, particularly in the North West.

Nearly all local services in the Liverpool, Blackpool, Preston, Wigan, Manchester and Rochdale areas are worked by these units, along with Class 150/1 and 150/2 Sprinters used on semi-fast and Trans-Pennine services. In the Leeds area, those allocated to Neville Hill work with the earlier Class 141 Leyland vehicles and Class 144 Alexander/B.R.E.L. units in service to Bradford, Scunthorpe, Skipton, York, Hull, Doncaster and Harrogate.

As well as problems on sharp curves and gradients, many of the units have had gear box problems, and a considerable number of units have been stored at Crewe and elsewhere awaiting modifications. The units can be seen over wide areas of the North of England and Wales, from Llandudno and Blackpool across to Manchester, Sheffield, Leeds and York.

When delivered, the first batch (Nos. 142.001-142.014) were painted in Greater Manchester orange/brown livery, and were allocated to Newton Heath (Manchester) to work local services to Rochdale (both routes) and New Mills/Romiley to the east.

The next batch (Nos. 142015-142027), were allocated to Laira (Plymouth) where they were named 'Skippers' for use on the Devon and Cornish branches still open. Unfortunately, the sharp curves and steep gradients did not suit the units, and most were subsequently replaced by older D.M.U.'s until more suitable Sprinters became available. These were painted in almost the G.W.R. livery of chocolate and cream, although, as mentioned previously, all were transferred to the North West.

The remainder of the units (Nos. 142.028-142.096) are all in Provincial sector two-tone blue livery, and are allocated to Newton Heath (except unit Nos. 142.071-142.095 which are at Neville Hill in Leeds).

Post Privatisation, the units have seen service with First North Western and Arriva Trains Northern, both of which are now absorbed into Northern Rail. Some Northern units carry Mersey Rail livery, others are in service with Arriva Trains Wales.

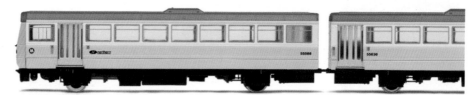

Hornby British Rail Class 142

Hornby introduced a ready to run OO model in 1987, and it is still currently available.

Class 150 Diesel Multiple Unit
British Rail

Introduced:	1984
Allocation:	British Rail Provincial Sector.
Unit Nos:	150001 - 150002, prototype units, designated Class 150/0, 3 car units built, 1984.
	150101 - 150150, designated Class 150/1, 2 car units built, 1985/1986.
	150010 - 150019, designated Class 150/1, 3 car units built, 1985-1987. Third car added 1995.
	150201 - 150285, designated Class 150/2, 2 car units built, 1986/1987.
	All built at British Rail Engineering Ltd., York Works.
Number Built:	146
Duties:	Passenger.

Technical Data:
Transmission: Mechanical.
Engine: Cummins NT855R5.
Horsepower: 570 2 car units; 855 3 car units.

British Rail Class 150 *Photograph courtesy of Milepost 92½*

In the early 1980s, British Rail was considering its options for producing replacements for its first generation diesel multiple units, some of which dated from the late 1950s. Utilising the Mark III body shell as a starting point, the British Railways Board commissioned two manufacturers to produce prototypes, which after testing would result in further orders. Its own British Rail Engineering Limited produced two x 3 car units (Nos. 150001 and 150002), and Metro-Cammell in Birmingham produced 2 units which were classified Class 151.

As a result, the Provincial Sector of British Rail commissioned British Rail Engineering Limited at York to build 147 units between 1984 and 1987. Provincial went on to become Regional Railways before Privatisation, and the units subsequently passed to new operators. A third car was added to 10 sets in 1995. The Class 150/2 variants had cab gangway connectors for use when working in multiple.

Following Privatisation, the Class 150 units entered service with Anglia Railways (later ONE), Wales & Borders (later Arriva Trains Wales), Central Trains, Arriva Trains Northern (later Northern), Valley Lines (later Arriva Trains Wales), ScotRail (now all transferred to Arriva Trains Wales), First North Western (now Northern), Silverlink (transferred from Central) and Wessex Trains (now First Great Western).

These units originally carried Provincial Sector livery, but since Privatisation they have carried the colours of the operators. A number of Wessex Trains units carried special promotional liveries for the area they served (Devon and Cornwall).

Bachmann are producing a Class 150 in both OO Guage and N Guage (Graham Farish range). These are due to be released in 2008.

Class 155 Diesel Multiple Unit
British Rail

Introduced:	1987
Allocation:	British Rail Provincial Sector and West Yorkshire Passenger Transport Executive.
Unit Nos:	155301 - 155335*, designated Class 155/0, 2 car units. *Rebuilt into 70 single car Class 153 units from 1991.
	155341 - 155347, designated Class 155/3, 2 car units.
	All built by Leyland Bus, Workington.
Number Built:	42
Duties:	Passenger.
Technical Data:	**Transmission:** Hydraulic **Engine:** Cummins NT855R5 per unit **Horsepower:** 570

British Rail Class 155 *Photograph courtesy of Milepost 92½*

The Provincial Sector of British Rail, which became Regional Railways, began an extensive programme of replacing its ageing fleet of first generation diesel multiple units and locomotive hauled trains with new vehicles.

As part of the programme, Leyland Buses in Workington were commissioned to build 35 two car 23 metre long diesel multiple units, using bus technology, which were classified as Super Sprinters.

These units saw service in the West Midlands, South Wales and the West of England, but were not very successful. They suffered reliability problems, and the decision was taken to rebuild them into 70 single car units. Conversion work commenced in 1991, and on completion the units became Class 153, which have been reasonably successful and many remain in service to date, seeing operations around the Bristol/West of England area.

A further 7 units were built in 1988 for use in the West Yorkshire Passenger Transport Executive (WYPTE) area on services around Leeds. The construction cost of these was funded by WYPTE, and as a result they originally carried WYPTE Metro Train livery, and are now in service with current operators Northern.

Hornby British Rail Class 155

> Dapol introduced a ready to run OO Gauge model in 1992. The model passed to Hornby in 1996 and was reintroduced in 1999. Whilst it is not in the current Hornby catalogue, it remains available.

Class 156 Diesel Multiple Unit
British Rail

Introduced:	1987
Allocation:	British Rail Provincial Sector (later Regional Railways). Later Anglia Railways (now ONE), Central Trains, Northern and ScotRail (now First ScotRail).
Unit and Coach Nos:	156401 - 156514 52401 - 52514 DMSL 57401 - 57514 DMS
Number Built:	114 x 2 Car Units, built by Metro-Cammell, Birmingham.
Duties:	Local and Regional Passenger.
Technical Data:	**Weight:** 36 tons DMSL; 35½ tons DMS **Transmission:** Hydraulic **Engine:** 1 x Cummins NT855R5 per vehicle **Horsepower:** 570 2 Car Units (285 per vehicle)

These units were designated 'Super Sprinter' when they were introduced by the Provincial Sector of British Rail between 1987 and 1989. All 114 units were built by Metro-Cammell (later Alstom) at Washwood Heath in Birmingham.

British Rail Class 156 *Photograph courtesy of Central Trains*

They were designed for longer distance regional services, and replaced locomotive hauled trains and first generation diesel multiple units. The last 14 units were funded by Strathclyde Passenger Transport Executive for services operating to and from Glasgow, and they were delivered in their orange and black colour scheme. This has subsequently been replaced by the red and cream livery currently in use in the Strathclyde operating area (services are operated on behalf of Strathclyde by First ScotRail).

The remaining 100 units initially carried Provincial Sector livery, but 20 units were subsequently repainted into Regional Railways Express livery.

Other than the sleeping car service to Fort William, Class 156 units now form all the Glasgow/Oban/Fort William/Mallaig services in First ScotRail livery.

Following Privatisation (from 1996), units were allocated to Anglia Railways (now ONE operated by National Express), First North Western (now Northern), Arriva Trains Northern (now Northern), Central Trains and ScotRail (now First ScotRail). Some exchange of units had occurred within owning franchise groups, for example some Central Trains units have been transferred to ONE, both owned by the National Express Group.

The current operators liveries are now carried, although some still retain their previous operators liveries pending repainting.

British Rail Class 156 *Photograph courtesy of Milepost 92½*

Hornby British Rail Class 156

Lima introduced a ready to run OO Gauge model in 1989, and it remained available until 2002. The tools passed to Hornby in 2005, and the model has been reintroduced into their range.

Class 158 Diesel Multiple Unit
British Rail Regional Railways

Introduced:	1990
Allocation:	Regional Railways, for later please see text.
Unit Nos:	158701 - 158872 (2 Car) 158901 - 158910 (2 Car) 158960 - 158976 (3 Car)
Number Built:	165 x 2 Car Units, and 17 x 3 Car Units, built by BREL, Derby.
Duties:	Express Regional Services.
Technical Data:	**Weight:** 38 tons per vehicle **Transmission:** Hydraulic **Engine:** 1 x Cummins NTA855R per vehicle (158701-158814); 1 x Perkins 2006-TWH per vehicle (158815-158862); 1 x Cummins NT855R per vehicle (158863-158872) **Horsepower:** 700 2 Car; 1200 3 Car

British Rail Class 158 *Photograph courtesy of Milepost 92½*

In the 1980s, after Sectorisation took place within British Rail, the Provincial Sector Services were operated either by locomotive hauled trains hauling elderly rolling stock, or by first generation diesel multiple units also nearing the end of their working lives.

Provincial Services later became Regional Railways, and an order was placed with British Rail Engineering Limited at Derby for 182 new 'Sprinter' units, of which 165 were 2 Car Units which could be worked in multiple when required, and the remaining 17 units comprised of 3 Cars. Delivery of the Class 158s allowed the withdrawal of many older coaches (Mark I and early Mark II), ageing diesel locos and first generation diesel multiple units. Unit Nos. 158841-158860 were fitted with Perkins 350 hp engines, whilst the rest of the fleet had Cummins engines fitted.

Introduced between 1989 and 1992, the Class 158s could be seen from Penzance to Wick. Not long after they were introduced, the Privatisation process was starting, and the units were soon sold to leasing companies, in turn finding their way to new operators.

Initially, the units were delivered in Regional Railways Express livery, although unit Nos. 158901-158910 were built for the West Yorkshire Passenger Transport Executive and carried WYPTE red and cream livery.

The 3 car units were generally used on the Trans Pennine Liverpool to Hull/Scarborough or Newcastle, these have now been replaced by the new Class 180s within the past year.

Following Privatisation, the fleet entered service with a number of operators. Virgin Trains inherited a small fleet of 5 Units for use on cross country services between the North West and Glasgow/Edinburgh, but these were withdrawn at the earliest opportunity and replaced by fleets of Classes 220 and 221, so the Class 158s were passed to other operators including Northern Spirit (later Arriva Trains Northern and now Northern), Central Trains, Wessex Trains (now First Great Western), ScotRail (now First ScotRail), Wales & West (later Wales & Borders and now Arriva Trains Wales), South West Trains (for conversion to Class 159/1) and TransPennine Express (operated by First Group). The various operators liveries were carried, and many of these have been reproduced in model form.

Thailand State Railways also purchased a number of units from BREL. These units were built at Derby and exported to Thailand, where they remain in service.

Bachmann British Rail Class 158

Graham Farish introduced a ready to run N Gauge model in 1992, which remained available until 2000 when the company was acquired by Bachmann. It was reintroduced in 2001 and remains available.

Bachmann introduced a ready to run OO Gauge model in 1997, and it remains available.

Class 159 Diesel Multiple Unit
British Rail Network SouthEast

Introduced: 1992

Allocation: British Rail Network SouthEast (South Western Division), later South West Trains.

Unit and Coach Nos: Set Nos. 159001 – 159022

53873 - 52894 DMCL
58718 - 58739 MSL
57873 - 57894 DMSL

Number Built: 22 x 3 Car Units by BREL in Derby and modified by Babcock Rail at Rosyth Dockyard.

Duties: Express Passenger.

Technical Data: **Weight:** 38 tons per vehicle
                                  Transmission: Hydraulic
                                  Engine: 1 x Cummins NTA855R3 per vehicle
                                  Horsepower: 1200 (400 per car)

Upon its formation in 1986, the Network SouthEast sector of British Rail inherited the former London & South Western route between London Waterloo and Exeter. The route had been operated jointly by the Southern and Western Regions, with Laira providing Class 50 locomotives which hauled Mark II coaches. Later, the Class 50 locos were replaced by Class 47 locos which were mostly transferred from Scotland.

Network SouthEast, under Chris Green, was actively replacing ageing rolling stock with new, and the almost forgotten route to the West of England was transformed, and with some imaginative marketing provided considerable passenger growth. Inhibited by infrastructure rationalisation that had been carried out west of Salisbury, there was little that could be done without accelerating services and reworking the timetable.

Regional Railways found that it had over estimated the number of Class 158 units required for its services. Network SouthEast was at the time looking at options for the Waterloo to Exeter route, so as a result, Network SouthEast agreed to take 22 of the Regional Railways order which was then under construction. Due to the contractual specifications, variation orders could not be issued, and the Class were delivered to the Regional Railways specification. Network SouthEast placed its own contract with Babcock Rail for modifications to be made at Rosyth Dockyard. Work included the fitting of toiler retention tanks, buffet area and First Class accommodation. The sets were also painted in Network SouthEast red, blue and grey livery.

To maintain the new fleet, a brand new depot was opened by Network SouthEast on the site of the former Great Western Railway terminus station at Salisbury. This had been located alongside the Southern station, and after closure was retained for goods traffic. Before the depot was constructed, its last role had been to house the British Rail Exhibition trains, which toured the country as mobile exhibition vehicles and were hired by many organisations.

Following Privatisation, the Network SouthEast South Western Division became South West Trains, part of Stagecoach. Since 2000, these units have been repainted into South West Trains livery. On summer Saturdays, trains are extended beyond Exeter to Paignton, Plymouth and Penzance. Trains operate in multiple as 6 or 9 car units, but were normally only 3 car units operating west of Exeter St. Davids when required. South West Trains supplemented the Class 159 fleet with 9 Class 170 units and 2 Class 158 units. The Class 170 units have subsequently been transferred to First TransPennine, and in return, First TransPennines 3 car Class 158 units are being refurbished and modified to Class 159 standard. These will be renumbered as Class 159/1 units. The work on these units is being carried out by Wabtec at Doncaster, and the first units completed reached Salisbury in late 2006.

Graham Farish introduced a ready to run N Gauge model of the Class 159 in 1992, and it remained available until 2000 when the company was acquired by Bachmann. It was reintroduced in 2003 and remains available.

Bachmann also introduced a ready to run OO Gauge model of Class 159 in 1998, and it remains available.

Class 166 Diesel Multiple Unit
British Rail Network South East

Introduced:	1992
Allocation:	Network SouthEast Thames & Chiltern Division, later Thames Trains, First Great Western Link and First Great Western.
Unit and Coach Nos:	Class 166/2 166201 - 166221 58101 - 58121 DMCL 58601 - 58621 MS 58122 - 58142 DMCL
Number Built:	21 x 3 car units, built by ABB York.
Duties:	Express Passenger (Suburban).
Technical Data:	**Weight:** 40 tons DMCL; 38 tons MS **Transmission:** Hydraulic **Engine:** 1 x Perkins 2006-TWH per vehicle **Horsepower:** 1050 (350 per car)

British Rail Class 166 *Photograph courtesy of Milepost 92½*

The Network SouthEast sector of British Rail began replacing its inherited fleet during the late 1980s. The suburban services operating on the non electrified routes out of London Paddington were in the hands of first generation diesel multiple units or loco hauled trains operating on the Oxford line.

The Network SouthEast rolling stock devised the Class 165 units for the then Thames & Chiltern Division, with the units split between the Paddington and Marylebone operations. For the longer distance services to Newbury and Oxford, they specified a similar unit but with air conditioning, more spacious interiors and carpets throughout the train. First Class had 2 plus 2 seating, and Standard Class had 2 plus 3 seating. There were 32 First Class and 243 Standard Class seats in total in the train. With the Class 165s working the higher density services between Reading and Paddington, local branches and the Marylebone to Aylesbury/Banbury routes, the Class 166s were designed to work with them and were operationally compatible, but operating normally on the longer distance services.

After Privatisation, they became part of the Thames Trains fleet operated by the Go Ahead Group. Following the amalgamation of the Great Western and Thames Trains franchises on April 1st 2004 and operated in the interim by First Group, The Class 166s carried First Great Western Link branding over the former Thames Trains logos. When the combined franchise was awarded to First Group on April 1st 2006, the trains became part of First Great Western. Some units now carry First Group corporate livery.

Bachmann British Rail Class 166

Bachmann introduced a ready to run OO Gauge model in 1999, which remains available.

Class 168 'Clubman' Diesel Multiple Unit Chiltern Railways

Introduced:	1997/2000
Allocation:	Chiltern Railways.
Unit Nos:	Class 168/0: 168001 - 168005 Total of 5 x 4 Car Units, built by Adtranz in Derby. Class 168/1: 168106 - 168107 (4 Car) 168108 - 168113 (3 Car) Total of 2 x 4 Car Units and 5 x 3 Car Units, built by Adtranz and Bombardier Transportation in Derby. Class 168/2: 168214 - 168219 Total of 5 x 3 Car Units, built by Bombardier Transportation in Derby.
Duties:	Suburban services.
Technical Data:	**Weight:** 43.7 tons DMSL **Transmission:** Hydraulic **Engine:** 1 x MTU 6R183TD13H per vehicle **Horsepower:** 1688 per 4 Car Set

Chiltern Railways Class 168 *Photograph courtesy of Milepost 92½*

The former Great Central route out of London Marylebone had been victim of the Beeching cuts in the 1960s and most of the route was closed. Passenger services remained between Marylebone and Aylesbury, and between Marylebone and Banbury via High Wycombe. Threatened again with rationalisation in the 1980s, and with the closure of its Marylebone terminus, the route survived and underwent a total route modernisation scheme under Network SouthEast with new track, signalling, depot and trains.

By Privatisation, the Chiltern route had been turned around from a closure candidate to the best London suburban route. Chiltern Railways was formed from a management buyout and continued the good work. Unprecedented growth and extension of services to Birmingham Snow Hill, Kidderminster and Stratford-upon-Avon demanded the building of additional trains, of which the Class 168 was the result.

Built in three batches, the first 5 units (Class 168/0) followed the Networker Turbo design (Class 165). The units were built at Derby during 1997/1998 and were the first new vehicles to be ordered post Privatisation, bringing much needed relief to the rail workshops who had not received an order since the process began in 1994.

For the next deliveries, the Turbostar (see Classes 170 and 171) design was adopted. By 2001, Adtranz had been taken over by Bombardier Transportation, and it was this company that delivered the units between 2001 and 2004.

Bachmann Chiltern Railways Class 168

The Class 168 units are fitted with Automatic Train Protection (ATP), and can only be coupled to Class 165 and 166 units due to the electrical connections formed through the couplers.

The units work between London Marylebone, Banbury, Birmingham Snow Hill, Stratford-upon-Avon and Kidderminster. The units carry Chiltern Railways livery.

Chiltern Railways was awarded a 20 year franchise extension in 2002. In addition to building new trains, it has invested considerably in infrastructure including the redoubling of the former Great Western/Great Central joint line north of Princes Risborough. The Class 168 units look set to continue for many years to come.

Bachmann introduced a ready to run OO Gauge model in 2003, and it remains available.

Class 170 Diesel Multiple Unit
Adtranz/Bombardier Transportation

Introduced:	1998
Allocation:	Anglia Railways (later ONE), Central Trains, First TransPennine, Midland Main Line, ScotRail (later First ScotRail), Hull Trains, South West Trains and Porterbrook Leasing.
Unit Nos:	Class 170/1: 170101 - 170117, 2 Car Units. Note that 170101 - 170110 were originally delivered as 2 Car Units before an additional vehicle was added in 2001.
	Class 170/2: 170201 - 170208, 3 Car Units. 170270 - 170273, 2 Car Units.
	Class 170/3: 170301 - 170308, 2 Car Units. 170392 - 170396, 2 Car Units. 170397 - 170398*, 3 Car Units. 170399*, 2 Car Units. * Denotes former Porterbrook demonstration units.
	Class 170/4: 170401 - 170424, 3 Car Units. 170425 - 170434, 3 Car Units. 170450 - 170461, 3 Car Units. 170470 - 170478, 3 Car Units.
	Class 170/5: 170501 - 170523, 2 Car Units.
	Class 170/6: 170530 - 170639, 3 Car Units.
	2 and 3 Car Units, built by Adtranz (later Bombardier Transportation) in Derby.

Duties: Express Passenger

Technical Data: **Weight:** 45 tons DMS; 44 tons DMC
                                     Transmission: Hydraulic
                                     Engine: MTU 6R183TD13H
                                     Horsepower: 422 per vehicle

The Privatisation process brought a stop to the procurement process for new trains. Following the passing of the 1993 Transport Act, the shadow companies could not order new stock, and the stock they owned and operated on 31st March 1994 passed to three new train leasing companies the following day.

Once the new operators had taken over the franchises, they were in a position to evaluate the rolling stock agreements, and so planned to remove old rolling stock and replace it with new to be provided by one of the leasing companies. The Class 170 was one of the new generation of diesel multiple units which met the post Privatisation criteria.

The Class 170 was developed by the former British Rail workshops in Derby, which by then was owned by Adtranz. This company was subsequently taken over by Bombardier Transportation in 2001.

The Class 170 units are known as 'Turbostars', and the first units were ordered by Midland Main Line to supplement HST services by running semi-fast trains between London St. Pancras and Leicester/Nottingham/Derby. The first units entered service in 1998, and for a period they were also used on services to York and Scarborough running on summer Saturdays only. The arrival of Class 222 'Meridian' units from 2004 resulted in the Midland Main Line units being transferred to another National Express franchise, Central Trains.

Two 3 Car Units (Nos. 170397 and 170398) and one 2 Car Unit were supplied in Porterbrook livery as demonstrators and were used on Central Trains, Midland Main Line and ScotRail in an effort to secure orders. Both were later absorbed into the Central Trains fleet.

Adtranz/Bombardier Transportation Class 170 *Photograph courtesy of Milepost 92½*

Anglia Railways was next to procure Class 170 units, taking delivery initially of eight 3 Car Units in 1999. When Anglia introduced a new Norwich to Cambridge direct service in 2002, it ordered four 2 Car Units specifically for this service. Following the award of the Anglia Railways franchise to National Express operator ONE in 2004, the Class have been repainted from Anglia livery and most now carry ONE livery. Four trains were initially leased to Hull Trains, in which Anglia had an interest, and these were used on open access services between London Kings Cross and Hull (see Hull Trains below).

Also in 1999, National Express operator Central Trains received a batch of 23 x 2 Car Units and 10 x 3 Car Units for use on services around the Midlands. In 2004, Central Trains also took over the three former Porterbrook demonstrator vehicles, which had also been used for spot hire. These three had initially carried a distinctive white and purple Porterbrook livery. The Central Trains fleet was further strengthened with the arrival of the 17 units from Midland Main Line, displaced by the new Class 222 'Meridian' units from Bombardier Transportation. The three former Porterbrook and the former Midland Main Line units initially had First Class accommodation, but as Central Trains does not provide First Class travel, all 20 units have had this accommodation declassified. The Central Trains units operate on non electrified services around Birmingham, Cardiff, Leicester, Norwich, Nottingham, Shrewsbury and Stansted Airport.

Open Access operator Hull Trains initially hired four units from sister company Anglia Railways. Hull Trains had four of its own 3 Car Units on order from Bombardier, and these were duly delivered during 2004 allowing the Anglia units to be returned to Norwich. First Group took over Hull Trains in 2005 and replaced the Class 170s with Class 222 'Pioneer' units (see Class 222), allowing the Class 170 units to be transferred to another First Group franchise, First ScotRail.

ScotRail took delivery of its first Class 170 units in 1999 when it was operated by National Express. In Scotland, the Class 170s operate between Edinburgh and Glasgow, and between the cities of Aberdeen and Inverness. They also work some local services around Edinburgh, including services to and from Fife. Originally the units were delivered in ScotRail 'Swoosh' livery, but this is now being replaced with the First Group corporate colours. Four additional sets have since been acquired from Hull Trains.

South West Trains, owned by Stagecoach, acquired eight 2 Car Units to supplement the Class 159 fleet for operating services between London Waterloo, Salisbury and Exeter. Following the delivery of some Class 158 units from elsewhere to South West Trains for upgrading to Class 159, the South West Trains units are now being transferred to First TransPennine Express. The units which carried the distinctive South West Trains livery are now being repainted in First Group corporate colours.

With 138 units in service with various operators, these units look set to be part of the railway scene for many years to come.

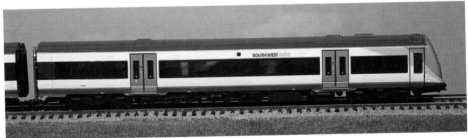

Bachmann Adtranz/Bombardier Transportation Class 170

Bachmann introduced a ready to run OO Gauge model in 2001, and it remains available.

Graham Farish introduced a ready to run N Gauge model in 2004, and it remains in their catalogue.

Class 171 Diesel Multiple Unit
Bombardier Transportation

Introduced:	2003
Allocation:	Southern Railway.
unit Nos:	Class 171/7 (2 Car Units): 170721 - 170726, later 171721 - 171726. 170727 - 170729, delivered as 171727 - 171729 (3 additional units) Class 171/8 (4 Car Units): 170731 - 170736, delivered as 171801 - 171806.
Number Built:	9 x 2 Car Units and 6 x 4 Car Units, built by Bombardier Transportation at Derby.
Duties:	Suburban Passenger.
Technical Data:	**Weight:** 45 tons per vehicle **Transmission:** Hydraulic **Engine:** 1 x MTU 6R 183TD per vehicle **Horsepower:** 844 for 2 Car Units; 1688 for 4 Car Units (422 per vehicle)

When the Strategic Rail Authority (SRA) abandoned its plans to electrify the Ashford to Hastings and Hurst Green to Uckfield routes in August 2002, it placed an order for 36 Class 170 units to replace its ageing Class 205/207 diesel units. The units are owned and funded by Porterbrook Leasing.

The Strategic Rail Authority's involvement had been forced by the poor performance of Connex, the French owned company that had been awarded both the South Eastern and South Central franchises. The South Central franchise was awarded for 7 years and commenced on 26th May 1996, and operated as Connex SouthCentral. On 24th October 2000, the SRA decided to terminate the Connex franchise on its expiry, and to award the new 20 year franchise to GoVia to take effect from May 2003. GoVias new franchise would operate as Southern, and trains would carry a two tone green livery.

On 29th May 2001, GoVia exchanged contracts with Connex to buy out the remaining 2 years of its franchise and completed the purchase on 26th August of that year, taking over operations from Connex.

The following year, the SRA abandoned its electrification plans for the only two non-electrified routes remaining in the former South Eastern and South Central divisions of the Southern Region. Following a change of plans, the SRA replaced the proposed 20 year franchise with a 6 year 7 months one. When the deal with GoVia was finalised in May 2003, the order for diesel units was increased by 3 x 2 car units.

The first unit was handed over to South Central by Bombardier Transportation at Derby Works on 9th July 2003. It was delivered on 6th August to Selhurst Depot and undertook test running on the Uckfield line. The new units entered service on 8th December.

Southern decided to have the six 4 car and the additional three 2 car units fitted with Dellner couplings in place of the BSI couplers. This made them compatible with the Class 377 electric multiple units, and they would be delivered with these fitted. It was also decided to retrospectively fit the six 2 car units with the same couplings. This resulted in the units being reclassified Class 171.

The Ashford to Hastings line went over to Class 171 operation on 10th May 2004. The first 4 car unit was exhibited at the 'Railfest' event at the National Railway Museum in York between 29th May and 6th June 2004. The remaining units were all delivered by the autumn, and the original 2 car units retro fitted with Dellner couplings. The additional three units were delivered to Southern in May 2005.

During the morning and evening peak, the Uckfield line services are extended to London Bridge. Outside the peak hour services, the Uckfield line service operates to and from Oxted.

The Class 171 units were delivered in Southern livery.

Bachmann Bombardier Transportation Class 171

Bachmann have produced Limited Edition OO Gauge models of the Class 171 units for ModelZone.

Class 220 Voyager
Virgin Trains

Introduced:	2001
Allocation:	Virgin Cross Country.
Locomotive Nos:	220001 - 220034
Number Built:	34
Duties:	Express Passenger.
Technical Data:	**Transmission:** Electric **Engine:** Cummins QSK1 **Horsepower:** 750 per vehicle

In December 1998, Virgin Trains placed an order with Bombardier Transportation for 78 new trains, of which 34 would be non tilt Voyagers and 44 tilting Super Voyagers. The order was worth £1.06 billion and included not just the purchase of the trains, but the maintenance of them until the end of the Cross Country franchise in 2007.

Virgin Trains Class 220 Voyager *Photograph courtesy of Milepost 92½*

They were designed at Bombardier's Bruges factory in Belgium, who also built the body shells. The Bombardier works in Crespin, France built the bogies. Final assembly, in many cases, was carried out at Wakefield where Bombardier purchased the former Procor wagon works as an initial British base, and commenced work converting it into a home for building passenger cars.

Using Computer Aided Design (CAD) to develop initially the concepts, and later the detail design drawings, these trains have been built to the highest possible engineering standards. From the onset, Bombardier took the project seriously and avoided many of the pitfalls that other new train builds had encountered in the post-privatisation railways in Britain.

Virgin became renowned for their high profile publicity launches, and on 6 December 2000 a large number of journalists and guests found themselves celebrating St Nicholas Day in Bruges. The event saw Sir Richard Branson and Stagecoach's Brian Souter receive an early Christmas present in the form of the first Voyager unit which was named Maiden Voyager. Bombardier had successfully tested the train over the previous two months on SNCB (Belgian National Railways) and took the whole assembly on a high speed run from Brugge to Ostend and back.

Such was the success of the train that it quickly cleared all the hurdles to secure a Railtrack safety case and was able to enter service just a few months later on 21 May 2001 between Birmingham and Reading via Oxford. They were soon extended to other routes as more trains were delivered at the rate of one per week. The last of the 34 trains was handed over to Virgin Trains by Bombardier at a ceremony at Wakefield on 13 December 2001, and after final testing and acceptance entered service early in February.

The Voyagers (Class 220) comprise 4 vehicles, each car with a 750hp Cummins QSK1 diesel engine. More cars can be added as demand requires it. A 4 car unit, therefore has 3000 hp of power, which compares very favourably with an express diesel locomotive, although the performance is enhanced by the power being spread down the length of the train and not just in the front! This enhances reliability and gives greater operating flexibility, as should a fault occur, individual engines can be shut down and the train still get home at line speed! In today's modern railway, where every minute of delay carries financial penalties, this is a very desirable attribute and it was responsible for much improved performance statistics.

Each of the 34 units has been named and proudly carries a distinctive red painted cast nameplate, manufactured to the same high standards by Newton Replicas as those from the days of steam.

Inside the train there is everything that the passenger could wish for. The First Class vehicle has its own catering facilities. For Standard Class passengers there is a self service shop from which magazines, books, drinks and snacks can be purchased. There are headphone sockets offering a range of on-board entertainment, laptop and mobile phone charging facilities through a three pin socket. Electronic seat reservations and information systems compliment this state of the art train. There are bike racks in the luggage area to cater for up to 4 bicycles per journey. Each 4 car unit encompasses 26 Club Class and 162 Standard Class seats.

The trains can already be seen at work on the extensive Cross Country network which stretches from Aberdeen to Penzance, and from the South Coast to Glasgow and Edinburgh. In July 2007, it was announced that the Cross Country franchise would be operated by Arriva Trains from the 11th November. A new livery is proposed.

Bachmann Virgin Trains Class 220 Voyager

Bachmann introduced a ready to run OO Gauge model in 2002.

Class 221 Super Voyager
Virgin Trains

Introduced:	2001
Allocation:	Virgin Cross Country.
Locomotive Nos:	221101 - 221144
Number Built:	44
Duties:	Express Passenger.
Technical Data:	**Transmission:** Electric **Engine:** Cummins QSK1 **Horsepower:** 750 per car

In addition to the 34 Class 220 non-tilt 4 car Voyager trains, Virgin Trains ordered a further 44 Class 221 tilting units which, at first glance, are identical.

Whilst they utilise the same body shells, they have completely redesigned bogies incorporating tilting equipment to enable the train to tilt. These are heavier than those fitted to the Class 220s, increasing the weight of each vehicle by 7 tonnes. Tilt provides an ideal solution to high speed operation over the curving West Coast Main Line, allowing Cross Country trains to operate at the same speed as the electric Pendolino fleet.

Virgin Trains Class 221 Super Voyager *Photograph courtesy of Colour Rail*

Each vehicle is powered by a QSK1 750 hp engine supplied by Cummins, giving an impressive 3,750 hp for a 5-car train and 3,000 hp for a 4-car unit.

Forty 5-car and four 4-car Super Voyagers were constructed by Bombardier Transportation for Virgin Trains. All body shells were built at Bruges, whilst Bruges and Wakefield shared responsibility for construction of the complete trains. The interior design and the on-board facilities are identical to the earlier class with the 5-car train having 250 seats (26 in First Class), and the 4-car trains having 188 seats (26 in First Class), the same as the Voyager trains.

Extensive testing was carried out both in Belgium and later in France, initially on the high speed TGV line to Le Mans and later on the curving SNCF route between Brive and Cahors. No.221101 was named 'Louis Bleriot' on 2 February 2002 at Cahors at a ceremony attended by members of the railway press.

The trains tilt is actuated by interface between track mounted balises and on board computer equipment. These tell the train how much it can tilt on each section of track. This is necessary in the UK due to the restrictive loading gauge - the other countries operating tilting trains have infrastructure built to the continental loading gauge allowing unrestricted tilting. Safety requirements in Britain stipulate that tilting trains have their neutral default position tilt locked, with the command for active tilt confirmed around every two miles or so by the positioning of balises between the rails. Further safety requirements demand that a speed supervision system is incorporated to prevent the train from taking curves above the maximum permitted speed.

The resulting TASS (Tilt Authorisation and Speed Supervision) system enables the computers on board the trains to receive messages from the balises between the rails. The computer reads three balises in advance and instructs the train how much it can tilt (up to 6 degrees maximum) and on its maximum speed. The balise also tells the train to stop tilting if approaching a tunnel or other structure with tight clearances, where civil engineers have been unable to enhance clearance. Tilt is automatically dis-enabled and the train reverts to non-tilt mode to operate in the same way as the non-tilting Voyagers. Once past the obstruction (of which in reality there are very few - due to extensive route modernisation), the trains computer searches for the next balise to restore tilt mode.

All 44 trains are named after famous explorers and voyagers in fact or fiction. Each train is fitted with an internal plaque above the payphone near the on board shop. This gives a brief biographical details of the person after whom the train is named. Externally the train carries a cast nameplate with 'Super Voyager' cast as an integral part of the nameplate. The background colour is blue to assist identification between the two train types, which can work together in non-tilt mode (Class 220 + Class 221). No.221130 was named 'Michael Palin' by the actor, broadcaster and super voyager himself at a ceremony held at Sheffield Station on 28 August 2002. This was followed by a press run over the Settle & Carlisle line to Carlisle.

The Class 221 Super Voyagers work alongside the earlier non tilt Voyagers (Class 220) on the Cross Country network between Aberdeen and Penzance and Brighton/Bournemouth to Glasgow/Edinburgh.

On the 10th July 2007, it was announced that the Cross Country franchise would be operated by Arriva Trains from the 11th November. Some units will be transferred to Virgin West Coast services, whilst some will be transferred to Arriva Trains. A new livery is proposed.

Bachmann introduced a ready to run OO Gauge model in 2003.

Class 222 Diesel Multiple Unit
Bombardier Transportation

Introduced: Meridians 2004; Pioneers 2005.

Allocation: Meridians on Midland Main Line, Pioneers on Hull Trains.

Unit Nos: Midland Main Line (Total of 23 units):

                         222001 - 222007, originally 9 car units, now 8 car units.

                         222008 - 222010, 4 car units.

                         222011 - 222017, originally 4 car units, now 5 car units.

                         222018 - 222023, 4 car units.

                         Hull Trains (Total of 4 units):

                         222101 - 222104, 4 car units.

Duties: Passenger.

Technical Data: **Transmission:**   Electric
                         Engine: Cummins QSK9R per car.
                         Horsepower: 750 per car

Following on from the successful delivery of the Class 220 Voyager and Class 221 Super Voyager fleets for Virgin Trains, Bombardier Transportation succeeded in winning further orders for units utilising the Voyager technology.

Midland Main Line did not, however, require a tilt capability, and decided to make full use of the non tilt British loading gauge. Midland Main Line ordered 16 x 4 car units and 7 x 9 car units. The Meridians, although a development of the earlier Voyager units, differ considerably internally due to the more generous allowances of the standard loading gauge, rather than the tilt version. The front end was restyled as Virgin retained the design rights to the Class 220/1 cabs. The first 4 car units entered service in 2004, with the 9 car units having been stored initially due to the cancellation of the Leeds to London St. Pancras services by the then Strategic Rail Authority. They eventually entered service as 8 car units, with the additional vehicles being used to be reconfigured into other units. The Midland Main Line fleet currently comprises of 7 x 8 car units, 7 x 5 car units and 9 x 4 car units.

Bombardier Transportation Class 222 *Photograph courtesy of Colour Rail*

A further order was secured for Hull Trains, whose 4 x 4 car Class 222 units are known as Pioneers. These entered service in mid 2005 and operated between Londons Kings Cross and Hull Paragon seven times every weekday in each direction. They differ slightly from the Midland Main Line Meridians internally. At present, one unit is out of service following accident damage sustained during a works visit.

Graham Farish are to produce an N Gauge version of both types.

Class 251 Blue Pullman Diesel Multiple Unit
British Railways

Introduced:	1959
Allocation:	British Railways London Midland and Western Regions.
Coach Nos:	Midland Pullman: 60090 + 60730 + 60740 + 60741 + 60731 + 60091 60092 + 60732 + 60742 + 60743 + 60733 + 60093 Formation of numbers DMBF, MFK, TF, TF, MFK, DMBF Western Pullman: 60094 + 60644 + 60734 + 60744 + 60745 + 60735 + 60645 + 60095 60096 + 60646 + 60736 + 60746 + 60747 + 60737 + 60647 + 60097 60098 + 60648 + 60738 + 60748 + 60749 + 60739 + 60649 + 60099 Formation of numbers DMBS, MS, TFK, TF, TF, TFK, MS, DMBS
Last of Class Withdrawn:	1973
Duties:	Express Passenger.
Technical Data:	**Weight:** 67 tons 10 cwt DMBF **Transmission:** Electric **Engine:** 1 x North British/MAN 1000 bhp V Type L12V18/2185 to each power car

British Railways Class 251 *Photograph courtesy of Colour Rail*

The London Midland Region operated 2 x 6 car units on its prestigious Pullman service between Manchester Central and London St Pancras using the the the Midland Main Line from 1959. The formation of the all First Class train comprised of a Driving Motor Brake First, Motor Kitchen First, 2 x Trailer Parlour First, Motor Kitchen First and Driving Motor Brake First. A total of 132 passengers could be seated in the luxurious accommodation which was aimed at the business market, the trains operating in both directions during the morning and evening peaks. They were the first trains to be fitted with air conditioning, double glazed windows and high levels of comfort. Performance was generally good, but the Swiss designed bogies gave a rough ride on occasions.

In 1960, the Western Region introduced 3 x 8 car units, which were operated on services from London Paddington to Birmingham, Bristol and South Wales. Each set comprised of a Driving Motor Brake Second, Motor Parlour Second, Trailer Kitchen First, 2 x Trailer Parlour First, Trailer Kitchen First, Motor Parlour Second and Driving Motor Brake Second. The Western Region sets could accommodate 108 First Class and 120 Second Class passengers.

Although these prestigious trains were popular with customers, they fell victim to modernisation of other routes. Electrification of the West Coast Main Line saw the London to Manchester services concentrated on the London Euston to Manchester Piccadilly corridor and the Birmingham services on to the Euston to Birmingham New Street route. The two units previously used out of St Pancras were put into storage in 1966, and the spare unit from the Western Region's Birmingham service was used as a spare for the Bristol and South Wales services.

In 1968, the former London Midland Region sets were converted for multiple working and some seats were reclassified to Second Class. These were used on the morning up service from Bristol Temple Meads to London Paddington. At Paddington the units were split and then operated a return trip separately to Oxford and Bristol, before reforming at Paddington for the down evening service to Bristol.

Tri-ang Hornby British Railways Class 251

Following the introduction of TOPS numbering, the Blue Pullmans were designated Class 251. They were not to remain in service much longer, and all were withdrawn in 1973.

The high speed multiple units had proved their operational worth and many lessons learned would be incorporated in the future High Speed Train fleet.

On delivery the units carried a very distinctive nanking blue and white livery. In 1968 this livery was replaced with the corporate British Rail blue and grey livery which was reversed for use on Pullman trains, the grey becoming the dominating colour.

> Tri-ang introduced a ready to run OO Gauge model in 1963. It passed to Tri-ang Hornby in 1965 and remained in the catalogue until 1972.

Class 252/253/254 Inter City 125 High Speed Train British Rail

Introduced:	1972
Allocation:	Western, Eastern and Scottish Regions. For post Privatisation please see text.
Set Nos:	Prototype: 252.001 - Formation: DMB 2TF TRUK 2TS TRSB 2TS DMB

Western Region:
253.001 - 253.017 - Formation: DMB 2TF TRSB 4TS DMB
253.018 - 253.027 - Formation: DMB 2TF TRUB 4TS DMB
253.028 - 253.041 - Formation: DMB 2TF TRUB 4TS DMB

Eastern Region:
254.001 - 254.015 - Formation: DMB 2TF TRUK 2TS TRSB 2TS DMB

Scottish Region:
254.016 - 254.020 - Formation: DMB 2TF TRUK 2TS TRSB 2TS DMB

Eastern Region:
254.021 - 254.032 - Formation: DMB 2TF TRUB 5TS DMB

DMB	Driving Motor Brake Nos. 43002-43198
TF	Trailer First Nos. 41003-41176
TRSB	Trailer Buffet Nos. 40401-40403 and 40414-40437
TRUB	Trailer Unclassified Buffet Nos. 40301-40327, 40331, 40332, 40355 and 40357.
TRFK	Trailer Kitchen First Nos. 40501, 40505, 40511 and 40513.
TRFM	Trailer Module Buffet First No.40619
TRBF	Trailer Buffet First Nos. 40700-40721, 40728-40730, 40733-40754 and 40756
TGS	Trailer Guard Standard Nos. 44000-44101
TS	Trailer Second Nos. 42003-42345

Power Cars built by B.R.E.L. in Crewe.
Coaching Vehicles built by B.R.E.L. in Derby.

Number Built:	96 Units
Duties:	High Speed Passenger services.
Technical Data:	**Weight:** 66 tons (power car) **Transmission:** Electrical **Engine:** Paxman Valenta 12 Cylinder 12RP V Type of 2250 bhp (1680 kw) per power car **Horsepower:** 2,250

British Rail Class 252/253/254 *Photograph courtesy of Milepost 92½*

Following successful trials with the prototype High Speed Train Set No.252.001 from its introduction in 1972, production versions were commenced in 1976 and the trains entered 'squadron' service on the Western Region in May 1977, with further diagrams introduced in October 1977.

These were initially used on the Paddington to South Wales or Bristol services, which includes through workings to Carmarthen, Taunton or Weston-super-Mare.

All Western Region sets (Series 253) consist of two power cars and seven trailer cars (as listed).

The next sets to be delivered were for the Eastern and Scottish Regions (Series 254), which consist of two power cars and nine trailers (as listed), and were put to work on the Kings Cross to Edinburgh/Aberdeen and Kings Cross to Leeds/Bradford services.

These very characteristic train sets have been a success wherever they have been introduced, due to their ability to run consistently at 125 mph. They are only restricted below this speed for temporary or permanent line speed restrictions; increased passenger loadings are causing overcrowding on some of these set formation trains.

On the Kings Cross to Edinburgh run, the H.S.T.'s took over the working from the Deltic diesels, and reduced the running time by some 45 minutes. Further sets were ordered for the important N.E./S.W. route. Other sets work the former Midland main line to and from St. Pancras.
The coaches used are standard B.R. MK III profile, although no buffing gear is carried, and they have special wiring for the through control gear. Special MK II coaches were branded as H.S.T. barrier vehicles for working the coaches to Derby Works for overhaul and maintenance.

311

New trailer second vehicles were built, which include a guards compartment in place of the end door, toilet and one bay of seating (following complaints of noise and rough riding in the small guards compartment), which also gave additional luggage space.

One alteration which has taken place, is the positioning of a smoke deflector about two inches above the top of the exhaust portion of the power car. This prevents downdraught from the exhaust in the trailing direction, covering the drivers windscreen with oily deposits which are difficult to remove. Power car Nos. 43014 and 43123 have had buffing and standard draw gear added, for use on the East Coast route for initial running with Class 91 locos before DVTs were delivered.

The prototype H.S.T. (No.252.001) which set a world record of 143 mph for diesel trains in June 1972, differed in several ways from the production series, having buffing gear and double vertical windows with central driving position, whilst the production series have single front screen and small trapezoidal windows in front of the cab door, and side-by-side seating for driver and second man. Prototype livery was overall grey with a blue band slightly deeper than the windows (running almost between the power car cab doors), and a full yellow panel. This unit has been withdrawn, the power cars having been used for part of the A.P.T. Programme which is also now defunct.

Following Privatisation, HSTs were split between Virgin, GNER, Midland Main Line and Great Western (now First Great Western). All Virgin units were withdrawn between 2002 and 2003, and some were transferred to other companies. Some have been stored, and some will be refurbished for use by Grand Central (due to commence operations in late 2007) between Sunderland and Londons Kings Cross.

Production series originally carried standard B.R. blue/grey livery with black roofs and underframe/bogies. Power cars have a very distinctive yellow skirt and front roof, with the blue band carried around slightly deeper than the drivers window, the remainder of the roof, underframe and bogies being black. Subsequently, the Inter City livery has been applied with swallow insignia added to the power cars. Most of these have also been named after a variety of subjects. Some units have been further refurbished for use as Pullman trains, viz 'The Master Cutler', 'Tees Tyne Pullman' and 'Golden Hind' amongst others with additional first class accommodation. Power Cars 43013, 43014 and 43062 (any two at one time) are used on the Network Rail Measurement Train and carry yellow livery.

Post Privatisation, a number of different liveries have been carried. Great Western, Midland Main Line and GNER have changed liveries at least once since 1994. GNER have had to have red doors painted to conform with the Disability Discrimination Act, otherwise the livery remains unchanged.

Further livery changes will occur in late 2007 when franchises see the fleet transferred to Arriva Trains, Cross Country, East Midlands (Stagecoach) and when East Coast National Express replace GNER.

Hornby British Rail Class 252/253/254

Hornby introduced a ready to run OO gauge model in 1977. It remains available.

Lima introduced their OO gauge ready to run version in 1982 which remained available until 2002. In 2005 the tools passed to Hornby, but it is unlikely to be reintroduced as Hornby already have the HST in their range.

Graham Farish introduced a ready to run N gauge model in 1981 which remained available until 2000 when the company were taken over by Bachmann. An upgraded model was introduced in 2007.

Class 73 Bo Bo Electro Diesel Locomotives
British Railways

Introduced:	1962 Class 73/0, 1965 Class 73/1.
Allocation:	Southern Region, later Gatwick Express, EWS, Eurostar, Merseyrail, FM Rail, GBrF, Railtrack, Network Rail and South West Trains.
Locomotive Nos:	E6001 - E6006, Type JA, built at Eastleigh. Re-numbered 73001 - 73006.
	E6007 - E6049, Type JB built by English Electric at Vulcan Foundry. Re-numbered 73101 - 73142* +.
	* E6027 was not re-numbered due to being withdrawn in 1972 after a collision.
	+ 12 locomotives used by the Inter City Sector have been taken from the Class 73/1 locos above and re-numbered in the series 73201-73212. As a result, Class 73/1 numbers no longer run consecutively.
Number Built:	49
Preserved Examples:	E6001 (73001) E6002 (73002) E6003 (73003) Sir Herbert Walker E6005 (73005) E6006 (73006) E6007 (73101) The Royal Alex E6016 (73110) E6022 (73116 & 73210) E6023 (73117) E6025 (73119) Kentish Mercury E6035 (73128) OVS Bullied CBE E6036 (73129) City of Winchester E6040 (73133) The Bluebell Railway E6043 (73136) Perserverance E6045 (73138) Post Haste E6047 (73140) E6019 (73113 & 73211) Used for spares
Duties:	Mixed Traffic.

Technical Data:

Tractive Effort:

Class	Electric Mode	Diesel Mode
73/0	42,000 lb	34,100 lb
73/1	40,000 lb	36,000 lb

Loco Weight: Class 73/0 76 tons; Class 73/1 77 tons.
Transmission: Electric
Engine: English Electric 4SRKT
Horsepower: 1600 Electric; 600 Diesel

British Railways Class 73 *Photograph courtesy of Milepost 92½*

The Class 73 (or ED for Electro Diesel as it was better known), was the most successful of Southern Regions locos in recent times. The ED's could perform on full power over the S.R. third rail electrified network, or on reduced power using diesel traction away from it. Since their introduction, the pockets of non-electrified track have been reduced, and there were only small sections (mostly freight and cross country routes) which were not electrified. They are, however, useful locomotives for the operating department, and did away with loco changes when leaving electrified lines.

The first six locomotives were built at Eastleigh and were of the JA Type (now designated Class 73/0). The remaining 43 locos were built by English Electric during the period from 1965 to 1967, and were known as the JB Type (classified Class 73/1 but some were reclassified 73/2, see above). Whilst there were differences inside the bodyshell, there were only small differences externally, the most notable being the positioning of grill panels and small windows on the bodysides. There were also minor details on the cabs, as the Class 73/1's had chequered kick plates at the top of the steps by the drivers doors, and had less cables fitted to the front/rear panels under the main windows.

The Class 73's were extremely versatile locomotives, and could be seen on a wide variety of duties ranging from freight, parcels and engineering trains to passenger trains. They could work in conjunction with both electrical multiple units or loco hauled coaching stock, and also in tandem with Class 33/1 diesel electric locos. They were used extensively around the Channel Ports, and from depots which have non-electrified lines in the vicinity.

Since the inauguration of 'Gatwick Express' services on May 10th 1984, they were used on the dedicated airport service, which was launched using Mk II coaches and a DVT (Driving Vehicle Trailing) modified from redundant HAP stock. To coincide with the launch, No.73123 was painted in the then new Executive (now Inter City) livery, and was one of the first locos to be so painted. Twelve locos were dedicated to the service, and were used solely for this and other Inter City duties on the Southern Region, including renting of the privately owned Venice-Simplon Orient Express (VSOE) operations. The Class were also employed on other push/pull operations, including Bournemouth line services prior to delivery of Class 442 'Wessex Electric' services.

Following Privatisation, The Gatwick Express services became pat of the National Express Group, and the Class were replaced between 2001 and 2005 by Class 460 electric multiple units which were built specially for this traffic.

EuroStar had two locomotives (Nos. 73118 and 73130) fitted with Scharfenberg couplings to allow them to rescue EuroStar units if the need arose.

English, Welsh & Scottish Railway (EWS) inherited a number of Class 73 locos, but these have now all been withdrawn and sold to other operators, or were sold for preservation. FM Rail purchased a number of redundant EWS locos, but following the recent closure of FM Rail, their long term future is unsure.

Merseyrail, at one time, had four Class 73/0 locomotives based at Birkenhead North for departmental work. All four were sold for preservation following withdrawal in 2002.

Freight operator GBrF (GB Railfreight) purchased six former Gatwick Express locomotives for use on freight trains, four of them being overhauled and returned to traffic at FM Rail in Derby.

Network Rail inherited two locomotives from Railtrack, and have subsequently acquired a third.

South West Trains have three locomotives for use as standy 'Thunderbirds'. These are placed at strategic locations should the need arise to rescue failed trains.

As the locomotives are withdrawn, many enter preservation and are popular with Heritage Railways.

On entering service, the Class 73/0 locomotives were delivered in green livery. It should be noted that this was not the standard diesel green livery, but S.R. loco green as more commonly applied to steam locos. A light green band ran along the bottom panel. The first of the Class 73/1 locos were delivered in the light electric blue livery, often referred to as XP64 Experimental 1964 Livery, but once the corporate livery had been established (the darker rail blue), the remainder were delivered in that livery. All locos not so treated were subsequently repainted to conform. Although variations appeared in the size of B.R. double arrow logo carried, the locos remained in overall blue until the arrival of the Executive livery in 1984, and many of the Class acquired this livery. Some of the Class have appeared in an allover blue livery, but the blue used appears to be the Network South East shade, presumably because it is readily available at S.R. depots. One locomotive (No.73101) was painted in Pullman Car livery for use on VSOE (Orient Express) duties.

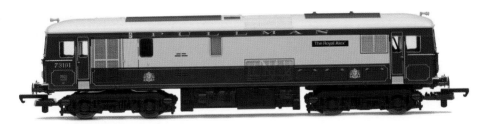

Hornby British Railways Class 73

Lima introduced a ready to run OO gauge model in 1986. It remained available until 2000. In 2005 the tools passed to Hornby who have reintroduced the model into their range.

Dapol introduced a ready to run N gauge model in 2004. It remains available.

Class EM2 (Later Class 77) Co-Co
British Railways

Introduced:	1953
Allocation:	British Railways Eastern and London Midland Regions. They were then sold to Netherlands State Railways in 1969 where they survived until 1986.
Locomotive Nos:	27000 - 27006

N.B.: 27005 was broken up for spares when sold to the Netherlands State Railways.

As they entered traffic for Netherlands State Railways in 1970/1971, they were renumbered as follows:
27000 became 1502
27001 became 1505
27002 became 1506
27003 became 1501
27004 became 1503
27006 became 1504

N.B.: Became Class 77 as withdrawn, and they were never renumbered in the series.

Number Built:	7
Preserved Examples:	1502 1505 returned to BR as No.27000
Technical Data:	**Tractive Effort:** 45,000 lb **Loco Weight:** 102 tons 10 cwt **Transmission:** Electric **Horsepower:** 2,490 **Power Source:** 1500 V DC Overhead Lines

British Railways Class EM2 (Later Class 77) *Photograph courtesy of Colour Rail*

Under the Manchester, Sheffield & Wath Electrification scheme announced in 1936, provision was made for 9 express passenger locomotives. Due to the Second World War, the programme was shelved, apart from building one EM1 loco (later Class 76), No.6701. However, following Nationalisation, British Railways ordered 27 locos in 1949, and these were to be numbered 27000-27026. As with the Class EM1, these new Class EM2s were to be constructed at Gorton, electrical equipment was by Metropolitan Vickers and installed at Duckinfield. The locos were to be a stretched EM1 with 6 motors to two bogies, similar to those fitted to the LMS prototype main line diesel electrics (Nos. 10000 and 10001), which were introduced in 1947. Unlike the Class EM1s, the buffers and drawgear was fitted to the body shell rather than the bogies. However, the order was cut back to just 7 locos in November 1950, as justification for 27 locos on a line only 41½ miles long was hard to prove, and a great deal of equipment was scrapped.

During 1959 to 1961 the locomotives received names of mythological Greek Goddesses. With the cut back of services prior to the closure of the MSW route to passenger traffic, the locos in Class 77 (none were ever renumbered) were withdrawn in October 1968, leaving all services to be handled by the Class 76s. In many respects this was sad, as the Class 76s would have been a far better loco had they been of Co-Co wheel arrangement.

The Class EM2s were occasionally used on freight traffic, but they did not have weight transfer switch to reduce slipping on starting, and the air operated sanding gear was not completely reliable, hence the locos were at a disadvantage to the Class EM1s. Regenerative braking was fitted, similar to the Class EM1s, but not the rheostatic system.

As with Class EM1s, upon the closure of Gorton in May 1963, maintenance was transferred to Crewe Works under the London Midland Region's Mechanical and Electrical Engineers.

The locomotives proved reliable in service, and records exist which show 'even time' running up rising gradients of 1 in 132/120/131 on the route over distances of 5.9 miles and 12.9 miles hauling 9 vehicles (285 tons gross).

In BR days, livery was initially lined black. However, in September 1956, No.27000 was turned out in green livery with orange/black lining. From 1966 the prefix E was applied to numbers, and the yellow warning panels were applied to the front of the cab, and either crest was carried according to the period.

After withdrawal, the locomotives were sold to the Netherlands State Railways (NV Nederlandse Spoorwegen). They were renumbered and repainted in the Dutch grey and yellow scheme, also used in this country for a period for locos used on P'Way work. The Class EM2 did some good work in Holland, and each of the 6 remaining locos ran approx. 2½ million miles. Although only 10 years of life was expected, they actually managed 16 years. Some modifications were obviously carried out to meet Dutch standards, and the most obvious was the fitting of pantographs, similar to the Stone-Faiveley type used in this country.

Tri-ang Hornby British Railways Class 73

Tri-ang introduced a ready to run OO Gauge model in 1961. It subsequently became available with Tri-ang Hornby and Hornby, but was withdrawn in 1971. It has not been available since.

As the prototype saw service in Holland, the Class attracted interest from Philotrain in 1989 and Kleinspoor (who introduced HO scale models) in 1998.

Class 86 Bo Bo Electric Locomotive
British Railways

Introduced:	1965. Rebuilt in 1972.
Allocation:	London Midland and Scottish Regions.
Locomotive Nos:	Class 86/0: Locomotives as built (E3101 - E3200)
	Class 86/1: 86101 - 86103. Locomotives with flexicoil suspension and revised electrical equipment (for passenger services).
	Class 86/2: 86201 - 86261. Locomotives with flexicoil suspension and SAB wheels (for passenger services).
	Class 86/3: 86311 - 86329. Locomotives fitted with SAB wheels to permit 100mph operation. Some capable of multiple working (for passenger services).
	Class 86/4: 86401 - 86439. Locomotives fitted with flexicoil suspension and SAB wheels. Used for Royal Mail duties (RES, later EWS). RCH TDM control fitted.
	Class 86/5: 86501 - 86509. Locomotives modified for Freightliner. Electric train heating equipment isolated. Locos converted back to Class 86/2.
	Class 86/6: 86602 - 86639. Freightliner locomotives. 75mph speed restrictions.
	Class 86/9: 86901 - 86902. Network Rail Loadbank locomotives.
	N.B.: No.86211 'City of Milton Keynes' was withdrawn following the Colwich crash in September 1986.
Number Built:	100
Preserved Examples:	86101 St William Stanier 86213 Lancashire Witch 86259 Peter Pan 86261 The Rail Charter Partnership

Technical Data:

Tractive Effort: 58,000 lb
Loco Weight: 83 tons
Transmission: Electric
Horsepower: 4,040
Power Source: 25kv AC Electrified Overhead Catenary

On electrification of the West Coast main line from London (Euston) to Manchester/Liverpool in the early 1960's, B.R. had acquired 100 AC electric locomotives, consisting of five Classes (81 to 85). This electrification scheme started between Crewe to Liverpool and Crewe to Manchester in the late 1950's, gradually moving southwards towards London, and reaching the capital in 1965/1966. To work the main trains, a new class was designed which incorporated all that had been gained from experience with the previous locos.

Construction of the new Class (originally designated Class AL6) was divided between B.R.'s Doncaster Works (who built 40 locos, Nos. E3101-E3140) and the English Electric Company's Vulcan Foundry Works (who built the remaining 60 locos, Nos. E3141-E3200).

Initially, all 100 locomotives were fitted with four nose suspended traction motors of the A.E.I. 282 AZ type. This was not an ideal arrangement, and they were replaced on rebuilding in 1972. Another cause for concern was the bad riding of the Class when running at high speed, which was caused by insufficient suspension on the bogies. Tests were made with loco No.E3173, which was fitted with the 'Flexicoil' secondary suspension system. This system was already in use on the Deutchse Bundesbahn Class 103 locomotives in West Germany, which ran without problem at 100 mph plus. Both traction motors and the suspension were becoming major problems. Track damage had been caused, particularly on 100 mph stretches. With electrification work in progress from Weaver Junction to Glasgow, it was obvious that the situation could not be tolerated for much longer.

To add to the problems, fractures were found in some bogie side frames which required treatment at Crewe Works.

British Railways Class 86 *Photograph courtesy of Milepost 92½*

Further tests showed that a rubber cushioned wheel would assist with the traction motor mounting problem. The SAB wheels, manufactured in Sweden and was in use on their railway systems, were so fitted for testing purposes to Nos. E3139 and E3173. Whilst the wheels showed a marked improvement on No.E3129, it was on the 'Flexicoil' fitted No.E3173 that the most dramatic changes were noticeable. As it was intended to fit the new Class 87 locos with these bogies/wheels, three further locos were treated. In all, some 58 locos have been rebuilt in this way. At the time they were rebuilt, opportunity was also taken to alter the traction motors to the A.E.L. 282 BZ type. On rebuilding, the Class were designated 86/2 and re-numbered in that series. The remaining 39 locos were rebuilt in a similar fashion and reclassified from 86/0 to 86/4.

Alongside the new Class 87's, the Class 86/2's work principal passenger trains from and to London (Euston) over the West Coast route. In their rebuilt form they are popular with train crews, who regard them as the best AC electric locos currently in use.

Following Privatisation, the class saw service with Anglia Railways for use between Liverpool Street and Norwich. These were withdrawn in September 2005. 15 locos went to EWS (English, Welsh & Scottish Railway) for use on freight, lasting until late 2003. Freightliner retain a number of locos at the present time.

Virgin trains inherited the baulk of the former Inter City fleet, but with the widespread introduction of new trains, the last was withdrawn in 2004.

Three locos are in service with Network Rail as mobile Load Bank Testing locos, which test the overhead line equipment. These are classified as Class 86/9.

FM Rail also acquired a number of these locos before its demise. A few remain in storage, and a few locos have been preserved.

When delivered, the Class were painted in light blue livery, with white cab window frames and white roofs over the cab ends. At first, warning panels were not painted on the front ends, but in accordance with B.R. policy, were later added. As locos moved through the workshops, the livery was changed to the darker B.R. blue. Front ends were painted yellow and roofs dark grey. Initially, cast numbers and B.R. lion and wheel crests were fiited, but these were later replaced by the B.R. arrow logo. Many of the Class 86 locos later carried Inter City Executive livery (no swallows), although Class 86/4 No.86401 carried Network South East livery. After Privatisation, the Class carried the various liveries of operators, the Network Rail locos carrying yellow livery.

Hornby British Railways Class 86

Wrenn Lima introduced a ready to run N gauge locomotive in 1967. After the arrangements with Wrenn ended in 1977, it was marketed under the Lima name from then until it was withdrawn in 1983. It has not been available since.

Hornby introduced a ready to run OO gauge model in 1981 which remains available.

Class 87 Bo Bo AC Electric Locomotive
British Railways

Introduced:	1973
Allocation:	London Midland and Scottish Regions.
Locomotive Nos:	Class 87/0: 87001 - 87035 Class 87/1: 87101
Number Built:	35
Preserved Examples:	87001 87035
Technical Data:	**Tractive Effort:** 58,000 lb **Loco Weight:** 87/0 82 tons; 87/1 78 tons. **Transmission:** Electric **Horsepower:** 5,000 **Power Source:** 25kv AC Electrified Overhead Catenary

British Railways Class 87 *Photograph courtesy of Milepost 92½*

An extension of the London Midland Region's 25kv electrified lines was authorised in 1970 from Weaver Junction (north of Crewe) to Gretna Junction on the Scottish border. In conjunction with this, the Scottish Region worked south from the electrified lines in the Glasgow area, to link up with the London Midland at Gretna Junction.

The West Coast main line includes the formidable climbs of Shap and Beattock. In steam days it was necessary to provide locos for banking trains over the summits, which was slow and time consuming. In providing a high speed service, it was essential that a loco was designed with a high tractive effort, capable of climbing steep gradients unassisted. The Class 86 locos met most of these requirements, but the opportunity to make various modifications was taken.

Whilst the Class 87's were a development of the Class 86 units, the new locomotives incorporated several improvements that resulted from problems experienced with the earlier designs. The axle suspended motor had been the main source of trouble on the Class 86, and a new prototype bogie and suspension was designed and fitted to Class 86 locos for trials; the new bogie (BP9) greatly reduced track wear. Other differences were the fitting of two cab windows, the Class 86's having three windows in the cab front, and the locos being wired for multiple operations; the locos are air braked only. The Class has been fitted with new style Browne Willis pantographs for 100 mph running.

In addition to the 35 units of Class 87/0, another locomotive (No.87101) was built as an experiment and was classified Class 87/1. In 1977 No.87001 was named 'Stephenson' by the Stephenson Locomotive Society, in connection with the 150th Anniversary of the Stockton & Darlington Railway. These nameplates were subsequently transferred to loco No.87101 when the rest of the Class 87/0 were named. No.87101 differed from the other locos in two respects, having been fitted with different traction motors, and having a thyristor control system which was later adopted for the advanced passenger train (A.P.T.).

On Privatisation, all 35 Class 87 locomotives were leased to Virgin Trains. With new Pendolino trains ordered, the Class 87s were withdrawn in mid 2005.

The sole example of Class 87/1 passed to EWS from Rail Express Systems, but it suffered a major failure in 1999 and was withdrawn from service. It was subsequently scrapped.

A number of freight operators have tried these locomotives on short term hire, including GB Railfreight (who retain two examples for current use), DRS and Cotswold Rail. Apart from the two GBrf examples, the rest have been stored. Two locos have subsequently been sold to a Bulgarian operator (and more may follow), and two have been preserved.

The Class 87's were painted in B.R. blue/yellow livery, and all 35 locos were named between 1977 and 1978. Many later appeared in the revised Inter City livery. Following Privatisation, the Class carried Virgin Trains livery. Four locos did see service with DRS for a while and carried the DRS blue livery. The two GBrf locos carry a modified version of the GBrf livery.

Lima British Railways Class 87

Lima introduced a ready to run OO gauge model in 1979. The tools passed to Hornby in 2005 following its acquisition of the Lima Group. It has not yet been scheduled for reintroduction.

Graham Farish introduced a ready to run N gauge version in 1998. It remained available until the takeover by Bachmann in 2000. An upgraded model was reintroduced in 2005 and remains available.

Class 90 Bo Bo AC Electric Locomotive
British Railways

Introduced:	1987
Allocation:	Eastern, London Midland and Scottish Regions, later Virgin Trains, ONE, EWS and Freightliner.
Locomotive Nos:	90001 - 90050
Number Built:	50
Preserved Examples:	None

Technical Data:

Tractive Effort: 58,000 lb
Loco Weight: 80 tons (estimated)
Transmission: Electric
Horsepower: 5,000
Power Source: 25kv AC Electrified Overhead Catenary

British Railways Class 90 *Photograph courtesy of Milepost 92½*

The building and development of this Class was announced in 1985, as further locomotives were being required to replace the remaining early build of 25kv electric locos of Classes 81 and 85.

The original order was for further Class 87's, and as details would vary slightly, classification would be 87/2. However, the designers altered the shape of the loco to such a degree, that changes were necessary internally as well as appearance wise. Eventually the locos were redesignated Class 90.

These locomotives were similar in concept to the Class 87/1 loco (No.87101 'Stephenson'), which was built with Thyristor control instead of the previously used tap changing control methods, and the design was developed by B.R.E.L. with G.E.C. providing the electrical components.

This class was used for express passenger and freight duties on the West Coast Main Line. It worked with driving van trailer, using the time division multiplex system (passing digital signals along train jumper cables, which is also used for train lighting and driver/guard communications), similar to those on the Class 47/7 locos formerly running on the Scottish Region between Glasgow and Edinburgh, to enable push/pull operations to take place. This reduced the number of locos necessary, by not requiring an additional loco to be coupled at the outer end of the train when a terminal is reached.

15 locomotives were owned initially by Inter City, the remainder by the Freight Sectors Network SouthEast and Rail Express Systems for parcels and mail traffic. On delivery, the Inter City locos carried Swallow livery, the remainder carried either Railfreight Distribution or Rail Express Systems. Network SouthEast livery was not carried as the locos were used on Inter City duties. In 1992, three locos were turned out for the Freight Connection Event in the liveries of DB (German Railways), SNCF (French Railways) and SNCB (Belgian Railways).

The Inter City locomotives were used on principal services between London Euston to Manchester, Liverpool and Glasgow. The freight locos were used on the Great Eastern section, the North London Line, East and West Coast main lines.

Following Privatisation, the 15 Inter City locomotives passed to Virgin Trains. The Railfreight Distribution and Rail Express Systems locos passed to English, Welsh & Scottish Railways (EWS). The remaining locos passed to Freightliner. EWS painted one of its locos in unbranded GNER livery for use on that operators services, but it was generally used on any freight service.

Following the introduction of Pendolino trains by Virgin, the Class 90 Virgin locos were returned to the leasing company. A number are now in service with ONE between London Liverpool Street and Norwich. EWS now provide Class 90 haulage on First ScotRail sleeper trains out of London Euston. A number of locos are being repainted in First Group corporate livery to operate these trains, they will be branded First ScotRail but will be operated by EWS who retain ownership.

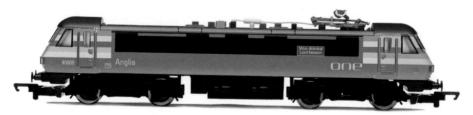

Hornby British Railways Class 90

Hornby introduced a ready to run OO gauge model in 1988 which remains available.

Graham Farish introduced a ready to run N gauge version in 1995. It remained available until the takeover by Bachmann in 2000. An upgraded model was reintroduced in 2005 and remains available.

Class 91 Bo Bo Electric Locomotive
British Railways

Introduced:	1988
Allocation:	Eastern and Scottish Regions, later GNER.
Locomotive Nos:	91001 - 91031
Number Built:	31
Technical Data:	**Loco Weight:** 84.1 tons **Transmission:** Electric **Horsepower:** 6,090 **Power Source:** 25kv AC Electrified Overhead Catenary

British Railways Class 91 *Photograph courtesy of Milepost 92½*

When originally announced as a design concept, these locomotives were designated 1C 225 (i.e. 225 kmph or 140 mph), later the name Electra was given to the Class 91. The design differs from the Class 90 by having a streamlined cab at the No.1 end, a continuous curved roof almost the full length to the No.2 end where the pantograph is located, and a blunt end cab.

In normal day time service on the East Coast Main Line, they are used with Mk IV coaches and driving van trailer (DVT), the locos will be at one end streamlined cab leading (normally the North end leaving London), and will pull or push accordingly, with through control using the Time Division Multiplex (TDM) system. The locomotives also differ from other electric locos to date (other than the A.P.T. power car), in that their motors are body mounted as opposed to being fixed to the bogies, with the final drive by cardan shaft.

Rheostatic brakes, as fitted to Classes 86, 87 and 90, are fitted as standard which can reduce speed to 45 kph (approx. 30 mph), at which point friction brakes come into operation.

The locomotives were delivered in the new Inter City sector white/red/grey livery with yellow ends, incorporating the Inter City logo and chrome swallow insignia. On Privatisation, all passed to Great North Eastern Railway (GNER) and they now carry GNERs blue livery. The awarding of the East Coast franchise to National Express Group on 14th August 2007, following financial difficulties within GNERs owning company (Sea Containers), will probably result in livery changes after 11th November 2007.

Hornby British Railways Class 91

Hornby introduced a ready to run OO model in 1988 which remains available.

Graham Farish introduced a ready to run N gauge version in 1990. It remained available until the takeover by Bachmann in 2000. An upgraded model was reintroduced in 2005 and remains available.

Class 92 Co-Co Electric Locomotive
British Rail / SNCF (French National Railways)

Introduced:	1993
Allocation:	Railfreight Distribution (later EWS), European Passenger Services (EPS), SNCF (French National Railways) and Eurotunnel.
Locomotive Nos:	92001 - 92046
	Built by Brush Traction, Loughborough.
Number Built:	46
Duties:	Freight Traffic via the Channel Tunnel.
Technical Data:	**Tractive Effort:** 81,000 lb **Loco Weight:** 126 tons **Engine:** Brush Traction motors **Horsepower:** 6760 in 25kV mode; 5360 in 750v DC mode

46 dual voltage electric locomotives were built for use on Channel Tunnel freight and night passenger services by Brush Traction, with the body shells being constructed by Procor at Wakefield and delivered to Brush at Loughborough for completion. The locos can pick up power from either 25kV overhead lines or from the former Southern Region 750 volt DC third rail system. The electrical systems on these dual voltage locos are extremely complicated, and following changes in legislation,

British Rail/SNCF Class 92 *Photograph courtesy of Milepost 92½*

they no longer meet European safety requirements. The Class 92 locos carry two pantographs, a requirement of Eurotunnel (the owners and main operators of the Channel Tunnel), although only one is in use at any one time, the other can be used if a problem arises with the other pantograph, avoiding delays whilst rescue operations are put into place in the tunnel.

The locomotives were extensively tested on the continent, with cold weather testing taking place in Vienna and the VUZ test track in the Czech Republic. Getting them into traffic in the UK was more difficult as deliveries became mixed up with the Privatisation of the British Rail businesses. Infrastructure passed to Railtrack who expressed concern about the amount of current the locos drew from the overhead electrification system and signalling interference. British Rail, having electrified the Redhill to Tonbridge line to handle Channel Tunnel freight traffic, then found Railtrack banning the locos from the route unless they were diesel hauled, the Class 92s using other routes to and from the tunnel.

Initially the allocation was split between Railfreight Distribution, European Passenger Services and SNCF (French National Railways) for operation between England and France via the Channel Tunnel, for which they are one of the few locos passed for operating through services.

Following Privatisation of Railfreight Distribution in November 1997, the 30 locos in their fleet passed to English, Welsh & Scottish Railway. They are deployed on Dollands Moor to Wembley workings, and are also used on freight trains on both the East and West coast main lines.

The 7 European Passenger Services locomotives were allocated for use on the planned overnight sleeper services between a number of British cities, and destinations in mainland Europe fell victim of both the rail Privatisation process and the introduction of low cost air services. Although a number of vehicles were completed, they never worked in revenue earning service and were eventually stored and later sold for service in Canada. This resulted in a number of EPS locos being stored, and in February 2007 five of the seven locos were sold to Eurotunnel after a lengthy period in storage.

Initially, all locomotives carried the two tone Railfreight grey livery, SNCF locos carried branding and the EPS locos had three silver rings of different sizes. Some have subsequently been repainted in EWS maroon and gold colours.

Hornby British Rail/SNCF Class 92

Lima and Hornby both introduced ready to run OO Gauge models in 1995. The Lima model remained available until 2003. Hornby now own both the tools following their acquisition of the Lima range in 2005. Whilst the model is not in the current Hornby catalogue, it remains available.

4 Car Suburban Electric Multiple Unit (4 Sub) Southern Railway

Introduced:	1925
Designed By:	R E Maunsell
Allocation:	Southern Railway, later British Railways Southern Region.

Set Number Series:

Motor Coaches		**Trailers**
4300 – 4325 (Western Section)	2-7 Compartment.	1-9 Compartment built at Eastleigh in 1925. 1-10 Compartment*.

* No.4313 has 9 Compartment all steel trailer.

4326/38, 4340/49 and 4351 – 4354 (Eastern Section)	2-8 Compartment.	1-10 Compartment built at Eastleigh in 1925/26.
4339 (Eastern Section):	1-7 Compartment 1-8 Compartment	1-9 Compartment built at Eastliegh in 1925/26. 1-10 Compartment.

Last of Class Withdrawn:	1963
Preserved Examples:	None
Duties:	Suburban Passenger services.
Technical Data:	**Transmission:** Electric **Horsepower:** 2 x 250 hp motors to each motor coach. **Power Source:** 650 volts DC Third Rail

SR 4 Car Suburban Electric Multiple Unit (4 Sub) *Photograph courtesy of www.southernrailway.net*

These units were the only all compartment electric stock built by the Southern Railway. These could be considered to be the first high density multiple unit trains, with six seats to each side of the compartment. The units were the first to be designed at the commencement of widespread electrification following grouping. Before grouping, two variations of electrification existed; The L.B.S.C.R. 6600 volt AC overhead system, and the L.S.W.R. 600 volt DC third rail system. At grouping, Sir Herbert Walker became General Manager, and being an L.S.W.R. man, he chose the third rail system. The lines for which these units were intended to run, were on the Western Section from Waterloo to Guildford via Claygate or Epsom, and on the Eastern Division to Orpington and Dartford from Holborn and Victoria. Charing Cross and Cannon Street to Orpington and Bromley North, together with branches to Addiscombe and Hayes, and the link to Beckenham Junction, were operable by the end of 1926.

On the Eastern Section, apart from these new units, some 537 coaches were rebuilt from 8' wide L.B.S.C. stock, by putting an additional foot in the centre of the vehicles, making a similar 9' vehicle.

The sets listed initially ran as three car units, and then had an additional vehicle added, often this being a Bullied vehicle with the distinctive top light in the doors. The units were made to be used in multiple operation as eight or twelve car sets, depending upon traffic requirements.

These vehicles were of wooden construction with steel panels, and were withdrawn in the early 1960's when the new all steel vehicles, designed for use on the Southern Region, were delivered.

In S.R. days, the units were in malachite green, whilst in B.R. days, they carried the slightly darker electric green livery. Towards the end of their service lives, they may have carried the small yellow warning panel below the cab windows. The circular BR crest was carried.

Tri-ang SR 4 Car Sububurban Electric Mutliple Unit (4 Sub)

Tri-ang introduced a ready to run 4-SUB in 1957. It was withdrawn in 1964. It was sold mainly as a 2 car unit.

5-BEL Electric Multiple Unit
Southern Railway

Introduced:	1933
Designed By:	Pullman Car Company, Preston Park, Brighton.
Allocation:	Southern Railway, later British Railways Southern Region.
Unit Nos:	3051 - 3053
	5 Cars: Motor Brake Second (MBS), Trailer Second (TS), Trailer Kitchen First (TKF), Trailer Kitchen First (TKF) and Motor Brake Second (MBS).
Last of Class Withdrawn:	1972

Preserved Examples:

52795 TKF	52875 TS
52805 TKF	52885 MBS
52815 TKF	52895 MBS
52825 TKF	52905 MBS
52835 TKF	52915 MBS
52845 TKF	52925 MBS
52855 TS	52935 MBS
52865 TS	

Duties:	Luxury Express Passenger.
Technical Data:	**Engine:** 4 x 225 hp British Thomson Houston Traction Motors to each power car **Power Source:** 750 volts DC Third Rail

SR 5 Bel *Photograph courtesy of Colour Rail*

The name Pullman has long been associated with the town of Brighton in Sussex. The American Pullman Car Company had its British headquarters at Preston Park on the outskirts of Brighton, and it was also the terminus for one of the worlds most famous trains 'The Brighton Belle'.

To commemorate the electrification of the Southern Railways London (Victoria) to Brighton Line, in the early 1930's, the Pullman Car Company built three 5 Car electric multiple units (classified 5-BEL) to replace the steam hauled stock used on 'The Southern Belle'. This train was inaugurated in 1908, although Pullman Cars were first introduced on services to Brighton in the 1890's. In peak times these units were run as ten car sets.

The new trains entered service amid great publicity on January 1st 1933, the first trains being given a carnival type reception. Until June 1934 these trains were named 'The Southern Belle', but from then on the new name of 'The Brighton Belle' was introduced.

'The Brighton Belle' offered a luxury service for which passengers paid a supplement. Meals were served to every table. Initially, trains were staffed by The Pullman Car Company, but eventually their British operations were acquired by The British Railways Board. Subsequently, all Pullman trains have been withdrawn. The Pullman concept had a brief comeback with Inter City, and the use of the name was more widespread. At first they offered revolutionary ideas, including air conditioning etc.. However, these features have now been incorporated in rolling stock designs over the years, and the building of new Pullman stock is no longer considered financially viable.

By 1972 the stock was approaching its 40th Birthday and coming to the end of its useful life. Its renewal could not be justified and the withdrawal of the train was announced. This did not prove popular, but attempts to gain a reprieve failed, the last trains running on April 30th 1972. Coaches from the train were put up for sale and several were purchased by individuals and private railways. No unit remained intact (i.e. all 5 Cars) as each coach was split into a different lot for the sale.

Until 1968 the trains were finished in the Pullman chocolate and cream livery. The six first class cars (two per train) carried the names 'Doris', 'Hazel', 'Audrey', 'Vera', 'Gwen' and 'Mona'. The units were repainted in blue/grey livery during 1968/1969. The words 'Brighton Belle' were applied in white in a distinctive typeface to supplement this.

All 15 cars were originally preserved, although one has subsequently been scrapped.

Wrenn SR 5 Bel

Wrenn introduced a ready to run OO gauge model in 1979. It was last available in 1992. Despite the tools passing to Dapol in 1993 and to G & R Wrenn (Mordvale) in 2001, the model has not been available since.

Class 411 (4 CEP) Electric Multiple Unit
British Railways

Introduced:	1956
Allocation:	British Railways Southern Region (750 volt third rail electrified lines).
Unit Nos:	7101 - 7211
	Later numbered 1501 - 1621, includes former 4Bep unit Nos. 7001-7022.
	Formation: DMBS (Driving Motor Brake Second) TC (Trailer Composite - Non Powered) TS (Trailer Second - Non Powered) DMBS (Driving Motor Brake Second)
Last of Class Withdrawn:	2005
Number Built:	120
Preserved Examples:	7105
Duties:	Passenger.
Technical Data:	**Weight:** DMBS 41 tons; TC 33 tons; TS 31 tons **Engine:** Traction Motors 4 x EE507 **Horsepower:** 1,000

British Railways Class 411 (4 CEP) *Photograph courtesy of Milepost 92½*

110 four car units were built at Eastleigh between 1956 and 1963, they were originally numbered 7101 to 7211. Designated 4Cep (later Class 411), the Cep coding referred to Corridor Electro-Pneumatic (brake).

They were a development of the Southern Railways 4COR units which were built in 1937. The 4 CEP's were built for the Kent Coast electrification scheme, and were designed using Mark 1 coaches as a basis. The first four units were initially used from 1956 on Central Division services. Operating on the British Railways Southern Region 650/750 volt DC third rail system, the units replaced steam operation on services from London to Margate, Ramsgate, Dover and Folkestone.

In 1975, unit No.7153 (which later became No,.1500) was refurbished with hopper windows, new interiors, and the Guards van was moved from behind the driving cab to the composite trailer. All units were refurbished at Swindon Works between 1980 and 1983, and were subsequently renumbered in the series 1501-1621, the additional units being provided from 4 BEP (Class 410) units.

Following the formation of British Rail sectors from 1981, the establishing of the London & South East sector to operate Londons commuter services, most of the Class 411 units carried L&SE 'Jaffa Cake' livery (two tone brown). L&SE became Network SouthEast in June 1986 and the distinctive blue, red and white livery was applied across the fleet.

Post Privatisation, most of the units saw service with Connex South Eastern (later South Eastern Trains). Connex South Central operated some units between 1995 and 1998 on the London Bridge to Brighton services. South West Trains (SWT) hired two units on a short term basis in 1996. More units were hired by SWT, who at one time operated 29 units on services from London to Portsmouth, Reading and Weymouth, pending arrival of new stock.

The first unit was withdrawn in 2002, and the last in 2005. Several vehicles have been preserved.

Bachmann British Railways Class 411 (4 CEP)

In 2006 Bachmann announced that it was to produce a OO Gauge ready to run model in its original condition (before refurbishment). The model is due for release in late 2007.

Class 370 Advanced Passenger Train
British Railways

Introduced:	1972 Gas Turbine (experimental). 1977 Electric (preproduction).
Half Unit Nos:	370001* 370002 370003 370004 370005 370006 * Was named 'City of Derby'.
Preserved Examples:	370003 The Gas Turbine Train (Experimental)
Technical Data:	**Transmission:** Electric **Horsepower:** 4,000 **Power Source:** 25kv AC Electrified Overhead Catenary

British Railways Class 370 APT *Photograph courtesy of Colour Rail*

The Advanced Passenger Train (APT) took some twelve years to develop. Experiments concerning the riding of conventional rolling stock bogies first commenced in 1967, and these allowed British Rail engineers to develop a tilting body/articulated bogie arrangement, which allowed trains to take curves at increased speeds.

In 1972, a 4 Car experimental gas turbine powered train (designated APT-E) commenced trials. It was subjected to very strenuous testing, which culminated in the setting of a new British speed record of 152 mph between Swindon and Reading in August 1975. The APT-E was useful in testing the concept of the tilting train, but the traction type was dropped in favour of a 25Kv AC electric version, and the APT-E was presented to The National Railway Museum at York.

Six preproduction 25Kv AC electric versions were introduced in 1977, for testing on services between London (Euston) and Glasgow (Central) which ran as three full trains. The electric trains were designated APT-P. The trains were again subjected to rigorous testing, and like all experimental and innovative technology, things did not always go well. The tilting sensation caused some discomfort to passengers, and the Press crucified the product for breaking down etc.. Despite this, one of the units did manage to reach 160 mph on the Scottish Region during trials in November 1979.

The trains themselves used electrical equipment derived from that fitted to Class 87 locomotives and No.87101 in particular. On H.S.T.'s the power car is part of the driving vehicle, and is located behind the driver, but on the APT's the power cars were marshalled centrally on the train. To maintain a 125 mph schedule, one power car was sufficient, but if increased speeds were required it was necessary to add a second power vehicle. The braking system was also revolutionary in that water turbine brakes were fitted, a set of conventional buffers and drawgear was fitted under the lifting nose, so that the train could be rescued by other locomotives without having to fit special drawbars (this system is used to rescue failed HST units). Sadly, the use of the equipment on APT-P's became a regular occurence.

Whilst the Press went to town on the trains failure, and the Sunday supplements contained colour photographs of the trains being broken up, many of the lessons learned and the technology tested, has been incorporated in more recent builds. The Class 91 locomotive has the same body mounting traction motors linked to the bogies by Cardan shaft, and the Classes 90 and 91 have the Thyristor control system.

The last surviving vehicles have been preserved at the Crewe Heritage Centre.

Hornby British Railways Class 370 APT

Hornby introduced a ready to run OO gauge model incorporating a tilt mechanism in 1980. It was last available in 1984. With the introduction of the Pendolino tilting trains by Virgin (see Class 390) there has been increased interest in this model of the pioneering tilting train.

Class 373 Eurostar
British Rail/SNCF/SNCB

Introduced: 1993

Allocation: Eurostar services between London Waterloo and Paris/Brussels. Please note that the opening of the Channel Tunnel Rail Link will see services transferred to/from London St. Pancras during 2007.

Unit Nos: 373001 - 373022 Eurostar (UK) operated units
373101 - 373108 SNCB operated units
373201 - 373232 SNCF operated units

62 x 10 Car Half Set Units were built by GEC Alsthom, and 14 x 8 Car Half Sets were built to provide 31 x 20 Car Trains and 7 x 16 Car trains.

Formation of 8 Car Half Units:
DM, MSO, TSO, TSO, TSO, RB, TFO, TFBO
10 Car Half Units have an additional TSO and TFO vehicle.

Duties: International Passenger.

Technical Data: **Weight:** 68.5 tons
Horsepower: 16,400 at 25kV ac & 7,388 at 750V dc

British Rail/SNCF/SNCB Class 373 Eurostar *Photograph courtesy of Milepost 92½*

The opening of the Channel Tunnel on the 6th May 1994 saw the introduction of Eurostar services between London and Brussels (Belgium) and Paris (France). These services were initially operated jointly by British Rail, French National Railways (SNCF) and Belgian National Railways (SNCB), but following Privatisation of British Rail the services in Britain passed to a new concern, London & Continental Railways, a consortium that at that time included National Express, British Airways and Virgin (no longer involved), with both SNCF and SNCB having 35% and 15% stakes respectively.

To operate these services a new train was devised, based on the successful TGV trains produced for SNCF by GEC Alsthom. Designated Class 373 Eurostar Trains, 62 Half Sets of 10 vehicles (31 full sets of 20 vehicles) which were preferred for GEC Alsthom (power cars built Belfort), Brush (traction motors), ANF, De Dietrich (trailer body shells), BN Construction and ACEC. These were built between 1993 and 1995 and are sometimes referred to as the 'Trans Marche' units.

The original plan (abandoned during the Privatisation plan) was to operate services beyond London to serve the regions. Yorkshire in particular had been instrumental in ensuring that this requirement was added during the passage of the bill through the parliamentary process. For this, 14 North of London Half Sets of 8 vehicles were ordered (7 full sets of 16 vehicles). Although units were tested on the North London Line, East Coast and West Coast main lines, and Eurostar lounges were built at Crewe and elsewhere, these plans were never fulfilled. The North London Line, which was to give access to both the West Coast and East Coast main lines, was modernised during the mid 1990s. Plans for overnight services from the regions were also abandoned, the specially built vehicles being subsequently sold to Canada having never been used for their intended purpose.

The Eurostar trains operate on three networks. Prior to the opening of the eventually built Channel Tunnel Rail Link in England, the services were restricted to the heavily used routes electrified at 750V dc using the former Southern Region third rail electrification scheme. The new link uses the 25kV overhead electrification scheme used elsewhere in Britain and France. The trains also carry provision for operating on the 3kV dc overhead electrification system in Belgium, and some are also capable of operation on the 1500V dc overhead system in France. The sets used on French domestic services have had their third rail equipment removed, and the opening of the new Channel Tunnel Rail Link in the UK will also render this equipment redundant, although it is not yet clear if it will be removed. In addition to coping with the four electrification systems, the Eurostar trains have to work with five different signalling systems across Britain, Belgium and France.

The abandonment of the North of London services rendered the 14 x 8 Car Half Units surplus to requirements. Three sets were placed on short term lease to GNER for use on London to Leeds and London to York services, and they carried GNER blue livery for the duration of the five year contract, which expired in December 2005. Six of the North of London full sets were subsequently utilised by SNCF on French domestic services.

In Britain the trains are currently maintained at North Pole Depot which is accessed from the West London Line through Kensington Olympia, the empty stock travelling from London Waterloo via the connecting chord east of Clapham Junction. The transfer of services from November 2007 to London St. Pancras has resulted in the construction of a new depot at Temple Mills in East London.

At the opening of the first phase of the new Channel Tunnel Rail Link on 30th July 2003, Half Units 3313/3314 set a new British speed record of 208 mph (334.7 kmh).

Eurostar trains operate between London and Paris or Brussels. There are also seasonal trains to the French ski resorts and to Disneyland Paris. Unlike France, where new high speed infrastructure was in place to coincide with the opening of the Channel Tunnel in 1994, the process has taken much longer and has been a far more painful route to achieve realisation.

When the Eurostar trains start operating in November 2007 on the newly opened high speed Channel Tunnel Rail Link, linking the tunnel near Folkestone and the capital at London St. Pancras,

Hornby British Rail/SNCF/SNCB Class 373 Eurostar

338

the trains will at last have infrastructure to match that on the other side of the Channel. The Eurostar's look set to dominate international traffic in and out of Britain for many more years to come.

The units have only carried Eurostar or GNER livery, in the case of the GNER units, vinyls were fitted over the existing Eurostar livery to allow easy removal after the short term lease expired.

Hornby introduced a HO Gauge model in 1995 which was made for Jouef by Mehano and was available under the Jouef label outside the UK. When Jouef became part of the Lima group (the then competitors to Hornby in the UK) the arrangement stopped. The model was then incorporated into the much larger Lima range.

Hornby tooled their own model to the more popular British OO scale in 1996, and this model remains available. Ironically, Hornbys acquisition of the Lima group (which includes Jouef) also gave them the tooling for the HO model, but it was not scheduled for reintroduction at the time of going to press.

Kato introduced a ready to run N Gauge model in 1996.

Class 390 Pendolino
Fiat Ferroviaria/Alstom/Virgin Trains

Introduced:	2002
Allocation:	Virgin Trains services on the West Coast Main Line to and from London Euston.
Unit Nos:	390001 - 390053
	Formation: DMS, MS, TPS, MS, TS, MF, TPG, MF, DMFK
Number Built:	53
Duties:	Express Passenger.
Technical Data:	**Engine:** 12 x Alsthom Onix 800

The awarding of the West Coast franchise to Virgin Trains in 1997 was without doubt the most demanding and yet exciting challenge faced by the new generation of railway companies. The modernisation of the West Coast Route had been proposed by Inter City, but had been abandoned indefinitely by the Privatisation process. Inter City's plans had included the building of new infrastructure, and although a Class 91 and Mark IV coach set had been borrowed from the East Coast Line, plans were abandoned.

A decade earlier, the tilting Advanced Passenger Train project had been abandoned, and the British Railways Board had been subjected to major press ridicule due to the high failure rate of test trains during the short period of passenger operation. The curvaceous West Coast Route required radical engineering solutions, and the tilt train was considered to be the answer. Just as a motorcyclist leans into the corners to maintain speed, the tilt train works on the same principles. When Britain abandoned the tilt train as a failure (although this was the perception, many of the features on these trains went on to be used in other builds without adopting the tilt technology), the Swedish and Italian

Fiat Ferroviaria/Alstom/Virgin Trains Class 390 Pendolino *Photograph courtesy of Milepost 92½*

train manufacturers simply developed it further. Since the early 1960s, Italian train manufacturer Fiat Ferroviaria had been experimenting with tilt through tilting seats rather than tilting vehicles. Eventually the company developed the Pendolino tilting train for domestic services in Italy, and this was to prove highly successful in the export market. Fiat has considerable experience in the automotive industry, and its operation included the highly successful Ferrari organisation.

Richard Branson's Virgin Trains did not inherit the baggage associated with the APT, but recognised that tilt was the only option to improve journey times over the West Coast Route. Free to buy from the world market, Branson's team opted for the Fiat package, with all assembly and final fitting-out taking place at Alstoms Washwood Heath plant in Birmingham. The completed bodyshells were assembled at Fiats Savigliano plant near Turin, and then they were shipped to Bristol Docks for onwards road movement to Birmingham.

Initially, 9 x 9 Car and 44 x 8 Car Units were ordered, but it soon became apparent that all trains needed the ninth car, so in October 2000 an order was placed for an additional 44 vehicles. Later deliveries came with the ninth car configured into the set, but the earlier units had to have them inserted at a later date.

The infrastructure package agreed between Railtrack and Virgin Trains was heavily delayed, and this led to the eventual demise of Railtrack. The engineering output was eventually managed by the Strategic Rail Authority and carried out by Network Rail. The first of the new trains was being tested in early2001 using the Old Dalby test track, which had been rebuilt and electrified by Alstom. The trains were stationed at a new test centre which incorporated the former Asfordby coal loading depot.

The onboard computer system (TASS) authorises the train to tilt (or not) through the reading of balises fitted to the track at regular intervals, the computer reading three in advance of the train.

Extensive testing was carried out both at Old Dalby and later on test site 'A' between Carnforth and Carlisle. The first train entered revenue earning service between Birmingham and Manchester during the Commonwealth Games in the summer of 2002. As further units were released into traffic and the infrastructure allowed it, old trains were replaced with Pendolino units.

In September 2004, the new Pendolino timetable was rolled out and officially launched by the Prime Minister (Tony Blair) during a ceremony at Euston Station. All old trains had been withdrawn, and seven years after taking over the West Coast franchise the new trains had all been delivered.

Pendolinos work all services from London Euston to the West Midlands, Liverpool, Manchester, Preston and Glasgow. They also currently work to Holyhead, but they are hauled by Class 57 locomotives between Crewe and the Welsh port. The Pendolino units are fitted with Dellner couplings, and the Class 57 locos have been fitted likewise. When trains are diverted due to engineering work, these arrangements also apply over non-electrified lines such as the Settle & Carlsile Line and the former Glasgow & South Western Railway route from Glasgow to Carlisle via Dumfries.

Such has been the success of the new trains and services that additional vehicles are now being considered to make them up to 10 cars.

There can be no doubt that the Pendolino has been the most successful of all new trains introduced since Privatisation. It has already become the icon of train travel in the 21st Century. The trains carry Virgin Trains silver livery.

Hornby Fiat Ferroviaria/Alstom/Virgin Trains Class 390 Pendolino

Dapol introduced a ready to run OO Gauge model in 2001. It remained available until 2004 when it was withdrawn.

Hornby produce a OO Gauge model, new in 2007.

Class 466 (Networker) Electric Multiple Units
British Rail Network SouthEast

Introduced:	1993
Allocation:	South Eastern Division (750 volt third rail electrified lines) of Network SouthEast (later Connex SouthEastern and South Eastern Trains).
Unit Nos:	466001 - 466043
	Formation: DMSO Driving Motor Standard Only DTSO Driving Trailer Standard Only 43 x 2 Car Units, built by GEC Alsthom, Birmingham

Number Built:	43 x 2 Car Units, built by GEC Alsthom, Birmingham
Duties:	Suburban Passenger
Technical Data:	**Weight:** 39 tons DMSO; 33 tons DTSO
	Engine: Traction Motors, 4 x Alsthom G352BY
	Horsepower: 804:

British Rail Class 465 with 466 behind (Cars identical) *Photograph courtesy of Milepost 92½*

As part of the Total Route Modernisation Scheme implemented by Network SouthEast for its South Eastern Division, the building of new trains was an integral part.

New 4 Car Units were built for the inner suburban services in the form of Class 465 units. These were supplied by two manufacturers, British Rail Engineering Ltd. (later ABB) in York who built the Class 465/0 and 465/1 units, and Metro-Cammell (later GEC Alsthom) who built the Class 465/2 units. To supplement these, and to enable trains up to 10 cars in length to run, 43 x 2 Car Units were supplied by GEC Alsthom for the Kent Link (now Metro Services). The delivery of the Class 465 and 466 fleets (collectively known as Networkers) enabled the old inner suburban fleet of EPB units to be withdrawn from service.

These inner suburban services, branded Kent Link and later Metro, operated out of London Cannon Street, Charing Cross and London Bridge stations, and initially served stations in South East London, Surrey and Kent. These include services to Sevenoaks (two routes), Orpington, Swanley, Dartford (three routes) and the branches to Bromley North and Hayes.

Following Privatisation, the South Eastern Division services passed to Connex, the French operator who branded these services Connex South East from the start of the franchise in 1996. Connex were not popular, despite being successful in many other countries, and were stripped of their South Eastern franchise by the Strategic Rail Authority (SRA) in June 2003, they also lost their South Central franchise in 2000. As an interim measure, the SRA took over the operation of these services themselves (operating as South Eastern Trains) pending the awarding of a new Intergrated Kent franchise, which included the operation of domestic services over the new Channel Tunnel Rail Link to London St. Pancras following completion of the work during 2007. In 2005, it was announced that GOVIA had been awarded the franchise, and they duly took over on 1st April 2006, and now operate as South Eastern Railway.

The Class 466 units were delivered in Network SouthEast livery, but a few carried revised Connex livery before their demise which was later adopted by South Eastern, although the name was deleted.

Having recently been refurbished by the new operators, the Class 466 units would appear to have another good 20 years of operation left in them!